Narratives of Annihilation, Confinement, and Survival

Culture & Conflict

Edited by
Isabel Capeloa Gil, Catherine Nesci and
Paulo de Medeiros

Editorial Board
Arjun Appadurai · Claudia Benthien · Elisabeth Bronfen · Joyce Goggin ·
Bishnupriya Ghosh · Lawrence Grossberg · Andreas Huyssen · Ansgar Nünning ·
Naomi Segal · Márcio Seligmann-Silva · António Sousa Ribeiro · Roberto Vecchi ·
Samuel Weber · Liliane Weissberg · Christoph Wulf · Longxi Zhang

Volume 14

Narratives of Annihilation, Confinement, and Survival

Camp Literature in a Transnational Perspective

Edited by
Anja Tippner and Anna Artwińska

DE GRUYTER

ISBN 978-3-11-076456-7
e-ISBN (PDF) 978-3-11-063113-5
e-ISBN (EPUB) 978-3-11-063098-5
ISSN 2194-7104

Library of Congress Control Number: 2019931984

Bibliographic information published by the Deutsche Nationalbibliothek
The Deutsche Nationalbibliothek lists this publication in the Deutsche Nationalbibliografie; detailed bibliographic data are available on the Internet at http://dnb.dnb.de.

© 2021 Walter de Gruyter GmbH, Berlin/Boston
This volume is text- and page-identical with the hardback published in 2019.
Cover image: Gulag Vorkuta, 1946. Sputnik / akg-images
Typesetting: Integra Software Services Pvt. Ltd.
Printing and binding: CPI books GmbH, Leck

www.degruyter.com

Contents

Anja Tippner and Anna Artwińska
Introduction: Camp Narratives in a Comparative Transnational Perspective —— 1

I: Comparing Camp Narratives: Theoretical Approaches

Leona Toker
Towards a Literary History of Concentration Camps: Comparative or "Entangled"? —— 13

Anja Tippner
Worlds Apart? Cross-mapping Camp Literature from the Gulag and Nazi Concentration Camps —— 30

II: Defining Camp Literatures: Overview

Eneken Laanes
Transcultural Memorial Forms in Post-Soviet Estonian Narratives of the Gulag —— 51

Ruxandra Cesereanu
Representations of the Gulag and Methods of Resistance: Romanian Detention Memoirs —— 71

Tadeusz Sucharski
Polish Literature of Soviet Prison Camps: An Outline of Issues —— 88

Davor Beganović
Between the Sun and the Stone – The Naked Body: Yugoslav "Re-education" Camps in Literary Representations —— 106

Anne-Berenike Rothstein
Presence through Absence: The Aesthetics of Blank Space in French Holocaust Literature and Film —— 127

Arkadiusz Morawiec
Konzentrationslager in Polish Literature: From Metaphorization to Metaphor —— 146

III: Witnessing and Remembering Camp Experiences: Comparative Case Studies

Silke Segler-Messner
The Grey Zones of Witnessing: Levi, Améry, Shalamov —— 169

Irina Sandomirskaja
The Ghetto of Leningrad, the Siege of Theresienstadt: A Comparative Reading of Enforced Communities —— 190

Doerte Bischoff
Uncanny Contingencies: Translation, Comparison, and Compassion in Herta Müller's *The Hunger Angel* —— 209

Anna Artwińska
A Communist Woman in the Gulag: Gender, Ideology, and Limit-Experience in Ginzburg and Budzyńska —— 231

Alexander Kratochvil
Trauma Narration as Adventure Fiction: Ivan Bahrianyj's Novel *The Hunters and the Hunted* —— 252

About the Authors —— 270

Index of Names —— 272

Index of Topics —— 279

Anja Tippner and Anna Artwińska
Introduction: Camp Narratives in a Comparative Transnational Perspective

The English historian Eric Hobsbawm coined the phrase "age of extremes" to describe the twentieth century. In his opinion, the years between 1914 and 1989 were marked by terrible catastrophes, man-made disasters, wars, and genocidal atrocities in an unprecedented way that called for new forms of documentation, representation, and cultural remembrance. The post-war cultural history of many European countries, and especially the period since 1989, can be understood as an intellectual and emotional struggle with the traumatic events of the Second World War, the Holocaust, Hiroshima, and the Gulag, as well as other effects of totalitarian rule. Historian Hayden White characterized the two world wars, the Holocaust, and Stalinism as "modernist events," that is as events that cannot be

> forgotten and put out of mind or, conversely, adequately remembered, which is to say, clearly and unambiguously identified as to their meaning and contextualized in the group memory in such a way as to reduce the shadow they cast over the group's capacities to go into its present and envision a future free of their debilitating effects. (White 1999: 69)[1]

The complicated and sometimes contradictory process of remembering these events often centers around accounts of camp experiences, since these occupy a singular place among the atrocities defining this century.

At this point in history, we are in possession of a vast archive of texts that deal with the effects of political violence and camp experiences in the twentieth century and that are devoted to conceptualizing the experiences of camp survivors. For a long time, literary criticism has largely focused on testimonial and fictional accounts of the Holocaust and Nazi concentration camps, and less on camp narratives that deal with Soviet and other socialist camps. The primacy of Holocaust camp narratives is understandable, given the importance of the Holocaust for the development of a transnational European memory. However, its predominance belies the fact that socialist labor and penal camps were transnational sites of terror in their own right and have also become transnational *lieux de mémoire*. After a period that was dominated mainly by acts of witnessing and

---

[1] This stands in contrast to what Alexander Etkind calls the "Fifty-Year-Effect," which is "how long it takes for literature [and science] to estrange the tragic past, process the experience, and elaborate a convincing narrative capable of gaining wide if not universal acclaim." (Etkind 2013: 3).

documenting, the literature of the Holocaust and the Gulag has moved on to memorialization and experimentation in describing the camp experience. In most cases, the act of writing texts on confinement, punishment and annihilation, as well as the reception of these texts, took place within the frame of specific national literary discourses that viewed camp experiences and the works they produced primarily within a narrow national frame. In many ways, this runs counter to the fact that the camp as a sign of modernity is a transnational phenomenon and was usually experienced as such. Still, few recent scholarly works that deal with camp literature as a philosophical, aesthetic, or sociological phenomenon take a comparative and transnational perspective.[2] This volume intends to fill this gap by providing a theoretical frame as well as an overview of several important European camp literatures and, last but not least, case studies of iconic camp narratives.

The concept of "camp narratives" rather than "Holocaust narratives" or "Gulag narratives" is based on the assumption that despite their obvious political and ideological differences, literary accounts of camp experiences share common traits, aesthetically as well as thematically. This book presents readings of camp literature that deal with extreme experiences, thus underscoring the similarity between the literature of Soviet Gulag, the literature of the Holocaust, and literature about other camp and prison experiences. As some of the contributors to this volume have noted, these similarities have not been lost on the survivors themselves. In many ways, literature about Nazi concentration camps serves as a point of reference for camp narratives in the same way that the Holocaust serves as a point of reference for other genocidal actions: "The emergence of Holocaust memory on a global scale has contributed to the articulation of other histories. Ultimately, memory is not a zero-sum game." (Rothberg 2009: 6)[3] The concept of multidirectional memory proposed by Michael Rothberg applies to camp narratives, since literature about Nazi camps raised the awareness of other camp experiences. Although texts dealing with the Gulag or socialist camps were not necessarily influenced by the aesthetics and conventions of Holocaust literature,[4] they are predominantly judged by these poetics.

One of the goals of this volume is to point out the ways comparison is used in depicting camp experiences and how the similarities between different types

---

[2] Considerations about the Gulag in the context of other camps and systems of annihilation can be found in *The Gulag. Evidence, Interpretation, Comparison*, edited by Michael David Fox. This important study focuses on a historical rather than aesthetical comparison between differences in camp experiences.
[3] This thought can be found in Huyssen (2003) and also Sucharski (2007).
[4] For the emergence of a specific aesthetic of Holocaust writing see Young (1988).

of camps are conceptualized. All too often, camp literature is associated mainly with one type of camp or *Lager*, either Nazi concentration camps or the Gulag. The narrowed concept of camps excludes many types of deathly penal camps in other countries, such as Romania, the ČSSR and Yugoslavia.[5] This is even more regrettable, since the discussion of these camps is not restricted to Romanian, Czech, or Yugoslav literatures, and representations of these camps can be found in German, English, and French literatures as well. Overcoming this narrow perspective is one of the objectives of this volume. To this end, we place camp narratives in the context of their national literary and cultural traditions, but also in the context of camp narrative as a genre and of transnational memorial cultures. The volume views camp narratives as "entangled" texts (see the contribution by Toker), which refer to other camp experiences and testimonies, but also to the literary canon, for example Dante's *Inferno*, through citation, allusion, and metaphor. In one of the first articles dealing with the concept of camp literature in Yugoslavia, Oskar Gruenwald stressed the importance of entanglement and cross-referencing in this type of literature (Gruenwald 1987). And in 1989, Matt F. Oja urged us to view camp experiences in a broader perspective:

> What we really need to define is not camp literature, but the camp experience. [...]. The definition must surely be universally applicable. [...] this experience need not literally involve a camp of the Stalinist or Nazi model; it may be set in a prison, a bamboo cage, the basement of city hall, or anywhere else. (Oja 1989: 273)

The question of comparison is a difficult albeit a necessary one. As Neil Levi and Michael Rothberg lucidly observed in their discussion of the "uniqueness" of the Holocaust and the Nazi camp system, there is a need to compare in order to fully fathom the depth of a historical event (Levi and Rothberg 2003: 441–442). We understand comparisons in this way, namely as a tool enabling us to put historical experiences into perspective. In doing so, we also acknowledge the assessments and insights of survivors and witnesses, such as Primo Levi, Margarethe Buber-Neumann, and Julius Margolin, who were comparing both types of camps in the first place. Thus, comparison here is not meant to parallelize different camps and the systems that produced them,[6] instead we want to look at the

---

[5] Our thanks go to Bernd Robionek for his important notes and observations about Yugoslav camp literature.
[6] With regard to history, the fundamental ideological and political differences between National Socialism and Stalinism must always be emphasized. See Traverso (2014: 112–162). On the opportunities and limitations of a historical comparison between these two systems see also Ganzenmüller (2012).

ways in which they are represented and interpreted retrospectively. This has been done, for example, with regard to Chinese camps, the *Laogai*, and the Gulag by the German historian Dieter Heinzig, who has pointed out: "At first glance, one could assume that the two types of concentration camp systems are similar if not identical. [...] after further investigation the differences also become visible [...]." (Heinzig 2007) Comparing thus is not a form of equalizing the political systems that established the camps, but rather sheds light on the similarities as well as differences in experiencing these camps.

A reference point for the comparative analysis of camp literature delivered here can be found in comparative genocide studies, which make extensive comparisons between different catastrophes, using the Holocaust as a paradigm "in a non-competitive comparative history" (Jinks 2016: 6). With the exception of the French and Italian experiences, most narratives originated in countries that had been occupied by or that allied themselves with Nazi Germany and were then incorporated into the Eastern bloc later on. When analyzing camp literature from these countries, it is apparent that for the majority of writers the experience of German and Soviet camps is deeply interconnected and that comparing them comes naturally. Comparison, Thimothy Snyder contends, is of the essence if we want to fathom camp experiences and their wider importance: "The Nazi and the Stalinist system must be compared, not so much to understand the one or the other but [to] understand our times and ourselves." (Snyder 2010: 380)

***

This volume presents essays on camp narratives by international scholars. It deals with camp narratives that relate to different types of totalitarian experience in Europe. The overall aim is to identify patterns in camp writing. In various ways, the essays in this volume discuss how to think about camp experiences and what representations of the camps look like within different national literatures in Europe. This approach is, by necessity, comparative, in as much as it is concerned with specific cases and their historical, political, and aesthetic contexts. The essays look for common patterns of camp writing regardless of the political circumstances that produced them.[7] The volume takes a predominantly European perspective, though the scope could easily be broadened by including writings about camp experiences from Latin America, namely Argentina or Chile, or China.[8] In contrast to most of the preexisting volumes on this topic, *Camp Narratives* takes Romanian, Ukrainian, and Estonian texts into account in

---

7 These circumstances might include Stalinism, forced labor, prisoners of war, the Ceaușescu regime, detention camp (e.g. Bereza Kartuska in the Second Polish Republic) or the Holocaust.
8 See, among others Domenach (1995), Frazier (2007), Perez (2014), Williams and Wu (2004).

order to show the ubiquity of the topic as well as the transmission of forms. Looking at different texts from a variety of literatures, however, patterns emerge in the representation of camp experiences. It is surely no coincidence that almost all contributors refer to the seminal texts by Primo Levi, Varlam Shalamov, Aleksandr Solzhenitsyn, and Imre Kertész in order to conceptualize camp experiences. To a greater extent than critics thus far have realized, these texts are cross-referenced among different camp narratives.

The first section of the book, "Comparing Camp Narratives: Theoretical Approaches," takes a more theoretical and systematic approach towards the topic. The first contribution to the section, "Towards a Literary History of Concentration Camps – Comparative or 'Entangled'?" by pioneering literary scholar Leona Toker, expands on her seminal work on the literature of the Soviet camps and her insights into the literature of Nazi concentration camps. Toker sets herself the goal of providing an overview of the most important literary texts on both types of camps and suggests possible future lines of inquiry. By collocating an episode from Imre Kertész's *Fateless* with episodes from the Gulag memoirs collected in *Voices from the Gulag* (edited by Solzhenitsyn) and Varlam Shalamov's story *The Lawyers' Plot*, Toker shows how accounts of the human experience under Nazi rule and in the Gulag can comment on one another in terms of the content of testimonial strategies. Anja Tippner also addresses the possibilities and benefits of comparison in her essay "Worlds Apart? Cross-mapping Camp Literature from the Gulag and Nazi Concentration Camps." She discusses some of the prominent arguments guiding the comparison of Nazi and Soviet camp testimonials, and then highlights differences between literary testimonies of both types of camps. She concludes with the observation that the different cultures of testimony drive the postmemorial treatment of camp narrative in official and popular memorial cultures and are consequential with regard to their place in a shared national and transnational memorial culture.

Eneken Laanes' chapter "Transcultural Memorial Forms in Post-Soviet Estonian Narratives of the Gulag" opens the second section of the book – "Defining Camp Literatures: Overview Articles." Laanes turns her attention to camp experiences that do not figure prominently in European cultural memory – those of the hundreds of thousands of people deported from the Baltic states to Siberia and Central Asia during the war years and immediately afterwards. With regard to Estonian witness accounts, she points out that these memories resurfaced publicly only after the *perestroika* and Estonian independence, linking them with discourses of the war and the Holocaust. She gives an overview of Estonian camp narratives, leading to what she terms the transnational turn in Gulag memories after the post-Soviet period. Her essay is centered on Imbi Paju's book and film of the same title, *Memories Denied*, an account of second-generation witnesses of

Soviet repression in the face of anti-Communist resistance after the Second World War.

In "Representations of the Gulag and Methods of Resistance: Romanian Detention Memoirs," Ruxandra Cesereanu concerns herself with camp experiences in Romanian literature, thus addressing a literary tradition that is often overlooked and seldom discussed within the frame of camp literature. In her examination of Romanian detention memoirs published after 1989, Cesereanu highlights several aspects, for instance the shame of survival (Tzvetan Todorov) or the delays in publishing due to interventions from state security. Her prism of memorial literature comprises *Gherla* by Paul Goma, *Jurnalul fericirii* ("The journal of happiness") by Nicolae Steinhardt, and Ion Ioanid's *Închisoarea noastră cea de toate zilele* ("Our daily prison"), which she lauds as the "most important book of memoirs about the Romanian Gulag," comparable to Aleksandr Solzhenitsyn's *The Gulag Archipelago*. She unfolds the testimonial character and the martyr-like heroism of these texts. Finally, Cesereanu uncovers methods for resisting the camp system, especially in works by female writers (e.g. Lena Constante).

Tadeusz Sucharski's chapter "Polish Literature of Soviet Prison Camps – an Outline of Issues" presents a much-needed analysis of Polish camp narratives from Soviet prison camps. He describes the Polish literature on Soviet prison camps that is primarily *émigré* literature, written in the years 1945–1989. Most of these texts are biographical or autobiographical, but many Polish authors break up the monopoly of factuality in traditional memoirs and turn to "novelizing" and fictionalizing their experiences. As Sucharski has shown, Polish literature on Soviet prison camps comprises the literature of forced exile (Pol. *zsyłka*), prisons, military prison camps, and *strojbaty* (construction battalions), and must be read in the ideological and aesthetical context "of national martyrdom." For the majority of Polish writers of the camps, Russia's image as "the land of slavery" was shaped by the patriotic literary school of the interwar period, where the Romantic notion of nineteenth-century deportations to Siberia predominated. Despite the fact that many of these texts combine a traditional pattern of Polish martyrdom with anti-Russian attitudes, the experience of "otherness" is thought-provoking, because besides suffering atrocities at the hands of the Soviets, the authors also encounter the humanistic tradition of nineteenth-century Russia. In the final part of his contribution, Sucharski analyzes the poetics of Polish literature on Soviet prison camps and discusses the role of the grotesque in the service of realism.

In his text "Between the Sun and Stone – the Naked Body: Yugoslav 'Re-Education' Camps in Literary Representations," Davor Beganović focuses on Goli Otok (Naked Island), the infamous concentration camp where renegade Communist Party members were kept prisoners after the Tito–Stalin split of 1948. Beganović analyzes the degrees of explicitness in Yugoslav camp literature about Goli Otok, exemplified by the works of Branko Hofman, Antonije Isaković, Dragoslav Mihailović, and Miroslav Popović. By placing Goli Otok within the broader context of totalitarian camp theories by Hannah Arendt and Giorgio Agamben, Beganović aims to stimulate further research on this topic, which has often been neglected. Anne-Berenike Rothstein's essay "Presence through Absence – the Aesthetics of Blank Space in French Holocaust Literature and Film" draws on Charlotte Delbo's testimony *Auschwitz and After*, Soazig Aaron's *Refusal*, Claude Lanzmann's *Shoah*, and Alain Resnais' *Night and Fog*. She demonstrates the need for close readings of well-known texts in order to bring into focus complex interrelations between these texts as well as between different types of media. Her contribution concentrates on the presentation and figuration but also on the non-representation of camps in French literature and film. Her point of departure is the social functions of the camp as an intermediate realm between life and death, its typical spatial structure, and also the symbolic implications of space and its narrative dimension. Her essay furthermore highlights spatial-semantic representations of the camps in literature and in film. Read in conjunction, the contributions in this volume provide insights into the shared elements of camp narratives and provide points of departure for further studies on camp experiences.

In his chapter "'Konzentrationslager' in Polish Literature: From Metaphorization to Metaphor," Arkadiusz Morawiec aims to identify the evolutionary stages of concentration camp literature in Poland. He focuses on Nazi German concentration camps and on works created before, during, and after the Second World War, both in and outside the camps. The main determinants of this evolution and its conceptualization include fact, theme, and metaphor. Narratives that focus on the concentration camp as a theme and metaphor were already being written during the German occupation of Poland. Immediately afterwards, however, the existence of the camps was deprived of its status as an autonomous topic and turned into a pretext for reflection of a moral, social, ideological, philosophical, historiosophical, and religious nature. With time, the concentration camp was understood both as a concrete historical phenomenon and as a productive literary theme – especially in the 1960s – suitable for the novel, drama, and poetry. Contemporary Polish literature (in the case of ideologically controlled historical and literary content, the abolition of censorship in Poland in 1990 is of crucial importance) shows that the theme is not only used time and again, but also abused.

The third part of the book, "Witnessing and Remembering Camp Experiences: Comparative Case Studies," is devoted to the analyses of seminal literary works on the camps. In her essay "The Grey Zones of Witnessing: Levi, Améry, Shalamov," Silke Segler-Messner examines the writings of Primo Levi and Varlam Shalamov, focusing on Shalamov's *Kolyma Tales*. She reads these two canonical texts of camp experiences with a special interest in the "grey zone." All three authors try to come to terms with the way in which the camp regime forced inmates and victims to compromise and ultimately to collaborate with an oppressive system. In "The Ghetto of Leningrad, the Siege of Theresienstadt: A Comparative Reading of Enforced Communities," Irina Sandomirskaja reveals the fluidity between the state of siege as experienced in Leningrad and the type of ghetto as it was created in Theresienstadt. What both had in common was that the extreme was the norm. What also made them similar was the "suspension" – in the case of Theresienstadt, suspension from extermination and, in Leningrad, suspension from Soviet heroism in the Great Patriotic War. Doerte Bischoff's "Uncanny Contingencies: Translation, Comparison, and Compassion in Herta Müller's *The Hunger Angel*" looks at Müller's 2009 novel, based partly on the experiences of her longtime friend and fellow Romanian *émigré*, Oskar Pastor, who was a forced laborer in a camp in post-war USSR. The book has been widely discussed but mainly with regard to its complicated writing process. Bischoff situates the text within the frame of German discourses of remembrance and forgetting. Her analysis also reveals that, even in narratives of atrocity that deal with violence and death as the consequences of biopolitics, homosexuality and sexuality in general often remain taboo. Anna Artwińska's chapter "A Communist Woman in the Gulag: Gender, Ideology, and Limit-Experience in Ginzburg and Budzyńska" examines a different type of camp narrative and the specific ethical as well as narrative problems it poses. She looks at camp memoirs written by members of the communist party, particularly Eugenia Ginzburg's *Into the Whirlwind* and Celina Budzyńska's *Shreds of a Family Saga*. Artwińska shows that though shaken and traumatized by the camp experience, these authors still cling to their communist beliefs. The ambivalence that marks these texts makes evident one of the fundamental differences between the accounts of Nazi camps and Soviet prisoner camps. Finally, in "Trauma Narration as Adventure Fiction: Ivan Bahrianyj's Novel *The Hunters and the Hunted*," Alexander Kratochvil tracks the complicated history of Ivan Bahrianyj's Ukrainian Holocaust novel, which is an inventive attempt to represent the unspeakable part of trauma and to construct a meaningful narrative through the medium of a popular genre, the adventure novel.

***

The spelling of names throughout the articles may vary, due to the different styles of transcription and transliteration adopted in the primary and secondary sources used throughout.

***

The publication of this volume would not have been possible without the generous funding from Hamburg University, for which we are grateful. Our special thanks go to our copy-editor and proofreader Katarzyna Trojanowska and our research assistants Luisa Dittrich, Elisabeth Kisner, Shahla Shahriari and Kristina Vogel, who were a great support in all matters of proofreading and text editing, as well as to Olga Stelter for her assistance in organizing the conference that laid the foundation for this volume. Finally, we would like to thank the editors of the Culture & Conflict series, Isabel Capeloa Gil and Catherine Nesci, for publishing our volume in their series.

Works cited

Applebaum, Anne (2003) *Gulag. A History* (London: Penguin Books).
Domenach, Jean-Luc (1995) *Der vergessene Archipel: Gefängnisse und Lager in der Volksrepublik China* [The forgotten archipelago. Prisons and camps in the People's Republic of China] (Hamburg: Hamburger Edition).
Etkind, Alexander (2013) *Warped Mourning: Stories of the Undead in the Land of the Unburied* (Stanford: Stanford University Press).
Frazier, Lessie Jo (2007) *Salt in the Sand: Memory, Violence, and the Nation-State in Chile, 1890 to the Present* (London: Duke University Press).
Ganzmüller, Jörg (2012) "Stalins Völkermord. Zu den Grenzen des Genozidbegriff und den Chancen eines historischen Vergleiches" [Stalin's genocide. On the limits of the genocide concept and the chances of a historical comparison], in *Holocaust und Völkermorde. Die Reichweite des Vergleichs*, ed. Sybille Steinbacher (Frankfurt and New York: Campus Verlag), 145–166.
Gruenwald, Oskar (1987) "Yugoslav camp literature: rediscovering the nation's past-present-future," *Slavic Review* 46.3–4, 513–528.
Heinzig, Dieter (2007) "Gulag and Laogai: Das sowjetische und das chinesische Lagersystem im Vergleich" [Gulag and Laogai: Soviet and Chinese camps in comparison], *Jahrbuch für Historische Kommunismusforschung*, 319–336. <https://kommunismusgeschichte.de/jhk/jhk-2007/article/detail/gulag-und-laogai-das-sowjetische-und-das-chinesische-lagersystem-im-vergleich/> (accessed 6 June 2018).
Hobsbawm, Eric (1996) *The Age of Extremes: The Short Twentieth Century* (London: Vintage).
Huyssen Andreas (2003) *Present Pasts: Urban Palimpsests and the Politics of Memory* (Stanford: Stanford University Press).
Jinks, Rebecca (2016) *Representing Genocide: The Holocaust as Paradigm* (London: Bloomsbury Academic).
Levi, Neil and Michael Rothberg (2003) *The Holocaust: Theoretical Readings* (New Brunswick, N.J.: Rutgers University Press).
Oja, Matt F (1989) "Toward a definition of camp literature," *Slavic Review* 48.2, 272–274.
Perez, Marianna Eva (2014) "The concentration camp and the 'unhomely home': the disappearance of children in post-dictatorship Argentine theater," in *Space and the Memories of Violence. Landscapes of Erasure, Disappearance and Exception*, ed. Estela Schindel and Pamela Colombo (London: Palgrave).
Rothberg, Michael (2009) *Multidirectional Memory: Remembering the Holocaust in the Age of Decolonization* (Stanford: Stanford University Press).

Snyder, Timothy (2010) *Bloodlands: Europe between Hitler and Stalin* (New York: Basic Books).
Sucharski, Tadeusz (2007) "Literatura Holocaustu i literatura Gułagu? Literatura doświadczenia totalitarnego!" [Literature of the Holocaust and literature of the Gulag? Literature of a totalitarian experience!], *Słupskie Prace Filologiczne* (Seria Filologia Polska) 5, 93–118.
Fox, Michael David (ed) (2016) *The Gulag. Evidence, Interpretation, Comparison* (Pittsburgh: University of Pittsburgh Press).
Traverso, Enzo (2014) *Geschichte als Schlachtfeld. Zur Interpretation der Gewalt im 20. Jahrhundert* [History as a battlefield. On the interpretation of violence in the 20th century], (Köln: Neuer ISP Verlag).
Williams, Philip F. and Yenna Wu (2004) *The Great Wall of Confinement. The Chinese Prison Camp through Contemporary Fiction and Reportage* (Berkeley and Los Angeles and London: University of California Press).
White, Hayden (1999) "The modernist event," in *Figural Realism. Studies in Mimesis Effect* (Baltimore: Johns Hopkins University Press), 66–86.
Young, James E. (1988) *Writing and Rewriting the Holocaust* (Bloomington: Indiana University Press).

I: Comparing Camp Narratives: Theoretical Approaches

Leona Toker
Towards a Literary History of Concentration Camps: Comparative or "Entangled"?

1 Narrative as historical testimony and artistic reflection

Narratives of the Nazi concentration camps and narratives of the Gulag are multifunctional.[1] Comparing them may serve to highlight their functions as historical testimony, shedding light on the human realities behind the historical data, and as artistic representations and refractions of those human realities. The yield of the former kind of inquiry is a better understanding of the individual experience in the two camp systems; the fruit of the latter is thickening the description of the typical and specific features of the translation of that experience into a narrative. At times, the distinction between the two types of inquiry, historical/psychological and artistic, becomes blurred.

2 Indirect reciprocal commentary in Holocaust and Gulag narratives

The third chapter of Imre Kertész's autobiographical Holocaust novel *Fateless*[2] tells of "something strange" (1992: 31): the protagonist narrator, a Jewish teenager living in Budapest, is taken off the bus, along with all the other Jewish passengers, on his way to work in Schell Oil Refinery on Csepel Island. There is just one policeman in charge of the operation at this particular city-border post, and he has turned it into a game: those taken off the earlier buses have been told to hide and enjoy the bewilderment of the new arrivals. The victims' understanding of the serial character of the operation is thus delayed. The policeman, who seems rather nice, acts as if he did not quite know what to do with the growing mass of people; he has not yet received further orders. As if to protect the assembled Jews from the elements, he suggests that they go to the customs house

---

[1] My view of the multifunctionality of literary works is based on Mukařovský's (1970). I was saddened to hear (from Wolf Schmid, in conversation) that in Prague University in the 1950s Ian Mukařovský had become a notorious Stalinist.
[2] A later translation is entitled *Fatelessness* (2004).

nearby. This is their first captivity; but they are slow to understand it, especially when their intelligence and discipline (Kertész 1992: 33) are appealed to. No one tries to escape yet: perhaps it might have been different if the arrests had been made after rather than before the workday. Waiting is tedious, but the captives are told that the impending document check is just a formality. By the end of the workday the policeman does seem to get new orders by telephone: "[We] overheard his hurried voice coming from his room, referring to some change of plans" (40). Eventually, the whole large group is marched back to the city, and blends with similar columns coming from other border posts. During this "beautiful clear summer afternoon," a dissonance is suggested by the reactions of the passersby: "a kind of hurried, hesitant, almost furtive curiosity" (41). Then a streetcar wedges in, and a few adults from the column take advantage of the confusion to escape – the protagonist does not understand why they should do so – for fun? He does not follow suit: "I had enough time for it, but still my sense of honor proved to be the stronger of the two urges" (42). The columns are taken to a makeshift prison – in retrospect, a threshold of hell. What had the change of orders been? Logistics of the march or the decision to send the workforce to concentration camps rather than straight into the Danube? (The latter option is not mentioned in the narrative, but Kertész's readers are expected to know about it.[3]) In addition to the ominous cognitive dissonance in this episode of the arrest, one of its striking features is an insight into the psychology of decorous non-resistance.

A contrasting change in orders is implied in the following recollection of the Gulag prisoner A.P. Butskovsky: after Stalin's death, he is transferred to Camp Nevelskoy, to work on the construction of a dock on the shore of the Tatar Strait. A tunnel to Sakhalin was to be built in secret under the Strait, but the project was eventually discontinued. "There was no stopping the rumor that this was the end of the line for us, that we were to die here building this dock. We got no letters, and all links with the world outside were cut off" (Butskovsky 2010: 199), evidently following someone's idea of the secrecy of the construction. Then something strange happens:

> [One] day we were taken into a small ravine with cliffs on either side; they set up machine guns on the heights and aimed them at us. I don't know what they had in mind for us, but in any case, they kept us here a very long time. Our guards fell back much farther than they normally did. We didn't do any work that day. They might even have been checking how

---

[3] Great numbers of Budapest Jews were shot on the bank of the Danube in the winter of 1944, their bodies falling into the river.

they could bury us after an execution. In any case, something was being planned against the politicals.

Two days after that incident we learned about the arrest of the Minister of Internal Affairs, Beria. The camp administration was in some confusion, but it was ready to carry out an order to eliminate political prisoners. (Butskovsky 2010: 199)

Apparently, someone in command sensed a change in the wind and did not sanction the massacre. The author records no feeling of relief after the prisoners are led away from the ravine: his memory seems to replicate the petrified state of the soul on a reprieve from a swift death handed to an exhausted prisoner.

This psychological phenomenon is also recorded in Varlam Shalamov's story *The Lawyers' Plot*. The police car carrying the prisoner to a retrial in Magadan winds uphill and stops at the gate of Serpantinnaia death camp:

> I was familiar with that name [...] This was "Serpantinnaia" – the famous interrogation prison of Kolyma, where so many people perished the previous year. Their corpses had not yet had time to disintegrate [...] I sat by the window and thought that my time too has come, my turn. It was as difficult to think about death as about anything else. I did not picture my own execution. I sat and waited. (Shalamov 2004: I, 194)[4]

Yet after a while the chief guard, having taken care of some official business or having found out about further orders (or a change of orders), signals to the protagonist that they are moving on:

> "Let's go."
> The car turned around; the "raven" sped away from Serpantinnaia.
> Soon, the glimmer of passing cars told me that we were back on the highway. (Shalamov 2004: I, 154)

The reprieve from torture and death receives no comment. The narrator says nothing about feelings of relief – they must have been de-energized, like most other emotions. At the end of that story, the protagonist and all the other people in "the lawyers' case" are released as a result of an internal purge in the ranks of the political police.[5]

---

4 Quotations from Shalamov are based on the 2004 edition; the translations, unless otherwise indicated, are mine. An English translation of a large portion of Shalamov's *Kolyma Tales* is available in Shalamov (1994). A new translation of the whole collection, by Donald Rayfield, has recently been published (Shalamov 2018).

5 The arrest of the chief interrogator of the case has led to the release of those to be retried according to his warrants, even though his arrest, a ripple of the purge in the ranks of the secret police that followed the replacement of Nikolai Yezhov by Lavrentii Beria as head of the People's Commissariat of Interior Affairs (NKVD), had nothing to do with them. That purge,

The "change-in-orders" episode in Kertész's book signifies a gradual descent into the inferno of the Holocaust, but those in Butskovsky's memoir and Shalamov's story foretell, conversely, a glimmer of light in the tunnel of the Gulag experience. Yet these episodes share a number of thematic (in fact, semiological) features. One of them is the helplessness of the victims – physical, psychological, and cognitive – as their fate is being decided, in distant quarters, by the local adherents of the *Führerprinzip*, the principle of divining the leader's unstated policies and translating them into the text of specific commands. Indeed, murder was not a matter of the inevitable tread of historical determinacies; it was a matter of decision, under circumstances that would have allowed for other responses as well.[6] Another issue transformed into a literary topos is the semiotic perplexity of the victims combined with a retrospectively organized, submerged catalogue of signs and symptoms that need deciphering. In Kertész's book, the unimaginable is beginning to happen: hindsight suggests that the protagonist is in denial about it, but could he, in his mid-teens, have known or imagined developments outside his cultural horizons? His very strengths – his sense of "honor," his habits of decorous conduct, his culture overlapping with that of the authorities – are what defeats him, turning him, to use an idiom with a long history, into a "sheep led to slaughter."[7] The story of his arrest might, moreover, be seen as a comment on the stories of non-resistance of Soviet citizens during arrests: decorous conduct (deplored by Solzhenitsyn in the first chapter of *The Gulag Archipelago*, the chapter devoted to the paradigm of arrests and effectively "arresting" the reader), the "sense-of-honor" self-delusion, and a denial of the inexorability of the change. Conversely, the elision of the expected sense of relief in stories of the reprieved Gulag prisoners may be a comment on the complex representation of reprieves in the memoirs of Holocaust survivors.

Thus, narratives do not merely shed light on one another but also provide an indirect comment on, or example of, broader issues. The dispassionate and elliptic character of Butskovsky's account supports Shalamov's representation of the surface indifference to life or death seen in depleted camp inmates,

---

unlike other similar operations, was accompanied by a small counter-wave, when a number of political prisoners, especially in pre-trial cases, were released.

6 Cf. Timothy Snyder's comparison (2010: 218–219) of Hitler's decision to exterminate the Jews in response to setbacks in the war against the Soviet Union and the decision of the Romanian authorities, in view of an impending defeat, not to speed up but, on the contrary, to decelerate the murderous drive against the Jewish population.

7 On landmarks in the history of the slogan "not as sheep to slaughter," re-launched by Abba Kovner in the Vilnius ghetto on 31 December 1941, see Feldman (2013).

which may, *mutatis mutandis*, have also been true of Auschwitz *Muselmänner*, utterly exhausted prisoners,[8] when they are (or are not) selected for slaughter by gas. Elsewhere (Toker 2008), under the influence of other related texts, I argue that this indifference is not a sign of *absence* of inner life in a "goner," but rather a part, a *feature*, of that inner life, which takes shapes that are different from the familiar human experience.

The "hide-and-surprise" game in Kertész's text can in retrospect be recognized as symbolic: manipulating the victims to make them participate in deceiving and betraying their fellow victims, knowingly or unwittingly collaborating with the perpetrators. Apart from probing the semiology of their immediate contexts, both episodes can also be seen as symbolizing aspects of the inhuman condition created by atrocity regimes. This symbolic load, which the reader tends to register even without immediately understanding its purport, is one of the artistic features of Kertész's crafted novel; but the power of Butskovsky's straightforward, non-artistic memoir is rooted in the weight of the human experience that it records, and in the appropriateness of the narrative stance to that experience.[9] The *sense of difficulty overcome* is one of the sources of our spontaneous appreciation of the quality of performance, visual or verbal. The surmounted difficulty need not be identified with the sophistication of the form of expression; it may also lie in the caliber of the experience rendered: the difficulty overcome was in living to tell about it, and summoning one's vital forces to do the telling, while maintaining the ethical position that harmonizes with the matters told. The intentness of attention that such texts command leaves little space for distinctions between the moral component and the touch of aesthetic appreciation in the reader's response to both texts.

3 The value and perils of comparison

The value of the comparative study of the literature of the Gulag and the literature of the Nazi-period ghettoes and concentration camps is, indeed, associated with the possibility that the literature of this aspect of the Holocaust and the KZ[10] and the literature of the Gulag can shed light on each other: the testimony

---

[8] The term used in Ravensbrück was *goldstück*, in Majdanek it was *gamel* (Warmund: 167).
[9] On the aesthetic effect of congruence of content and stance, see the Romantic poet William Wordsworth's discussion of plain-folk epitaphs (1810 [1974]: 48–99).
[10] KZ stands for Nazi concentration camp, from the German *Konzentrationslager*.

of one corpus complements and illuminates the testimony of the other.[11] The testimony concerns events, camp conditions, and the human experience. In the context where other historical sources are available, narrative testimony to the facts can become redundant, but the relevance of testimony to the specificities of experience survives historiographical redundancy. Its impact is enhanced by the artistic qualities of the text, which move to the foreground of our attention when the narratives in question no longer have to be read "for the facts."

A great number of historical studies have compared Stalin's and Hitler's regimes and the types of political persecution and genocidal waves for which each was responsible; they were eventually complemented by literary-critical studies, such as those by Terrence Des Pres and Tzvetan Todorov.[12] I regard literary studies as important for historiography because they are better adapted to evocation of the human experience involved. The inevitable complexities of judgement and of suspending judgement demand humility in writing about the camps.[13] On the other hand, any responsible mental operation in processing the material may complicate, refine or modify our model approximations of concentration camp experience and its contexts.

Of course, irrespective of the so-called "uniqueness debate," drawing *analogies* is among the most perilous of analytic procedures (if all cats are gray, it is because the perceiver is benighted), yet it can be justified if the prominent features of one term provide a comment on the veiled features of the other. That which is explicit in the semiotics of the Nazi camps can elucidate what remains veiled in the Gulag – and conversely: that which is systematically explored in the literature of the Gulag may remain understated, almost overlooked in the

---

[11] As Jakob Lothe has put it (in conversation with the author, 2015), "the disnarrated" (see Prince 1988) of one corpus can become "the narrated" of the other.

[12] In addition to comparatively brief remarks in more general historical works, e.g. Conquest (1990: 195–206), see, for instance, Bullock (1992), Kershaw and Lewin (1997), Rousso (1999), Snyder (2010). The interdisciplinary field that combines studies of literature of the Gulag and the Holocaust includes Bernadette Morand's (1976) book, which places the two bodies of literature within the broader genre of political prisoners' writing; Terrence Des Pres's *The Survivor* (1976), which uses both the Nazi Konzentrationslager and the Gulag materials to construct the sociology of camp experience and revise traditional values (of heroism or conformity) in its light; Alain Parrau's (1995) study, which juxtaposes several separate aspects of the *Konzentrationslager* and Gulag testimony; and Tzvetan Todorov's *Facing the Extreme* (1991 [1996]), which offers further ethical reflections. My forthcoming study (Toker 2019) is mainly devoted to the issues of artistic representation and concentrates on cases where the context that each body of literature provides for the other proves to be particularly illuminating.

[13] See reflections on this cognitive inaccessibility of the experience of the victims in, for instance, Jurgenson (2003), Liu (2009), Clendinnen (1999), and the introductory chapter to Lothe et al. (2012).

literature about Nazi camps. The same relationship may obtain between the literary representations of the so-called red camps and the so-called brown ones.

Jürgen Kocka describes historiographical comparisons as discussing "two or more historical phenomena systematically with respect to their similarities and differences in order to reach certain intellectual aims"; these aims may be "heuristic, descriptive, analytical, and paradigmatic" (2003: 39). The heuristic method, one in which comparison helps "to identify questions and problems that one might miss, neglect, or just not invent otherwise" (Kocka 2003: 40), is of special value in the comparative study of concentration camp literature.

Yet the methodology of comparative history may be supplemented by that of the so-called "entangled history." We should remain alert to the question of causal connections, vast or small, between the terms of comparison. To what extent and in what ways did the Nazi or Soviet authorities learn from or imitate each other? Comparison may shed light on the scant evidence of this too: the two systems may have owed some of their features to what the theory of historiographical comparison calls "reciprocal observation and transfer" (Patel 2005: 18). Mainly, I believe, things that were unthinkable in one of the systems may have become "thinkable" because they were practiced in the other: each of the systems of atrocity provided the *Zeitgeist* background to the other.

The issue of the legitimacy of comparisons is, of course, complicated by "Holocaust uniqueness" debates that have consumed much intellectual energy over at least three past decades.[14] There are prominent features that single out the Holocaust from other atrocities, including the Armenian genocide of 1915 or the events in Rwanda; there are features of the Stalinist Great Terror that find themselves repeated in Pol Pot's Cambodia, but these features do not recur as a full syndrome; those other catastrophes developed singular syndromes of their own: "every country and every region has its own *Sonderweg*" (Kocka 1999: 48).

---

[14] On the uniqueness debate," see, for instance, the collection of essays *Is the Holocaust Unique? Perspectives in Comparative Genocide*, ed. Alan S. Rosenbaum, first published in 1996 and reprinted twice since; the reflections of Wlad Godzich (2009) and a very useful critical survey of the issue in Gavriel D. Rosenfeld's *Hi Hitler!* (2015: 78–121). The topic is an intellectual minefield: even the fascinating symposium on "Jewish values in the post-Holocaust future" (*Judaism* [1967]: 266–99) seems at some point to have slipped into a wasteful debate for and against the particularity or generality of the Holocaust, at the expense of attention to illuminating statements by, for instance, Emil Fackenheim, George Steiner, and Elie Wiesel. An insightful philosophical treatment of the issue of "uniqueness" is provided in Bernard Harrison's "The uniqueness debate revisited" (Harrison 2015), which lends support to Gunnar Heinsohn's argument that Hitler sought to exterminate the Jews as bearers of the belief in the sanctity of human life, that he thus sought "a genocide for the purpose of reinstalling the right to genocide" (Heinsohn 2000: 424) in preparation for capturing his *Lebensraum*.

Sustained attention to the history and significance of each is a moral imperative. What I propose is not to link the Gulag and the Holocaust, or, for that matter, the Armenian genocide and Hiroshima, in order to broaden our concern with humanity,[15] but to concentrate on those issues whose understanding is improved by a comparative discussion of selected aspects of events if and when they comment on each other's import.[16] Of help here may be Marcel Detienne's (2000) method of comparing what a literary critic may call selected micromotifs of "incomparable" anthropological formations.

The challenge remains to not allow the discussion of analogies to lead either to a "comparative suffering" discourse or to "Holocaust obfuscation" (Robbins 2010), and to not allow it to promote either trivializing the Gulag or "normalizing" the Holocaust. Comparing the incomparable, to borrow the title of Detienne's book, need not be detrimental to the terms in the juxtaposition. At the same time, the phenomena which, by a kind of conceptual shorthand, we can refer to as the Holocaust and the Gulag, form an entangled complex because, among other things, they were deployed over overlapping spaces and times (Snyder 2010: 377) and may represent similar developments in contiguous moral climates.

I shall illustrate some of the above statements through a comparison of a short story by Varlam Shalamov and a chapter by Primo Levi. This comparison will suggest that the very fact that some features of institutions and of the existential position of inmates are clearly evident in one of the systems and obfuscated in the other can also carry a semiotic load: the case is not only of analogies bringing distinctions into higher relief but also of distinctions competing against analogies for retrospective attention.

3.1 *Selektion* in the Gulag: Varlam Shalamov

Varlam Shalamov's short story *Odinochnyi zamer* ("An individual assignment"; 1955) from the first cycle of *Kolyma Tales*,[17] is set in a convict-worked gold mine of Kolyma. The overseer announces to prisoner Dugaev, a 23-year-old and already exhausted former student, that the next day he will be working alone. Dugaev is glad that nobody will hustle him, but the reaction of the other people around him is strange. The foreman suddenly falls silent and raises his eyes to

---

15 As Marie L. Baird put it in talking about Todorov's comments on Primo Levi (Baird 2005: 203), the "truth" about human nature "should not have to be purchased at so high a price."
16 This may be regarded as a literary-critical version of the method of comparative history described by Marc Bloch in 1928 (1963: 16–40).
17 For a reading of that story in the context of the cycle see Toker (2000: 151–152).

the evening star that has, symbolically, appeared over a hill. Dugaev's partner Baranov starts fussing mildly. The two obviously understand what Dugaev and the first-time reader do not, namely, that when a prisoner works alone, without a partner, the amount of his own production can be measured exactly and compared to the set quota. In the fateful year of 1938, when the story is obviously set, the results of such measurement could be fatal.

Shalamov's references to landscape and natural environment are usually sparse and symbolic[18]: the foreman's raising his eyes to the sky may be a sign of his embarrassment and wish to avoid looking at Dugaev, but the evening star is a symbol of Dugaev's fate, still unknown to him; it is written in the stars – he is now a dead man walking. In Kolyma prisoners were buried in mass graves dug under the hills[19] –the foreman's glance at a waning star above the hill may remind the reader of KZ prisoners' glances at the smoking chimney of a crematorium. Yet the difference in the visual and emotional content of the objects of the glance is one example of the way a structural analogy may belie an incommensurability of objects in terms of actual human experience.

After the evening meal Baranov unexpectedly offers Dugaev a hand-rolled cigarette, which on first reading we may fail to recognize as one of the items in the classical repertoire of the last wishes of the condemned. Dugaev is surprised at what in a camp is a generous gesture, but his attention is diverted from its unusual character by Baranov's standard proviso: have a smoke, but "leave me some" (1994: 21). A subversive recycling of a literary topos is thus joined with an item in a specific semiotic code. By gesturing towards camp semiotics, Baranov, who seems to understand the situation very well, is actually collaborating with the authorities in keeping Dugaev unaware of his fate, while paying tribute to that fate in his own way.[20] Yet for all we know, he may have simply wanted those few residual puffs; and for all we know, he may have been the one who has informed on Dugaev and is now facing the consequences of his act.

Exerting himself the next day, Dugaev produces 25 percent of the quota. In 1938 achieving less than 30 percent of the quota could have meant "sabotage"; but Dugaev does not know this.[21] In the evening he is called to an interrogator but asked only standard questions. The following day he again works with

---

[18] On Shalamov's rejection of landscape for its own sake in fiction that doubles as testimony, see a brief discussion of the poetics of "new prose" in Toker (2000: 150–160).
[19] In Shalamov's story *Po lendlizu* (*Lend-Lease*, 1994: 275–283) a spring landslide uncovers such a burial ground, with corpses preserved whole by the permafrost.
[20] Cf. Frankl (1962: 8) on the condemned person's "delusion of reprieve."
[21] Paradoxically, fulfilling 30 percent and getting only part of the rations often turned out to be a better way to survive than fulfilling the whole quota and getting the full ration, which still did

Baranov; in the evening he is led away behind the fence, to the area from which the tractor has been heard roaring at night. The punchline of the story is that, "having understood what the matter was, Dugaev regretted that he had labored to no purpose, on that last day" (2004: 63). His deepest last wish might have been for a day's reprieve from slave labor.

Death, even one's own, is thus presented as a matter-of-fact eventuality. The prisoner emerges as reduced emotionally and intellectually to such an extent that even in his final moments he can think of and regret nothing more than having missed a chance to rest on his last day, after his fate had been sealed by the previous day's production measurements and the pro forma interrogation. This is Shalamov's ironic recycling of another topos – that of a person's whole life passing in review at the last moments before death; here, a whole life contracts to the dim memory of an exhausting workday. Yet Dugaev may be seen as achieving a transcendent insight after all, in so far as, together with the reader, he seems to understand not only what is in store for him but the whole procedure, including the use of the tractor to jam the sound of the shots and the cynicism with which the regime squeezes the last pounds of gold-bearing sand out of the condemned.

The use of a condemned man as the center of consciousness shapes the story as clearly fictional.[22] Yet, as the hint at Dugaev's final insight may suggest, with the tractors roaring every night, and with the people around him clearly in on some veiled regularities, Dugaev's case is typical, and the story can be read as testimony: its implicit representativeness goes a long way to deactivating the "as if" convention.[23] Shalamov's scattered autobiographical notes show that he himself had first-hand familiarity with the constituents of Dugaev's experience (the actual moment of Dugaev's execution is not described – this no one has returned to narrate): he had himself become skeletal, working in the gold mines, he had narrowly escaped in-camp execution at least twice, both times in conditions similar to Dugaev's and involving similar apparent indifference to life or death. Later in his camp life he was given an individual assignment with the view to reducing his food rations – that, however, happened in later years, not in

---

not replenish the calories spent. This irregularity is also repeatedly confirmed by Solzhenitsyn. Julius Margolin's memoir likewise alludes to his struggle to achieve at least 30 percent of the quota; yet he too eventually becomes a "goner." The 2016 version of Margolin's book contains chapters and passages reconstituted by Luba Jurgenson's archival research; these materials had been elided in the 1952 Chekhov Publishing House (NY) edition. The recent French translation by Jurgenson, *Voyage au pays des Ze-Ka* (2010), includes the elided materials, as does the Hebrew edition (Margolin 2013). The book is still awaiting publication in English.

22 On "signposts of fictionality" see Cohn (1999: 109–132).
23 See Iser (1993: 12–23) on the role of the "as if" convention in constituting "the fictive."

the fatal year of 1938. Whatever other effects the fictionalization of camp experience may produce, in this story its main impact is an enhanced sense of the seriality of Dugaev's fate.

All this, and more, one can gather on reading the story by itself and in its Soviet context. Yet if one reads it in the context of the literature of the Holocaust, one can see in it a Kolyma version of KZ in-camp *Selektion*. In 1938, exhausted Gulag prisoners, whose production yields were low, were executed almost as surely as the depleted prisoners in the KZ, only the selection was carried out not in a nightmarish pageant, the to-the-left/to-the-right division on arrival in Birkenau or the inspection of naked bodies within the camps, but in an inconspicuous, matter-of-fact, callous but not sadistic manner, under the cover of a pseudo-legal procedure with pro forma interrogations and protocols and a summary verdict in absentia. In 1938 hundreds of thousands of new prisoners were due to arrive in remote camps from mainland prisons. Room had to be made for them, and not only by building new barracks. Of course, in the Nazi camps mass executions of prisoners to make space for new transports were much quicker, more massive, and less ceremonious.

3.2 *Selekcja* in Auschwitz: Primo Levi

Chapter 13 of Primo Levi's *If This is a Man* presents a story of an Auschwitz *Selekcja*.[24] This is a first-person narrative of a survivor, but it is deployed in such a way as to achieve an effect of seriality, by narrative means different from Shalamov's. The event is preceded by rumors of its imminence, which prove to be true. A multiple non-choice of possible outcomes is evoked, and a paradigm of responses to the results of the *Selekcja* is constructed. When the day comes, the prisoners walk naked in front of SS men. It is not themselves but their registration cards that are then divided into two piles: those of the condemned go "to the left," a thin euphemism for the *schlechte Seite* ([the bad side], Levi 1990: 134). The documents are sorted not away from the prisoners' eyes, as in the Gulag, but in a more immediate manner, so that the prisoner can catch a glimpse of his fate. The split second of the SS decision creates a kind of a "disnarrated:" what does not happen to Primo and his friend Alberto does happen to others, in particular to the still strong René who stoops a little and wears glasses.[25] The SS judgment of the

---

[24] Here I respect Primo Levi's transliteration, *selekcja* (1990: 130). The word means the selection of those to be sent to the gas chambers.
[25] A token of an intellectual, spectacles used to provoke derision or hostility of the guards in both Nazi and Soviet camps.

prisoners' condition is not infallible: "René passed the commission immediately in front of me and there could have been a mistake with our cards. I think about it, discuss it with Alberto, and we agree that the hypothesis is probable. I do not know what I will think tomorrow and later; today I feel no distinct emotion" (Levi 1990: 134). The life of one intellectual has been randomly spared by the condemnation of another in his stead. We do have Levi's book as a result; but perhaps had René survived, we might have had another.

"I feel no distinct emotion" resonates with the blank indifference of Shalamov's protagonist on being driven away from the execution site of Sepantinnaia in *The Lawyers' Plot*. Nor is the theme of the last wish elided in the episode. By local initiative, those selected to die are given a double ration of soup, but they sometimes have to exert themselves and beg for it, less or more obtrusively:

> Ziegler holds out his bowl, collects his normal ration and then waits there expectantly. "What do you want?" asks the *Blockältester*: according to him, Ziegler is entitled to no supplement, and he drives him away, but Ziegler returns and humbly persists. He was on the left, everybody saw it, let the *Blockältester* check the cards; he has the right to a double ration. When he is given it, he goes quietly to his bunk to eat. (Levi 1990: 135)

As in Shalamov's *An Individual Assignment*, the episode stages a tension between knowing and ignorance, possession or lack of semiotic proficiency. One of the condemned (also by "mistake") is Sattler, a Transylvanian peasant, still strong, newcomer to the camp:

> Sattler does not understand German, he has understood nothing of what has taken place, and stands in a corner mending his shirt. Must I go and tell him that his shirt will be of no more use? (Levi 1990: 135)

In Levi's sarcastic comment – as, clearly, in his experience – knowledge predominates: most of the victims will "depart" for the gas chambers in full awareness of going to death.

The story of *selekcja* ends with a glimpse of a person who does have "distinct emotion" on finding himself on the "good" side[26]:

> I see and hear old Kuhn praying aloud ... Kuhn is thanking God because he has not been chosen.
> Kuhn is out of his senses. Does he not see Beppo the Greek in the bunk next to him, Beppo who is twenty years old and is going to the gas chamber the day after tomorrow and knows it and lies there looking fixedly at the light without saying anything and

---

[26] The discussion of this episode is, to a large extent, my response to a paper by Manuela Consonni presented at a Jerusalem conference on Elie Wiesel in October 2013.

without even thinking any more? Can Kuhn fail to realize that next time it will be his turn? Does Kuhn not understand that what has happened today is an abomination, which no propitiatory prayer, no pardon, no expiation by the guilty, which nothing at all in the power of man can ever clean again?

If I was God, I would spit at Kuhn's prayer. (Levi 1990: 135–136)

The violence of the narrator's language in respect to Kuhn almost belies his earlier statement "today I feel no distinct emotion." His anger at Kuhn is overdetermined.[27] The most obvious reason for it is Kuhn's tactlessness in the presence of a condemned young man on the bunk next to his, though Levi would also like to imagine Beppo as no longer thinking or hearing. Yet this somewhat violent response ("I would spit at Kuhn's prayer") may also be a defense against the realization that he himself is glad not to have been "chosen" like Beppo or René. Recollecting Shalamov's "goners," it makes sense to imagine Beppo as a *Muselmann* who is "not even thinking any more": the protagonist of *The Lawyer's Plot* is likely to have treated an execution warrant with the same surface indifference with which he treats the reprieve. Notably, however, Primo Levi's narrator does not even dare to imagine what the "young and robust" René (Levi 1990: 134) may be going through in the awareness of his fate. Yet the "goner's" indifference to life and death may spell not his loss of wish to live but his realization of his total inability to actively influence his own fate.

3.3 Narrative axiology

The touch of sarcasm is strong in *An Individual Assignment*, but the pathos of Dugaev's fate is almost completely suppressed. Dugaev is Beppo, whose partner/neighbor Baranov (Kuhn) is both sorry for the condemned and glad that death has so far chosen another rather than himself. The literature of the *Konzentrationslager* can also allow us to imagine Dugaev's body, hidden as it is by the padded clothing of a Gulag inmate. The people around Dugaev seem to treat him with some basic respect, largely erased in Auschwitz by a greater proximity of underclad bodies. Dugaev's sympathetic partner is likely to have been the one to inform on him. Sycophantically, or perhaps out of sheer nervousness, Baranov starts cleaning the already clean trench when he realizes the overseer's plans for

---

[27] In chapter 4 of *House of Dolls*, Ka-Tzetnik similarly presents communal anger against a woman who loudly praised God for having spared her in a recent *Aktion*, when others were taken (see a discussion of this episode in Rogovin 2016: 288–90).

his doomed team mate.[28] Shalamov's story appeals to the cognitive aspect of reading, and creates semiotic proficiency in the reader, like a boat that is being built while sailing it: it makes us reenact and surmount Dugaev's initial lack of understanding. It is the resulting network of ironies that downplays pathos. And yet some of the nature of the camp experience is forced on us through the first-reading shock at the end of the story, when seemingly humdrum acts suddenly turn out to have been leading up to a case of serial execution. The axiology of survivor narratives is largely responsible for staging the ineffable, for giving us a whiff of the experience that is not amenable to plain discursive representation.

4 Comparison and the issue of "entanglement"

Whereas the comparison of the representation of *Selekcja* by Shalamov and Primo Levi is an argument for comparative literary history of the camps, it may bear traces of entangled history as well. In 1955, when Shalamov is believed to have written *An Individual Assignment*, he could hardly have escaped familiarity, not with Primo Levi, but with the historical realities that Levi's book represents, including in-camp *Selekcja*. One cannot know whether or to what extent this familiarity was reflected in the artistic choices behind that story. It seems, moreover, that for many years the entanglement of Gulag literature and the literature of the Nazi concentration camps was negative: they competed for the readers' attention. After the French writer David Rousset, member of the Resistance and survivor of Buchenwald and Neuengamme, started his campaign against Stalin's concentration camps (which were going strong after the German camps were closed), the second and third books (*Les Jours de Notre Mort [The Days of Our Death]* and *Le Pitre ne rit pas [The Clown Does not Laugh]*) of his Buchenwald trilogy did not get the same publicity as his first book, *L'Univers concentrationnaire* ("The Concentrationary Universe"). The situation changed after Khrushchev's unmasking of some of Stalin's crimes at the 20th Congress of the Soviet Communist Party, and, in particular, after the publication of Solzhenitsyn's *One Day in the Life of Ivan Denisovich* in 1962, but perhaps the most dramatic moment in the entanglement of the two strands of literature was the reading of Solzhenitsyn's novella, as well as of Shalamov's *Kolyma Tales*, and of other Gulag works by the French-Spanish writer Jorge Semprun. Semprun wrote some of his

---

28 If he did inform on Dugaev, it may have been because their common output was low due to Dugaev's physical condition and, consequently, the rations that they both received were also very low.

work almost in response to Solzhenitsyn, and his play *The Return of Carola Neher* actually mentions glimpses of the actress in the Gulag narratives of Eugenia Ginzburg and Margarete Buber-Neumann. The study of the entanglement between the two strands of literary history is complicated by the fact that for many years, especially from 1948 to 1956, the Holocaust was a taboo subject in the Soviet Union, and that in the West stories of the Gulag were often written off as instruments of Cold War propaganda. In addition, writers who remained in the Soviet Bloc, such as Tadeusz Borowski and Imre Kertész, having survived Nazi camps, were still liable to find themselves in one or another version of the Gulag. At the present state of scholarship, the causal entanglements between the Gulag and Nazi camps have not been brought to light; much is left to future fact-finding. The same is true for the likelihood of reciprocal influence between literature of the Gulag and literature of the Holocaust; a comparative study may turn out to be a step in that direction, while retaining value in its own right.

Works cited

Baird, Marie L. (2005) "'The gray zone' as a complex of tensions: Primo Levi on Holocaust survival," in *The Legacy of Primo Levi*, ed. Stanislao G. Pugliese (New York: Palgrave Macmillan), 193–206.
Bloch, Marc (1928) [1963] "Pour une histoire comparée des sociétés Européennes" [Towards a comparative history of European societies], in *Mélanges historiques* (Paris: S.E.V.P.E.N.), 16–40.
Bullock, Alan (1992) *Hitler and Stalin: Parallel Lives* (New York: Knopf).
Butskovsky, A. P. (2010) "The fate of a sailor," in *Voices from the Gulag*, ed. Aleksandr Solzhenitsyn, trans. Kenneth Lantz (Evanston: Northwestern University Press), 171–218.
Cohn, Dorrit (1999) *The Distinction of Fiction* (Baltimore: The Johns Hopkins University Press).
Clendinnen, Inga (1999) *Reading the Holocaust* (Cambridge: Cambridge University Press).
Conquest, Robert (1990) *The Great Terror: A Reassessment* (Oxford: Oxford University Press).
Des Pres, Terrence (1976) *The Survivor: An Anatomy of Life in the Death Camps* (Oxford: Oxford University Press).
Detienne, Marcel (2000) *Comparer l'incomparable* [Comparing the incomparable], (Paris: Seuil).
Feldman, Yael S. (2013) "'Not as sheep led to slaughter?' On trauma, selective memory, and the making of historical consciousness," *Jewish Social Studies* 19.3, 139–169.
Godzich, Wlad (2009) "The Holocaust: questions for the humanities," *Partial Answers: Journal of Literature and the History of Ideas* 7.1, 133–148.
Frankl, Victor (1962) [1946] *Man's Search for Meaning: An Introduction to Logotherapy*, trans. Ilse Lasch (Boston: Beacon).
Harrison, Bernard (2015) "The uniqueness debate revisited," in *Deciphering the New Antisemitism*, ed. Alvin H. Rosenfeld (Bloomington: Indiana University Press), 289–325.
Heinsohn, Gunnar (2000) "What makes the Holocaust a uniquely unique genocide," *Journal of Genocide Research* 2.3, 411–430.

Iser, Wolfgang (1993) *The Fictive and the Imaginary: Charting Literary Anthropology* (Baltimore: The Johns Hopkins University Press).

Jurgenson, Luba (2003) *L'expérience concentrationnaire est-elle indicible?* [Is it possible to convey concentration camp experience?], (Paris: Rocher).

Kershaw, Ian' and Moshe Lewin (1997) *Stalinism and Nazism: Dictatorships in Comparison* (Cambridge: Cambridge University Press).

Kertész, Imre (1992) [1975] *Fateless*, trans. Christopher C. Wilson and Karharina M. Wilson (Evanston: Northwestern University Press).

Kocka, Jürgen (1999) "Asymmetrical historical comparison: The case of the German *Sonderweg*," *History and Theory* 38.1, 40–50.

Kocka, Jürgen (2003) "Comparison and beyond," *History and Theory* 42.1, 39–44.

Levi, Primo (1990) [1987, 1958] *If This is a Man. The Truce*, trans. Stuart Woolf (London: Abacus).

Liu, Sarah (2009) "The illiterate reader: aphasia after Auschwitz," *Partial Answers: Journal of Literature and the History of Ideas* 7.2, 319–342.

Lothe, Jakob, Susan Rubin Suleiman and James Phelan (eds) (2012) *After Testimony: The Ethics and Aesthetics of Holocaust Narrative for the Future* (Columbus: Ohio State University Press).

Margolin, Julius (2010) *Voyage au pays des Ze-Ka* [A voyage to the land of camps], trans. Luba Jurgenson (Paris: Broché).

Margolin, Julius (2013) *Masa l'Eretz Haasirim* [A voyage to the land of camps], trans. Idit Shaked (Jerusalem: Carmel).

Margolin, Julius (2016) *Puteshestvie v stranu zeka i Doroga na zapad* [A voyage to the land of camps and The path to the West], ed. Misha Shauli (Jerusalem: Studio Click), 2 vols.

Morand, Bernadette (1976) *Les Écrits des prisonniers politiques* [The writings of political prisoners], (Paris: Presses Universitaires de France).

Mukařovský, Jan (1970) *Aesthetic Function, Norm and Value as Social Facts*, trans. Mark E. Suino (Ann Arbor: University of Michigan).

Parrau, Alain (1995) *Écrire les camps* [Writing the camps], (Paris: Belin).

Patel, Kiran Klaus (2005) [2003] *Soldiers of Labor: Labor Service in Nazi Germany and New Deal America, 1933–1945*, trans. Thomas Dunlap (New York: Cambridge University Press).

Prince, Gerald (1988) "The disnarrated," *Style* 22.1, 1–8.

Robbins, Wendy (2010) *Heart and Soul: The Holocaust Deniers*, episode 2. BBC World Service 12 December. <http://www.bbc.co.uk/iplayer/episode/p00c74k5/Heart_And_Soul_The_Holocaust_Deniers_Episode_2/> (accessed 14 September 2015).

Rogovin, Or (2016) "Ka-Tzetnik's moral viewpoint," *Partial Answers: Journal of Literature and the History of Ideas* 14.2, 275–298.

Rosenfeld, Gavriel D. (2015) *Hi Hitler! How the Nazi Past is Being Normalized in Contemporary Culture* (Cambridge: Cambridge University Press).

Rousso, Henri (ed) (1999) *Stalinisme et nazisme, histoire et mémoire comparée* [Stalinism and Nazism: comparing history and memory], (Brussels: IHTP/CNRS).

Shalamov, Varlam (1994) *Kolyma Tales*, trans. John Glad (Harmondsworth: Penguin).

Shalamov, Varlam (2004) *Sobranie sochinenii v 6-ti tomakh* [Collected works in 6 volumes], (Moskva: Terra).

Shalamov, Varlam (2018) *Kolyma Stories*, trans. Donald Rayfield (New York: NYRB).

Snyder, Timothy (2010) *Bloodlands: Europe between Hitler and Stalin* (New York: Basic Books).

Todorov, Tzvetan (1991) [1996] *Facing the Extreme: Moral Life in the Concentration Camps*, trans. Arthur Denner and Abigail Pollak (New York: Henry Holt).

Toker, Leona (2000) *Return from the Archipelago: Narratives of Gulag Survivors* (Bloomington: Indiana University Press).

Toker, Leona (2008) "Znaki i simvoly Varlama Shalamova" [Varlam Shalamov's Signs and Symbols], in *Puti isskustva. Simvolizm i evropeiskaia kul'tura XX veka: materialy konferentsii* [Paths in Art: Symbolism and European Culture in the 20th Century], ed. D. M. Segal and
N. M. Segal (Rudnik) (Moskva: Vodolei), 380–390.

Toker, Leona (2019) *Gulag Literature and the Literature of Nazi Camps: An Inter-Contextual Reading* (Bloomington: Indiana University Press), forthcoming.

Warmund, Joram (2005) "The Gray Zone Expanded," in *The Legacy of Primo Levi*, ed. Stanislao G. Pugliese (New York: Palgrave Macmillan), 163–176.

Wiesel, Eli (1967) "Jewish values in the post-Holocaust future: a symposium" (1967) *Judaism* 16.3, 266–299.

Wordsworth, William (1810) [1974] "Essays upon epitaphs," in *The Prose Works of William Wordsworth*, ed. W. J. B. Owen and Jane Worthington Smyser (Oxford: Clarendon), II: 48–99.

Anja Tippner
Worlds Apart? Cross-mapping Camp Literature from the Gulag and Nazi Concentration Camps

1 Introduction

Narratives of confinement and extreme suffering in different kinds of camps constitute an important part of the twentieth-century library of life-writing. Works by Primo Levi, Eugenia Ginzburg, Varlam Shalamov, Ruth Klüger, or Gustaw Herling-Grudziński confront their audiences with accounts of extreme experiences, dehumanization, survival, and strength. These authors as well as many others describe acts of witnessing and documenting the camp experience in writing as a driving force for survival and a moral obligation. Camp narratives like Is *this a Man?* by Primo Levi or *Into the Whirlwind* by Eugenia Ginzburg not only provide us with testimony and insights into the *conditio humana*, they are also important contributions to discussions of totalitarianism, political violence, and the human condition in the twentieth century.

Fictional and documentary representations of confinement and imprisonment, camp narratives provide readers with insight into a secluded and closely guarded world that is now gone, at least in Central Europe. Some of the camps were built as penitentiary and/or labor camps, but often their main purpose was annihilation through work, cold, and terror. In some aspects camp narratives overlap with the older genre of carceral or prison narratives, a genre that has been well established and popular since Romanticism. Both prisons and camps are far removed from everyday life and share metaphors and literary topoi. Camp literature confronts us with many, if not all, aspects of life in the camps and with experiences of incarceration from the point of view of captives and victims who have committed no other crime than the "crime" of being Jewish, of belonging to a minority being, a dissident, or wrongly accused. Testimonial life-writing about the camps most often not only aims to inform about and document the camps, but is also driven by the need to promote resilience and resistance and by the wish to prevent history from repeating itself and expose the ideologies and politics that helped to build the camps.

Definitions of camp literature are as manifold as the camps themselves and partially overlap with narratives of imprisonment and other types of involuntary confinement. Some researchers define the genre as including only testimonies and texts that originate from eye-witness accounts of personal experiences

(Oja 1989: 272). Others are more encompassing in their definition, including texts that try to fathom and depict everyday camp life through fictional accounts of camp experiences or novelization and pseudo-memoirs, in order to "reflect upon the human condition" in prisons and camps (Segel 2012: 2). Finally, while most of the time memoirs from both types of camps are perceived as two separate entities, Polish literary scholar Tadeusz Sucharski argues that Gulag narratives as well as Nazi camp narratives should be classified under one header, as literature that documents and testifies to the camps as an experience of totalitarianism (Pol. *literatura doświadczenia totalitarnego*).

All in all, the camp experiences described by Levi or Solzhenitsyn come to serve as symptoms and symbols of psychic and physical events that traumatize whole societies and nations. This is in no small part due to the influential writing of sociologists and philosophers such as Zygmunt Bauman, Hannah Arendt, or Giorgio Agamben, who have explored the relationship (and to some extent, interdependence) between the camps and modern society within the conceptual frameworks of biopolitics and totalitarianism. Agamben has been particularly influential in this respect, contributing to the de-contextualization and universalization of the Holocaust. His plea to regard the camp "not as [...] an anomaly that – though admittedly still with us – belongs nonetheless to the past but rather in some sense as the hidden matrix and *nomos* of the political space in which we still live" (Agamben 2000: 37) has resonated widely within the humanities and arts.

The "camp" has become a cipher as well as a global reference for the atrocities and disasters that plagued the twentieth century and due to this capacity, different types of camps seem to have become almost similar. This has led to a surge of historical and political studies that do not discuss the comparability of the camps but take it as their point of departure. Even more interesting from the point of view of a literary scholar is the fact that historians, such as Timothy Snyder, Anne Applebaum, and Karl Schlögel, turn to memoirs and testimonial narratives by Holocaust and Gulag survivors to bolster their arguments, citing from Solzhenitsyn without commenting on the literariness of these sources. In contrast, literary studies – with the notable exception of Leona Toker – very rarely view both kinds of camp narratives together, even if they make use of biopolitics as a frame of reference. This chapter will take a different stance, in explicitly comparing or "cross-mapping" literary devices and narratives in order to determine what camp narratives about the Holocaust and Stalin's gulag share with each other and with other carceral narratives, and where they differ. Consequently, my purpose is to acknowledge and analyze structural and thematic similarities in camp narratives without classifying them in terms of "influence" or "appropriation" of a narrative model. I will focus on texts by primary witnesses, such as memoirs, as well as on auto-fiction and prose, but I will not discuss postmemorial texts or texts by secondary witnesses.

2 The difficulties and benefits of comparison

In her memoir *Still Alive. A Holocaust Girlhood Remembered*, Ruth Klüger reflects on the need to compare in order to get a grasp on her experiences, to put them into perspective, and to fully understand them. She writes: "We would be condemned to be isolated monads if we didn't compare and generalize, for comparisons are the bridges from one unique life to another." (Klüger 2001: 64) Though she does not explicitly focus on the comparison of different types of camps, she declares comparison to be a way out of the impasse of unsayability and also a means of conceptualizing her experience. Questions of uniqueness and the possibility to compare have long been a bone of contentment in Holocaust studies. In his seminal book *Writing and Rewriting the Holocaust*, James E. Young observes that "[i]t is ironic that once [the Holocaust as] an event is perceived to be without precedent, without adequate analogy, it would itself become a kind of precedent for all that follows: a new figure against which subsequent experiences are measured and grasped" (1988: 99). In the struggle for recognition victims' groups strive for an analogy of their suffering to the persecution of the Jews and parallelize offenders and perpetrators with the Nazis (Levy and Sznaider 2006: 188). In a paradoxical twist, the "uniqueness" of the Holocaust is reaffirmed in the mode of comparison. Or, in the words of Michael Rothberg, the "assertion of uniqueness [...] actually produces further metaphorical and allegorical appropriations" (2009: 11). This in turn heightens the value of the Holocaust as archetype and metaphor, furthers Holocaust remembrance, and cements its conventions and rituals. Within the logic of Rothberg's concept of multidirectional memory, it is precisely the mode of comparison that helps raise awareness of other events and triggers new memorial cultures. Due to the fact that the Holocaust as such was not a frequent topic of public discourse in the Soviet Union and that very few testimonials or literary representations of Nazi camps were being published before the 1970s, Russian authors of this period could only make scarce use of this analogy. As Holocaust awareness in Russia grew, alongside the need to develop a Russian discourse on terror and the camps as well as an impulse to measure up the Gulag experience to those of the Holocaust, Holocaust comparisons emerged too. Interestingly, Alexander Etkind has also suggested that it is the very idea of uniqueness that is alien "[t]o the scholars of Stalinism, [...] and [that] the reason for this is not only the desire to receive the proper recognition for the victims of

Stalinism but also the intuitive understanding of the multitudes of repression – genocides and democides – that constitute Stalinism" (2013: 11).

This does not mean that these scholars deny the uniqueness of the Holocaust; instead, they use the Holocaust as a foil for comparison (Levy and Sznaider 2006: 115). The *"Historikerstreit"* (historians' dispute) (Augstein 1987), a debate that went on in Germany in the mid-1980s, and centered around the question whether Soviet camps were the model for Nazi camps and whether a comparison was justifiable at all. Whereas Jürgen Habermas refuted Ernst Nolte's claim that the Holocaust was an "Asiatic deed" comparable to Stalin's Gulag or the Turkish genocide of Armenians as inacceptable, contemporary historians such as Timothy Snyder and Jörg Baberowski frequently engage in a comparison of both camp systems. The comparisons that were put forth in the 1980's debate initiated by Habermas, Nolte, Andreas Hillgruber, and Michael Stürmer, among others, were perceived as an attempt to reinterpret and revalidate German history and underplay German guilt. However, contemporary comparisons made after 1989 are based on the argument that there is a common trait to the political and legal structures of state terror and politics of annihilation. According to German historian Jörg Baberowski, historical studies should not be preoccupied with motives or ideological reasoning, but should rather search for spaces of enablement that allow totalitarian terror. These spaces of enablement establish an extraordinary relationship between bodies and language, between individuals and bureaucracies. And what is more important from our perspective, they are indifferent to the ideological foundations that created them.

In his history of post-war Europe, Tony Judt also argues in favor of comparison or, more precisely, of taking an overall view that does not discriminate between Nazi and Soviet camps, stating that:

> Even if Nazism and Communism were utterly different in intent – and even, if in Raymond Aaron's formulation, "there is a difference between an ideology whose logic is monstrous and an ideology that can be given a monstrous interpretation" – that was scant consolation to their victims. (Judt 2007: 826)

What he essentially means is that "[h]uman suffering should not be calibrated according to the goal of the perpetrator" (Judt 2007: 826). Literary scholar Tzvetan Todorov reasons along the same lines. He even devotes a whole chapter to the question to his decision to include both regimes in "the same category, that of totalitarianism," as he does in his book *Facing the Extreme. Moral Life in the Concentration Camps* (Todorov 1997: 132). He contends that "with respect to the camps, whether one stresses differences or similarities [...] depends on one's perspective again." He then notes that "from the inmate's point of view, the Communist and Nazi camps were often identical," choosing

Margarete Buber-Neumann and her testimony in *Under Two Dictators*, which was first published in 1949 as his crown-witness. Since Buber-Neumann was incarcerated in both types of camps, she seems to be particularly well placed to compare them. Interestingly though, she refrains from doing so most of the time, and when she does, it is always with regard to a specific phenomenon such as the treatment of prisoners in the sick bay or prisoner informers. Buber-Neumann's memoir shows very clearly that in the end the difference between being incarcerated for racial or political reasons, because of anti-Semitism or class warfare, can lose its significance. But human suffering can also be calibrated according to the beliefs of the victim. Thus, Polish writer Gustaw Herling-Grudziński insists in his memoir *Inny świat* (*A World Apart*) that every type of prisoner had his or her own camp experience, depending very much on their political, national, and moral attitudes, pointing out that Polish prisoners of war had a very different experience in the Gulag than in the Nazi camps. He was also convinced that the Polish experience in the Gulag differed from the Russian one (Herling-Grudziński 1951: 190–210), as did the German-Jewish communist experience of the Gulag. Herling-Grudziński develops his understanding of the camp experience in dialogue with canonical authors such as Dante and Dostoevsky, but also with his contemporary Tadeusz Borowski, who wrote about his experiences in the Nazi camps in *Kamieny świat* (*World of Stone*). In a similar vein, Etkind argues that the subjective experience of victimization – for example, agreeing with the identification as a "Jew" but disagreeing with the identification as an "enemy of the people" – makes a great difference in terms of resistance or loyalty to the regimes that victimized people (Etkind 2013: 204). Several Gulag memoirists, most notably Eugenia Ginzburg, were at least initially convinced that their arrest and confinement were to a mistake, and remained staunch communists even after the Gulag experience (Artwińska 2019). Ginzburg proclaimed herself a Leninist even after her camp experience (in the epilogue to her memoir [2002: 417]), thus still partly identifying with the system that imprisoned and almost killed her.

3 Differences and similarities between the two camp narratives

It is apparent that within the conceptual frame of comparison prevalent today, Holocaust narratives serve as the backdrop against which any other camp narrative is written and measured. Nancy K. Miller and Jason Tougaw propose that

[if] the Holocaust supplies the paradigm of modern, incommensurable suffering, many of the ethical and aesthetic, moral and formal dilemmas involved in bearing witness to the horrors of the Holocaust reappear and are reconfigured in different national and political contexts. This is not to suggest that other kinds of disaster should be compared in literal ways to the Holocaust as a limit event. (Miller and Tougaw 2002: 4)

They argue that the Holocaust has "produced a discourse" and provided our culture with narrative forms, metaphors, and concepts of truth and authenticity that are now applied to the representations of other forms of traumatic or extreme experiences and that serve as a model for witness accounts, from 9/11 to Sarajevo (Miller and Tougaw 2002: 4). This leads us to an important point when comparing and cross-mapping camp narratives from Nazi and Stalinist camps: Holocaust testimonies were not part of the Soviet literary canon and thus could not function as a frame of reference for Soviet authors who wanted to describe their own camp experiences. On top of this, trauma as a interpretative concept was mostly absent from Soviet and even Post-Soviet discourses on the camps and the Holocaust (Tippner 2018). What is more, Gulag memoirs could hardly give each other context and influence each other's poetics, let alone form a discourse or tradition, since the first camp narratives could only circulate orally and in a clandestine manner. Anne Hartmann has suggested that, in a way, Gulag memoirs "fell out of time," since they were written during Soviet times but not published, and when they could finally be published during the *perestroika* they seemed to have lost some of their societal importance (2016: 159–160). Hence the significance of Solzhenitsyn's *One Day in the Life of Ivan Denisovich*; its publication in 1962 made it the sole camp narrative available to a broader audience in the Soviet Union. In this respect Russian texts differ greatly, for example, from Polish testimonial narratives of both types of camp which were published after the war, enabling a comparison of both types of biopolitics, and comprised both types of camp narrative. In the Soviet Union there were almost no witness accounts and memoirs available for a wider public, and authors did not have access to the privileged discourse and the poetic rules for conveying the trauma that existed in the West, thus expectations to be published were low (Toker 2000: 123). Testimonies were passed on orally and the few literary accounts tended to be fashioned after the dominant model of Socialist realism and integrated parts of the Socialist realist narrative. This is the case with Masha Rol'nikaite's memoir *I Have to Tell* or with Anatolii Rybakov's documentary novel *Heavy Sand*. It is thus safe to assume that the paradigms of narrating trauma developed in Western European Holocaust literature in the 1970s and 1980s only became widely available in the Soviet Union and some parts of Eastern Europe after the *perestroika*. Therefore, the perceived similarities between Holocaust camp narratives and Gulag narratives from before the *perestroika* are most likely due to the subject matter and not to intertextual references to canonical Holocaust authors, such as Primo Levi or Elie Wiesel. Although witnesses of the Soviet camps might refer to similarities in the Nazi and Soviet camp systems, they overwhelmingly do not refer to Holocaust literature since its seminal texts were not available to them at the time of writing.

The different literary contexts of writing about trauma and the camp experience thus notwithstanding, it is apparent that testimonies of survivors, both of Nazi camps and of the Gulag system, share common traits. First and foremost, it is the impulse to bear witness and to speak out, especially for those who are not able to do so any more, that fuels both types of camp narratives. Another notable similarity concerns feelings of isolation and solitariness, but also exposure, that overwhelm victims and that are expressed in both types of camp narratives. Victims' testimonials also share descriptions of feeling objectified through extreme cold, hunger, and pain, feelings of loss and disorientation. The underlying structure of the camps and the logistics of totalitarian bureaucracies result in shared themes, such as the trauma of traveling into the unknown, exploitation and destruction through work or the effects of extreme hunger. Leona Toker has established a set of nine topoi which are displayed to a greater or lesser extent in Gulag camp narratives: arrival, dignity, stages of adaptation, escape, moments of reprieve, blind spots, chance, the zone and the larger zone, end-of-term fatigue. In many ways they mirror the stages of adaptation to camp reality, which Bruno Bettelheim identifies in his essay "Individual and mass behavior in extreme situations" (1943) written shortly after his emigration to the USA. Bettelheim, who was imprisoned in Dachau and Buchenwald during 1938–1939, took a scientist's approach towards the camps and tried to describe their impact on prisoners. As the author points out, this approach towards the camps was a coping mechanism in itself, which helped him to survive.

Some of the similarities between Gulag camp narratives and Holocaust camp narratives may be the result of shared literary references. Most authors discussed here reside firmly within the Western literary canon, with Dostoevsky's *Notes from the House of the Dead*, Dumas's *The Count of Monte Cristo*, and Dante's *Divine Comedy* being the classic texts of confinement and punishment cited most often. Some of the structural and topical similarities between both kinds of camp narratives can be partly traced back to the classics of carceral literature and prison narratives, which also revolve around images of loss of faith, conversion, and redemption that are linked to the liminal quality of the confinement experience. One prominent motif that can be found in many prison narratives is conversion and finding one's true self (Duncan 1988: 1225–1230, Cesareanu 2019: 77). This leads us to a question that authors of both types of camp narrative discuss, namely, whether anything can be learned *in* the camps and *from* the camps. Perhaps the most prominent example of this controversy is documented in the correspondence between Shalamov and Solzhenitsyn, which goes to show that even experiences of extreme violence, suffering, and exposure to the state of exception within the same totalitarian system are open to interpretation (e.g. Shalamov 2009: 641–652), with Shalamov arguing that the camps have no epistemological value, while Solzhenitsyn argues that they do. Even though, this dispute has its historical roots in Russian literature since Tolstoi and Chekhov first wrote about prisons and camps (Medhibovskaya 2017), it is also due to the varying conditions in different camps and different attitudes of the incarcerated towards their imprisonment. There is not *one* camp narrative, because experiences vary, whether within Holocaust literature or Gulag literature, mostly depending on the camp experience itself but also on the time and place of remembering and writing as well as on the cultural discourse of remembrance. As Shalamov famously declared, "Solzhenitsyn doesn't know the camp and he does not understand it."

Even inmates of the same camp may have made vastly different experiences and approached the camp with different attitudes. Camps can be perceived as a disaster that leads to the loss of moral values and dignity, or they can be seen as a lesson, an opportunity to learn something about humankind. In his memoir *If This is a Man*, Primo Levi wrote: "We are in fact convinced that no human experience is without meaning or unworthy of analysis, and that fundamental values, even if they are not positive, can be deduced from this particular world which we are describing." (1959: 99) To the Italian survivor, the camps were a "gigantic social and biological experiment" (Levi 1959: 99) that led some men to grow beyond themselves, while others "drowned" and were annihilated. Levi's view is in accord with Solzhenitsyn's but stands in contrast to Shalamov, who declares: "I am convinced: the camp is a negative experience – entirely. If one spent but an hour there – it would be an hour of moral corruption. The camp has never given anything to anyone – and never could. Everyone, both prisoners and civilians, are corrupted by the camp." (2004–2005: 265) In contrast, Solzhenitsyn confesses that for him the camp had a redemptive quality, that after hitting rock bottom he resurfaced a stronger man (Solzhenitsyn 1978: 98). In contrast to Levi or Solzhenitsyn, Shalamov could not see any redemptive quality in the camp experience. Ruth Klüger agrees with the latter. She cites a short conversation she had with German students who were disappointed by the politics of an Israeli Holocaust survivor:

> How can someone who comes from Auschwitz talk like that? the German asks. I get into the act and argue, perhaps more hotly than need be. What did he expect? Auschwitz was

> no instructional institution, like the University of Göttingen, which he attends. You learned nothing there, and least of all humanity and tolerance. Absolutely nothing good came out of the concentration camps, [...] and he expects catharsis, purgation, the sort of thing you go to the theater for? They were the most useless, pointless establishments imaginable. (Klüger 2001: 65)

Once again, one needs to stress that comparing these structural similarities and discussing analogies established by the authors themselves does not mean that the Nazi camps and Socialist labor camps are one and the same phenomenon. And it is by comparing survivor testimonies that the differences become apparent: The topos of end-of-term fatigue, proposed by Toker, points us towards the most pronounced difference between the Jewish experience of Nazi concentration camps and the Gulag experience. Whereas Gulag narratives revolve around a sentence – regardless of how unjust and arbitrary it may have been – the concepts of sentence, re-education, and correction do not figure in testimonies of Jewish survivors from the Nazi camps. Thus, while the imprisonment in the Gulag was finite, death was the only imaginable fate for Jewish prisoners in the Nazi camps. As Primo Levi has noted in *If This is a Man*: "For us, on the contrary, the *Lager* is not a punishment; for us, no end is foreseen and the *Lager* is nothing but a manner of living assigned to us, without limits of time, in the bosom of the Germanic social organism." (1959: 94) Even if the designated day of release seemed to be an eternity away for many Gulag prisoners, there was a release date and all of the most prominent Gulag witnesses (Ginzburg, Solzhenitsyn, Shalamov) lived to see it. Margarete Buber-Neumann also ponders this difference and concludes that the fact that even for non-Jewish captives there was "no term [...] fixed for release" was "one of the worst features of German concentration camps" (2008: 183).

Another crucial difference between both types of camp narratives concerns the position of victim and perpetrator. According to Daniel Levy and Natan Sznaider, the dichotomy of helpless but morally virtuous victims and cruel perpetrators, "the clear ethical boundaries [...] between good and evil" that characterized Nazi camps, offered moral guidelines and certainty (2006: 159). After 1989 this may be one of the last ultimate certainties in an uncertain world. The identification with victims contributes to the popularity of the camp narratives in contemporary culture. This dichotomy has been abundantly problematized, most importantly by Primo Levi in his 1986 essay collection *The Drowned and the Saved*. Here, Levi notes that the space that separates perpetrators from victims is not empty. A perception, he adds, which is pertinent not only to Nazi camps but also to the Gulag and other extreme situations (Levi 1989: 40). He introduces the concept of the "gray zone" in order to depict the moral dilemmas that were engendered by the structure of the camps, especially the way in which the Nazis assigned privileges or recruited victims as helpers and forced them to move into this zone of moral ambivalence. Soviet camps never allowed for such a clear-cut opposition and veered towards the uncertain territory of the gray zone again and again. As historian Lynne Viola noted about perpetrators in Soviet history:

> The "gray areas" of victimhood and perpetrator status were multiple and far more complex than in the case of Nazi Germany, where, regardless of the racial absurdities of concrete definition [...], the Jew was a Jew unless somehow dangerously cloaked within the official order. The enemy was clearly the "other." In the Stalinist context, the enemy was internal. He could be anyone. (Viola 2013: 10)

One of the defining traits of Gulag culture is in fact the complicated and unstable distinction between perpetrators and victims, since perpetrators can become victims and victims may have been perpetrators before their imprisonment. Even seemingly clear-cut distinctions at the time of the events, become hazy in retrospective, as shown, for example, by Ginzburg with regard to several protagonists, including the narrator herself. In the concluding pages of her book, Ginzburg writes:

> In our times, the boundary between perpetrators and victims is blurred, it is almost nonexistent. This is a big difference to the year 1905 for example, were *they* were on one side of the barricades and *we* were on the other. How many of those, who forced me into the Stalinist abyss, were later thrown into it themselves. (Ginzburg 2008: 784)

The blurred lines and the complicated after-thoughts and after-history of the camps mean that the Gulag is much more difficult to assimilate into the cultural memory. The ambivalent nature of the Gulag itself, as well as the fact that Soviet labor camps have not only been condemned as hell on earth but also praised as a means of Socialist re-education, add to the complexity. Even if books such as the infamous collection on the Belomorkanal are deemed to be pure propaganda, there existed a "dual image" of the camp in Russian public discourse, as Dariusz Tołczyk (1999) has shown. The "rotation" of perpetrators and victims within the Soviet culture of terror and persecution as well as the ambivalent perception of the camps make it more difficult, if not impossible, to "reach a historical, philosophical [...] – in fact, any rational – understanding of these events at all" (Etkind 2013: 7–8). This fact may also explain why it was, and still is, difficult to turn Soviet camps into a universal cipher of persecution and annihilation parallel to the Nazi camps.

Last but not least, another marked difference in the conceptualization and narration of Nazi and Soviet camps concerns their distinct topographies. A comparison of Nazi camp narratives and Gulag testimonials reveals that a crucial element of the Soviet camp is the zone, as Leona Toker has shown (Toker 2000).

Although both camp cultures share common traits, such as watch towers, barbed wire, and cramped barracks, the outlines of Soviet camps are at once less pronounced, more permeable, and much more expansive than those of the Nazi camps. Some of the Soviet camps did not even need fencing due to their localization. In his essay *GULAG kak tsivilizatsiia* ("The camp as civilization"), Russian writer Andrei Bitov points out: "The camp is a model of our (that is the Soviet) world" (1997: 6), thus echoing Agamben, yet at the same time diverging from the much more encompassing understanding of the camps in the works of the Italian philosopher. In other aspects, Bitov's exploration of the Soviet space follows Agamben's, for example, his notion that the camp symbolizes a "dislocating localization" (Agamben 2000: 44), even if its application is restricted to the Soviet experience.

The experience of being dropped on another planet, in another world, as suggests the title of Herling-Grudziński's memoir, is shared by inmates of both types of camps alike. It is thus more than a coincidence that David Rousset's testimony of Buchenwald and Neuengamme *L'Univers concentrationnaire* ("The Concentrationary Universe"; 1946) was given the same title in the Englisch translation (Rousset 1951). The alien quality of the camps gains a double significance in testimonies by Western European prisoners in the Soviet system, as Izabela Sariusz-Sząpska has pointed out in her study on Polish gulag testimonies, among them those of Herling-Grudziński. She underlines the fact that the Russian chronotopos is different in its ambivalence, since Russia is traditionally conceived of as space without frontiers and borders and shaped by its geographical expansion, a trait that contrasts the confinement of the gulag as well as ways in which the landscape is used to discipline the inmates (Sariusz-Skąpska 2012: 40). In the Russian context, this dislocation is reflected in the Russian word *zona* (the zone), which denotes the space of the camp marked by fences, barbed wire, and watch towers, but also any other space that stands in opposition to freedom (Etkind 2013: 9). This enables the Russian differentiation of *malaia zona* (the small zone), which denotes the camp, and *bol'shaia zona* (the great zone), which denotes the USSR as a whole. Regardless where the found themselves, former inmates never felt truly "free" again. Reading the Gulag memoir of Eugenia Ginzburg, especially the chapter devoted to her time in Magadan which was not a camp but still somewhat exterritorial and camp-like, can serve as an illustration to this fact.

The special topography of the Soviet camps and the complicated relationship between the small zone and the great zone engender another difference of Soviet and Nazi camp narratives, first noted by Leona Toker:

> The double-edged effect of Gulag literature – raising the consciousness of the target audience and presenting free instructions to the Lubyanka – distinguishes the history of this

corpus from that of the Holocaust literature, which came into being after the Nazi *Lagers* had been turned into museums. (Toker 2000: 76)

Herling-Grudziński, who experienced the Gulag but as a Pole was eventually allowed to leave the Soviet Union and the zone, adds an epilogue to his camp memoir *A World Apart*, in which he stresses the difference between life in the camps and life outside. He remembers an encounter with a former fellow prisoner, who confesses that he had informed on four other prisoners, eventually executed, in order to save his own life. Now, in June 1945 in Rome, he craved for Herling-Grudziński's absolution and forgiveness, something the Polish author could not grant. For him granting absolution and proclaiming understanding, would have meant to return, mentally, to the camp, to accept the morality of the camp. In contrast to Soviet authors, Herling-Grudziński insists on the difference between life in the zone and life outside the zone: "The days of our life are not like the days of our death, and the laws of our life are not the laws of our death. I had come back among people, with human standards and conceptions, and was I now to escape from them, abandon them, voluntarily betray them?" (1951: 247) He could do so because he was a free man in a free country, and did so because he wanted to stress this difference. In this aspect, his text is closer to narratives about Nazi camps, which were mostly written when the system that had built the camps had been destroyed and the camps with it, while Gulag camp literature was usually written while the camps were still very much a fact of Soviet life.

4 Conclusions

Narratives of confinement and captivity written during or after the camps share many common aspects. These similarities can be explained partly through recourse to older forms of carceral narratives and the tropes and devices these texts established, and partly with the shared extreme and traumatic experiences that are beyond human comprehension and that characterize both types of camps. The differences in both types of camp narratives are to a great extent due to the systemic and ideological differences between Nazi and Soviet systems.

The differences between Gulag and Nazi camp narratives have a strong influence on the way both types of camps are perceived, remembered, and re-narrated today. The different memorial cultures and the different memorial forms in which these two types of camp narratives are embedded and which shaped them, brought about a diametrically divergent postmemorial culture. First, Gulag camp narratives are still not part of a European culture of remembrance in the same way as Nazi camp narratives are. This is very much evidenced by attempts of countries like the Baltic States, Poland, or Hungary to implement gulag remembrance in the curricula of European schools and to introduce a day of remembrance for the victims of communism. Despite these efforts, the topic has not succeeded in getting the attention of a wider audience, and is often met with contempt and resentment.

Within the Russian context this might also be due to the fact that not only the testimonies are absent but also material objects that could compensate this blank space and tell the same story, like the iconic objects of the Holocaust such as suitcases, children's toys or glasses. Thus, it does not come as a surprise that camp narratives do not make part of the Russian culture of remembrance (Shcherbakova 2015). These differences in the presence and reception of the erstwhile primary testimony lead to differences in their postmemorial perception and re-presentation through secondary or intellectual witnesses. This might be one of the reasons for the failed attempts to position the experience of the Gulag as parallel to that of Nazi concentration camps. Svetlana Boym has suggested that "[whereas] the experience of Auschwitz profoundly influenced western political philosophy [and popular culture] of the twentieth century, [...] the experience of the Soviet gulag did not" (2008: 343). Even if this is perhaps exceedingly absolutist, the critical response to Solzhenitsyn in the 1970s was overwhelming and helped change attitudes of a whole generation of left thinkers in the West towards the USSR, it is still true that the Soviet camp system does not engage the cultural imagination in the same way the Nazi camps do. This can be seen as a problem but also an opportunity, since it will allow the postmemorial literature about the Gulag to form without the convention or economical strictures that have long accompanied camp literature about the Holocaust. In his discussion of desired reactions to narratives and representations of the camps and the Holocaust, Dominick LaCapra has put forth the concept of "emphatic unsettlement." He develops this concept with regard to Claude Lanzmann's film *Shoah*, declaring that the secondary witnesses, be they writers, critics or readers, are supposed to "reactivate and transmit not trauma but an unsettlement [...] that manifests empathy (but not full identification) with the victim" (LaCapra 1997: 267). The idea of "emphatic unsettlement" may also be seen as a reaction to the commercial success of films such as *Schindler's List, Life is Beautiful,* or *The Pianist* that moved audiences and turned the Holocaust into a spectacle, as a reaction to its uneasy coexistence with the "enjoyment [and pleasure] we associate with fiction [or films]" (Parks 2014: 37). The disconnect between the historical experience and pop-cultural facts seems to be less evident in the Gulag, where there are so far very few fictionalized accounts and even fewer feature films, none of which can claim a comparable success in movie theatres to films about the Holocaust. One exception might be the wave of crime stories and thrillers that use the Gulag as a backdrop, such as the novels by Tom Rob Smith or Martin Cruz Smith (Frieß 2016). One has to note though, that despite efforts at authenticity, these novels do not adhere to the same rules of factuality in depicting the Gulag as do novels about the Holocaust. The fact that a combination of crime story and the Gulag seems to be feasible points us again to a notable difference in the reception of and knowledge about different types of camp narratives. Thus, the necessities of testimonial dialogue and the ways in which it is warded off vary depending on the emotional, cultural, and political needs of different societies. Often, testimony and camp narratives serve several functions – they aid the writer in his/her personal recovery, they help a society to come to terms with a difficult past, or they help establish a collective discourse on a topic that had been taboo for a long time: "Testimony records a movement from individual experience to the collective archive, from personal trauma to public memory. But when testimony located on a national stage is riven by conflicting aims among those bearing witness, such a transformation is impeded." (Miller and Tougaw 2002: 13)

To this day, Russian society has only just begun to look for these testimonies and to incorporate them in the cultural imaginary. Despite the significant number of Gulag memoirs that were published after the *perestroika* there are still very few texts of this genre that make part of the Russian literary canon, and one might add, the Polish or Czech literatry canon as well. The same holds true for the integration of gulag experiences in the communicative or family archive. Here too, as evidenced in Orlando Figes book *The Whisperers* (2007) circulation and public forms of remembrance are scarce. In sum, this makes postmemorial representations and evocations difficult, as is documented by the reception of Zakhar Prilepin's novel *Obitel'* (*Abode*; 2014) which treats the Solovki gulag. One of the few exceptions is Sergei Lebedev's novel *Oblivion* (2015) which deals with Russia's need to come to terms with the gulag and its violent past. Ann Rigney has stated that "scarcity" is a defining trait of all memory work, but one can see that in comparison Russian authors in particular have much less material at hand if they wish to re-narrate and re-create the Gulag experience for contemporary readers. Only through "recursivity," that is "visiting the same place, repeating the same stories" (Rigney 2005:20), can cultural memory be created. As noted above, memory work and recursivity are made more complicated, if there are only few stories available for retelling. Whereas post-catastrophic narratives that deal with the Holocaust can take a certain knowledge of the facts for granted, Gulag narratives by secondary witnesses have to establish their subject matter again and again, since the facts have not taken hold within a public memorial culture. The scarcity of camp narratives from communist camps is part of the problem and one of the fundamental differences between both types of camp literature.

Works cited

Agamben, Giorgio (2000) "What is a Camp?" in *Means without Ends. Notes on Politics* (Minneapolis and London: University of Minnesota Press), 37–48.
Artwińska, Anna (2019) "A communist woman in the Gulag: Gender, ideology, and limit-experience in Ginzburg and Budzyńska" in *Narratives of Annihilation, Confinement, and Survival. Camp Literature in a Transnational Perspective*, ed. Anja Tippner and Anna Artwińska (Berlin/Boston: De Gruyter), 231–252.
Augstein, Rudolf (ed) (1987) *Historikerstreit: Die Dokumentation der Kontroverse um die Einzigartigkeit der Judenvernichtung* [The historians' dispute: documentation of the controversy about the uniqueness of the Holocaust], (München: Piper).
Bal, Mieke (2002) *Travelling Concepts in the Humanities. A Rough Guide* (Stanford: Stanford University Press).
Baberowski, Jörg (2016) *Scorched Earth: Stalin's Reign of Terror* (Cumberland: Yale University Press).
Bettelheim, Bruno (1943) "Individual and mass behavior in extreme situations," *The Journal of Abnormal and Social Psychology* 38.4, 417–452.
Bitov, Andrei (1997) "GULAG kak tsivilizatsiia" [GULAG as civilization], *Zvezda* 5, 3–31.
Borowski, Tadeusz (1980) *This Way for the Gas, Ladies and Gentlemen* (Harmondsworth: Penguin Books).
Boym, Svetlana (2008) "'Banality of evil', mimicry, and the Soviet subject: Varlam Shalamov and Hannah Arendt," *Slavic Review* 67.2, 342–363.
Bronfen, Elisabeth (2003) "Cross-mapping. Kulturwissenschaft als Kartographie von erzählender und visueller Sprache" [Cross-mapping: cultural studies as a cartography of narrative and visual language], in *Kulturwissenschaften. Forschung, Praxis, Positionen*, ed. Lutz Musner and Gotthart Wunberg (Freiburg: Rombach Verlag), 121–151.
Buber-Neumann, Margarete (2008) *Under Two Dictators. Prisoner of Stalin and Hitler* (London: Pimlico).
Carnochan, W. B. (1995) "The literature of confinement," in *Oxford History of the Prison: The Practice of Punishment in Western Society*, ed. Norval Morris and David J. Rothman (New York: Oxford University Press), 381–407.
Cesereanu, Ruxandra (2019) "Representations of the Gulag and methods of resistance: Romanian detention memoirs" in *Narratives of Annihilation, Confinement, and Survival. Camp Literature in a Transnational Perspective*, ed. Anja Tippner and Anna Artwińska (Berlin/Boston: De Gruyter), 71–88.
Duncan, Martha Grace (1988) "Cradled on the sea: positive images of prison and theories punishment," *California Law Review* 76.6, 1201–1247.
Etkind, Alexander (2013) *Warped Mourning. Stories of the Undead in the Land of the Unburied* (Stanford: Stanford University Press).
Ferretti, Maria (2011) "The Shoah and the Gulag in Russian memory," in *Clashes in European Memory: The Case of Communist Repression and the Holocaust*, ed. Muriel Blaive, Christian Gerbel and Thomas Lindenberger (Innsbruck: StudienVerlag), 23–37.
Figes, Orlando (2007) *The Whisperers: Private Life in Stalin's Russia* (New York: Metropolitan Books).

Fischer von Weikersthal, Felicitas and Karoline Thaidigsmann (2016) "Introduction," in *(Hi-)Stories of the Gulag. Fiction and Reality*, ed. Felicitas Fischer von Weikersthal and Karoline Thaidigsmann (Heidelberg: Universitätsverlag Winter), 9–21.

Frieß, Nina (2016) "'From Russia with blood.' Stalinist repression and the Gulag in contemporary crime fiction," in *(Hi-)Stories of the Gulag. Fiction and Reality*, ed. Felicitas Fischer von Weikersthal and Karoline Thaidigsmann (Heidelberg: Universitätsverlag Winter), 281–303.

Fludernik, Monika (1999) "Carceral topography: spatiality and liminality in the literary prison," *Textual Practice* 13.1, 43–77.

Ginzburg, Eugenia (2002) *Journey into the Whirlwind* (New York: Harcourt).

Ginzburg, Eugenia (2008) *Krutoi marshrut. Khronika vremen kul'ta lichnosti* [Journey into the Whirlwind], (Moskva: Astrel').

Hartmann, Anne (2016) "Erschöpft und usurpiert. Plädoyer für ein erweitertes Konzept von Gulag-Literatur" [Exhausted and usurped. An argument for a wider concept of Gulag literature], in *(Hi-)Stories of the Gulag. Fiction and Reality*, ed. Felicitas Fischer von Weikersthal and Karoline Thaidigsmann (Heidelberg: Universitätsverlag Winter), 159–175.

Hartman, Geoffrey (1998) "Shoah and the intellectual witness," *Partisan Review* 65.1, 37–48.

Herling-Grudziński, Gustaw (1951) *A World Apart. The Journal of a Gulag Survivor* (New York: Roy Publishers).

Hirsch, Helga (1993) "Der Holocaust ist nicht einmalig: Gespräch mit dem polnischen Soziologen Zygmunt Bauman" [The Holocaust is not singular: in conversation with the Polish sociologist Zygmunt Bauman], *Die Zeit* 23 April, 17.

Judt, Tony (2007) *Post War: A History of Europe since 1945* (London: Penguin).

Kegel, Sandra (2011) "Im Schlamassel der Erinnerung" [In the muddy waters of memory], *Frankfurter Allgemeine* 16 November. <http://www.faz.net/aktuell/feuilleton/buecher/autoren/herta-mueller-und-ruth-klueger-im-schlamassel-der-erinnerung-11530909.html> (accessed 3 March 2018).

Klüger, Ruth (2001) *Still Alive. A Holocaust Girlhood Remembered* (New York: Feminist Press).

LaCapra, Dominick (1997) "Lanzmann's *Shoah*: here there is no why!" *Critical Inquiry* 23, 231–269.

Lebedev, Sergej (2015) *Predel Zabveniia* [Oblivion], (Moskva: Èksmo).

Levi, Primo (1959) *If This is a Man* (New York: Orion Press).

Levi, Primo (1989) *The Drowned and the Saved* (New York: Summit Books).

Levy, Natan and Daniel Sznaider (2006) *The Holocaust and Memory in the Global Age* (Philadelphia: Temple University Press).

Medzhibovskaya, Inessa (2017) "Strafe und Menschlichkeit: Was wir von Hannah Arendt, der russischen Literatur und Lev Tolstoj lernen könne" [Punishment and the human condition: what is to be learned from Hannah Arendt, russian literature, and Leo Tolstoy], in *Extreme Erfahrungen. Grenzen des Erlebens und der Darstellung* [Extreme experiences. The limits of life and representation], ed. Anja Tippner and Christopher F. Laferl. (Berlin: Kadmos Verlag), 199–225.

Miller, Nancy K. and Jason Tougaw (2002) "Introduction: Extremities," in *Extremities: Trauma, Testimony, and Community* , ed. Nancy K. Miller and Jason Tougaw (Urbana: University of Illinois), 1–25.

Norris, Stephen (2011) *Wanted: A Good Gulag Film*. <https://www.rbth.com/articles/2011/02/14/a_good_gulag_film_12455.html> (accessed 3 March 2018).

Oja, Matt (1989) "Toward a definition of camp literature," *Slavic Review* 48.2, 272–274.

Parks, Tim (2014) "The ultimate koan," *New York Review of Books* LXI.6, 37–39.
Prilepin, Zakhar (2014) *Obitel'* [Abode], (Moskva: AST).
Rigney, Anne (2005) "Plenitude, scarcity and the circulation of cultural memory," *Journal of European Studies* 35.1, 11–28.
Rothberg, Michael (2009) *Multidirectional Memory. Remembering the Holocaust in the Age of Decolonization* (Stanford: University Press).
Rousset, David (1951) *A World Apart* (London: Secker and Warburg).
Ruge, Eugen (2013) *In Times of Fading Light* (London: Faber and Faber).
Sariusz-Skąpska, Izabela (2012) *Polscy świadkowie GUŁagu. Literatura łagrowa 1939–1989*. [Polish witnesses of the GULag. Polish camp literature 1939–1989], (Kraków: Universitas).
Schmid, Ulrich (2007) "Nicht-Literatur ohne Moral. Warum Varlam Schalamov nicht gelesen wurde" [Non-literature without ethics. Why Shalam Varlamov has not been read], in *Osteuropa* 6, 87–105.
Segel, Harold B. (ed) (2012) *The Walls behind the Curtain: East European Prison Literature, 1945–1990* (Pittsburgh: University of Pittsburgh Press).
Shalamov, Varlam (1978) *Kolyma Tales* (New York: W. W. Norton).
Shalamov, Varlam (2009) "Perepiska V. Shalamov – A. I. Solzhenytsin" [Correspondence V. Shalamov – A. I. Solzhenytsin], in *Neskol'ko moikh zhiznei. Vospominaniia, zapisnye knizhki, perepiska, sledstvennye dela* (Moskva: Eksmo), 641–680.
Shalamov, Varlam (2004–2005) "O novoi proze" [About the new prose], in *Sobranie sochinenii v shesti tomakh*, vol. V (Moskva: Terra), 157–160.
Shalamov, Varlam (2009) "Chto ia videl i poniial v lagere" [What I saw in the camps], in *Neskol'ko moikh zhiznei. Vospominaniia, zapisnye knizhki, perepiska, sledstvennye dela* (Moskva: Eksmo), 263–268.
Shcherbakova, Irina (2015) "Gulag Memory Map: Problems and Gaps." *Laboratorium: Russian Review of Social Research* 7, 114–121. <http://www.soclabo.org/index.php/laboratorium/article/view/512/1266> (accessed 3 March 2018).
Solzhenitsyn, Aleksandr (1978) *The Gulag Archipelago, 1918–1956. An Experiment in Literary Investigation* (New York: Harper & Row).
Sucharski, Tadeusz (2007) "Literatura Holocaustu i literatura Gułagu? Literatura doświadczenia totalitarnego!" [Literature of the Holocaust and literature of the Gulag? Literature of a totalitarian experience!], *Słupskie Prace Filologiczne* (Seria Filologia Polska) 5, 93–118.
The Way Back (2010) Dir. Peter Weir (National Geographic Films).
Thun-Hohenstein, Franziska (2005) "Auszug aus der Lagerzivilisation. Russische Lagerliteratur im europäischen Kontext" [Moving out of camp civilization. Russian camp narratives in a European context], in *Auszug aus dem. Zur Überwindung des modernen Raumparadigmas in der politischen Philosophie*, ed. Ludger Schwarte (Berlin: Transcript), 180–201.
Tippner, Anja (2013) "The writings of a Soviet Anne Frank: Masha Rol'nikaite's Holocaust memoir 'I Have to Tell' and its place in Soviet literature," in *Search and Research: Lectures and Series*, vol. XIX: Representation of the Holocaust in Soviet Literature and Film, International Conference "The Holocaust and the Jews in the Second World War in Soviet Literature and Film" 2013 (Jerusalem: Yad Vashem), 59–80.

Tippner, Anja (2018) "Conflicting Memories, Conflicting Stories: Masha Rol'nikaite's Holocaust Novels and the Soviet Culture of Holocaust Remembrance," *East European Jewish Affairs. Special Edition: Post Cultures, The Many Ways of Bearing Witness and the Yearning for Jewish Survival*, 48.3 doi 10.1080/13501674.2019.1566999.

Todorov, Tzvetan (1997) *Facing the Extreme* (New York: Henry Holt).

Toker, Leona (2000) *Return from the Archipelago. Narratives of Gulag Survivors* (Bloomington: Indiana University Press).

Tołczyk, Dariusz (1999) *See No Evil: Literary Cover-ups and Discoveries of the Soviet Camp Experience* (New Haven: Yale University Press).

Uhl, Heidemarie (2017) *Holocaust Memory and the Logic of Comparison*. <http://www.enrs.eu/sk/articles/1749-holocaust-memory-and-the-logic-of-comparison> (accessed 24 June 2018).

Venclova, Tomas (1979) "Prison as a communicative phenomenon: The literature of Gulag," *Comparative Civilizations Review* 2, 65–73.

Viola, Lynne (2013) "The question of the perpetrator in Soviet history," *Slavic Review* 72.1, 1–24.

Within the Whirlwind (2009) Dir. Marleen Gorris (Corinth Films).

Young, James E. (1988) *Writing and Rewriting the Holocaust. Narrative and the Consequences of Interpretation* (Bloomington: Indiana University Press).

Zotov, Igor' (2014) *"Obitel'" Zakhara Prilepina* [Abode by Zakhar Prilepin], <http://www.kultpro.ru/item_233/> (accessed 3 March 2018).

II: Defining Camp Literatures: Overview

Eneken Laanes
Transcultural Memorial Forms in Post-Soviet Estonian Narratives of the Gulag

1 Trauma as a transcultural memorial form

When the documentary *Memories Denied* by Imbi Paju, an Estonian filmmaker, was first shown in Tallinn in 2005, it marked a new era in the remembering of Stalinist repressions and perhaps even the whole Soviet period in Estonia. The film caused a cultural shock and provoked strong emotional reactions, both from many prominent figures in the arts and culture sectors and from the general audience, almost as if it told the story of Soviet deportations and the Gulag for the first time.[1] There was a feeling that despite nearly two decades of probing at the most painful experience associated with the Soviet regime, it was Paju who had finally managed to capture the profound effect it had on people's lives. This chapter is inspired by the question of why the film's approach was perceived as novel in Estonia after a long period of public attention to the memories of state terror.[2]

There are a number of reasons for the unprecedented impact of the film. Firstly, it is a very personal story of the director and her mother and aunt, twin sisters who were imprisoned in 1948, at the age of eighteen, for alleged collaboration with the Forest Brothers, the anti-Soviet military resistance movement that emerged after the Second World War, and were sent to the Gulag in the Arkhangelsk Oblast. The film is primarily about the profound effect that the untold story of the mother has had on the director, who in the course of the film tries to make sense of her experience by reconstructing the story with the help of survivor and expert testimonies and archival research, by situating it into a larger historical context of the Second World War and the Soviet occupation of Estonia. Secondly, the film is unique because it gives an account of Stalinist repressions from a gendered experience of women, focusing on sexual humiliation and violence under state terror. Thirdly, Paju makes use of the powerful visual medium of documentary film, only rarely utilized in narratives about personal experiences of the Gulag before. And finally, the film, produced in

---

[1] See, for instance, a review by one of the most esteemed Estonian poets, Viivi Luik (2005).
[2] Research for this chapter was funded by the Juris Padegs Fellowship of the MacMillan Center for International and Area Studies, Yale University, and the institutional research project no. IUT28-1 of the Under and Tuglas Literature Centre of the Estonian Academy of Sciences.

https://doi.org/10.1515/9783110631135-004

Finland and Estonia, seems to be consciously turned outwards, trying to tell the Estonian story to a wider international audience. All these features contributed to its success, both in Estonia and abroad.

By focusing on *Memories Denied* in this chapter, I am interested in what I see as a transnational turn in Estonian memories of the Gulag more generally. I will show how the Estonian culture of remembrance of Stalinist repressions was transformed in the past decade due to the transnational developments in the global culture of memory. The proliferation of memory discourses related to the Second World War in the early 1980s, augmented by various anniversaries of this major historical event of the twentieth century, by the early 1990s has led to the universalization of the Holocaust memory as the central aspect of the war. In the process, the Holocaust memory was developed into a global memory imperative for addressing human rights violations in the present (Levy and Sznaider 2006) and into a universal trope for multidirectional remembering of other histories of violence (Huyssen 2003: 14; Rothberg 2009). One of the most significant changes that the Holocaust memory and its universalization introduced into global memory culture was its focus on individual experiences of trauma and suffering, articulated in public by new cultural forms, such as survivor and witness testimony (Huyssen 2003: 8; Wieviorka 2006; Hirsch and Spitzer 2009).

In their landmark study, *The Empire of Trauma*, Didier Fassin and Richard Rechtman charted the ways in which in the past three decades trauma has emerged as the central moral category for making sense of our relationship to the past. They argue that the movement of individual suffering into the heart of historical understanding was not a result of scientific advancements in psychiatry, but that it came about through the shifts in moral values and sensibilities that arose in the context not only of the Holocaust memory but also of the women's rights and Vietnam War veterans' rights movements (Fassin and Rechtman 2009: 6). Whereas in the first half of the twentieth century the psychological trauma of injured workers or wounded and shell-shocked soldiers was attributed a negative moral value, starting from the 1960s the individual experience of suffering was re-evaluated as able to testify to the violent history of our age. Since then the legitimized individual victim has moved from a peripheral role into the center of the historical understanding of political conflicts and repressions.

Part of that change has also been the detachment of the concept of trauma from its clinical context and its move into everyday language, but also onto the collective level. On the collective level the metaphorical notion of trauma denotes large-scale violent events, be it political conflicts and repressions or natural catastrophes, that have left a wound on the collective memory. The double concept of trauma establishes a mutually reinforced link between the psyche and culture: "The collective event supplies the substance of trauma which will be articulated in individual experience; in return, individual suffering bears witness to the traumatic aspect of the collective drama" (Fassin and Rechtmann 2009: 18). The connection between the individual and the collective has made the historical trauma universalizable. As according to Fassin and Rechtmann individual experience of suffering is universal, so one's personal experience of suffering allows one to empathize with and understand the violent histories of others.

Fassin and Rechtman's social history of trauma as a universalizing moral category is interesting for me here because it maps a change of moral vocabularies. It reminds us that trauma has not always been the only language through which to make sense of political conflicts and injustices, something that is amply demonstrated by the Estonian memories of the Gulag.[3] In the next section, I will explore how in the past decade Estonian memories of the Gulag have come to be dominated by the discourse of trauma, largely absent from the past memory culture. The first part of the chapter gives an overview of Estonian camp memories before *Memories Denied*: how they emerged, starting from the 1970s, in the *émigré* communities in the West and from the second half of the 1980s in Estonia, by using the discourse of injustice and survival, sometimes resistance. I will show that the first attempts to publicly remember deportation and the camps were local in nature and made use of cultural forms and the language of commemoration available at the time. Even if the transnationalization of the Holocaust memory and the emergence of trauma as a universal moral category, which is relevant for many legacies of suffering independent of their historical or geographical context, are dated around the same time that the Estonian memories of the Stalinist repressions first emerged, in the 1990s they remained largely untouched by the discourse of trauma.

If, from the perspective of trauma discourse, non-traumatic representations of the Gulag could be accounted for in terms of latency, Fassin and Rechtman's account suggests to us that it may truly be a different way of interpreting the experience of suffering that is based on the sensibilities and values of the time and specific cultural context. Catherine Merridale, who has studied the social memory of Stalinist repressions in Russia, questions the usefulness of the trauma paradigm in this context: "The point is not to question the ubiquity of suffering and trauma in Soviet Russia, but to see that people regarded them

---

[3] Fassin and Rechtman suggest that trauma has replaced the discourse of oppression and resistance used in many parts of the world before. They draw attention to how the change of idiom influences the ways in which people perceive themselves as political subjects (2009: 162, 212).

differently" (Merridale 2010: 381). She maintains that even if suffering is universal, the responses to it may be culture specific.

It is only in the new millennium that trauma emerges in Estonian memory culture in reference to Stalinist repressions, imported, as I would like to argue, by memorial forms developed in the context of the Holocaust memory. I take the concept of memorial form from Ann Rigney, who noted that even though the past of different groups is always specific to those groups, the mnemonic technologies and memorial forms used to remember the past are often borrowed from other groups and recycled (Rigney 2005: 24). The transnational or transcultural memory studies have increasingly drawn attention to how narratives, images and mnemonic forms travel across cultures and are appropriated in order to articulate historical experiences that are politically and historically diverse (Erll 2011: 4). In this case, I am particularly interested in survivor testimony as a memorial form that personalizes and psychologizes historical experience and elicits an emotional response (Fassin and Rechtman 2009: 211).

In the second part of this chapter I will show how *Memories Denied* differs from previous ways of remembering the Gulag in that it uses the "postmemorial" form of testimony that tells a highly gendered story of personal experience of suffering by focusing on the familial trope. Starting from the film, the discourse of injustice and survival in remembering deportation and the Gulag has been gradually replaced by trauma. As I will argue, the change was partly the result of various transnational pressures on local memory culture that led to the need to explain local history to a wider world. In the remainder of the chapter I will chart the consequences of that change. I am particularly interested in the profound effect that these stories, consciously told for an international audience, have on local memory culture and what happens if memories that are deterritorialized by the use of a transnational idiom of trauma are reterritorialized and renationalized in the local context.

2 Memories of the Gulag before *Memories Denied*

Needless to say, the question of Soviet deportations of Estonians and the Gulag[4] was one of the greatest taboos of Soviet Estonian public discourse and

---

[4] Post-Soviet Estonian memories of Stalinist repressions focus on two mass deportations of Estonians: on 21 June 1940 and 14 March 1949, with 10,000 and 21,000 people deported respectively (Pettai and Pettai 2015: 55). In 1941 people were mainly sent to the Gulag, whereas in 1949 they were mostly resettled to the northern or northeastern rural regions of the Soviet

cultural representations throughout the second half of the twentieth century. The first texts about Stalinist repressions started to appear in Sweden in the 1970s, published by Estonian *émigré* community. These accounts were authored either by the very few people who were able to emigrate after their release from the camp, or written in Estonia and smuggled out to the West.⁵ These texts served the consciousness-raising efforts among the *émigré* community and aimed at the most detailed documentation of the ordeal of starvation, destitution and deterioration of health in the Gulag and in forced resettlement. These personal, matter-of-fact accounts do not psychologize the experience, but are framed by the discourse of injustice rather than trauma.⁶ As only a handful of these texts have been translated into other languages, they remained within the bounds of the *émigré* community, and even if some were smuggled back to Estonia, their impact on the public sphere was limited until the very end of the 1980s.

During the political turn at the end of the 1980s memories of Stalinist repressions formed the core of the renewal of society. The counter-memories of the Gulag and the deportations that had survived in the private sphere of family memory flooded the public space through literature, media, and first historical surveys (Anepaio 2002). The first legal initiatives that dealt with Stalinist repressions, commemorative practices that focused in particular on the 50th anniversary of the 1949 deportation in March 1989, and first fact-finding missions further supported the emergence of these legacies of Stalinism.⁷ In late 1980s literature played a crucial role in bringing memories of the Gulag into the

---

Union. As the experience of the camp and forced resettlement both include displacement into a foreign cultural context, confinement and forced labor, the memories form a common corpus in post-Soviet Estonian memory culture and therefore will be discussed together.

5 Maria Kopperman, *Minu 12 aastat Siberis* ("My 12 years in Siberia"; 1972); Rutt Eliaser, *Passita ja pajata* ("Without passport and cauldron"; 1985), *Üheksa ametit* ("Nine jobs"; 1986); Aili Helm, *Kuradil ei ole varju* ("The devil has no shadow"; 1979). Maria Koppermann was deported twice, first to the Gulag in 1941 and then resettled in 1949. She was released in 1955 and emigrated to Sweden in 1968. Rutt Eliaser was also deported and resettled twice, and emigrated to Sweden in 1977. Aili Helm is a pseudonym used by Hilja Rüütli, who was arrested in 1945, spent eleven years in the Vorkuta camp and wrote her fictionalized memoirs in collaboration with Helmut Tarand.

6 Kopperman, who focuses on the miracle of survival, also uses the discourse of divine providence. Helm presents her experience of the Gulag in a sarcastic and militant discourse of resistance.

7 The first law on Stalinist repressions was passed by the Supreme Soviet of the Estonian Soviet Socialist Republic (ESSR) in December 1988. The two mass deportations (14 June 1941 and 25 March 1949) have been officially commemorated since 1994. The first State Commission for the Examination of Repressive Policies and Crimes Against Humanity was founded by the Supreme Soviet of the Republic of Estonia in March 1992. See Tamm (2013).

public space. Three texts in particular stand out: Heino Kiik's *Maria Siberimaal* ("Maria in Siberia"; 1988) and Arvo Valton's *Masendus ja lootus* ("Depression and hope"; 1989), which deal with the 1949 deportation and exile, and Raimond Kaugver's *Kirjad laagrist* ("Letters from the camp"; 1989), which is based on his experiences in the Vorkuta camp.[8] All these narratives give a fictional account of the experience, a choice strongly influenced by the time of writing. As most of the texts had been written long before their publication, the only way to retain the hope of being published for their authors was to claim artistic license (Toker 2000: 123).[9] Thus, to a certain extent, the fictional form also functioned as a device of self-censorship and the choice of the genre strongly influenced the way testimony could be given. Even if these texts differ quite significantly, what they have in common is that they do not focus on traumatic suffering.

The first and most influential representation of deportation of the Estonians, Kiik's *Maria Siberimaal*, is based on the experiences of the author's mother and younger brother, who were deported in 1949 and exiled to Novosibirsk Oblast. The novel is a straightforward, realist, third-person account of the various aspects of deportation and resettlement focalized through its protagonist, Maria. Even if it does highlight the fears and the pain related to starvation and death of children, these are not represented in a traumatic key. Rather, it is a progressive narrative of a struggle for survival from an initial situation of extreme deprivation to a gradual building up of one's life from scratch in a foreign country. It is also a story of the Estonian peasant community, which successfully created an agricultural oasis based on their own ethics in the midst of the Soviet collective farm. The novel was met with ambivalent reception. Some critics argued that even if it was written too early (to be published), once it finally came out it came too late. Its mitigated representation of a harsh reality and its reconciliatory tone were seen as having paid too much tribute to (self-)censorship (Mikli 1987: 4; Uibo 1989: 125). However, the ambivalence shown by critics did not diminish the impact of the novel as the first coherent public account of the experience of deportation.

Valton's *Masendus ja lootus*, based on the author's experiences as a child survivor of the 1949 deportation, is a bleaker account of long years of hunger and destitution in a deportee community in Novosibirsk Oblast, but its focus again is not on suffering.[10] As a third-person panorama novel that shifts

---

[8] In addition to literature, various theatre productions (e.g. by Jaan Kruusvall, Rein Saluri and Merle Karusoo) acquired a legendary status.
[9] "Maria in Siberia" was written in 1978 and disseminated through Samizdat. "Depression and hope" was written in 1983–1984 and still denied publication in 1987.
[10] In a recent interview, Valton (2013) suggested that his not entirely pessimistic picture of the deportations might be attributed to his young age at the time.

internal focalization through numerous characters, it gives an extensive overview of the diversity of the social world of the deportee community and different ways of adapting to the experience of exile. Valton concludes his novel with the words "How was he supposed to sum up these years spent in Siberia? He could not say other than that nobody benefited from it. [...] There was no need for it, one should not regard it as inevitable. An awful injustice had been done to people and it was unforgivable."[11] (1989: 606) However, his narrative, which focuses predominantly on young people and children, and their pursuit of education and living their life against all odds, has a sense of hope.

Kaugver's *Kirjad laagrist*, a collection of short stories, is arguably based on the letters he sent to his family from Vorkuta, where, after a short period in the mines, he was part of the medical personnel. In the introduction he proclaims the testimonial value of everything told, but also stresses the literary character of the stories. Indeed, they are highly artistic, often anecdotalizing various incidents that have taken place in the camp. In some cases, the narrative pleasure is clearly in conflict with extreme violence and horror of the subject matter. Lack of a moral reflection achieved by a clash of perspectives (of the narrator and of the focalizer) characteristic of Gulag memoirs made some critics uncomfortable (Hinrikus 1990). However, this choice of style may also testify to the harsh world of moral adaptation necessary for survival in the camp. As the narrator states, compassion was sometimes a luxury one could not afford.

The same non-traumatic stance is characteristic of camp memoirs written during the Soviet period and published after the disintegration of the Soviet Union. The most remarkable of these is *Võõrsil vastu tahtmist* ("Abroad against one's will"; 2011) by Arnold Susi, minister of education in the four-day Estonian government formed in the interregnum between the German and Soviet occupation in September 1944. Susi was imprisoned in 1944 and spent eight years in various camps and five years in forced exile. Next to being one of the highest state officials surviving the repressions, his story is interesting because in 1945 in Lubyanka prison he befriended Solzhenitsyn and later, between 1965 and 1967, hosted him in Estonia, where Solzhenitsyn worked on *The Gulag Archipelago* (Solzhenitsyn 1997: 42–58). Susi's own memoir, written at the end of 1950 in exile in Abakan and partly used by Solzhenitsyn for *The Gulag Archipelago* (Solzhenitsyn 1997: 52), is a very sober and reserved, personal, but not personalized, account of his experiences. Its main function is to document the Soviet repressive system, the topography, and the routine of the camp in as detailed a manner as possible. Susi's is the most comprehensive Estonian memoir

---

[11] This and all subsequent translations from Estonian are mine (E.L.).

exhibiting all the characteristics of a Gulag memoir, such as the link between the individual and the communal, and the presence of different topoi, such as imprisonment, hunger, and destitution, the violence of criminal convicts, and the terror of juveniles (Toker 2000: 74). Written in the 1950s with no wider perspective available, his narrative is enclosed in a claustrophobic world of the camp. However, as a lawyer Susi is interested in the (perverted) juridical side of Soviet repressions and hence, as if writing for an imaginary court of justice, he frames his account within the discourse of injustice.

Throughout this inevitably cursory overview of the first fictional and factographic accounts of the deportations and the Gulag, I have argued that the main aim of their authors has been to document the experience that had been present in the social memory of the afflicted communities, but whose details were largely unknown to the wider public. When embarking on a documentary mission, they draw on traditional Estonian literary genres or modes of autobiographical narration, but those that hardly focus on traumatic suffering (Hinrikus and Kõresaar 2004: 20), so familiar to us in the contemporary culture of remembrance. Instead of the psychological side of the experience, these accounts highlight the circumstances of survival or, less frequently, adopt the stance of militant resistance as a way of processing them. The first comprehensive texts about deportation and the Gulag emerging in late 1980s were extremely important, because they largely prefigured the ways in which Stalinist repressions were remembered in the 1990s in post-Soviet Estonia.

In the 1990s the main medium for processing memories of deportations and the Gulag in the public were life stories, written down and systematically gathered since the late 1980. As the repressed gained increasing visibility through legal and commemorational initiatives, while comprehensive historical accounts of Estonian experience of the Gulag and deportations were slow to emerge, personal life stories were valued highly as something that could fill the "blank spots" of Soviet history writing. The life stories of the repressed were collected with the help of public appeals and life story competitions organized by the Estonian Heritage Society, the Cultural History Archive of the Estonian Literary Museum and, since 1996, by the Estonian Life Stories Association founded specifically for that purpose, and published both in popular and in academic editions.[12]

Even if the life stories give an account of painful experiences of family separation and destruction, prolonged starvation and exhaustion, of a harshness

---

[12] On the life story collection, dissemination and research, see Hinrikus and Kõresaar (2004). Estonian life stories are accessible in English in Kirss et al. (2004) and Kirss (2009).

that goes far beyond that of the fictionalized accounts of the 1980s, the language of trauma is still largely absent from them. Tiina Kirss argues that the life stories resist interpretations based on the concept of trauma, because the writers staunchly refuse to relinquish their subject position as active agents. Kirss' claim with regard to one such writer that "her focus is on [...] the delineation of a defiant, even dissenting attitude of moral poise, a definition of herself as an active agent rather than a passive victim," (2004: 123) seems to characterize most of the authors of that genre.

This brave mode of representation may be associated with normative restrictions of the particular genre of a solicited life story. Public calls and competitions in the 1990s were framed by the discourse of nationalism that placed individual life histories and their collection in the context of the recovery of a collective national history (Kõresaar 2004: 89). As a result, authors have interpreted their experiences in the context of communal identity, and stressed personal and collective survival and resistance (Kurvet-Käosaar 2013: 132). Catherine Merridale, who has questioned the usefulness of the trauma paradigm for understanding the memories of the Gulag in the Russian context, equally regards the collective focus as the main prerequisite for a successful survival of the Gulag experience in memory (2010: 381). Whereas for Kurvet-Käosaar the collective anchor functions as a screen that covers the traumatic experiences that must be present, but remain hidden in the narrative,[13] Merridale suggests that the communal narrative has indeed helped to come to terms with the memories of the Gulag. What seems to be at stake here is the idea that the modes of addressing and working through suffering are historically and culturally variable.

Tiina Kirss argues that Estonian life stories are influenced by the "culturally significant and historically specific interpretative filters and metanarratives about selfhood, agency, gender, and membership in a larger collective." (2004: 114) Vielda Skultans has highlighted the importance of national literature as such an interpretative filter in Latvian life stories of the Gulag (1998: xii). In the case of Estonia it seems that in the 1990s the accounts of former deportees were in no small part premediated by the first factographic and fictional accounts of the Gulag experience, in particular by *Maria Siberimaal*. In divergence from the fictional texts of the late 1980s and the life stories of the 1990s, *Memories Denied* makes use of a different interpretative filter and focuses on the damaging effect of the experiences of deportation and on victimhood.

---

[13] Käosaar argues that authors consciously downplay their traumatic experiences for the sake of preserving their national identity built on endurance and survival. By doing so, she reads trauma into the narratives where she admits to not finding it, hence testifying to the power of the lens of trauma.

3 *Memories Denied* as an act of postmemory

Imbi Paju's documentary introduces the discourse of trauma into the Estonian memories of the camp by employing a cultural form that Marianne Hirsch, referring to aesthetic objects in the context of the Holocaust memory, has called "postmemory." Postmemory describes "the relationship of children of survivors of cultural or collective trauma to the experiences of their parents, the experiences that they 'remember' only as the narratives and images with which they grew up, but that are so powerful, so monumental, as to constitute memories in their own right" (Hirsch 1999: 8). *Memories Denied* is an act of postmemory because it is a second-generation journey into the past, as Paju herself is present in the film, as a narrative voice that clearly positions itself as a victim of repressions. She begins the film by telling how as a child she suffered by being awakened by her mother's nightmares of the Gulag. She explains:

> As a child I often couldn't sleep because my mother had nightmares and cried out for help in her sleep. The horrors of her dreams were Stalin's forced labor camps and the Soviet soldiers who threatened her life. In these nightmares, she never made it back home to her mother. The nightmares stirred me as a child. It was then that the scenario for this story began to form in my mind. Forced labor camps and death camps penetrated my unconscious through my mother's nightmares [...] Feelings of all kinds can flow from mother to child. I didn't know then that my mother was suffering from what might be called "remembrance." I felt helpless. (Paju 2005)

Paju is also present in the film as a character, as she accompanies her mother and aunt on their visits to their former places of suffering. Rather than through narratives and images, what forms the traumatic memory of the camps in the film is silence. The film is an act of postmemory because it tries to make sense of the suffering of the first generation of survivors, who do not want to recall the past, a fact made obvious in the film – Paju's mother and aunt repeatedly say they prefer not to talk about their experiences.

Like many postmemorial aesthetic objects of the Holocaust memory, Paju represents traumatic experiences through what Claire Kahane has called the familial trope. Kahane argues that in the Holocaust memory, the destruction of the mother–child relationship that forms the protective shield of subjectivity in psychoanalysis, has come to represent an extreme historical event: "If we understand the first trauma of infantile life to be the trauma of maternal loss, the use of a traumatic breach in the mother–child relation to figure an unrepresentable historical trauma has a logical inevitability as well as a universal affective power." (Kahane 2000: 164) In the film the historical trauma that is rendered through a mother–child relationship does not pertain only to the relationship between the filmmaker and her mother. The trauma of the first generation of survivors in the film is also, first and foremost, a trauma of separation from the mother and later, of separation of twin sisters; recalling the memory of that separation is emotionally the most difficult moment in their testimony.

However, the main reason I evoke Hirsch's concept of postmemory is because it highlights the major role of cultural mediation in the second-generation accounts of past suffering, something that is extremely important in Paju's film. Hirsch argues that the second generation not only uses the memories of the first generation, which are virtually unavailable if they are silenced, but it also relies to a large extent on cultural mediation, as well as on imaginative investment, projection, and creation (1999: 8). Precisely because her mother does not want to remember, Paju is forced to take recourse to family photos, files from the NKVD archive, Soviet archival footage as well as testimonies of experts and other victims, to try to uncover her mother's story.

The reasons why the protagonists of *Memories Denied* prefer not to recall the past are related to the issues of gender. As my cursory overview of Estonian memories of the camps showed, the perspective of women was strongly represented, partly owing to the fact that more women than men were deported and more women survived.[14] However, as the post-Soviet Estonian memory culture of the 1990s foregrounded resistance to the Soviet regime, gendered experiences were included only so far as they supported the metanarrative, leaving unaddressed many experiences unique to women during the repressions (Kurvet-Käosaar 2003; Kirss 2005: 17). The singularity of women's experiences in Paju's film, which might have been incompatible with the masculine heroism of the memory culture of the 1990s, includes the questions of sexual humiliation and violence against women. As a painful topic, it was completely absent from Estonian memory culture before Paju's film.[15] Even Paju cannot address the question directly. Her mother and aunt recall instances of sexual humiliation, but they also leave many things unsaid and keep silent on issues of sexuality.

In order to approach the question of sexual violence that her mother and aunt refuse to address directly, Paju composes an archive of testimonies by interviewing other women who were imprisoned in the NKVD headquarters and in the Patarei prison in Tallinn. These are excruciating accounts. The most

---

[14] Most of the men deported in 1941 experienced a more than 50 percent death rate; they were executed or sent to a prison camp, whereas many women were resettled (Pettai and Pettai 2015: 46, 55). In 1949, three-quarters of the Baltic deportees, mostly resettled, were women and children (Strods and Kott 2002: 20).

[15] Tiina Kirss has shown that the threat of and attempts at sexual violence are sometimes addressed in written life stories, but with a lot of discretion (2005: 30).

remarkable is that by Hilja Rüütli (Aili Helm), author of a fictionalized memoir published by the *émigré* community, *Kuradil ei ole varju* ("The devil has no shadow"). In the film, as in her book, Rüütli describes her personal experiences of violence, torture, and sexual humiliation in a characteristically grotesque and defiant manner that clearly seems to be her way of coping with these memories.

Despite the explicit nature of Rüütli's testimony, the question of sexual violence still seems to haunt the filmmaker. Hence, she supplements the testimonies with drawings from the Gulag, created by Danzig Baldaev (2010), fill in, through visual images, the lacunas of the unsaid in women's narratives. The use of Baldaev's images highlights the importance of cultural mediation and imaginative investment in aesthetic acts of postmemory. The visual public archive of the Gulag in Estonian culture is limited. Until very recently, Estonians were used to read and listen to stories about deportation and the camps, but not to view them. Therefore, the desire for a visual supplement to the testimonies is all the more pressing. However, Baldaev's images are not an unproblematic find for Paju, not only because of the ambiguous position of the artist,[16] but also owing to his ways of representing (sexual) violence and torture in the Gulag.

Baldaev uses images to tell the story of the Soviet regime. More than 130 drawings gathered into a book focus in particular on the detailed account of different methods of torture the NKVD used to break its victims. Baldaev's images of torture and sexual violence are extremely graphic, to the extent that some have considered them prurient (Brown 2010). Even if the critics cast doubt not so much on the authenticity or "factuality" of Baldaev's work as on his representational choices, his British editors have anticipated the former by corroborating many images with relevant testimonies from Russian Gulag literature (Solzhenitsyn, Shalamov, and others). Thus, far from being a transparent visual evidence of Soviet repressions, as they are used in Paju's film, these images seem to need supplementation by textual sources.

One of Baldaev's representational choices that seems problematic is his extensive focus on the perpetrators and the pleasure they appear to derive from torture. The visual emphasis on the perpetrator is further strengthened by the textual component of Baldaev's images that create an interplay between the visual and the textual, quite apart from the editors' footnotes. The drawings frequently include direct speech by the perpetrators, giving them a voice, whereas the victims are often mute and faceless, sexualized bodies.

---

16 Danzig Baldaev (1925–2005) was a prison guard in Kresty, an NKVD prison, and in the Gulag system (Baldaev 2010: 5).

The discussion is relevant to Paju's use of these images because she is interested precisely in the testimony they can give about sexual violence against women in the Gulag, even though she also borrows other images by Baldaev that evoke Estonia and help to highlight the aspects of Stalinist repressions relevant to her family.[17] By showing images of sexual humiliation and violence, Paju mitigates the potentially problematic aspects of Baldaev's sketches by breaking them up with the help of the camera's movement. She focuses mainly on victims and shows the whole image only at the end. Her scrutiny of these images as a background to oral testimonies highlights the role of cultural mediation in making sense of survivors' suffering by subsequent generations. Ultimately, what seems to be the most painful for the filmmaker in this postmemorial act of remembering is a gnawing uncertainty about the exact nature and extent of her mother's suffering, the question of where to place her experience in the context of the narratives and images she has gathered while making the film.[18]

In this part of the chapter I have tried to show how Paju introduced a radically new memorial form into the Estonian memories of the Gulag by looking at them from the perspective of second-generation survivors and highlighting the personal psychological side of suffering with a strong emotional appeal. The fact that the memorial form was borrowed from transnational memory culture was immediately recognized by one of the first reviews of the film, entitled "So late came the first Estonian Holocaust doc." This is how the critic explains his choice of the title: "the lingua franca of modern historical documentary is obviously the Holocaust film [...] but here [in Estonia] the language that would pave the way to the academic or public realm is spoken only by a few." (Rooste 2005: 14) He writes further: "The topic of the film is the Estonian counterpart to the Holocaust: the destruction, discontinuation and disruption of the trajectory of human life, the humiliation and devastation of individuals, the haunting legacies left to the next generation." While the film does not refer to the Holocaust, the critic has recognized that it is told in a language that has been developed in the context of the Holocaust memory, a language that can be used to talk about other histories of violence because it focuses on individual traumatic experiences.

---

[17] Paju has picked the image of deportation where a cattle car bears the inscription "Tallinn" and the image of "the enemy of the people," the charge applied to her family (Baldaev 2010: 24, 180).
[18] In her book *Memories Denied* that accompanies the film and broadens its scope, Paju repeatedly mentions how tormented she was by uncertainty (2009: 286).

4 Transnational memory as translation

The ways in which the Holocaust memory has become formative in remembering other histories of violence has in recent years been most aptly rendered by Michel Rothberg's concept of multidirectional memory. Rothberg shows that even if claims for remembering slavery in the United States or the legacies of European colonialism have often been made in competitive terms in reference to the Holocaust, on the cultural level the Holocaust memory has contributed immensely to the emergence of these histories by offering a consciousness and a language to address them (Rothberg 2009).

Since the collapse of the Soviet Union, Eastern Europe has been another region where comparative discourses about the Holocaust and in this case communist crimes have proliferated. As already said, the liberalization of the former Eastern bloc coincided with a particular moment in the development of global memory culture – the transnationalization of the Holocaust memory that had various reverberations in Eastern Europe. Above all, it put pressure to the new or restored nation states to incorporate the global Holocaust memory into the newly shaped national memories of the Second World War and to deal with local histories of the Holocaust and collaboration with the Nazis. In the 1990s the call was resisted in many Eastern European countries, because there was a feeling that the legacies that needed to be addressed most urgently were those of Soviet repressions (Pettai 2011: 159; Blacker and Etkind 2013: 4). The discrepancy between transnational pressure and local interests and concerns often resulted in comparative and at times competitive discourses about the Holocaust and Soviet repressions, and about Nazism and Stalinism more generally.

In addition, at least in the Baltic States, Russia's prolonged denial of the illegal annexation of these countries in 1940 and its unwillingness to work through the legacy of Stalinism (Etkind 2013) led to the search for international recognition of local historical legacies in order to establish historical justice. The enlargement of the European Union in particular has given the Eastern European countries the chance to make their voices heard on the European forum. Since then, there have been various attempts to condemn crimes against humanity committed by the Soviet Union, pushed mainly by these countries, some of which have been successful. The initiatives have used the Holocaust as a template for seeking recognition for their particular historical legacies of the Second World War by putting their demands in universalist terms – as an attempt to construct a common European memory of its totalitarianisms (Mälksoo 2014: 89). However, despite universalist claims, the demand for equal recognition through the paradigm of "double genocide" has sometimes sled into competitive discourses about the equality and symmetry of the experiences

(Rothberg 2013: 91).[19] Furthermore, a universalist demand for the recognition of communist crimes has not always been accompanied in these countries by an equal eagerness to deal with the issues of collaboration, both in the Holocaust and with the communist regime itself (Blacker and Etkind 2013: 8).

Whereas on the political level the comparative discourses of the Holocaust and the crimes of communism have been highly visible, in the cultural field the influences of global memory culture have been subtler. As I have shown, the cultural process that positioned the Holocaust to become the prism through which to look at the legacy of Stalinist repressions has been slow in Estonia. The first attempts to remember Soviet labor camps were localized and drew on cultural forms that were inherited from the earlier cultures of writing and remembering. The crucial change that *Memories Denied* introduced in Estonian culture of remembrance of the Gulag consisted in its use of a privileged transcultural memorial form of testimony in its postmemorial version. Hence, covertly, the film is an act of multidirectional memory. It does not make any explicit references to the Holocaust; however, its narrative is strongly indebted to the Holocaust memory in terms of memorial forms and modes, and the aesthetics of remembrance more generally.[20] Even if there are no obvious references to a different historical memory, the ways of remembering may nonetheless be borrowed. Paju's approach to the memories of Stalinist repressions was perceived as groundbreaking in Estonia and has been successful internationally because it uses the memorial form of trauma and its testimony, a form that is familiar to the international audience, but one that was to a certain extent new in Estonian post-Soviet memory culture.

Of particular interest in Paju's case is not only the way in which she makes use of transcultural mnemonic forms to articulate historically specific local experiences, but how these forms make local memories travel transnationally. Paju is a filmmaker, writer, and journalist who is based both in Finland and Estonia. The documentary was co-produced by Finnish filmmakers and was first released in Finland. The narrative, with its extensive outline of the historical background, is itself consciously turned outwards and tells the story of Stalinist repressions to an international audience. As such, the story translates Estonian memories of the Gulag into a language of trauma and testimony that is understandable in the contemporary global context.

---

19 For the importance of the recognition of asymmetry in multidirectional remembering, see Rothberg (2011: 526).
20 In her book Paju credits Imre Kertész, Primo Levi, Claude Lanzmann and others as her sources of inspiration, thereby making an explicit link to Holocaust memory (2009: 73, 230).

In the past decade the transnationalization of Estonian camp memories can be described precisely as their translation into a transcultural language of commemoration. One of the most remarkable examples of such a translation is Martti Helde's recent feature film *In the Crosswind* (2014); it follows the trend set by Paju in that it stages an emotionally engaging testimony of personal experiences of suffering and trauma. It tells of the deportation of an Estonian woman, Erna, to a Siberian exile in an uninterrupted series of still images, black and white *tableaux vivants*.[21] The thirteen *tableaux vivants* that render different stages of the experience of deportation and resettlement are accompanied by the protagonist's voice-over, who talks about her experiences in letters to her husband. This highly experimental form that represents the freezing of time in exile enables the director to tell a deeply moving story that has caught the interest of many major film festivals and made a profound effect on audiences. However, the film's international success may also be attributed to the distinctly transnational language of trauma and testimony that it deploys.

The element of translation is most visible in the iconography of the film and in its end credits that dedicate it to "the victims of the Soviet Holocaust." The dedication makes a clear reference to the Holocaust memory, used here as a global icon[22] that helps the director draw attention to a different legacy of suffering. Next to the dedication the film appropriates such Holocaust iconography as a pile of shoes of murdered prisoners. On the one hand, by building such a frame of reference what the film seems to do is not so much compare the Soviet deportations to the Holocaust or make the two compete, as to make a reference that is known to an international audience, and through that reference bring an unknown historical reality closer to the experience of the audience. On the other hand, however, such references, the transnational iconography of suffering and occasional "simplifications" that seem to be the prerequisite for global travel of memories also impoverish the memory of specific historical experiences.[23] Fassin and Rechtman argue that the language of trauma has the virtue of universalization, but it also renders "histories without history" (2009: 214).

---

21 The film combines *tableaux vivants* with a moving camera.
22 Aleida Assmann argues that the Holocaust is appropriated as a global icon if it is disconnected from its historical context and "travels easily without impediments along the informal channels of global communication. In the format of canonical images, this de-contextualized historical reference is circulated, cited, indirectly evoked and understood all over the world." (2010: 113).
23 One of the examples of such a simplification in *In the Crosswind* is the merging of two phases of deportation, 1941 and 1949, into one. In the film the deportation is dated 1941. However, in her voice-over the protagonist regrets "not having fled across the sea" to escape the deportation. This is a reference to the escape of 70,000 Estonians across the sea in September

It blurs the specificity of historical contexts and prevents their historical and political analysis in the past and present. The recognition darkens the optimism of such approaches in transnational memory studies as that of Alison Landsberg's, who argues that "prosthetic" memories generated by experiential sites produced by commodification and technologization, such as the cinema, enable one to "remember experientially" things that one has actually not lived through and that are not linked to the particularities of one's identity, hence offering an opportunity to create empathy across different identities (Landsberg 2004: 2–3). Even if the great advantage of prosthetic memories is that they resist essentialist claims over memory, they are inevitably diluted. In order for a historical experience to become a prosthetic memory for an audience, it has to be translated into a language that the audience can understand. But perhaps the assimilation is not too high a price to be paid for the global travel of historically specific experiences.

The final facet of the transnationalization of the Estonian memories of the Gulag that I would like to discuss in relation to the two films is the reterritorialization of their accounts of Stalinist repressions in the local context. In the past decade the aesthetic acts of memory that have been addressed outwards, to an international audience, have had a strong impact on the way the deportation and the Gulag were remembered locally in Estonia. Paju's film was met with great interest both in the country and abroad. In Estonia, on the one hand its new, emotionally engaging way of presenting Stalinist repressions corresponded to the sensibilities and values of new generations of Estonians whose families were affected, in one way or another. On the other hand, however, the film, precisely because it was successful abroad, was quickly embraced by official publicity and turned into a cultural product that represented Estonian suffering under Soviets on all kinds of forums, ranging from cultural festivals to public screenings in the European Parliament.[24] The rapid renationalization of memories, made transportable by the use of a transcultural memorial form, highlights the recent claim that in contemporary world the diaspora may be the most prolific field of national memory (De Cesari and Rigney 2014: 7).[25] Considering the great difficulty and resistance with which Paju, for the first time,

---

1944 that could be regretted as a missed opportunity only by people who were deported in 1949.

24 Estonian president Toomas Hendrik Ilves wrote the foreword to the book version of the film. The film was screened in the European Parliament in November 2009 and at many events organized by Estonian embassies all over the world.

25 Another remarkable example of national memory produced in the transnational language of trauma in the diaspora is the international bestseller *Purge* (2008) by Estonian-Finnish

brought into the open the highly gendered experiences of sexual humiliation and violence under state terror, it is somewhat surprising that they were so readily embraced by national politics of memory as representative experiences of the Soviet period. The transnational language of trauma and suffering, as helpful as it has been for highlighting individual experiences, has also reinforced the overarching collective victimhood paradigm and the externalization of all responsibility for repressions that has been characteristic of post-Soviet Baltic memory culture (Pettai and Pettai 2015: 58, 63).

Works cited

Anepaio, Terje (2002) "Reception of the topic of repressions in the Estonian society," in *Whose Culture?* ed. Pille Runnel (Tartu: Eesti Rahva Muuseum), 47–65.

Assmann, Aleida (2010) "The Holocaust – a global memory? Extensions and limits of a new memory community," in *Memory in a Global Age: Discourses*, Practices, *Trajectories*, ed. Aleida Assman and Sebastian Conrad (Basingstoke: Palgrave Macmillan), 97–117.

Baldaev, Danzig (2010) *Drawings from the Gulag* (London: FUEL).

Blacker, Uilleam and Alexander Etkind (2013) "Introduction," in *Memory and Theory in Eastern Europe*, ed. Uilleam Blacker and Alexander Etkind (New York and Basingstroke: Palgrave MacMillan), 1–22.

Brown, Roland Elliott (2010) "Drawings from the Gulag by Danzig Baldaev – review," *The Guardian* 17 October, 4. <https://www.theguardian.com/world/2010/oct/17/drawings-gulag-danzig-baldaev-review> (accessed 1 October 2015).

De Cesari, Chiara and Ann Rigney (2014) "Introduction," in *Transnational Memory: Circulation, Articulation, Scales*, ed. Chiara De Cesari and Ann Rigney (Berlin: De Gruyter), 1–21.

Eliaser, Rutt (1985) *Passita ja pajata* [Without passport and cauldron], (Lund: Eesti Kirjanike Kooperatiiv).

Eliaser, Rutt (1986) *Üheksa ametit* [Nine jobs], (Lund: Eesti Kirjanike Kooperatiiv).

Erll, Astrid (2011) "Travelling memory," *Parallax* 17.4, 4–18.

Etkind, Alexander (2013) *Warped Mourning: Stories of the Undead in the Land of the Unburied* (Stanford: Stanford University Press).

Fassin, Didier and Richard Rechtman (2009) *The Empire of Trauma: An Inquiry Into the Condition of Victimhood* (Princeton and Oxford: Princeton University Press).

Helm, Aili (1979) *Kuradil ei ole varju* [The devil has no shadow], (Lund: Eesti Kirjanike Kooperatiiv).

Hinrikus, Rutt (1990) "Proosamaastik 1989; Unustada või loota" [Prose landscape 1989; to forget or to hope], *Looming* 4, 551–559.

Hinrikus, Rutt and Ene Kõresaar (2004) "A brief overview of life history collection and research in Estonia," in *She Who Remembers Survives. Interpreting Estonian Women's Post-Soviet*

---

writer, Sofi Oksanen. For wide-ranging public debates around the reterritorialization and renationalization of her representation of the Soviet period in Estonia, see Laanes (2012).

Life Stories, ed. Tiina Kirss, Ene Kõresaar and Marju Lauristin (Tartu: Tartu University Press), 19–34.

Hirsch, Marianne (1999) "Projected memory: Holocaust photographs in personal and public fantasy," in *Acts of Memory: Cultural Recall in the Present*, ed. Mieke Bal, Jonathan Crew and Leo Spitzer (Hanover: University Press of New England), 3–23.

Hirsch, Marianne and Leo Spitzer (2009) "The witness in the archive: Holocaust studies/ memory studies," *Memory Studies* 2.2, 151–170.

Huyssen, Andreas (2003) *Present Pasts: Urban Palimpsests and the Politics of Memory* (Stanford: Stanford University Press).

In the Crosswind (2014) Dir. Martti Helde (Allfilm and Baltic Pine Films).

Kahane, Claire (2000) "Dark mirrors: a feminist reflection of Holocaust narrative and the maternal metaphor," in *Feminist Consequences: Gender and Culture*, ed. Elizabeth Bronfen and Misha Kavka (New York: Columbia University Press), 161–188.

Kaugver, Raimond (1989) *Kirjad laagrist* [Letters form the camp], (Tallinn: Eesti Raamat).

Kiik, Heino (1988) *Maria Siberimaal* [Maria in Siberia], (Tallinn: Eesti Raamat).

Kirss, Tiina (2004) "Three generations of Estonian women: selves, lives, texts," in *She Who Remembers Survives: Interpreting Estonian Women's Post-Soviet Life Stories*, ed. Tiina Kirss, Ene Kõresaar and Marju Lauristin (Tartu: Tartu University Press), 112–143.

Kirss, Tiina (2005) "Survivorship and the Eastern exile: Estonian women's life narratives of the 1941 and 1949 Siberian deportations," *Journal of Baltic Studies* 36.1, 13–38.

Kirss, Tiina (ed) (2009) *Estonian Life Stories* (Budapest and New York: Central European University Press).

Kirss, Tiina, Ene Kõresaar and Marju Lauristin (eds) (2004) *She Who Remembers Survives: Interpreting Estonian Women's Post-Soviet Life Stories* (Tartu: Tartu University Press).

Kopperman, Maria (1972) *Minu 12 aastat Siberis* [My 12 years in Siberia], (Stockholm: Harta).

Kõresaar, Ene (2004) "Private and public, individual and collective in Linda's life story," in *She Who Remembers Survives: Interpreting Estonian Women's Post-Soviet Life Stories*, ed. Tiina Kirss, Ene Kõresaar and Marju Lauristin (Tartu: Tartu University Press), 89–111.

Kurvet-Käosaar, Leena (2003) "Other things happened to women: World War Two, violence, and national identity in 'A Sound of the Past' by Kabi Laretei and 'A Woman in Amber' by Agate Nesaule," *Journal of Baltic Studies* 34.3, 313–331.

Kurvet-Käosaar, Leena (2013) "Voicing trauma in the deportation narratives of Baltic women," in *Haunted Narratives: Life Writing in an Age of Trauma*, ed. Gabriele Rippl, Philipp Schweighauser, Tiina Kirss, Margit Sutrop and Therese Steffen (Toronto and Buffalo and London: University of Toronto Press), 129–151.

Laanes, Eneken (2012) "Sofi Oksanen's 'Purge' in Estonia," *Baltic Worlds* V.2, 19–21.

Landsberg, Alison (2004) *Prosthetic Memory: The Transformation of American Remembrance in the Age of Mass Culture* (New York: Columbia University Press).

Levy, Daniel and Natan Sznaider (2006) *Holocaust and the Memory in the Global Age* (Philadelphia: Temple University Press).

Luik, Viivi (2005) "Tõrjutud mälestused" [Memories denied], *Eesti Ekspress* 3 November, B5.

Mälksoo, Maria (2014) "Criminalizing Communism: transnational mnemopolitics in Europe," *International Political Sociology* 8, 82–99.

Memories Denied (2005) Dir. Imbi Paju (Fantasiafilmi and Allfilm).

Merridale, Catherine (2010) "Soviet memories: patriotism and trauma," in *Memory: History, Theories, Debates*, ed. Susannah Radstone and Bill Schwarz (New York: Fordham University Press), 376–389.

Mikli, Marika (1987) "Arvustus," [Review], *Sirp ja vasar* 25 December, 4.
Oksanen, Sofi (2010) *Purge*, trans. Lola Rogers (New York: Black Cat).
Paju, Imbi (2009) *Memories Denied* (Helsinki: Like).
Pettai, Eva-Clarita (2011) "Establishing 'Holocaust memory' – a comparison of Estonia and Latvia," in *Geschichtspolitik im erweiterten Ostseeraum und ihre aktuellen Symptome*, ed. Oliver Rathkolb and Imbi Sooman (Göttingen: V&R unipress), 159–173.
Pettai, Eva-Clarita and Vello Pettai (2015) *Transitional and Retrospective Justice in the Baltic States* (Cambridge: Cambridge University Press).
Rigney, Ann (2005) "Plenitude, scarcity and the circulation of cultural memory," *Journal of European Studies* 35.1, 11–28.
Rooste, Jürgen (2005) "Nii hilja valmis siis Eesti esimene holokaustidokk!" [So late came the first Estonian Holocaust doc], *Sirp* 4 November, 14.
Rothberg, Michael (2009) *Multidirectional Memory: Remembering the Holocaust in the Age of Decolonization* (Stanford: Stanford University Press).
Rothberg, Michael (2011) "From Gaza to Warsaw: mapping multidirectional memory," *Criticism* 53.4, 523–548.
Rothberg, Michael (2013) "Between Paris and Warsaw: multidirectional memory, ethics, and historical responsibility," in *Memory and Theory in Eastern Europe*, ed. Uilleam Blacker and Alexander Etkind (New York and Basingstroke: Palgrave MacMillan), 81–101.
Skultans, Vieda (1998) *The Testimony of Lives. Narrative and Memory in Post-Soviet Latvia* (London and New York: Routledge).
Solzhenitsyn, Aleksandr (1997) *Invisible Allies* (London: The Harvill Press).
Strods, Heinrihs and Matthew Kott (2002) "The file on operation 'Priboi': a re-assessment of the mass deportations of 1949," *Journal of Baltic Studies* 33.1, 1–36.
Susi, Arnold (2011) *Vöörsil vastu tahtmist* [Abroad against one's will], (Tallinn: Eesti Päevaleht).
Tamm, Marek (2013) "In search of lost time: memory politics in Estonia, 1991–2011," *Nationalities Papers* 41.4, 651–674.
Toker, Leona (2000) *Return From the Archipelago: Narratives of Gulag Survivors* (Bloomington and Indianapolis: Indiana University Press).
Valton, Arvo (1989) *Masendus ja lootus* [Depression and hope], (Tallinn: Eesti Raamat).
Valton, Arvo (2013) "Interview to Martin Pau," Tartu Postimees 58 (25 March), 2.
Wieviorka, Anette (2006) *The Era of The Witness* (Ithaca: Cornell University Press).
Uibo, Udo (1989) "Siber Maarjamaal: sotsialistlik realism" [Siberia in Maria's land: socialist realism], *Looming* 1, 125–126.

Ruxandra Cesereanu
Representations of the Gulag and Methods of Resistance: Romanian Detention Memoirs

1 Memoirs of detention in the Romanian Gulag

The vast majority of Romanian detention memoirs on the autochthonous (and sometimes also Soviet) Gulag aim to be anatomies of power and totalitarianism.[1] A few are written in a documentary (reportage) style, whereas most rank as confessions or revelatory records of "how I suffered back then." Some authors, anticipating criticism of the literariness of their work, ask readers to excuse their "clumsy wording," claiming it is not literature, but a true testimony. The Western reader may have been acquainted with this type of literature, but the Eastern European reader in general and the Romanian reader in particular had to do some catching up due to a politically induced ethical delay. Since the fall of Communism and of its dominant "hypocritical literature," readers have been exposed to the "literature of infernal truth," to "the monotony of terror," eventually getting used to the horror of the Gulag (Baltă 1994).

The memoirs of communist detentions have the same importance as Holocaust testimonies: they represent "the inferno that testifies," as André Glucksmann has put it (1991: 15). Romanian witnesses tend to display two of the three forms of shame distinguished by Tzvetan Todorov (1996). Along with the shame to have survived, survivors from the Pitești prison (where systematic torture was inflicted between 1949–1951, especially on student inmates, and many were forced to become torturers in turn) often feel the shameful memory of having been tortured and having become torturers, as well as the shame of being human.

Some of the detention memoirs were confiscated, the authors having to start a second version of the "hostile" manuscript from scratch. Nicolae Steinhardt's *Jurnalul fericirii* ("The journal of happiness," 1991) is the third version, revised, completed, and corrected by the author, based on two previous manuscripts, the first of which was confiscated by the authorities (it was returned to the author eventually). Similarly, Belu Zilber's *Monarhia de drept dialectic* (*The Monarchy of*

---

[1] This study examines Romanian detention memoirs published after 1989.

Dialectical Right), published in 1991 under the pseudonym Andrei Şerbulescu, was confiscated by the Securitate and then re-written. In the ensuing years, the Humanitas Publishing House, which had published *The Monarchy of Dialectical Right*, recovered the first version of the memoir and printed it under the title "Actor in the Pătrăşcanu's trial," this time with the author's real name on the cover: Herbert (Belu) Zilber (1997). The two versions differ, not only in nuances and details, but as a whole and with regard to the writing style.

With a few exceptions, the majority of these memoirs were written after release from detention. One such exception is the prison camp diary kept by Onisifor Ghibu (1991). It owes its unique status to the fact that in 1945, at the time Ghibu was serving time in the Caracal prison camp, the Romanian Gulag was not yet properly conceived and organized. Another exception is the memoir written by the Greek-Catholic bishop Iuliu Hossu, who wrote his memoirs while in monastery arrest (paradoxically though, in the period in which the bishop wrote his memoirs, repression was at its peak in communist Romania). There are some cases when diaries of deportation were kept while in confinement.

Some testimonies on detention are disguised, but the concealment acts as a see-through mask. Literary scholar Adrian Marino distinguishes two essential manners of approaching detention as a literary topic: "through literarization, stylization, the entire set of typical literary procedures, and through direct, documentary testimony, as objective as possible." (Marino 1993: 3); a possible hybrid formula could "recuperate cold reporting as 'literature'" (1993: 3). While warning against three misleading aspects that are likely to alter the memories of communist detention – "the author pretending to be a hero, emphatic embellishing and amateurish 'literarization'" (Marino 1996: 40) – Marino conducts his enquiry by focusing his attention on the "congenital defects" of the detention testimonies. The critic thus rebukes "the extremely annoying tendency of ostentatiously representing oneself in the best light, of transforming oneself into a hero, of excessive moralization, aggressive resentments, conventional literarization, and abundance of stereotypes" (Marino 1996: 3).

Ion Cârja, a primary witness of Gulag atrocities, considers his testimony to be more of a draft than a finished work. This self-deprecating tone is characteristic of the modesty of a non-writer; yet, an eye witness and established writer, Paul Goma writes in *Gherla* (1990a) about the "true truth" contained in this type of memoir, which, even if subjective, does not challenge the veracity of narrated events. In other words, they are subjective and honest, but nevertheless only *versions* of the truth. On the other hand, one of the characters in Goma's novel *Ostinato* (1991) represents a certain brand of heroism in political detention:

> [...] with them, with the political detainees, detention was... how should I put it? I dare say: fake – only there did the honest citizen X find out that he was a hero; until he got there, he, poor guy, had no idea who he was: once he got there, he started taking on, gradually, not only the appearance, but especially the psychology of a hero (a political hero, obviously); as far as I know, in there, those who had really handled guns, explosives, or... whatever (as one would say "men of action") were looked down upon with disdain, considered intruders by the "non-aggressive ones;" former dignitaries, "men of power," "agitators;" even the students, who dropped like flies, not because they had "committed" something, but because it was assumed that they might have intended to "commit" something evil. From this point of view, Marian [a former political detainee] is enviable: he had the chance to pass through that place where you're up to your neck in "heroism," where there were imprisoned not those who represented a real danger to society, but common people, who only there, and from that moment, learnt to represent a risk to society. (Goma 1991: 396)

There are also novel-like memoirs of detention, such as Marcel Petrişor's memoirs (1994), Costin Merişca's *Tărîmul Gheenei* (*The Land of Gehenna*, 1993), and others. Petrişor uses third-person narration and changes the names of the detainees who are still alive. Merişca also employs third-person narration, changing only the name of the protagonist – himself.

Stylistically, emotionally, and structurally, the memoirs of the Romanian Gulag are very diverse. *Gherla* by Paul Goma (1990a) is disguised by pseudo-dialogue that includes memories of detention. Goma writes in an uneasy, radical style, typical of a pamphleteer. His article of faith is a life-writing that captures suffering as it was experienced, without resorting to any form of embellishment. Some memoirs of detention are written in a melodramatic style and appear to be counterfeits, lacking any sort of rhythm and forging ahead demagogically, in anti-concentrationary, wooden language. Others are chained in "the iron circle of hate." Nicolae Mărgineanu's testimonies, *Amfiteatre şi închisori* ("Amphitheaters and prisons," 2002) are, interestingly, pre-selected, the author refraining from mentioning the horrors that happened during his detention, out of patriotic embarrassment. He draws a distinction between a memoir written by a well-known individual and a humble person's testimony; unassumingly, he includes his writings in the latter category. Similar classifications are advanced by Gabriel Bălănescu, Constantin Cesianu (a meticulous researcher of the Danube–Black Sea Canal labor camp), and Ioan Victor Pica. The last also pleads testimony, undertaking to write a "book of fire" on anti-Communist resistance in the mountains: "Others will certainly write history, I have a much easier role, namely that of saying what I saw, heard and felt." (1993: 9) Towards the end of his book, he stresses the importance of testifying: *"The biggest guilt is not to say the truth, when you know it!"* (1993: 177; author's emphasis).

For historical accuracy, Constantin C. Giurescu uses the scholarly term "testimony" (Rom. *testimoniu*) in order to render the sense of evidence offered by an objective document. He states that he has composed his prison memoirs without any hate or bias, but only with a historical purpose in mind. Political detainees are history, since they belong to history. Giurescu cherishes all memories that acquire the role of a testimony. Generally, imprisonment on political grounds acts like an inner protection screen or, as Al. Mihalcea calls it, the "background canvass of thoughts." (1994: 206) For Ion D. Sîrbu, it is the miniature metaphor of the world, both during detention and after release (Sîrbu 1996: 178).

Some other depositions display a narrative flair. One example is Maxim Holban's epistolary testimony (he got to know Siberia in its extreme in Kolyma) embedded in his son's Ioan's story, "Father in a steel shirt" (Holban 1995). Another is Doina Jela's *Bildungsreportage* on the Danube–Black Sea Canal camp (*Nichita Dumitru*, Jela 1995), which creates a collage of various documentary sources: minutes from meetings "unmasking the enemies of the people," denouncements, fragments of contemporary diaries, letters from victims' relatives, short interviews with the surviving prisoners and guards, etc.

Some texts are written in an elaborate, almost baroque style, such as *The Journal of Happiness* by Nicolae Steinhardt (1991), *Drumul crucii* ("The way of the cross") by Aurel State (1993) (who views his testimony as an ascent of Mount Tabor, with writing considered as a sacred gesture), or *Jurnalul unui figurant* ("The journal of a figurehead") by George Tomaziu (1995). Others, to the contrary, are written in a plain style: the primitive and naive picturesque style of Anița Nandriș-Cudla's memoir (1991), for instance, echoes Henri Rousseau's paintings, transposed on the Siberian landscape. Monica Lovinescu sees in this naive style "a language not tarnished by knowledge, which existed before the tree of good and evil. In fact, [it is] the language of Paradise" (1996: 303). Similarly, Elizabeta Rizea's story, although fluid (hers is a spoken book), is inventive and spontaneous. The witness perceives her deposition as an animal "growl," which produces a cathartic effect. She distinguishes between this "growl" and the human cry or outcry – only a growl, not a decorative cry, can awaken the indoctrinated souls and minds: "'Cause I wanna growl, not cry, 'cause I can't bear it anymore" and "I'd like to moo like a cow because of all I've been through" (Nicolau and Nițu 1993). Similarly, the dialogue between Oana Orlea and Mariana Marin is very intense (Orlea 1993). In order to render the atmosphere of prison, Orlea, a former political detainee, uses rude, expletive-ridden language, linguistically reminiscent of the Gulag experience.

Quite different from Nandriș-Cudla's or Rizea's accounts are Lena Constante's refined, albeit cruel memoirs. Between these two ends of the spectrum, there is Adriana Georgescu's brief reportage (1992), which does not achieve a "moderation" of the testimony; rather, she views figures of speech only as rhetorical flowers of the actual testimony; or else, pain is just pain, that is all there is to it, no metaphors.

The most important book of memoirs about the Romanian Gulag is Ion Ioanid's *Închisoarea noastră cea de toate zilele* ("Our daily prison"). Like Aleksandr Solzhenitsyn's *The Gulag Archipelago*, Ioanid's memoir is a panoramic viewing of Romanian prisons realized with real finesse. The structure of his memory resembles that of an archive, where each prison represents a book of life written with narrative impartiality. The area of each punitive space and especially the microcosm of the cell are described in careful detail. According to Alex Ştefănescu, it is a memory that "is in itself a heroic form of opposition against the communist regime." *Our Daily Prison* is a "report addressed to a supreme authority (God, history of humankind, or conscience)." Ştefănescu sees Ioanid's memoirs as succeeding in creating a sense of "nostalgia for prison," since they instill the sensation that "everything we read represents our own memories" (Ştefănescu 1991: 5).

> What's also characteristic of Ioanid's writing is that the time of writing is that of prison; the never-ending day of suffering. And in order to make it bearable, it has to be fragmented in gestures and occupations. In such a time, there is place for all the details, for the remains of everyday life that most of us sift out from the essential, the event. (Lovinescu 1996: 340)

Far from being bland, Ioanid's writing is captivating through its touch of a saga-novel and nuanced conciseness. The author also suggests drawing up a list of names of all anti-communist political detainees in Romania. There are some other, similarly Sisyphean attempts, none of which equals Ioanid's in narrative excellence and panoramic range. Ion Pantazi (1992), for instance, likens his memories to a screen on which a film about detention is played out. Pantazi, too, considers producing a synthesis of the prison regime (in the last part of his memoirs), with classifications according to type of detention, age, and social class, elaborating hierarchies of portraits and behaviors, but his work falls prey to exaltation.

2 Strategies of survival adopted in the Romanian Gulag

2.1 Secular strategies

In order to survive inside the communist camps and prisons, prisoners created a philosophy of detention in order to compensate the long-lost outside universe, which was now, and perhaps forever, beyond their reach. This philosophy served as a substitute for the real, but also as a self-contained and versatile world-engendering survival strategy.

A prime example for this type of text is by Nicolae Steinhardt, namely his well-known "Political testament," which prefaces *The Journal of Happiness* (Steinhardt 1991). Steinhardt proposed three methods of resistance in the carceral universe: "the Solzhenitsyn solution" – considering oneself dead or numbed and hence beyond the reach of the apparatus of oppression; "the Zinoviev solution" – playing the part of a lunatic or vagrant who was structurally maladjusted to the system; and "the Churchill–Bukovsky solution" – valiantly fighting against the concentration camp system. Steinhardt did not indicate whether these methods were applicable inside or outside the Gulag, and his references to the concentration camp system were, more or less, general; therefore, they should be brought back into discussion. For instance, the Solzhenitsyn approach was obviously applicable, especially inside the Gulag (it would not have made any sense on the outside), and the Zinoviev or Churchill–Bukovsky methods were applicable particularly outside the Gulag (Bukovsky, however, also resorted to it when in the Gulag). Insofar as the third solution is concerned, I believe that Steinhardt exaggerated by labeling it the Churchill solution; whereas Aleksandr Solzhenitsyn, Aleksandr Zinoviev and Vladimir Bukovsky had a connection to the Gulag and to communist totalitarianism, invoking Churchill was hardly conclusive or appropriate, and appears to be an honorary mention more than anything else. Moreover, the parity that the author of the "Political testament" established between the three approaches was strained, since the Zinoviev approach was more escapist than the other two, which were more trenchant.

2.2 Resistance through faith

Steinhardt did not exhaust all the methods of resistance, nor did he intend to do so; with his own life he embodied yet another approach – that of faith. This was a nuanced approach that comprised two aspects: one that was relatively common, in the sense of faith in tradition, and the other that was mystical. The latter entailed a spiritual adjustment of the concentration camp universe to the archetypal Christian scenario that a prisoner might face: after experiencing the revelation of faith in caverns and abysses, he could believe, at first, "only in half- or quarter-measures, or even less, almost not at all." (Steinhardt 1991: 39) Steinhardt had overcome the first stage, approaching detention in the manner of a mystic. In his relation to others, he reached *agapé*, Christian love, being permanently marked after baptism by an indestructible inner elation.

The fact that detention bore certain fruits for Nicolae Steinhardt may be attributed to his conversion to Christianity (he repeatedly stated that prison was a "place of fulfillment") and to his strong moral edifice, which required that he make use of psychological weapons that were tantamount to those of his opponent (the investigator, the torturer), training himself up for these confrontations. Aware that a single prison was small when compared with the country at large as a prison, Steinhardt refused to become a traitor or collaborator, and gave himself up to the organs of repression at a time when the authorities merely wanted to test him psychologically. Steinhardt's *Christomorphosis* was revealing to the extent that detention amounted to resuming an ordeal of salvation. This inspired term was coined by Vlad Pavlovici, who comments as follows:

> N. Steinhardt incessantly proves his lucidity in prison. He even displays a sort of *trezvie* (intense wakefulness), as he understands everything and accepts everything. What he accepts, above all, is his destiny. The more tragic it is, the more disturbing his suffering, the more evident it becomes that his power of overcoming suffering is by converting it into happiness. The emphasis is on the freedom of experiencing the religious sentiment and his suffering is transfigured. [...] The blessing of the Calvary he faces, the transformation of the most atrocious source of suffering into a source of joy, the terrible will to retrace, to reiterate the passions of the Savior – all these converge, in N. Steinhardt's book, towards a proposed *Christomorphosis*. (Pavlovici 1993: 25)

Once he was released from detention and attained inner salvation, Steinhardt no longer posed the question of forgetting evil (he had already solved the problem of forgiveness). Beyond loneliness, disillusionment and old age, his gift remained the freshness of Christianity. Steinhardt's case was all the more interesting as he was not a professional dispenser of the faith, which would have legitimized the mystical solution he had adopted.

In his notes about prison, the Greek-Catholic Bishop Iuliu Hossu testified, in turn, to a form of innate and instinctual resistance through *Christomorphosis* (although he did not use this particular term). Despite repressions, the atmosphere was one of communion and acceptance of the ordeal in the sense of becoming one with God and rising from the dead through suffering. Hossu focused on the idea of a "spiritual feast" in detention: a luminous, albeit powerful delicacy marked the bishop as a diaphanous warrior, who had immersed himself into the intricacies of faith with a devotion that was outstandingly rare. In addition to prayer, Hossu also found a way of enduring his ordeal: he programmatically and strategically recollected his peregrinations as a bishop and a free individual in his diocese, his canonical visitations, the consecrations of churches, the sermons he had delivered during holidays, thus re-living what he referred to as his "archpastorate." He was the sole prisoner incarcerated for having remained true to his conscience in whom

I have encountered this unique attitude of resistance, which allowed him to escape the barbed-wire enclosure in his mind. In the Sighet prison Hossu silently recited the liturgy every day, adapting it according to the holidays to be celebrated, and conceived new prayers together with the other prelates. The movement was katabatic, of the *descensus ad inferos* type, but redemptive: "the tougher the restrictions against externalization, the deeper I descended into the recesses of my soul, deeper and deeper, turning everything I experienced in the dungeons of Sighet into holy prayer and offering it with humility to the Lord Jesus." (Hossu 2003: 236) Prayer was perceived as the "supreme university" and a "vocational school." Although, out of humility and gentleness, he had never presumed to envisage himself as a "chosen vessel of Christ," Iuliu Hossu was just that, abundantly. His memoirs about imprisonment could be said to amount to a second *The Journal of Happiness*, because the only other prisoner in whom the sweetness of suffering and the firmness of a crusader could be encountered is Nicolae Steinhardt. It is worth noting, however, that Hossu's memories and experiences in detention are to be understood as a form of liturgy.

An interesting case was that of Richard Wurmbrand, a Protestant pastor, whose book *With God in Prison*[2] is not only a testimony by a clergyman who endured the Romanian Gulag for fourteen years, but also a manual of how faith can be tested through temptations, revelations, visions, and so forth. The variant of faith proposed here is refined: "beyond faith and love, there is joy unto the Lord: a profound, extraordinary ecstasy of happiness, unparalleled in this world" (Wurmbrand 1994: 7), differentiating mystical joy from faith and love. Wurmbrand applied this attitude especially in isolation. He prepared mentally for detention and torture, like a soldier, even though immediately after his arrest he considered suicide. This testimony is crucial, because here the entire carceral ordeal was perceived as a threshold for testing his faith. Morally, the solution to rise above torture and all forms of aggression was for Wurmbrand a Christian acceptance of death as resurrection; when suffering must be forgotten or when the danger of madness must be overcome, the prisoner resorts to a whirling dance, like that of the dervishes, or to prayer "in the heart." Wurmbrand's book is strange for a cleric also because the author confessed at length to his hallucinations and temptations (for instance, of slaying the demon of lust with the help of the demon of pride). He described the physical degradation that, by way of compensation, led him directly towards an intense spiritual life. During nearly three years of isolation, Wurmbrand felt haunted and literally

---

[2] First published in English in 1968 and subsequently translated into Romanian (Wurmbrand 1994) [Ed.].

tested by the devil, whom he overcame through deeds of faith and sometimes through poetry. His moral structure was, above all, that of an astute missionary (in this last aspect, it is interesting to recall the strange relationship between the investigated and the investigator, which led to the latter's Christian conversion: at first enticed with Marxist ideas applied in a Christian manner, the investigator ultimately confessed to the investigated, like in a scene from a Dostoevsky novel). While in collective detention, the pastor always spoke in parables and exercised his pedagogical vocation, because in prison witty stories and advice with cathartic effect proved to be essential: "I would often speak for hours on end, although I was sick and dizzy with hunger: a story could keep a man's life going just as well as a piece of bread could." (Wurmbrand 1994: 89)

When referring to resistance through faith, Richard Wurmbrand spoke of a Christian approach "in a living form"; he did not want to experience missionizing and faith in a rigid way, but in a manner that was adapted to the context, for all suffering has something of Christ's suffering, he claimed, converting prisoners of all ages and from all walks of life (his great converts were the young and the Marxists). Sometimes the pastor's sermons were rejected, and then he made up stories with brigands, which were nonetheless grafted upon writings with a Christian touch of Tolstoy and Dostoevsky, and always featured a moralizing subtext. The cells that Wurmbrand walked through were regarded as "parishes." During the second period of his detention, the pastor met those who had been re-educated by torture in Pitești prison and irretrievably hardened prisoners, whom he was unable to reach. His attitude was that of an indefatigable missionary: he did not seek vengeance, nor did he give up preaching, for he managed to bring people on the brink of suicide onto the path of faith. I would say that as a shift from one extreme to the other, from murder to repentance and holiness, Dostoyevskianism was a characteristic of Pastor Wurmbrand's converts, even though their readiness to convert was ambiguous: "Prison turned some into saints and others into brutes and it was hard to predict who would become a saint and who a brute; but one thing was certain – that most prisoners would continue to live as if in a vacuum." (Wurmbrand 1994: 232) Wurmbrand's last battle with the devil consisted in his refusal to accept "brainwashing" (during prison sessions of self-criticism and verbose masochism, with hysterical overtones) through a Faustian dramatic inner dispute.

2.3 Individualized forms of resistance

There were also other, less trenchant or spectacular, but still valid ways of resistance. Nicolae Mărgineanu revealed the secret of his resistance in simple terms: "The great advantage of the Romanian intellectual who had ended up in prison was this: the richness of his life prevented him from feeling alone wherever he was." (Mărgineanu 2002: 155) After seventeen years of imprisonment, Mărgineanu attributed his physical and moral resilience to his clear conscience, to a self-imposed intense thought regime and, last but not least, to the camaraderie in detention.

Ion Ioanid also referred to resistance inside the Gulag: he was a tenacious and farcical fighter, a master of games whose aim it was to mislead informers and authorities alike. Describing life in the labor camps, Ioanid attested that although brutalized and exhausted, political prisoners succeeded in sabotages that defied the organs of repression, and managed to impose their holidays, even though persecution intensified. At another stage of detention, the challenges of the administration triggered an organized opposition, with Ioanid's group launching a hunger strike as a means of defying repression. To jolt the prisoners out of their apathy, the strike was meticulously organized and layers of strikers were involved – the old and infirm, hesitant and resistant. At first, the administration was indifferent; then the prison authorities became conciliatory, but attempted to break the strike; then followed bribes, surrenders, and isolating the "Mohicans," who were averse to the idea of force feeding. In order to pacify the protesters, the prison regime and the guards' behavior improved, but everything was ephemeral. After a new avalanche of penitentiary despotism, when the strike was defeated, the elderly were demoralized, but the young exhibited the same radicalism against the system: while living with the hope of liberation, which was perpetually crushed, not in utopia but in reality, the youngest political detainees became, in a sense, a kind of long-distance runners.

Ion Ioanid distinguished between two types of resilient individuals who endured in the Gulag: the "intransigent knights," who had a strict code of honor, and the "adapted moderates," those who used the same (moral, psychological) weapons as the authorities, sometimes even finding compromise solutions (the author considered himself as the latter). Both the intransigent knights and the adapted moderates found a constant, self-defining temptation in defying the measures adopted by the administration. Ioanid himself engaged in risky acts, arising from the insane courage of his youth. To obtain up-to-date political information, he pretended to need dental surgery; on another occasion, he stole a Communist brochure from the commander's mantle or pretended to be sick so as to be isolated in quarantine with a friend from another cell. Finally, he even pierced the cell wall with an improvised drill to get in touch with his mother, located somewhere outside the prison, but in a spot visible from the cell. The spirit of resourcefulness and imagination often saved prisoners who, despite strict surveillance, initiated a manufacturing industry on a minuscule scale, managed to establish paradoxical networks of communication.

One thing necessary in detention, the memoirist said, was black humor, a barely optimizing element that nonetheless enabled a sort of ironic adjustment to hell. There is a memorable scene in *Our Daily Prison*: after catching hundreds of flies, the prisoners attached strings of colored yarn to their legs, shocking guards and investigators who could sense a large-scale sabotage and were made to feel guilty for lacking vigilance with this display. While being interrogated about a problematic period of his life, Ioanid concocted a genuine *mise en scène*, adopting the position of a trickster. First, he secured the guards' neutrality, impersonating the perfect, docile prisoner; then, to avoid torture, he played the role of a sick man, learning to control both his mimicry as a Molièresque character and the inexpressiveness necessary to screen his thoughts.

In prison, Ion Ioanid witnessed a true communion between very different individuals, whose common experiences had shaped their characters. This mutual understanding regardless of the squalid conditions in detention proved that the Gulag was a space in which the prisoner's character and conscience were put to the test.

> An ordinary snob slept under the same blanket as a peasant from Bukovina; the critical spirit of the cold and realistic intellectual was faced with petty-bourgeois prejudices and superstitions; the believer ate from the same bowl as the atheist; the sentimentalist was forced to listen to the cynic's stories, and so on. Under the circumstances, this compost was more than explosive. And yet, humaneness and wisdom prevailed. (Ioanid 1991: 348)

During a difficult moment of his detention, when his cell was infested with the plague of opportunism, Ion Ioanid managed, with the patience of a schemer, to organize a miniature *coup d'état*, changing the bleak atmosphere in the cell and imposing a moral code of camaraderie. The fact that we will not encounter demoralization in Ion Ioanid's prison memoirs was a result of the pact the author has made with himself, coupled with a strong instinct for survival and defensive optimism.

Alexandru Paleologu considered detachment as one of the methods of resistance in prison: neither confronting the guards, nor mentally accepting that you had become a *nobody*; as he confessed: "That a guardian humiliated me, that he hit me was, of course, a physical inconvenience, but that did not prevent him from remaining an imbecile and a brute, and I was still a man who had read Plato and Mallarmé." (1991: 131) What essentially saved the incarcerated individual, however, were his intellectual resources and his intellectual-histrionic vocation: "I strove to turn the cells into salons where discussions were held and civility reigned. My method gained followers and achieved some success." (Paleologu, 1991: 131) To quote another example:

> Everyone was talking about what they knew. Some recounted a movie or a novel [...]. Others held actual conferences they had prepared beforehand, or even delivered cycles of talks. I also gave several series of lectures on Proust, Balzac, Stendhal, with some success, which encouraged me to reiterate them in other prisons to which I was transferred. I think that in this way, I orally converted a number of people to literature. (Paleologu 1991: 132)

On another occasion, Paleologu talked about how he filtered the prison experience through humor, noting the comic side of detention and highlighting both aspects of tragic and self-pity, which to him were anathema. What he discovered in the Gulag, especially in the labor colonies, was grotesqueness of the Rabelaisian and Aristophanic type; his perspective did not sublimate the tragedy and the cruelty of the experience, but incorporated them in the grotesque. Paleologu's laughter was perceived by other prisoners in two ways – it was either valued as comforting or criticized as cynical and reprehensible. As a beholder of grotesqueness in detention, Paleologu saw the Gulag through the carnivalesque lens, a world turned upside down, in keeping with the Grand Guignol and clownish models (Paleologu 1996: 163, 170, 172, 181).

Paul Goma's resistance was different. It was loud. Having been abused in the Gherla prison, his response to violence was a defiant howl, his revolt was non-silence. The prisoner no longer protected only his head or genitals, the bodily parts where he was regularly assaulted, but also his mouth. While objectors usually do so with words, the tortured Goma only had a howl at his disposal. Later, in a 1977 inquiry, Paul Goma's body remembered. Independently of its owner's natural fear, it adapted to being incarcerated and his mind only followed suit later. Goma survived the interrogation because his body had turned out to be a shield, a hardened shell:

> Flesh and innards, with their memory intact, followed, in parallel, the pathways of a re-arrested prisoner. A parallel, subterranean road, like a platform on tracks, buried underground. The cells had refused to listen to me, they had reorganized themselves according to the well-known, well-learned formula from twenty years ago (and repeated daily, for twenty years). (Goma 1990b: 245)

Not infrequently, resistance in prison occurred through extraordinary pedagogical dedication, such as that demonstrated by George Manu, an inmate and professor of nuclear physics who taught in the Zarca Aiudului prison. Professor Manu, nicknamed the Rector, represented a model of intellectual survival, resorting to various tricks in order to initiate his students: lessons on the history of France and England written on a bar of soap or the bottom of a tin, scholarly commentaries on English and French literature etched on wax plates, lessons about the great geographical discoveries on hand-drawn maps, the US Constitution. Ingenuity led him to discover the Morse communication method using thread, which is how he taught *If*, a poem by Rudyard Kipling which he considered to be a model of resistance against the vicissitudes of life.

Another prisoner, Oana Orlea, belonged to the category of passionate fighters. She believed that women could cope with detention better than men could, by virtue of being inured to pain. Orlea's detention was hard. Turbulent, Orlea was often placed in isolation and endured the carceral regime, went on hunger strike – which she considered to be a code of honor – and simulated suicide to avoid solitude. Her attitude to resistance in prison was that of relentless revolt, even though she committed the sin, in her words, of gratuitous heroism. Orlea considered herself to be morally, albeit not physically, resistant and concluded that prison could not change anybody completely; torture could.

Adriana Georgescu was a fighter, too. While subject to unrelenting torture and living an endless nightmare, she found two methods of resistance: on the one hand, by accepting death (the Solzhenitsyn approach) and on the other hand, by sublimation of fear (a solution she was not able to apply) (Georgescu 1992). There were two equally dangerous types of fear that could bring a prisoner to her knees: mental and visceral. Georgescu managed to overcome the latter, but gave in to the former and obsessed with torture.

A simple soul, Anița Nandriș-Cudla (1991), outlined the three kinds of feelings that had inspired and fueled her resistance in the Siberian exile: patriotism, Christian faith, and love of the family. In her case, there were no ups and downs of the soul, no shades of gray, but only a fatalistic resistance and naive-primitive peasant toughness.

Confessing that she had hidden under a mask in detention, Elisabeta Rizea admitted that owing to this mask, her patience and typical peasant shrewdness, and despite her severe averseness to betrayal, she was able to survive inside the Gulag. Admittedly, the mask had also been imposed upon her by the ordeals to which she had been subjected. Calling herself a "rag doll," Rizea mimicked obedience to the authorities, but never gave up, the secret of her resistance being faith (many crosses with the tongue and prayers in the heart!) and silence as divine grace (Cordoș 1993). When she was arrested for the second time, she was already an initiated practitioner of intransigence and a camouflaged warrior: although she was risking a death sentence, being put in chains and thrown into isolation, she was determined to resist (Nicolau and Nițu 1993).

Understanding that not obedience but revolt, albeit not raucous rebelliousness, was the solution and feeling the need to confront the external pressures and isolation, Lena Constante built a compensatory imaginary world during the first stage of her detention, resorting to "ceaseless intellectual gymnastics" (Lovinescu 1996: 148). She took aesthetic refuge within – sometimes she would build a utopian house in her mind's eye, at other times her evasion consisted in compiling a mental dictionary of disparate lyrics. The other world, opposed to investigations and detention, was poetry, solitude being overcome by a huge recuperative aesthetic gesture; still, her mental escape was difficult. As a detainee, she made up stories, manufactured dolls, composed fairy tales and theater plays, drew and managed to create, by visually devouring an object, no matter how small, a real landscape, a new world; and when she could not see it, being prohibited to do this, she attempted to see through her hearing, like the blind. A rustle, a murmur, any kind of noise became the lines and colors of a cosmos that she painstakingly reconstructed. Everything happened, however, at a purely mental level, because to externalize her inner world could have proved fatal for her. Since the periods of respite alternated with those of torture, Constante hoped for death as a last resort, but then understood that death was inaccessible to her since she was a crucial witness in the Stalinist lawsuit brought against the Communist leader Lucrețiu Pătrășcanu (one of the few real intellectuals among the Romanian Communist leaders; he was put on trial by Stalinist authorities and was executed in the Jilava prison on 17 April 1954). The thought of suicide fortified her, but her spiritual crisis became acute when persecution erupted to an absurd level. However, Constante did not give in, she opted for calm tenacity: "Sadness makes you weak. Anger, stronger. I chose resistance. I made the decision not to weep ever again and I never wept again. To admit hope and I exceeded hope. I found a new confidence within me. The certainty that I would find freedom, joy, my family." (Constante 1992: 201–202) During the first stage of her detention, Constante's idea of resistance was that of salvation through aesthetic means. Her revelation was foundational: "The power of words. I had words and I had time." (1992: 56) Sanda Cordoș does not believe that Constante's approach was bookish, but rather that it was existential, using the "frail body of words;" she likens Constante's inner escape with a "state of grace [...] comparable, on its solar route, with that achieved, also while in custody, by N. Steinhardt." (Cordoș 1993: 30)

Lena Constante's "black book," *Evadarea tăcută* ("A silent escape"), which succeeded in overcoming detention because she had found refuge in the imaginary, was followed by the "gray book," *Evadarea imposibilă* ("The impossible escape"), in which the idea of an aesthetic escape was abandoned. In turn, the ephemeral, Solzhenitsynian escape from *A Silent Escape* was replaced by tricking death and its helpers through an underground, tempered battle. Relinquishing her mental escape, Constante entered into a dialogue with other prisoners; still she maintained a certain tactical (psychological) distance and did not completely discard the cold mask that concealed her inner reactions.

Collective resistance often manifested itself through symposia, dissertations, foreign language lessons, in other words, through a penitentiary "university," as attested by most memoirists. For instance, Constantin C. Giurescu meticulously inventoried conferences and lectures given in prison, making a list of references that specified the topics, the cell where the discussion had taken place, the author of the lecture, etc. Because time was a torturer, the word that summed up life in prison was "wait." A word spoken snappily by the guards and experienced to the point of despair by prisoners. The latter became remotely controlled automatons, conditioned by the opening of a door and the motivation underlying this event. The prison cell was studied under a magnifying glass, like a matrix, with its two key elements: the window (an opening to the outside of the prison and a means of escape for the gaze) and the door (an opening to the inside of the prison), with the annex of the visor (a double spy: an eye of the guard, but also an eye of the daring detainee). A prisoner like Giurescu sharpened his memory and survived mainly due to the mental training to which he subjected himself, both in solitude and in front of an audience.

The imprisoned individuals exhibited varying degrees of psychological resistance: they could be optimistic, naive, skeptical, pessimistic, or cynical; all of them, however, regardless of the personal survival methods they had adopted, acknowledged, as a collective solution, the university atmosphere of the cells, the barracks etc. "The thirst for knowledge was, in fact, a disguise of despondency, our refusal to become brutes," as put by a witness (Pavlovici 2001: 196–197). Thus, the detention space had come to replace, to some extent, the library, the cultural salon, the lecture amphitheater, or even the house of prayer.

Works cited

Bălănescu, Gabriel (1994) *Din împărăția morții* [From the kingdom of death], (Timișoara: Editura Gordian).
Baltă, Nicolae (1994) "Sertarul și tipăriturile" [Drawer and print], *Luceafărul* 16–17, 7.
Bănuș, Max (1991) *Cei care m-au ucis* [Those who killed me], (București: Editura Tinerama).
Cârja, Ion (1993) *Canalul morții* [The death canal], (București: Editura Cartea Românească).
Cesianu, Constantin (1992) *Salvat din infern* [Saved from the inferno], (București: Editura Humanitas).
Constante, Lena (1992) *Evadarea tăcută. 3000 de zile singură în închisorile din România* [A silent escape. Three thousand days in Romanian prisons], (București: Editura Humanitas).
Cordoș, Sanda (1993) "Vorbind din adăpostul tăcerilor" [Speaking from the shelter of silence], *Vatra* 10, 31.

Georgescu, Adriana (1992) *La început a fost sfîrşitul. Dictatura roşie la Bucureşti* [In the beginning was the end. The red dictatorship in Bucharest], ed. Micaela Ghiţescu (Bucureşti: Editura Humanitas).

Ghibu, Onisifor (1991) *Ziar de lagăr. Caracal 1945* [A concentration camp newspaper. Caracal 1945], ed. Romeo Dăscălescu and Octavian Ghibu (Bucureşti: Editura Albatros).

Giurescu, Constantin, C. (1994) *Cinci ani şi două luni în penitenciarul de la Sighet (7 mai 1950–5 iulie 1955)* [Five years and two months in the prison from Sighet (7 May 1950–5 July 1955)], ed. Lia Ioana Ciplea, introd. Dinu C. Giurescu (Bucureşti: Editura Fundaţiei Culturale Române).

Glucksmann, André (1991) *Bucătăreasa şi Mîncătorul de oameni. Eseu despre raporturile dintre stat, Marxism şi lagărele de concentrare* [The cook and the man-eater. An essay on the relations between the state, Marxism and concentration camps], trans. Mariana Ciolan (Bucureşti: Editura Humanitas).

Goma, Paul (1990a) *Gherla* (Bucureşti: Editura Humanitas).

Goma, Paul (1990b) *Culorile curcubeului '77 (Cutremurul oamenilor)* [The color of the rainbow '77 (The earthquake of the people)], (Bucureşti: Editura Humanitas).

Goma, Paul (1991) *Ostinato* (Bucureşti: Editura Univers).

Holban, Ioan (1995) "Tata în cămaşă de oţel" [Father in a steel shirt], in *Basarabia în Gulag*, ed. Serafim Saka (Chişinău: Editura Meridianul 28, Editura Uniunii Scriitorilor).

Hossu, Iuliu (2003) *Credinţa noastră este viaţa noastră. Memoriile cardinalului Iuliu Hossu* [Our faith is our life. The memoirs of Cardinal Iuliu Hossu], ed. Fr. Silvestru Augustin Prunduş (Cluj-Napoca: Editura Viaţa Creştină).

Ioanid, Ion (1991) *Închisoarea noastră cea de toate zilele* [Our daily prison], (Bucureşti: Editura Albatros), vol. I, II.

Jela, Doina (1995) *Nichita Dumitru. Încercare de reconstituire a unui process comunist, 29 august–1 septembrie 1952* [Nichita Dumitru. An attempt to reconstruct a communist trial, 29 August–1 September 1952], (Bucureşti: Editura Humanitas).

Lovinescu, Monica (1996) *Insula Şerpilor. Unde scurte VI* [Serpent Island. Short Waves 6], (Bucureşti: Editura Humanitas).

Mărgineanu, Nicolae (2002) "Amfiteatre şiînchisori" [Amphitheaters and prisons], in *Mărturii asupra unui veac zbuciumat*, ed. Daniela Ţăranu-Mărgineanu (Bucureşti: Editura Fundaţiei Culturale Române).

Marin, Mariana (1991) *Ia-ţi boarfele şi mişcă!* [Take your rags and move! An interview with Oana Orlea], (Bucureşti: Editura Cartea Românească).

Marino, Adrian (1993) "O carte de sertar" [A book kept in the drawer], *Tribuna Ardealului* 68, 3–4.

Marino, Adrian (1996) "Represiune şi confesiune," [Repression and confession], *Revista* 22, 28–30.

Merişca, Costin (1993) *Tărîmul Gheenei* [The land of Gehenna], (Galaţi: Editura "Porto-Franco").

Mihalcea, Al. (1994) *Jurnal de ocnă* [Prison journal], (Bucureşti: Editura Albatros).

Nandriş-Cudla, Aniţa (1991) *20 de ani în Siberia. Destin bucovinean* [20 years in Siberia. The destiny of a woman from Bucovina], (Bucureşti: Editura Humanitas).

Nicolau, Irina and Theodor Niţu (eds) (1993) *Povestea Elisabetei Rizea din Nucşoara. Mărturia lui Cornel Drăgoi* [The story of Elisabeta Rizea from Nucşoara. The testimony of *Cornel Drăgoi*], introd. Gabriel Liiceanu (Bucureşti: Editura Humanitas).

Paleologu, Alexandru (1991) *Minunatele amintiri ale unui ambasador al golanilor, Conversations with Marc Semo and Claire Tréan* [The wonderful memories of an ambassador of the gallows], trans. Alexandru Ciolan (Bucureşti: Editura Humanitas).

Paleologu, Alexandru and Stelian Tănase (1996) *Sfidarea memoriei (Convorbiri), aprilie 1988–octombrie 1989* [The defiance of memory (dialogues), April 1988–October 1989] (București: Editura DU Style).
Pantazi, Ion (1992) *Am trecut prin iad* [I've been through hell], (Sibiu: Editura Constant), vol. I.
Pavlovici, Vlad (1993) "Imitatio Christi" [Imitating Christ], *Steaua* 8–9, 25.
Pavlovici, Florin Constantin (2001) Tortura pe înțelesul tuturor [Torture for everyone], (Chișinău: Editura Cartier).
Petrișor, Marcel (1991) *Fortul 13 Jilava. Convorbiri din detenție. Memorii I* [Fort 13 Jilava. Talks from prison. Memories I], (București: Editura Meridiane).
Petrișor, Marcel (1994) *Secretul Fortului 13. Reeducări și execuții. Memorii II* [The secret of Fort 13. Reeducations and executions. Memories II], (Iași: Editura Timpul).
Pica, Victor Ioan (1993) *Libertatea are chipul lui Dumnezeu* [Freedom is the image of God], (Tîrgu-Mureș: Editura Arhipelag).
Șerbulescu, Andrei (1991) *Monarhia de drept dialectic. A doua versiune a memoriilor lui Belu Silber* [The monarchy of dialectical right. The second version of Belu Silber's memoirs], (București: Editura Humanitas).
Sîrbu, Ion. D. (1996) *Jurnalul unui journalist fără jurnal* [The diary of a diarist without a journal], ed. Toma Velici and Elena Ungureanu (Craiova: Scrisul Românesc), vol. II, 178.
Solzhenitsyn, Alexandr (1997) *Arhipelagul Gulag. 1918–1956. Încercare de investigație literară* [The Gulag Archipelago. 1918–1956. An experiment in literary investigation], trans. Nicolae Iliescu, postface by Alexandru Paleologu (București: Editura Univers), vol. I.
State, Aurel (1993) *Drumul crucii* [The way of the cross], (București: Editura Litera), vol. I, II.
Ștefănescu, Alex (1991) "Amintiri despre vremuri mai pure" [Remembering more chastely times], *România literară* 39–40, 7.
Steinhardt, Nicolae (1991) *Jurnalul fericirii* [The journal of happiness] (Cluj-Napoca: Editura Dacia).
Todorov, Tzvetan (1996) *Confruntarea cu extrema. Victime și torționari în secolul XX* [Facing the extreme. Victims and perpetrators in the twentieth century], trans. from the French Traian Nica (București: Editura Humanitas).
Tomaziu, George (1995) *Jurnalul unui figurant, 1939–1964* [The journal of a figurehead, 1939–1964], trans. Mariana and Gabriel Mardare, preface and postface Gabriel Mardare (București: Editura Univers).
Wurmbrand, Richard (1994) *Cu Dumnezeu în subterană* [With God in prison], trans. from English by Marilena Alexandrescu-Munteanu and Maria Chilian (București: Editura "Casa Școalelor").
Zilber, Herbert (Belu) (1997) *Actor în procesul Pătrășcanu. Prima versiune a memoriilor lui Belu Zilber* [Actor in the Pătrășcanu trial. The first version of Belu Zilber's memoirs], ed. G. Brătescu (București: Editura Humanitas).

Tadeusz Sucharski
Polish Literature of Soviet Prison Camps: An Outline of Issues

1 Origins and chronology

Polish literature on Soviet prison camps constitutes one of the most important and richest accounts of Soviet war experience. It comprises, in part, the literature of forced exile (Pol. *zsyłka*), prisons, military prison camps, and *strojbaty*.[1] Polish literary historians rarely make these distinctions, perhaps because it is not always possible to classify unequivocally a particular literary work, as they often reflect the experience both of the Soviet prison camps and of exile. Therefore, attempts to offer a general overview of this type of literature tend to cover all works, regardless of the forms of repression depicted (and experienced) by the author, with a single definition: either of *literatura łagrowa*,[2] i.e. Soviet prison camps literature (Czaplejewicz 1992: 7–20), or *literatura zsyłkowa*, i.e. exile literature (Taylor-Terlecka 1997: 261–280). As a consequence, it is far too easy to bring disparate forms of repression (both on the basis of the Soviet Criminal Code and the experiences of victims) to a common denominator. Despite the fact that *literatura łagrowa* has been present in the official Polish historical consciousness for over a quarter of a century (it was banned by communist censorship until 1989, while currently it is included in school literary canon), there are still gaps in our knowledge about the specifics of Stalinist repression. The terms *łagier* [forced labor camp] and *zsyłka* usually appear interchangeably. This can be explained by the fact that both Soviet prison camps (in the official Soviet terminology called "correctional labor camps," *ispravitel'no-trudovye lageria*, ITL) and deportation were dramatic experiences often

---

1 *Strojbaty* is short for *stroitelnye bataliony* in Russian (construction battalions), responsible for building and maintaining military facilities. They were forced labor divisions that drafted non-Russian men of various origins (Central Asians, fugitives from Polish territories annexed into the USSR, Russian Germans etc.).
2 Translator's note: The adjective *łagrowy*, to the Polish ear, immediately evokes the worst of the Soviet era, while *zsyłkowy* brings back both Soviet and the earlier Tsarist experience of deportation and exile. It is important to notice, however, the specificity of the term *zsyłka*. While the verb *zsyłać* might apply equally well to Napoleon's exile on the island of Elba and Joseph Brodsky's exile to Siberia, the noun in Polish has an immediate connotation with Siberia (*zsyłka na Sybir*).

referred to, especially in the tradition of national martyrdom, as "Polish Golgotha of the East."

Repressions against Poles and Polish citizens (Jews, Ukrainians, and Belarusians resident in the Second Polish Republic) were a consequence of the Ribbentrop–Molotov pact of 23 August 1939, enforced in Poland after the Soviet aggression of 17 September 1939, which resulted in Soviet occupation of up to 52% of the total interwar territory of Poland. To this day disputes continue about the number of Poles who experienced repression at the hands of Soviet authorities. Early migration researchers estimated the number of Poles imprisoned in camps, held in detention camps and prisons, and deported deep into the Soviet Union between 1939 and 1941 to have ranged between 1,442,000 and 1,700,000 (Wielhorski 1956: 14–16; Siedlecki 1990: 46; Zamorski and Starzewski 1994: 101). In the early years of post-communist Poland (after 1989), these estimates were raised by domestic investigators up to 1,875,000 (Żaroń 1990: 132). After research done in the 1990s in the Soviet archives (both by Russian researchers from the "Memorial" association and by Polish historians) that number was substantially reduced, by as much as three to four times. The most recent estimates determine the number of deportees alone (excluding prison camp inmates) to have been 330,000. In labor camps and prisons, not counting prisoner of war camps, there were around 250,000–300,000 imprisoned Poles and Polish citizens (Hryciuk and Sienkiewicz 2008: 16–22). This included a large group of writers, university professors, and journalists.

From the perspective of Polish martyrology,[3] Soviet (Stalinist) actions against the Poles were a continuation of nineteenth-century Russian repressions. However, to fully realize the extent of Stalinist crimes – and this is very important in the context of Polish literature of Soviet prison camps, which is basically anti-Communist, but not anti-Russian – these crimes have to be weighed against the effects of the policy of exile in tsarist Russia. Over the period spanning more than half a century (1823–1877), including the Decembrist Uprising, Polish uprisings and the beginnings of revolutionary-terrorist activity, Russia was known as "the biggest open-air prison in the world" – nearly 600,000 people were exiled to Siberia. Stalin and the NKVD took a little over a year to imprison, lock up in camps, and deport a similar number, or perhaps twice as many, of Polish citizens. The effectiveness of the Stalinist apparatus in solving the "Polish problem" compelled many researchers to suspect that the

---

3 "Polish martyrology" is a term used to refer to the sufferings of the Poles at the hands of Germans and Russians, beginning with the partitions of Poland (end of the eighteenth century).

process of deportations to the Soviet Union of the rest of the Polish population living under Soviet occupation would have been completed, "inevitably, over the next five years" (Siedlecki 1990: 47). Before that could come to pass, however, on 22 June 1941 the Nazis invaded its former ally.

The war between the Third Reich and the USSR, two totalitarian states that in 1939 had shared the sphere of influence in Europe, initiated a process of fundamental change: it caused a reversal of existing political alliances, which in turn allowed for the creation of an anti-Hitler coalition. It was also of paramount importance for the Poles living within the borders of the Soviet Union. A little over a month after the Nazi invasion, on 30 July 1941, General Władysław Sikorski (Prime Minister of the Polish Government in Exile and the Supreme Commander of the Polish Armed Forces) and the ambassador of the USSR in Great Britain, Igor Majsky, signed a treaty restoring diplomatic relations between Poland and the Soviet Union that had been severed after the attack of 17 September 1939. Less than two weeks later (12 August 1941) the Presidium of the Supreme Soviet issued a decree (announced in the protocol attached to the treaty) about "an amnesty" towards Polish citizens resident within the boundaries of the USSR, and on 14 August an agreement was signed authorizing the creation of the Polish Army in the USSR. The army was made up of former prison camp inmates and exiles, and the commander was General Władysław Anders (himself a prisoner of the notorious Moscow Lubyanka prison). The Polish Army was supposed to fight the Germans alongside the Soviet Army. However, the failure by the Soviet authorities to fulfill their obligations toward the new army (military equipment shortcomings, drastic food shortages), diseases spreading among the soldiers who made their way to the army in a state of extreme physical exhaustion – all this eventually caused the evacuation of a 70,000-strong army to Iran. Soldiers were accompanied by civilians – women and children on their way.

The total number of Poles evacuated in 1942 from the Soviet Union was close to 115,000. Among them were writers who were to become the most renowned authors of Polish literature of the camps, those who created the very canon: Gustaw Herling-Grudziński, Beata Obertyńska, Herminia Naglerowa, Anatol Krakowiecki, Wacław Grubiński, Tadeusz Wittlin, Witold Olszewski, and many others. The group also included Józef Czapski, author of *Na nieludzkiej ziemi* (1990; an English translation, *Inhuman Land*, is to be published in 2018), one of the most important literary testimonies to the Polish fate in Soviet Russia, even though it only indirectly concerns Stalin's camps. Almost immediately after leaving the "house of bondage," these writers called for "writing down their memories" (Obertyńska 1991: 356) and set to work on documenting and reflecting on the Polish fate in Soviet "inhuman land." Some of these works had been written during the war and were published immediately after: a volume of short stories entitled *The Oppressed People* by Herminia Naglerowa, which appeared in Rome in 1945, and less than a year later, Beata Obertyńska's *In the House of Bondage*. After the war, all of the authors mentioned above remained in exile, unwilling to return to Poland in the grip of communist power. Therefore, Polish literature of the Soviet camps is primarily, though not exclusively, *émigré* literature, written in the years 1945–1989. The most important works were created outside Poland in the first decade after the war, the period most important in the development of this type of literature. In addition to those already mentioned, examples of these works include Wacław Grubiński's *Między młotem a sierpem* ("Between a hammer and a sickle;" 1948), Witold Olszewski's *Budujemy kanał: wspomnienia kierownika biura planowania* ("We are building a canal. Memoirs of a planning manager"; 1947), Anatol Krakowiecki's *Książka o Kołymie* ("A book about Kolyma"; 1950), Tadeusz Wittlin's *Diabeł w raju* ("The devil in paradise"; 1951), Marian Czuchnowski's *Tyfus, teraz słowiki: powieść* ("Typhoid fever, now nightingales: a novel"; 1951), and finally, the *magnum opus* of not only Polish camp literature, but literature on Stalinist repression as such, *A World Apart* by Gustaw Herling-Grudziński.[4] In subsequent years, fewer texts of significance appeared, but the ones that did carried an artistic value previously absent from prison camp prose. These were primarily Leo Lipski's short stories from the volume *Dzień i noc* ("Day and night"; 1957) and Paweł Mayewski's texts from the collection *The River* (1960), first published in English.[5]

The breakthrough of 1989/1990 marked a turning point in Polish literature of Soviet prison camps. From then on, the most important books written in exile began at long last to be published in Poland. At the same time, books that had been written in communist Poland started to emerge. Poland was ruled by a satellite of Moscow's Communist Party and enforced restrictive (and preventive) censorship, especially towards works (and potential authors) that represented the Soviet Union in a critical light. Stalinist repression was never officially referred to in Poland, even in an Aesopian, figurative language, and not even after the publication of Aleksandr Solzhenitsyn's *One Day in the Life of Ivan Denisovich* in the USSR in 1962.

This does not mean, however, that such texts did not exist. They were written "for the drawer" (i.e. never published) or published under pseudonyms in

---

4 Pol. *Inny świat*. The English translation came out in 1951 in London, while the Polish original appeared in London two years later, in 1953; only in 1988 was the book finally published in Poland.
5 I refer to the Polish translation.

exile. Their authors returned to Poland having experienced Soviet prison camps. Most of them were arrested in 1944, when the Red Army entered onto the territory of the Second Polish Republic. This was the fate of Barbara Skarga, who was arrested in Vilnius in 1944 by the NKVD for her role in the underground Home Army, and sentenced to ten years in a labor camp. Having completed her sentence, she spent two more years in exile. After returning to Poland and writing her memoirs, she published them in Paris under the pseudonym Wiktoria Kraśniewska, with a painfully ironic title *Po wyzwoleniu... 1945–1965* (*After the Liberation...*). Needless to say, this was because such "liberation" was brought to Poles by the victorious march of the Red Army.

2 Axiology

2.1 Writing as a sense of duty

Polish literature of the Soviet camps fully recognized, as General Anders wrote, "the duty towards its own people and to the entire civilized world" (Anders 1990: 7). Polish authors not only preserved the memory of the Polish fate, but felt a moral obligation to the millions of suffering camp prisoners of other nationalities. The national perspective did not obscure the general human perspective. Most of the texts are thus a *sui generis* indictment and resemble testimony rather than literature. The author is usually represented as a victim, a witness for the prosecution and the prosecutor in one, a miracle survivor, dedicating his or her book "to those who died and still die there...". The "mission" adopted by Polish writers was best expressed in the title of Jerzy Gliksman's book published in English as *Tell the West* (1948). But an awareness of this duty finds its expression in almost every prison camp text, as testified by the words of a prisoner left behind in the camp and quoted as a motto of Witold Olszewski's *We are Building a Canal*: "Be damned, those of you [who] leave here and remain silent" (1947: 5). Polish writers seem to be guided by three creative "imperatives": the personal, the national, and the universal human imperative. At the first level, through the voice of a newly liberated slave, the author expresses his/her/their own individual pain and suffering. But they inscribe it, at a higher level, into the national experience, the Polish fate. Beyond these two planes there is yet another mission: to spread the knowledge about the Soviet Union gained "in the inhuman land" to the entire civilized world. The "amnesty" experienced by inmates was regarded as a kind of miracle, because no one, especially not the prisoners, had the right to leave the Soviet "prison civilization." But the Poles saw it, got to know it, and left. They accepted, therefore, the responsibility to communicate to the world the truth about the Soviet "liberator," to reveal the true face of the Soviet empire. They looked for a way to communicate this that would make the world believe their testimony and would enable the world to understand, and understand quickly, the threat posed by Communism. Polish literature of Soviet prison camps can, therefore, be seen as a kind of outpost to Solzhenitsyn's *The Gulag Archipelago*. A helpless outpost, because the Western world did not want to accept the truth certified by experience, treating it instead as an expression of the "Polish Russophobia."

The "mission" adopted by Polish literature of Soviet camps did not gain appropriate resonance in the West, gripped by a profound fear of embarrassing a powerful ally and of the fact that "one criminal was defeated with the help of another" (Applebaum, 2005). Certain books by Polish authors fell victim to those attitudes: Józef Czapski's *Wspomnienia starobielskie* ("Starobielsk memoirs") did not immediately obtain consent for publication because of the English censorship. Bertrand Russell's foreword to *A World Apart* (1951), emphasizing not so much the book's artistic value as the authenticity of the facts it contained, was included alongside letters from Soviet communists, who claimed that the camps described by Herling "do not exist." The words of the great philosopher, author of one of the earliest diagnoses of Bolshevism (*The Practice and Theory of Bolshevism*, 1920), which were supposed to offer an *imprimatur*, were probably intended by the publisher as an answer to those letters. Even if the letters did not directly contest the veracity of Polish testimony, then their inclusion certainly indicated a desire to preserve (extreme) "objectivity" by the same people who did not question, as Anne Applebaum writes, the texts of Elie Wiesel and Primo Levi.[6] But it would have been considered criminal to attempt similar latitude were Nazi officials to protest.

Herling was well aware that Polish books on Stalin's prison camps might not be able to "immediately open the West's eyes to the plight of millions of people tortured slowly to death in the Soviet house of the dead" (Herling-Grudziński 1993: 181). But he was absolutely convinced that "as long as this disgrace of modern slavery is not wiped off of the face of the earth, every writer who [...]

---

6 It should, however, be noted that "the world" was just as reluctant to accept the literary testimony of the Holocaust, the best evidence of which was the fate of books by the very authors cited by Applebaum (2005: 12–16). The manuscript of Primo Levi's debut book *Survival in Auschwitz* was rejected by a major publishing house in 1947 and released by a little-known publisher. Elie Wiesel's memoirs *And the World Remained Silent* met a similar fate: given the absence of interest in Europe, the book was published in Buenos Aires in 1956.

can reveal it in its bare horror before the eyes of his readers, will not only render a service to humanity, but will also continue the best traditions in literature" (1993: 181). Thus, the author emphasized the non-artistic, but still undoubtedly weighty significance of aforementioned books. They had to meet a specific, almost utilitarian, purpose. They sought to expose the lies of the Soviet propaganda and aimed to reveal the criminal system of the red empire (to which such luminaries of the European culture as Anatole France, George Bernard Shaw, Lion Feuchtwanger and Henri Barbusse had turned a blind eye). They also attempted to inform the free world of the crimes that were still being committed in thousands of camps of the Gulag, to open the Western eyes to this "archipelago," to appeal to its conscience.

Therefore, it may be said that the literature of the camps was to serve a cognitive function. And it did. It should be emphasized, however, that Polish writers found themselves in a situation that had not been envisaged even by the most perceptive theoreticians of realism – but still they tried to describe, actually to reconstruct, "another world," an "inhuman land," a reality beyond the horizon of the readers' expectations, but also beyond the descriptive abilities of writers. How is it possible to render a mimesis of an "inhuman," "different" reality and to pass it on to readers who have no idea about such a world? Nazi camps had been photographed, filmed, and in a way "tamed" by the recipients of *Lager* literature. The Soviet prison camp civilization not only remained unknown, but hardly anyone was interested in finding out about it. Polish writers tried to overcome their powerlessness and undertook an effort to name the elements constituting this "infernal" reality, but often ended up surrendering to it. Almost every text contains explicit evidence of helplessness that years later was also voiced by Solzhenitsyn and Varlam Shalamov.

Gustaw Herling-Grudziński, the most prominent representative of Polish literature of the Soviet camps, pointed out an aspect directly unconnected with the reality of the Stalinist world, namely, that literature "can never be indifferent to all that is human" (Herling-Grudziński 1993: 181). He broadened the horizons of its "cognitive" aspect and mission: to know the world, but also to know the human being. To describe the reality of both the "small" and the "great" Soviet *zona*, but also to show human beings subjected to its mechanisms, to understand their greatness and pettiness, cowardice and heroism (Sucharski 2002). The description of a world knowable empirically must be accompanied by an attempt to offer insight into the world of spiritual experiences. Only through this approach, through the fusion of both those elements, can we talk about the cognitive character *par excellence* of this literature. In this statement Herling-Grudziński revealed the basic premise of Polish camp literature authors, who, in a virtually identical manner, expressed in their work their axiomatic system guided by a similar hierarchy of values (Naglerowa 1956: 1). They sought the fullest representation of the reality of the prison camps, and certainly did not want to and could not be impartial. They wanted to do justice to the tortured, and that eliminated neutrality and objectivity. The mirror of their prose, which included the zone, the barracks and the *lesopowały*,[7] was, however, directed towards and focused on the inner world of the inmates, as others tried to deprive them of their human dignity. Polish writers wanted to restore the inmates' humanity and that is what they did. As witnesses of the civilization of prison camps they undertook to develop a blueprint narrative and description, in which a realistic vision of the outside world ("hell") accompanies the creation of the spiritual world, the realism of the experience of its prisoners. Czapski expected a "new Proust" or a "new Tolstoy," capable of expressing Soviet reality (Czapski 1990: 104). Stanislaw Swianiewicz stressed that "to penetrate the atmosphere of the camps requires genius equal to [Dostoevsky's]" (1990: 193).

This approach is also apparent in the portrayal of death. Polish literature of the camps (as in Shalamov's *Kolyma Stories*), which recreates the reality of mass killing in camps and prisons, at the same time avoids images of mass death, defies its ordinariness, objects to stripping it of individuality, holiness, uniqueness, and finally – deprivation of humanity. Thus, Polish writers evoke cases that restore the importance of both death and the dying human being, cases which by their "uniqueness" try to break out of the machinery of mass destruction. In choosing their subjects writers do so perhaps out of a subconscious belief that showing death as "sloppy" or "dirty" can make them participants in the crime of throttling a human being, depriving him or her of their last human right – the "right to a beautiful death." (Herling-Grudziński 1993: 118)

2.2 Polish writers and the "otherness" of Russia

In an attempt to reconstruct the axiology of Polish prison camp writers one cannot ignore their attitude towards Soviet Russia and its people. In the preface to the Russian translation of *A World Apart* Herling-Grudzinski stressed how important in his work is the "shared suffering" of Poles and Russians, two nations most marked by Soviet Communism, because from a common martyrdom "a common hope is born" (Kudelski 1992: 333). The attitude towards Soviet

---

[7] The word, originally Russian, entered the Polish language through the literature of the Soviet camps and refers to the place where trees are logged.

Russia is best reflected in titles, which indicate not only the repressive character of the reality described in the books, but above all the world of anti-values, an anti-humanist anthropology: *Ludzie sponiewierani* ("The oppressed people," Naglerowa), "In the house of bondage" (Obertyńska), *Through the Land of Bondage* (Jan Kazimierz Umiastowski), *Inhuman Land* (Czapski), *A World Apart* (Herling-Grudziński). The attitude toward the state is not, however, synonymous with the attitude towards its people. The paradox of Polish prison camp literature lies in the fact that in this "other world," hostile by definition, writers find "another Russia," whose "otherness" is revealed, moreover, on several levels.

For the majority of Polish writers of the camps, a vision of Russia as "the land of slavery" had been shaped by the patriotic literary school of the interwar period, where the romantic tradition of deportation to Siberia was predominant. These writers stressed the generational continuity of suffering and often included stories of their ancestors, who had been sent into remote lands of tsarist Russia. The myth of Siberia replaced the knowledge of Russia. The term "Siberia" in the political, not geographical, sense served as a kind of spatial synecdoche of a slavery system that stretches from the eastern Polish border to Vladivostok and Chukotka. Therefore, in Polish camp prose one will rarely encounter the term "Gulag"; instead, terms such as "a house of bondage" or "a different world" are used, thus incorporating the experience of hundreds of thousands of Polish citizens in the twentieth century into the centuries-long continuum of Polish suffering in Russia.

Russia was for Poles almost always the "other," different from their own world. It was an unembraceable space, with another time, another faith and another human mentality, another authority and another attitude towards subordinates. The otherness also stemmed from the perceived gap between the material culture of the, after all not so rich, world from which they were uprooted and that into which they were thrust by force. Maria Janion brilliantly surmises that "Polish self-identification usually takes effect by presenting Russia as a not fully valued but dangerous Other" (2007: 226–227). What Polish writers attempted to convey in this category of otherness is the incomprehensibility of the world, its decrepitude, but above all to express hostility, alienation, and anxiety. However, if in the works embodying the traditional pattern of Polish martyrdom combined with anti-Russian attitudes "otherness" covered the broadest range of negative experience, in the works of most of the Polish prison camp writers the experience of "otherness" becomes a positive experience.

The point of reference, however, is different here: the experience of otherness ascends to another level. For, if in the first case the material poverty of Russia was contrasted with Poland, later it is universal humanism that becomes the reference point for the depraved Soviet anthropology. This does not happen immediately; rather, it is a process that is gradually illuminated in the most important Polish books of the Soviet experience. First and foremost, *A World Apart*, which is, even before Solzhenitsyn's *In the First Circle*, a perfect witness to the discovery of new attitudes that herald the birth of a new Russian formation in Stalinist labor camps (Sucharski 2002: 37–40). But this is only one aspect of Herling's Bildungsroman. Before Herling (and his ilk) made this discovery, he had gone through a process of initiation in Russia. However, unlike most writers, he did not stop at the conclusion of typical "otherness." In the camps he encountered Russians whose moral stance assured him of the victory of good over evil, saving humanity in an anti-human system. Therefore, if a "world apart" means the world of "an inverted Decalogue" (Skarga 1997: 203), the "other Russia" in "a world apart" means the Russia of a restored Decalogue, Russia that is spiritually close to Polish prison camp inmates, sharing similar values (Sucharski (2008: 27–29)).

The anti-Soviet sentiments of "Polish witnesses of the Gulag" (Sariusz-Skąpska: 1995) do not signify, therefore, a new version of traditional russophobia. On the contrary, they are a proof that national burdens and constraints can be overcome, leading and encouraging to seek attitudes in the Soviet "prison civilization" that were faithful to the humanistic tradition of nineteenth-century Russian thought. "Soviet" is therefore not synonymous with "Russian" and Soviet "inhuman land" does not equate to Russia.

3 Poetics

As an epigraph to the last part of *A Book about Kolyma*, Anatol Krakowiecki borrows a quotation from Zofia Kossak's Auschwitz memories entitled *From the Abyss*: "God has allowed some people to behold hell in their lifetime and then to return to bear witness to the Truth" (Krakowiecki 1950: 239). Prose that originated in the camps, especially in the post-war period, was characterized by poetics subject to the imperative of "bearing witness." The documentary character of those works in a sense *demanded* fidelity in reconstructing the world of prison camps, so that in the lawsuit that literature brought against the oppressors no one would accuse it of false testimony. In a sketch summarizing her decade in the camps Herminia Naglerowa emphatically stressed that "the nagging proximity of the material at hand, the urgency of the writer's own experiences [...] impose [...] dutiful, nearly report-like accuracy and thoroughness" (Naglerowa 1956: 1). The reliability and truthfulness of this literature, as well as the opportunity to confront the facts it contains with various documentary evidence, is one of its characteristic traits (Taylor-Terlecka 1997 272; Danilewicz-Zielińska 1999: 95). The unquestionable integrity of this literary testimony also allowed it to enter the history of national martyrdom, so that it became an invaluable record of the "Soviet Golgotha" of the Polish people.

Therefore, in the period immediately after the authors' leaving the Soviet Union, literature was dominated by testimony, as shown by the extraordinary popularity (among both writers and readers) of documentary texts. "Soviet" books, backed by the seal of authentic experience, had to speak "to the reader's imagination much more vividly than any tale that consciously used artistic effects" (Markiewicz 1965: II, 19). That documentary trend was initiated by Melchior Wańkowicz's *Dzieje rodziny Korzeniewskich* ("Korzeniewski family history;" 1991), the first book devoted to the Polish experience in the Soviet Union written by an author who had himself been spared this experience. Wańkowicz used a fictional story but he propped it up with an authentic diary of a settler in exile and a story of a survivor from the "house of bondage." He intended it to serve as "one of the thousands of bloody documents that talk about death, about the agony of hundreds of thousands of people, documents that you will need to throw in the face of this naive world clapping at every appearance of Stalin on the screen." (Wańkowicz 1991: 166) Although it might be difficult to claim complete accuracy concerning genre, at the forefront of prison camp prose stand traditional memoirs (*Starobielsk Memoirs* by Józef Czapski; *Receding time* by Marian Czuchnowski), various types of diaries (*In the House of Bondage* by Beata Obertyńska; *A Book about Kolyma* by Anatol Krakowiecki), memoirs based on notes and a journal with a diary (*Through the Land of Bondage* by Jan Kazimierz Umiastowski), excerpts from diaries and letters (*Soviet Justice* by Kazimierz Zamorski and Stanisław Starzewski), reportage, and finally "a mixture of diary with reportage on current affairs" (Stanisław Skrzypek, "The Russia I saw. *Memoirs of the years* 1939–1942"). There are also some attempts at fictionalizing the experience (*Tell the West* by Jerzy Gliksman) or fictionalizing while dramatizing the documentary medium (*Between a Hammer and a Sickle* by Wacław Grubiński). Even if the work was fictional, which in the immediate post-war years happened extremely rarely, it was preceded by a note explaining that somehow fiction was "justified," as was the case with Witold Olszewski's novel *We are Building a Canal* (1946). These texts differ in the degree of intimacy, the way they show the relationship between the "I that remembers" and the outside world. However, the first-person narrator predominates and the texts tend to have the character of a directly autobiographical report, supported by a documentary record of events, often interwoven with other inmates' stories, "biographical micronovellas" (Bolecki 1994: 98–99). This applies equally to both "documentary" and "fictionalized" literature, because even the latter "had to keep all the ingredients real. Fiction, therefore, did not transform the material, it only differentiated the way in which it was used, or reduced it to a framework." (Naglerowa 1956: 1)

The autobiographical character of the works became one of the most effective ways to assure the reader of their truthfulness. Certainly, in this case the referential pact ("I promise to tell the truth") was supported by the autobiographical pact. The truth of the reconstructed image of the "house of bondage" seemed to confirm the "I" of the author, the narrator emphasizing his identity as the author and protagonist of the narrative, not as a fictional storyteller. Each book contains information, either expressed directly or veiled, allowing the reader to identify the narrator with the author. Authors actually compel the reader to read their books as a record of personal experience. Using their own name was like a signature on a testimony "before the petrified conscience of the world" (Krakowiecki 1950: 5) in a symbolic lawsuit against the *tiuremnaja ciwilizacja* ("prison civilization") by the surviving Poles on their own behalf and on behalf of all of its victims. If the author did not include the name of the narrator-protagonist in the narrative, they smuggled other biographical details, thus forcing the reader to identify the narrator with the author. In conversations or in excerpts from testimonies, authors included their name and *otchestvo* (patronymic), so prevalent in the Russian formula of addressing the interlocutor.

Books that focused almost exclusively on providing documentary truth clearly revealed their fundamental deficiencies that were keenly picked apart by Herling-Grudziński. He accused them of "noble haste," of "a desire for an immediate [...] need to be an emissary of the truth," which for him was a sign of "utilitarian" writing (Herling-Grudziński 1993: 11). He instead advocated processing a formless "mass of facts and experiences of the Soviet Union" into a "lasting monument." A great, painful subject should culminate in work that would give it justice. Essential to this, however, is "the wise and sentient eye of the artist" (Herling-Grudziński 1993: 27). The perspective of a chronicler, into whom the liberated slave tried to morph, was not enough. After a wave of "documents" there came a time for "literature."

The gradual silencing of the imperative to testify to the truth was closely associated with changes in the meaning of the "ontology" of memories, to quote from the introduction of Czapski's *Inhuman Land*. Namely, he distinguished between a "report" and "a mixture of experiences and reactions which is affected not only by the length of time described, but by an entire life" (1990: 47). It was according to this principle that he wrote his memoir from the "inhuman land." Skrzypek also emphasized that "against the background of memories" he was going to describe "some fundamental problems of Soviet life" and make a "rational attempt to explain them." And, despite the book's title, he presented Russia not so much "as he had seen it" but as "he had thought it" (Skrzypek 1949: 9). Decades after writing *A World Apart* Herling said that he "kept from the beginning to the end [...] the idea that these memories do not have to be a pure document based on reality alone" (Herling-Grudziński and Bolecki 1997: 116). He emphatically insisted that he would never have written a book that would be limited only to a bare report of imprisonment in a camp. What is needed is a "literary *récit*" (131), because Soviet prison camps cannot be presented in a dry, businesslike manner. The act of creation exempts one from the obligation to be fastidious about conveying the facts; however, it does not abolish the principle of credibility of the message. Much later, Barbara Skarga adopted similar poetics. She defined her work as a memoir, but said it resembled a "story"[8] in the same sense as Herling-Grudzinski's *A World Apart* did.

The changing views on the "house of bondage" narrative formula resulted in significant genre differences. The desire to break up the monopoly of traditional memoirs led to the "novelizing" and fictionalizing of expression. Attempts at fictionalizing documents were made and fictional works were created on the canvas of memories. In the novel *Typhoid Fever, Now Nightingales*, Czuchnowski returned in fiction to the events described earlier in the memoir *Cofnięty czas*. Tadeusz Wittlin, in *The Devil in Paradise*, used material reminiscent of his earlier *Radosne dni* ("Joyous days"). He embellished his performance as the narrator with the figure of "a reluctant traveler in Russia," as announced by the subtitle to the English translation. This figure provided a sense of humor and satirical distance to the presented reality. By undermining the credibility of the report, however, Wittlin pointed to the possibility of liberating literature from the rigors of serving an absolute historical truth. He directed it instead towards artistic truth. And yet, both novels met with a hostile reception of the Polish readers, who were expecting further literary testimonies documenting Polish fate in the USSR. *The Devil in Paradise* enjoyed a greater popularity among foreign readers. There were also some cases of a novel or a story arising out of notes taken in a camp, provided the author managed to conceal and later smuggle them out, as in the case of Andrzej Romański's *Prisoners of the Night* (1956).

Faced with this attitude of Polish readership, it is not surprising that a number of fictional texts devoted to the Soviet prison camp experience was first published abroad in translation, and only then in Polish. Such was the fate of Romański's book published as *The Prisoners of the Night* in the United

---

[8] Skarga writes: "There's something in my story that irritates me today and yet the story is true." (2000: 132).

States (1948); the author had to wait another eight years for a Polish edition. The same happened with Paweł Mayewski's stories from the volume *The River* – they were first published in *The Partisan Review* and *The Prairie Schooner*. A Polish translation of Sławomir Rawicz's *The Long Walk* (1956) was released with a nearly forty years' delay with respect to the English edition. Rawicz's book, which enjoyed an enthusiastic reception around the world, became one of the biggest bestsellers of adventure-travel literature, and was translated into twenty-five languages.[9] It is mainly because of that book that a wide circle of the Western public got to know the reality of the Soviet war. Also of note is the case of Jerzy Gliksman's *Tell the West* and its two language versions. In the Polish version, entitled *Powiedz Zachodowi*, the author pared down the emotional layer, pushed aside its artistic values and impoverished the language, depriving it of its characteristic poetization evident in the English version.

In his "poetics of doom," formulated *ex post* and determined by a critical reading of the literature of the camps (both Hitler's and Stalin's camps), Herling expressed the belief that words would be "all the harder, the fewer they are" and would be "echoed all the louder, the calmer they are spoken" (1995: 318). The literary works from the first decade of the Soviet experience poignantly illustrate the process of working out a formula to express this reality, constituting a record of the search for a prison camp language and realism. It is in those works that all the most important varieties of expressing "the inexpressible" were tested; it is to those forms that authors who came later will continue to look back. In most memoirs respecting the canonical rules of the genre, the author retains a two- or three-pronged composition that reflects the respective stages of the Soviet experience: life under occupation up to the arrest, imprisonment, and the camp, and finally life "in so-called freedom."[10] They differ, however, in the language of narration and dialogue. Naglerowa's texts are full of pathos and naturalistic imagery, while Grubiński and Wittlin employ satirical and ironic language, bordering on farce; Obertyńska's sharp, sometimes vulgar language is accompanied by subtle poetic imagery; Krakowiecki interweaves a brutal narrative style with a transparent style of a discreet commentary, close to the classicistic appeal of psychological realism; Olszewski demonstrates extraordinary artistic skill in his use of Soviet newspeak while Czuchnowski, in his heavily lyricized narrative, reaches for poetic prose.

---

9 In 2010 Australian director Peter Weir made a film – a Polish co-production – based on Rawicz's book (*The Way Back*, starring Jim Sturgess, Colin Farrell and Ed Harris).
10 The title of a chapter of Beata Obertyńska's *In the House of Bondage*.

The poetics of the main literary text of the literature of the camps, *A World Apart*, deserves particular attention. The text is a culmination of the struggle of Polish prose with the experience of prison civilization. Herling-Grudziński combined a veristic method of description, a calm and collected narrative style punctuated here and there with an almost poetic language, with extreme "psychological inquisitiveness" (Burek 1991: 13–14). That inquisitiveness is close to the introspective efforts of Fyodor Dostoevsky's *The House of the Dead* that Herling-Grudzinski read in a Soviet labor camp. It was there he realized that "within the framework of full realism" he is confronted with the task of "finding the human being within the human being" (Bakhtin 1970: 92). Herling-Grudzinski also relied on a foundation of realism developed by Daniel Defoe in *A Journal of the Plague Year*. By combining the formula of seeking "the human being within the human being" and therefore focusing on a single prisoner, with the formula of "hell of an inevitable doom" that depicts mass death, Herling-Grudzinski achieved "full realism" in *A World Apart*. In his later elaboration he placed equal weight on Dostoevsky, master of a psychological analysis of the imprisoned man, and Defoe, precursor of the depiction of "the dying of entire nations and cities." (Herling-Grudziński 1993: 168)[11] Polish prose of the camps after Herling-Grudzinski demonstrates, however, that none of the later authors came close to the poetics of *A World Apart*, to its "higher realism." Most writers headed toward "photographic realism," a concept that brought them closer to the initial documents rather than looking for a new formula for "a text-monument." Alternatively, attempts were made in parallel to employ the grotesque in the service of realism. Many works of prison camp literature from Poland defined the Soviet Union as "a world of utter absurd" (Skarga 2000: 5), "the greatest country of paradoxes" (Wittlin 1990: 233), "an invented country" (Lipski 1998: 33), but at the beginning the full force of the grotesque was applied only in Olszewski's novel *We are Building a Canal*. The author creates a global vision of the world after a victorious Second Patriotic War, in which collective farmers from Tahiti, deserving dairy workers from the Netherlands and professional sportsmen from Punjab all coexist. Thanks to the use of Soviet newspeak, which the first-person narrator uses in his *skaz*-like story,[12] Olszewski reveals the greatest crime – the depravation of language and the Sovietization of consciousness.

---

[11] I discuss the significance of both Dostoevsky and Defoe in Sucharski (2002: 59–70).
[12] *Skaz* is a Russian literary term that refers to a story told by a fictitious narrator. Nicolai Leskov is widely recognized as the master of the *skaz*.

Subsequent literary efforts used the grotesque, understood both in terms of Mikhail Bakhtin and Wolfgang Kayser, much less consistently. The "ludic carnival" formula plays out on various levels of the world represented in Wittlin's *The Devil in Paradise*. Grubiński uses certain elements of the grotesque prison camp formula in his memoir *Between a Hammer and a Sickle*. In these works the grotesque, as "laughing freedom," is the antidote to slavery, an expression of inner freedom, projected onto the world of the prison camp.

Kayser's concept of the grotesque, in which an absolutely hostile world evokes a sense of awe and horror, dominates the short story *Day and Night* by Leo Lipski. Contrary to the thesis that an "imaginary"[13] country like the USSR cannot be deformed, the author undertakes such a risk with a vengeance. He does not pretend to understand that world, but neither does he try to make sense of it. In the process of creating an "imaginary" world of the camps, the author attempts to exorcise the demonic, and this resembles Kayser's liberation factor. But Lipski can also be a realist, skillfully using contrast and counterpoint, seeing in the apparently uniform world of the camps its different faces. He is able to find a lost sense of equilibrium in the "colorful" world of imprisoned women, in the beauty of their bodies that produces more of an aesthetic than an erotic experience. And this beauty becomes an antidote to the ragged world of the camps. In the short stories from his collection *The River*, Mayewski on the other hand consistently creates a repulsive space possessed by forces of perpetual darkness in the metaphysical sense. It sometimes resembles the world of Kafka's *The Trial* and *The Castle*, with only a few hints at the reminiscences of the camps and the deportation. This imprecise, but intricate and suggestive, created space allows for a near sensual experience of the ferocity of the world. It is a world of absolute alienation, misunderstanding, and utter inability to understand.

***

Seventy years have passed since the publication of the first Polish works narrating the Soviet prison camp experience. This is sufficient time to have assessed their value. We have the good fortune of reading them at a time when their extraliterary reality has become a "closed era," but also when there is no denying the existence of "the Gulag archipelago." Polish writers made a significant contribution to the deepening of awareness in the western world and to the representations of Soviet prison camp civilization. Thus, they have fulfilled their responsibilities to the world and to universal values. They have also fulfilled their duty towards their nation. Today, their books are in the canon of required reading for Polish

---

13 The term borrowed from Leo Lipski's *Day and Night* (1998: 33).

pupils and students. While appreciating the factual and documentary value of Polish literature of Soviet prison camps, whose worth no one disputes today, it is time to evaluate its artistic level, assessing the writers' commitment to literature. Undoubtedly, many of these works are permanently inscribed in the history of Polish literature, even though nobility of intention is not always accompanied by aesthetic values. Herling-Grudzinski's *A World Apart*, however, belongs to the history of world literature. Enclosed in an impeccable form, his novel has become, alongside the works of Solzhenitsyn, Shalamov and Vladimov, a poignant monument-testimony to the Soviet "wolf century" and its totalitarian disgrace.

Works cited

Anders, Władysław (1990) "Wstęp" [Introduction], in *Diabeł w raju* [The devil in paradise], Tadeusz Wittlin (Warszawa: Polonia).
Applebaum, Anne (2005) *Gułag* [The Gulag], trans. J. Urbański (Warszawa: Świat Książki).
Bakhtin, Michaił (1970) *Problemy poetyki Dostojewskiego* [Problems of Dostoevsky's poetics], trans. Natalia Modzelewska (Warszawa: Państwowy Instytut Wydawniczy).
Bolecki, Włodzimierz (1994) *"Inny świat" Gustawa Herlinga-Grudzińskiego* [Gustaw Herling-Grudzinski's "A World Apart"], (Warszawa: Wydawnictwa Szkolne i Pedagogiczne).
Burek, Tomasz (1991) "Cały ten okropny świat. Sztuka pamięci głębokiej a zapiski w *Innym świecie* Herlinga-Grudzińskiego" [All that horrible world], in *Etos i artyzm: rzecz o Herlingu-Grudzińskim*, ed. Seweryna Wysłouch and Ryszard Kazimierz Przybylski (Poznań: "a5").
Czaplejewicz, Eugeniusz (1992) *Polska literatura łagrowa* [Polish literature of Soviet prison camps], (Warszawa: Wydawnictwo Naukowe PWN).
Czapski, Józef (1990) *Na nieludzkiej ziemi* [Inhuman land], (Warszawa: Czytelnik).
Danilewicz-Zielińska, Maria (1999) *Szkice o literaturze emigracyjnej półwiecza 1939–1989* [Essays on émigré literature of the half-century 1939–1989], (Wrocław, Warszawa and Kraków: Zakład Narodowy im. Ossolinskich).
Herling-Grudziński, Gustaw (1993) *Wyjścia z milczenia* [Exits from silence], (Warszawa: Biblioteka "Więzi").
Herling-Grudziński, Gustaw (1995) *Dziennik pisany nocą 1973–1979* [Diary written at night], (Warszawa: Czytelnik).
Herling-Grudziński, Gustaw and Włodzimierz Bolecki (1997) *Rozmowy w Dragonei* [Conversations in Dragonea], (Warszawa: "Szpak").
Hryciuk, Grzegorz and Witold Sienkiewicz (eds) (2008) *Wysiedlenia, wypędzenia i ucieczki 1939–1959. Atlas ziem Polski. Polacy, Żydzi, Niemcy, Ukraińcy* [Expulsions, exiles and escapes 1939–1959. An atlas of polish lands. Poles, Jews, Germans, Ukrainians], (Warszawa: Demart).
Janion, Maria (2007) *Niesamowita Słowiańszczyzna. Fantazmaty literatury* [The uncanny Slavonia. Literary phantasmatics], (Kraków: Wydawnictwo Literackie).
Krakowiecki, Anatol (1950) *Książka o Kołymie* [A book about Kolyma], (London: Katolicki Ośrodek Wydawniczy "Veritas").
Kudelski, Zdzisław (1992) "Posłowie" [Postcript], in *Upiory rewolucji*, Gustaw Herling-Grudziński (Lublin: FIS).

Lipski, Leo (1998) *Dzień i noc. Na otwarcie kanału Wołga-Don* [Day and night. For the opening of the Volga-Don canal], (Lublin: Wydawnictwo Uniwersytetu Marii Curie-Skłodowskiej).

Markiewicz, Zygmunt (1965) "Literatura dokumentarna" [Documentary literature], in *Literatura polska na obczyźnie 1940–1960*, ed. Tymon Terlecki (London: B. Świderski), v. II.

Mayewski, Paweł (1960) *Rzeka* [River], tr. from the English by J. Kempka, introd. J. Wittlin (London: Oficyna Poetów i Malarzy).

Naglerowa, Herminia (1956) "Komu i czemu służą" [Whom and what they serve], *Wiadomości* 521, 1.

Obertyńska, Beata (1991), *W domu niewoli* [In the house of bondage], (Warszawa: Instytut Wydawniczy Pax).

Olszewski, Witold (1947) *Budujemy kanał. Wspomnienia kierownika biura planowania* [We're building a canal. Memoirs of the planning bureau manager], (Warszawa: Instytut Wydawniczy Pax).

Russell, Bertrand (1951), Preface, in *A World Apart: The Journal of the Gulag Survivor*, Gustav Herling, (London: Arbor House), IX–X.

Sariusz-Skąpska, Izabela (1995) *Polscy świadkowie GUŁagu. Literatura łagrowa 1939–1989* [Polish witnesses of the GULag. Literature of the Soviet Prison camps 1939–1989], (Kraków: Towarzystwo Autorów i Wydawców Prac Naukowych UNIVERSITAS).

Siedlecki, Julian (1990) *Losy Polaków w ZSRR w latach 1939–1986* [Poles in the USSR 1939–1986], (Gdańsk: Gryf Publication).

Skarga, Barbara (1997) "Świadectwo *Innego Świata*" [A testimony of "A World Apart"], in *Herling-Grudziński i krytycy. Antologia tekstów*, ed. Zdzisław Kudelski (Lublin: Wydawnictwo Uniwersytetu Marii Curie-Skłodowskiej).

Skarga, Barbara (2000) *Po wyzwoleniu... 1945–1965* [After the liberation...1945–1965], (Warszawa: Fundacja Aletheia).

Skrzypek, Stanisław (1949) *Rosja jaką widziałem. Wspomnienia z lat 1939–1942* [The Russia I saw. Memoirs of the years 1939–1942], (Newtown: Montgomeryshire).

Sucharski, Tadeusz (2002) *Dostojewski Herlinga-Grudzińskiego* [Herling-Grudziński's Dostoevsky], (Lublin: Wydawnictwo Uniwersytetu Marii Curie-Skłodowskiej).

Sucharski, Tadeusz (2008) *Polskie poszukiwania „innej" Rosji. O nurcie rosyjskim w literaturze Drugiej Emigracji* [Polish search of the "other" Russia: The Russian question in Polish post-World War II émigré literature], (Gdańsk: słowo/obraz terytoria).

Taylor-Terlecka, Nina (1997) "Literatura zsyłkowa" [Deportation literature], in *Literatura emigracyjna 1939–1989*, ed. Marek Pytasz (Katowice: Śląsk), vol. I.

Swianiewicz, Stanisław (1990) *W cieniu Katynia* [In Katyn's shadow], (Warszawa: Czytelnik).

Wańkowicz, Melchior (1991) "Dzieje rodziny Korzeniewskich" [Korzeniewski family history], in *Klub Trzeciego Miejsca. Kundlizm. Dzieje rodziny Korzeniewskich*, (Warszawa: Wydawnictwo Polonia), 139–187.

Wielhorski, Władysław (1956) *Los Polaków w niewoli sowieckiej (1939–1956)* [The fate of the Poles in Soviet prison camps], (London: [s.n.]).

Wittlin, Tadeusz (1990) *Diabeł w raju* [The devil in paradise], (Warszawa: Polonia).

Zamorski, Kazimierz and Stanisław Starzewski (1994) *Sprawiedliwość sowiecka* [Soviet justice], (Warszawa: Alfa).

Żaroń, Piotr (1990) *Ludność polska w Związku Radzieckim w czasie II wojny światowej* [Polish population in the Soviet Union during World War II], (Warszawa: Państwowe Wydawnictwo Naukowe).

Davor Beganović
Between the Sun and the Stone – The Naked Body: Yugoslav "Re-education" Camps in Literary Representations

1 The Yugoslav Gulag: Historical background

The story of Yugoslav camps begins in June 1948. Until then Yugoslavia blindly followed Stalin's vision of establishing socialism in Eastern Europe. However, some tendencies toward increasing independence from the Soviet Union, especially in international relations, put in question the rule of the almighty Secretary General of the Soviet Communist Party. After the dissolution of Comintern in 1943 the international socialist movement became decentralized. It was not until 1947 that, on Stalin's initiative, an organization named Communist Information Bureau (Cominform) was founded with the aim of coordinating the activities of communist parties in "people's democracies" and to bring them into closer cooperation in the newly formed Eastern Bloc. The Yugoslav Communist Party (KPJ), which was initially seen as the most reliable Soviet ally, was accused of going its own way, dissenting from the countries that were to establish the Warsaw Pact only a few years later. On 28 June 1948[1] the Information Bureau released a resolution. Its aim was to condemn the alleged "rightist deviations" in the Yugoslav Communist Party and to initiate a purge to remove Yugoslavian leadership, including Tito,[2] from power. That attempt, coordinated by Stalin himself, failed, but the political, military, and economic pressure was enormous. It was sustained mostly from the outside but still there were a great number of people in Yugoslavia itself who thought that Tito's decision to break with Stalin and the Soviet Union was a mistake. According to the Yugoslav communist leadership, it was necessary to isolate those people. They were stigmatized as "enemies inside," and an unrelenting and unsparing fight against them began on a massive scale.

A seemingly precise line of division between those who were loyal to KPJ and the Party's enemies emerged around the question "Are you for or against

---

[1] The 28th of June is a date of great symbolism, especially in Serbian history. It was the date of the Battle of Kosovo in 1389 and the day when the successor to the Habsburg throne, Archduke Franz Ferdinand, was assassinated in Sarajevo in 1914. It was not a coincidence that the Soviet officials chose that day for their declaration.
[2] The most reliable source regarding that period is still Petranović (1981). In the German-speaking world it is Sundhaussen (2012); in English it is Lampe (2000).

the resolution of the Cominform?" All who came out for Stalin and against Tito were declared foes and put in prison; later, when a system of camps was set up, they were moved into camps, mostly those on Goli Otok (the Naked Island). The other, "ideologically pure" people, remained on the outside.

Regarding the problematic of the personality cult, it is crucial to discuss the ideological contents impersonated in its bearer. The Tito/Stalin division line compresses two versions of socialism that differ at first sight with regard to political leadership and the manipulation of the life world, but also reflect more or less hidden points of contact and coincidence. The most important point was certainly the Stalinist settling of accounts with former communist comrades. First individuals were imprisoned already in the autumn of 1948, mostly without any juridical process. The system by then was far from completed, but it was fully realized the following year, and Goli Otok became its symbol, a place that metonymically represented the Yugoslav Gulag in its entirety.

I would like to offer just a short outline of the history of Goli Otok[3] and then discuss its organization and its representation in literature. I will not consider these three elements separately, but try to connect them and show how interwoven they are.

The order to establish concentration camps came, according to Milovan Đilas, from Tito himself (Đilas 1983: 272). The decision to place the largest camp on the deserted island in the vicinity of Rab was more or less accidental. Sculptor Anton Augustinčić[4] was searching for marble that could be used for his monumental works celebrating the partisan victory in the Second World War. Goli Otok appeared as a possible source, particularly as General Dušan Simović[5] had entertained the idea of building a prison for political convicts (in the Kingdom of Yugoslavia they were naturally mostly communists) there before the war. Augustinčić shared his thoughts with the minister for internal affairs, Stevo Krajačić, who connected the enjoyable with the useful and informed Tito about the convenience such a place could offer. Tito's approval came promptly and the new camp was born. The idea to extract marble was not

---

[3] Statistical and historical facts about Goli Otok and Yugoslav concentration camp system are mostly drawn from Jezernik (2012), unless stated otherwise.

[4] Augustinčić was the most prominent proponent of socialist realist art in post-war Yugoslavia. He was commissioned to produce most of the monuments memorizing the heroic fight of the partisans against the occupiers.

[5] General Simović was a commander of the Yugoslav Royal Air Force who led the coup d'état against the pro-fascist government in March 1941. Nazi Germany immediately declared war on Yugoslavia and attacked the country.

very successful, but this was of secondary importance. The essence was in any case hidden in the futility of unproductive and non-creative jobs.

2 The camp on Goli Otok

2.1 Camp setting and organization

The first group of prisoners arrived on the uninhabited island on 9 July 1949. It consisted of 1300 of the regime's political adversaries. By the end of the year their number had increased to 3663. Until 1954, only civilians were confined there, but later there was an influx of military personnel, mostly officers, who had previously been detained in Bileća. From 1956 onwards, Goli Otok was no longer a camp exclusively for political prisoners. Ordinary criminals were confined there too, which gave rise to discontent among the adherents of Informbiro (Cominform), who saw themselves as pure idealists and approached any possibility of mixing with criminals with indignation, revulsion and near-loathing. After 1958 a group of only 100 or so incorrigibles remained. All in all, according to official records, a total of 16,000 detainees had gone through the camp, although the unofficial numbers were much higher, at 31,000 to 32,000. A total of 413 prisoners died of illness, suicide or from torture. There was no systematic killing on the island. The camp was closed down in 1988, but by that time it had already lost its role as a political prison. Now it is open to the public as one more tourist attraction on the Croatian coast.

Prisoners were sent to camps via two different juridical processes. The first was a "normal" verdict, delivered by a court; convicts were usually sent to ordinary prisons. The second group, however, found themselves in a grey area of camp life. Theirs was an administrative sentence, generally of two years, but it could be extended to what to some prisoners felt like eternity. Extension was possible if the investigator was not convinced that the prisoner had changed (the official term was "revised") his enemy position. In that case they were sent to the coast, only to be detained there again and returned to the island for two more years. Such people were ironically called *dvomotorci* (a person with two engines) or *tromotorci*, if their position had still not been "revised" after four years. One can certainly feel a sense of "evil eternity" here and imagine the terrible psychological pressure experienced by inmates.

There were no security measures in the camp. Anything could happen, but the prisoners were not able to intervene or do anything that could possibly change their fate. The only way out was through a full confession, and even that was sometimes not enough. The interrogators were the final authority when it came to deciding whether a prisoner deserved a release or not, and they acted with extreme arbitrariness. Depending on their capricious will, they could deem that a prisoner was ready to leave the island or that they still had not achieved the illuminated status of a person who is aware of their own faults.

Let us look briefly at the structure of the camp. There has been some research into this topic, but the results leave much to be desired. However, I can refer to some important findings, especially those of Božidar Jezernik. Perhaps the most interesting discovery is the particular status of victims within the *Lager* system. As already evident in the first phase of camp development, victims were also perpetrators. Based on a perfidious concept developed by the administration and implemented by the secret police, a system existed in which the prisoners themselves were the torturers and other prisoners' watchdogs. To some extent, this set-up can be compared with the role of the capo in Nazi concentration camps. However, the economic aspect of camp management was more broadly applied to the everyday lives of inmates, something impossible in the slavery of the Nazi system. The idea behind inmate-led administration was that the rules in the camp should reflect the newly developed ideology of Yugoslav self-management. Inmates should make decisions concerning the economic "development" of the camp themselves. Of course, it was highly ironic that self-management was first tested on Goli Otok.[6]

The self-management system was thus twofold. On the one side was the political dimension, concerning the regulations of camp life; on the other side was the economic dimension, with inmates, or their representatives, making decisions concerning the production and distribution of products on the market in the free world. The organization was strictly hierarchical, so that inmates who had been broken first, mostly those who were old and verifiably communist, could assume the role of a proxy administration while the actual administration remained hidden from view.

2.2 Camp theory

At this point it seems appropriate to compare the Yugoslav Gulag with its Soviet and Nazi counterparts, with some theoretical insights into the system of

---

[6] On this point, see Jezernik (2012: 125–138). Jezernik refers to Đilas (1982, especially pp. 97–103) and Milomir Marić, a Serbian journalist who in the 1980s wrote extensively about the Goli Otok in the journal *Duga* ("Rainbow"). Marić's theses are strongly influenced by ideology. In his model the whole of Yugoslavia is a prison and the system of self-management is the foundation of that state of slavery (Jezernik 2012: 138).

totalitarian ideology. I would like to introduce two important theories into our deliberations, though at first glance they may seem difficult to bring together. This merger of theories should not be thought of as a *sine qua non*, but it might testify to the singularity of Yugoslav camps in the broad construct of the Gulag, which spread everywhere on the world map. I am referring to the theories of Hannah Arendt and Giorgio Agamben. Arendt is crucial because she was the first to differentiate between the Nazi and Stalinist camp systems, whereas Agamben was the first to employ the concept of a "state of exception" (or emergency), which was central to the political philosophy of right-wing German jurist Carl Schmitt in a novel, postmodern (or post-fundamentalist) context.

According to Arendt, the secrecy of totalitarian rulers, their efforts at hiding the very existence of camps, is a characteristic factor that can be found in Nazism as well as in Stalinism:

> Just as the stability of totalitarian regime depends on the isolation of the fictitious world of the movement from the outside world, so the experiment of total domination in the concentration camps depends on sealing off the latter against the world of all others, the world of the leaving in general, even against the outside world of a country under totalitarian rule. This isolation explains the peculiar unreality and lack of credibility that characterize all reports from the concentration camps and constitute one of the main difficulties for the true understanding of totalitarian domination, which stands or falls with existence of these concentration and extermination camps; for, unlikely as it may sound, these camps are true central institutions of totalitarian organizational power. (Arendt 1986: 438)

Arendt shows us that the aim of both totalitarian systems is, first of all, to avoid discussing the camp, to convince the external world of the absurdity of the very *idea* of its possible existence, and to suppress the fact of the existence of institutions that could put any sort of moral blemish on the pure ideological premises on which the camps were built. However, it is even more important to remove the "unconsecrated," people who are initialized and thus not able to comprehend the intrinsic appropriateness of a process that might on the surface seem ethically reprehensible, but that is full of true meaning for those who execute it and who approach it on the cognitive level. Thus, the totalitarian systems are doubly protected: on the outside, they are secured off from their devotees, who do not have to know every detail of how they function, and on the inside, they avoid the transparency that could lead to rebellion or provoke moral outrage and damage the small populist stratum formed on their surface.

Yet another component of life in the camp is essential for Arendt. While the particular veiling is a tactic used to appease the internal and external "neutral" observers, camp inmates are treated by their tormentors and ideological commanders to a strategy of forgetting. In contrast to "ordinary" murder, in which a life is annihilated, but not the traces of the victim's existence, which remain a source of mourning for his/her/their kin, murder in the camp is aimed at a complete destruction and anonymity brought by death. The end result is the destruction of the prisoner's personal identity and his oblivion. This neutralization of identity eliminates the feeling of moral responsibility on the perpetrator's side:

> The real horror of the concentration and extermination camps lies in the fact that the inmates, even if they happen to keep alive, are more effectively cut off from the world of the living than if they had died, because terror enforces oblivion. Here, murder is as impersonal as the squashing of a gnat. Someone may die as the result of systematic torture or starvation, or because the camp is overcrowded and superfluous human material must be liquidated. Conversely, it may happen that due to a shortage of new human shipments the danger arises that the camps become depopulated and that the order is now given to reduce death at any price. (Arendt 1986: 443)

Arendt's description can easily be applied to Goli Otok. Oblivion plays a role, as well as the economic aspect. The *Vernichtungslager* (extermination camp) never functioned economically. Its main aim was the annihilation of human material that was seen as inferior. Stalinist and some Nazi camps were places of exploitation of slave labor. Yugoslav camps assimilated this function with that of re-education, which made them unique in the world of concentration camps.

Agamben starts from a different premise. The three books that formed the core of his magnum opus, *Homo Sacer*, are the eponymous *Homo Sacer*, followed by *State of Exception* and *Remnants of Auschwitz*.[7] What is the state of exception? Roughly, it is a suspension of the transfer of power and its concentration in the hands of one person or a group of people acting as one corpus. For the sake of my argument, it is crucial that the state of exception prevails in the context of Yugoslavia in the 1940s and 1950s. Only this accounts for the swift and almost perfect transition from a totalitarian society without a complex isolation system to the construction of a camp world. According to Agamben, the state of exception renders the politics and its underpinning ideology plausible. Thus, the camp appears as the quintessence of modern society itself. "From this perspective, the camp – as the pure, absolute and impassable biopolitical space (insofar as it is founded solely on the state of exception) – will

---

[7] The "Homo sacer" project developed further and is still being pursued. However, Agamben has abandoned his interest in totalitarian communities and is now attempting to document the spiritual history of Europe, tracing theological ideas from the Middle Ages to modern times.

appear as the hidden paradigm of the political space of modernity, whose metamorphoses and disguises we will have to learn to recognize." (Agamben 1999: 123) The state of exception is implemented by the government, which uses, or misuses, its influence in order to isolate the real as well as potential enemies:

> [If] the essence of the camp consists in the materialization of the state of exception and in the subsequent creation of a space in which bare life and the juridical rule enter into a threshold of indistinction, then we must admit that we find ourselves virtually in the presence of a camp every time such a structure is created, independent of the kinds of crime that are committed there and whatever its domination and specific topography. (Agamben 1999: 174)

The suspension of human rights, the country's constitution and laws, or changing them in a sense that corresponds with the state of exception, leads to the suspension and leverage of juridical structures. People lose their individuality and identity; they become bearers of their bare lives and nothing more.

Still, camps are populated with real people, albeit reduced to the bare, or naked, life and we have to see who they are and how they react to the situation they are exposed to. Some are reduced to the condition that can be interpreted as the most radical reaction to the state of exception. This can be observed in the figure of the *Muselmann*.[8] Nazism and Stalinism intersect exactly at this point and the differences between the two totalitarian political systems – one created on racial, the other on ideological assumptions – become surmountable, porous, gradually obscure, to ultimately merge in an act of annihilation of biological life. One might say that both regimes meet in the process of Muselmann creation. What is, according to Agamben, so important in the figure of Muselmann? The philosopher implements the early insights of Bruno Bettelheim, who spent a year in Nazi camps in Germany and used his experiences to develop a therapy for autistic children after he had been sent into exile in the USA. Bettelheim states: "What was external reality for the prisoner is for the autistic child his inner reality. Each ends up, though for different reasons, with a parallel experience of the world." (Agamben 1999: 46) If Arendt stresses the historical and political dimension of camps and thereby neglects their human component, Agamben, relying on Bettelheim, emphasizes exactly that element. In this way his analysis takes on a strong ethical impetus: "[The] Muselmann in some sense marked the moving threshold in which man passed into non-man and in which clinical diagnosis passed into the anthropological analysis."

---

[8] Muselmann is most thoroughly defined and described by Primo Levi in his two classic books on the Holocaust (Levi 1966, 2013).

(Agamben 1999: 47) The neutrality of the medical position gives way to the necessity of an ethical one. It is impossible to watch a Muselmann without taking a moral stance. That precisely is the source of reflection for another crucial figure, even more so than Bettelheim, Agamben's main reference – Auschwitz survivor, Primo Levi:

> The new ethical material that he [Levi – D.B.] discovered in Auschwitz allowed neither for summary judgements nor distinctions and, whether he liked it or not, the lack of dignity had to interest him as much as dignity [...] In Auschwitz ethics begins precisely at the point where the Muselmann, the "complete" witness, makes it forever impossible to distinguish between man and non-man. (Agamben 1999: 47)

Agamben postulates conclusively:

> At times medical figure or an ethical category, at times a political limit or anthropological concept, the Muselmann is an indefinite being in whom not only humanity and non-humanity, but also vegetative existence and relation, physiology and ethics, medicine and politics, and life and death continuously pass through each other. This is why Muselmann's "third realm" is the perfect cipher of the camp, the non-place in which all disciplinary barriers are destroyed and all embankments flooded. (Agamben 1999: 48)

But Agamben is careful when comparing Stalinist and Nazi camps. He does not even mention the former, although they were equally successful in creating the Muselmann as were the latter. Therefore, I have to ask whether there is any uniqueness in Soviet and *eo ipso* Yugoslav camps that would bring forward the discussion about the differences between the two major twentieth-century totalitarian systems.

We may be inclined to equate the two, but one difference remains compelling. The choice of Muselmann in the Nazi destruction camp is arbitrary. Following Primo Levi, it is possible to conclude that humans are reduced to such a condition in a certain biological selection process dominated by evolution components. Everybody can become a Muselmann, as long as they have the physical endurance that enables them to deteriorate or decline gradually. Nazi destruction camps consistently produce the Muselmann through conscious neglect of elementary human needs, based on an unprecedented indifference embedded in their racial ideology. What is horrific is the slow pace of the process. It is difficult to see how arbitrariness is mixed with deliberation here. At least to a certain degree, communism shifts the last instance of human life from contingent arbitrariness to ideological determination. Communist tormentors have enough time to destroy their enemies, themselves mostly old communists and therefore their ideological brethren. "Brainwashing" is accompanied by physical maltreatment in a subtle, monstrous construct of interrogation or court procedure. Its aim is to give a semblance of a judicial system, pretend to abolish chance as a principle, and represent everything that happens to the victim as a rational outcome that is inevitable in its social determination, and finally, in the best manner of pseudo-Marxism, historically necessary, too. Of course, that determination hides elementary voluntarism. The lie, as a leading anthropological principle of the whole Stalinist system of destruction of those who think differently, enters into the structure of state organization and takes over the function of an ideological determinant of social streams in the negative context of a carnivalesque[9] world turned upside down. Therefore, the most disturbing scenes of violence in the memoirs of Yugoslav camp survivors are descriptions of people on the verge of becoming a Muselmann – especially those who were exposed to the "boycott." "Boycotted" are those who are excluded from the collective and as such declared unprotected game. Everybody was given the opportunity to torture them and encouraged to do so, even punished if they refused.

2.3 The role of forgetfulness

To further analyze the camp as cultural construct, it is necessary to take a closer look at those in the Yugoslav-Stalinist-Titoist Gulag system who had the power to manipulate others through intense widening of the world of lies and deceit. Those were members of camp administration and *udbaši*, a label assigned to members of the secret police that originates from UDBA, the acronym for a state security institution.[10] Perpetrators must not have their own voice and must not defend themselves when accused. Therefore, they are important as subjects only in the focus of a dialogue between the interrogator and the interrogated. Outside of that focus they dissolve into figures that lose importance, figures that can fulfill a role only in a given context. Other than that, they exist as anonymous evildoers, who are only effective as part of an obscure collective. This strategy is underpinned by a dual tendency to hide and forget. First, the external world had to be isolated from all comprehension of what happens behind the "closed doors," and at the same time a perfidious psychological method was developed that enabled individuals to forget those who disappeared on the other side of the curtain. The minds of those who were left on the outside were manipulated in such a way that they did not remember the missing persons at all. They, as

---

9 For the concentration camp as a place of a perverse carnival see LaCapra (1998).
10 For the special role of the secret police in the construction of camps and their art of interrogation, see chapter "Everything goes by, except the interrogation" in Jezernik (2012: 285–298; in Slovene).

"people from beyond," ceased to be part of the ordinary world and moved into an imaginary realm unapproachable by reason for those who were luckily left outside. Consequently, that world was eliminated from their view. The strategy of imposed forgetting appears truly tragic in cases where those who had to be forgotten were family members or close friends. Moments of breaking down the most intimate relationships may cause disintegration of the protagonist's psyche. A particularly poignant picture of such a breakdown was given by Dušan Jovanović in the drama *Karamazovi*,[11] in which a conflict between three brothers – a theme of one of the most important novels of Russian realism – is transposed to a scene of a downfall of a Yugoslav family during the resolution of Cominform.

Besides this, let me call it psychological suppression, the authorities resorted to more obvious means that are effective in creating forgetfulness. They are related to methods of transport. Prisoner transports are a metonymy of the whole social system. Darkness, silence, secrecy mirror the symptoms of totalitarian societies: to cover and make the obvious – unobvious, the possible – impossible, the allowed – forbidden. What hovers above was uncertainty, a constant that determined the whole Gulag system. The priority was to force inmates to accept an insecure tomorrow, to erase their future, but at the same time to convince those who might feel compassion that the future as a projective time dimension had become illusory for inmates. The cruelty of transport to Goli Otok continued in horror arrival scenes and the "receptions" were followed by beatings whose main actors were other serving inmates.

The strategy by which prisoners were forced into "beneficial" forgetting – this time based on their own ideological assumptions – entails suppressing their guilt and repeating the phrase that "they know why they are where they are." The revelation of sins came at the peak of a torturous interrogation process. The same matrix was repeated upon arrival in the camp. Boycotting was followed by intense brainwashing in an oral and literal search for ideological digression that, as a consequence, had the concrete use of newly acquired false ideology in the service of an internal and external enemy. Covering up the actual guilt, insisting that the victim uncovered and understood it himself/herself/themselves, the supposed purging through the process of revealing one's sins and the final act of forgetting, forgetting everything, past and present, and concentrating upon their isolated pieces – all this had one result: destruction of individual identity and its unquestioning drowning in the collective, whose member the person became in

---

11 As theater play, *Karamazovi* is not the focus of this chapter. It deals with a family tragedy that happened as a consequence of time served on Goli Otok rather than with the camp itself. More about this drama can be found in Borovnik (2006).

the process of forced, extorted forgetting. Once they were released from the camp, prisoners were asked to forget everything they experienced there. That was the final moment of liberation, but it was not liberation in a true sense. What followed the release was only a simulacrum of real life.

3 Literature on the Yugoslav Gulag

3.1 Verisimilitude *versus* veiling

At this point it seems justified to cross the thin line between history and art and enter the world of literary representations of Goli Otok. They existed long before writers (and film-makers) were allowed to speak directly about this place of horror. It was only in the comparatively liberal 1960s that first attempts were made to approach this sensitive topic. Consequently, the only way to talk about the forbidden was to use the strategies of the ineffable. The most prominent example of such a narrative about Goli Otok is the novel *Kad su cvetale tikve* (1968; an English version, *When Pumpkins Blossomed*, was published in 1971) by Serbian author Dragoslav Mihailović.[12] It is indicative that in the novel, which tells a story of growing up on the peripheries of Belgrade, Goli Otok appears only through the protagonist's father's and brother's disappearance. Both old communists and members of the resistance movement, one night they leave their family and come back two years later, completely changed and broken men. There is not one word in the novel about their whereabouts, so that one can imagine a reader who is not familiar with Yugoslav history wondering what had happened to them. However, every Yugoslavian would immediately know what their fate was. The whole tragedy, the decay of the patriarchal family, is inscribed in that imprisonment. After his return, the father finds destruction – a daughter who was raped, a younger son who has abandoned his promising boxing career and only thinks about vengeance, an environment that has become strange and unrecognizable. What is worse still is that he is not able to

---

[12] Dragoslav Mihailović (born 1930) was himself as a young man a prisoner on Goli Otok. He became the most prominent representative of the *stvarnosna proza* (reality prose) in Serbian literature of the 1960s. It is important to note that the book, with its strategy of veiling, was published without any significant difficulties. However, its stage adaptation caused a real scandal and brought censorship out of its hiding place. The play was banned and Mihailović went into exile. He claimed that this ban was imposed by Tito himself. The reason for this was, he believed, that in the play Goli Otok was mentioned directly, without the hidden narrative measures that worked so successfully in the novel.

help. All his strength, physical and moral, was destroyed on Goli Otok. There is just one way out of this impasse – death, but not volitional death. Suicide is taboo in patriarchal society, but it can happen through alcohol abuse and subsequent depression. The younger son kills the man who raped his sister, escapes to Sweden, and spends his life dreaming of coming back to his home country. Goli Otok remains a dark shadow lingering over the story.

Interestingly, Emir Kusturica applied the same method in a well-known film, *When Father was Away on Business*.[13] Although shot in the 1980s, when first literary works dealing with concentration camps for political prisoners had already appeared, the film follows a technique of disguise typical of other, more ideologically challenging, periods of Yugoslav history. But film was seen as a more important medium than literature and was consequently subject to stricter censorship than literary texts. It is important to note that Mihailović had himself been a prisoner on Goli Otok. The father of Abdulah Sidran, Kusturica's screenwriter, was a prisoner, too. Autobiographical writing is thus an essential part of camp prisoner literature in Yugoslavia as well as in Russia.

Yet the real breakthrough in camp prisoner literature in Yugoslavia was not associated with the memoirs of former inmates, at least not in the beginning. The two novels that paved the way for the forthcoming series of memoirs were written by a Slovene, Branko Hofman, and by a Serbian author, Antonije Isaković. Neither was a prisoner on Goli Otok. *Noč do jutra* ("Night till morning"), Hofman's novel, was first published in Slovenia in 1981 and a Croatian translation followed in 1984. *Tren II* ("Moment II") by Isaković appeared in 1982. The latter is of particular importance because Isaković was a prominent member of the Communist Party and a partisan fighter during the Second World War. He was therefore extremely exposed and credible as a voice for the disenfranchised. Despite this, he faced significant problems in publishing his novel. However, after this literary breakthrough, survivors' memoirs started appearing either in journals or as books.

3.2 Factography and fictionality in the literature of the Gulag

Leona Toker makes one of her numerous classifications of Gulag literature by following the criteria of the proximity of narrative instance to the narrated events.

---

13 *When Father was Away on Business* was awarded the Palme d'Or at the Cannes Film Festival in 1985. It was the second international success of the young director, following the Golden Lion for the best first film for *Do You Remember Dolly Bell?* in Venice in 1981. In both films a strong tone was set by intensely lyrical poetics of the screenplay written by a Sarajevo poet, Abdulah Sidran.

For her, "proper" Gulag literature is that solely written by survivors. Only they can achieve the small distance that enables them to represent the given space with verisimilitude. Still, she allows for fictionality to penetrate into the literary corpus she tends to consider as a distinct genre. "From the very beginning, narratives that dealt with political imprisonment in Soviet Russia bifurcated into the predominantly factographic materials in *émigré* publications and the predominantly fictional ones in official Soviet literature." (Toker 2000: 28–29) Does it mean that *Lager* literature shows particular resistance to fiction? Yugoslav examples seem to point in a different direction. As we have seen, fiction came first, preceding the memoirs. However, it is possible to envisage that the authors of the two groundbreaking texts had sources who helped them to achieve a certain level of truthfulness or at least to diminish the gap between fiction and fact. One, yet more important, difference that may be drawn between Soviet camp memoirs and Yugoslav camp fiction and memoirs is that Soviet camps contained a mixture of ordinary criminals and political prisoners, whereas in Yugoslavia prisoners were communists, who were almost exclusively left to themselves. That led to a yet more pronounced ethical dimension of these texts. The question "How can like minded-persons have done this to us?" lingers in its unanswerability over all of the narratives, and precludes any sort of positive conclusion. Thus, the tension between ethical and aesthetic, pronounced by Toker, reaches another dimension.[14]

One of the prominent examples of Yugoslav fictional camp narratives is Hofman's *Noč do jutra* which tells two – are at first glance incompatible – stories: One takes the shape of a crime story, whereas the other is a psychological narrative, reconstructing the life of a disillusioned communist intellectual, Peter. What links them is an investigative judge who was, as becomes obvious very soon, Peter's interrogator on Goli Otok. He comes to the village where Peter lives in seclusion with his brother and sister-in-law, to investigate an alleged murder of a young woman. Retrospective narration slowly goes back into Peter's past. From studies in Paris, via a teaching job in pre-war Slovenia, involvement with the Communist Party, to the partisan war against the Germans and Italians, and finally to his high position in the newly formed Slovenian government: everything reflects the evolution of a typical socialist revolutionary career. Instead of certain success, however, different fate awaits him: failure and defeat brought about by his inability to accept the fact that the former highest authority – Stalin – is seen as the archenemy under the changed circumstances. This denial results in Peter's

---

[14] "Because of similarities in their subject matter and in the writer's motivation for the narrative act, Gulag memoirs tend to display the following common morphological features: [...] tension between the *ethical* drive and an *aesthetic* impulse, closely associated with the bi-functionality of Gulag narratives as acts of witness-bearing and as a work of art" (Toker 2000: 74).

eight-year imprisonment on Goli Otok. The new quality recorded in *Noč do jutra* is a direct speech about the events that happened in custody and on the island itself. Hofman had obviously done intensive research among former prisoners and tells a rather realistic story of torture and humiliation:

> He stepped into the emptiness, fell on his head, lay in the water and thought at first: a well. Water was shallow. With shackled hands, he barely managed to stand up. For a long time, he couldn't find his bearings: windows were nowhere to be seen, no light, nothing. He leaned against the wall with his back – concrete. He moved right – concrete. Left – concrete. Concrete floor, but not the usual one: it was sloping, it fell from door to the back wall at a thirty-degree angle, the lower third of the floor under water. No table, no chair, no bed. A bunker. And himself.
> He was there (who knows for how long).
> He heard the chattering of teeth first: loud, almost unstoppable. Some time had passed (who knows how long) until he understood: his teeth, although he pressed them together spasmodically. He tried to get out of the water: he turned to the door, dropped on his back, the cuffs cut his flesh, he moaned. When he got accustomed to the pain, he raised himself, helping himself with elbows. And with legs. It went slowly, centimeter after centimeter. His legs were already in the dry part of the cell, he was close to the door, when he fainted again and slid on the sloping floor. The cold water felt pleasant on the swollen hands. But not for long. He trembled, not from the cold but only so. He tried again. And again. Again. And he slid back again, and he slid again, and again, and again, and... He was caught by awe, he screamed. (Hofman 1984: 111–112)

This type of waterboarding is only one method used by torturers to break stubborn ideological opponents depicted in the novel. However, it cannot be said that this is a realistic novel. The main mode of narration is modernist, with the breaking up of temporal levels, discontinuity that overlaps the borders of past and present, free floating of events without any attempt to bind them in a causal and chronological order. Such a narrative process makes it possible to bring together, following the dominant principle of contingency, the former *udbaš* and his victim. When this is achieved, it has devastating ethical effects. The very difference between the perpetrator and victim seems to be abolished:

> He said to himself, *all of us are stigmatized*, and he thought how the violence is in reality a double-edged sword, because it doesn't only hit the victims, but the perpetrator too, him even more, because time has a literary inflational impact on their arguments that justified violence. (Hofman 1984: 124)

The story is set in the deep Slovenian province where Peter lives, withdrawn in his brother's inn, and where judge Kovač comes to interrogate the alleged murderer of a young peasant's daughter. This murder, which is finally uncovered as a suicide, is the real tragedy of the novel. The daughter of conservative peasants who is driven to suicide parallels in a strange way Peter's destiny of being betrayed by his kin: his wife, his friends, and the Communist Party itself. The final meeting of Kovač and Peter results in a grotesque rumble, in which neither emerges as a winner. All that is left are two defeated men, each carrying the burden of his own past in his own way. That is the sad message of the story, presenting a lost generation of failed revolutionaries and cynical winners of a battle against like-minded enemies that ends in ethical ruin.

Isaković's *Tren II* uses a different narrative technique. In the tradition of Serbian new realism, the story is told in the mode of *skaz*.[15] In traditional Russian literary studies, *skaz* is bound to the narrative perspective because it substitutes the author's or narrator's speech with the speech of a character. *Skaz* insists on the oral quality of speech. It allows a semblance of authenticity to emerge, leading to polyphony, the merging of different voices, especially if there is a collocutor who, rather than being passive, actively participates. Serbian new realism re-discovered *skaz* as a technique appropriate for enhancing the natural qualities of literary texts. Therefore, characters using *skaz* come mostly from the lower classes that are more prone to dialectal coloring of the speech. The most important enthusiast of this narrative technique is Dragoslav Mihailović.[16]

Isaković's *skaz* is interesting insofar as he uses it in a double refraction. As the subtitle of his book indicates ("Narrating to Čeperko"), there is a person (Čeperko – it could be the author himself) who is listening to the stories told to him by an anonymous person, the carrier of the *skaz*. In another complication, the story concerning Goli Otok is told by a stranger – a fellow passenger on the winter train – who launches into it out of the blue:

- It is dark. I can't see your hands. You haven't been there?
- You have?
- Yes.
- Naked...
- We were naked. (Isaković 1982: 37)

The story starts as a misunderstanding that is not actual, but ironical. The narrator asks the other passenger whether he was on Goli Otok and the man answers that they were naked. Rhetorically, a toponym is substituted by an adjective. This strategy underlines the impossibility of comprehending what happened "there": "Say, what was it like there? / One cannot say." (Isaković

---

15 For a more in-depth description of *skaz* see Titunik (1977).
16 For a discussion of *skaz* by Mihailović see Hodel (1992).

1982: 38) The impossibility to tell is the core of the narrative,[17] but it is broken by the *skaz* narrator, who has an almost involuntary drive for telling. The story is already almost a topos in Yugoslav camp literature, one of torture and disintegration of communist ideological values. It culminated in an amalgamation of drastic body representations and a treatise of treason on the one side and steadfastness on the other. This matrix may also be found in later memoirs, but here it is underlined not so much with factography, as with fictionality.

One inmate, Toma, starts with an outrageous claim: "We all are sons of the Party." (Isaković 1982: 52) This is heretical, because inmates are traitors who lost the right to see themselves as members of a collective. A violently cruel punishment, a stoning sentence, follows:

> Then a horrible scream could be heard. Somebody was hit in the middle of the quarry. Blood ran from my nose, then mouth. Slowly I became blessed; nobody can harm me any more. Nothing at all, I rise to heaven. Death uncovered me, it came to pick me up and lift me up from this world. [...]
>
> We arrived in the main harbor part of the quarry. Our formation is ordered as one arch, cut in two by a transversal shadow. Heat blinks, in it the sparks of stone corns. At last I saw: a man sits pressed against the smooth rock, almost covered with stones. And I recognize him: Toma, he is stoned.
>
> Everything tears to pieces in the moment, your eyes open, a window is created in the dust: Toma's head is whole, eyes open, looking embarrassed, not much, face more than calm – there is no vengeance in it. The whole left arm is free, and both legs, to the knees, protrude out of the pile of stones. (Isaković 1982: 52–53)[18]

Thus, perspectives are multiplied, which enables a multitude of reflections, experiences, and interpretations. Different layers come to the surface; we are confronted with violence in various shapes. Apart from the narrative technique, it is important to see one innovation on the thematic level of narrative. As I have already mentioned, the violence in *Tren II* is extreme. Descriptions of torture lose every abstract quality. They become completely body-focused. This, too, is made possible through the technique of *skaz*,[19] but it is now more than a mere

---

17 Of course, this impossibility will disappear in the course of the narrative. Goli Otok is talked about, indeed, at length.
18 It is difficult to ignore how religious discourse, almost incompatible with the communist one, gets the overhand. Religious metaphor is embedded in the vocabulary ("blessed," "harm") and in the typical scenes of ascension to Paradise. It seems that the words of the author are subverting those of the narrator, as if he intervened in the narrative without being invited to do that.
19 The most important representative of Gulag literature, Varlam Shalamov, should not, according to Toker, be seen as an author who uses more traditional, realistic, narrative techniques such as *skaz*: "Though a careful student of Chekhov, Dostoevsky, Leskov, and Bunin,

technical innovation: it opens up a completely different approach to Goli Otok, one which could best be described as testimony[20] and closely related to it – a memoir.

While *Noč do jutra* insistently emphasizes the fictional moment of the story and is constructed as a psychological novel concentrated on the innermost feelings of the main protagonist, *Tren II* dismisses this approach and turns almost exclusively to the documentary. It is not vital that the story told is a confession of a real inmate. What matters is the realistic potential generated by the *skaz* and realized at the thematic level by a cruel representation of the inhuman everyday life of prisoners and their guards. A space was now open for a new kind of literature that dominated Yugoslav *Lager* discourse from the end of the 1980s onwards. Isaković's role in launching this kind of discourse is unquestionable, but there is one more author whose contribution in this area is ineffaceable – Miroslav Popović.[21] His hybrid text *Udri bandu* ("Batter the Gang") is the first that portrays Goli Otok complex from the perspective of a direct participant. Popović simultaneously writes his testimony and his confession. He is embittered but still tries not to lose objectivity. He knows that this is the only way to keep enough self-restraint to give the reader sufficient information to believe him – and that is the *sine qua non* of literature of testimony. This concept is apparent in particular chapter titles. Except for one, they are one-word titles concentrating on different aspects of life in the camp or on the suffering inflicted upon prisoners: "Composition," "Pencil and its consequences," "Chase," "Lynch" and "Illnesses." Rhetorical sparsity tends to enhance their veracity. It is obvious that Popović intended to write some sort of encyclopedia, but his work was cut short by his untimely death. There is a quest for definition, but it cannot be fulfilled. The text, driven by

---

Shalamov regarded the modernist Andrei Bely as the most significant influence on his work. Like most modernist works, his texts challenge the reader not to seek a meaning but to help create it." (Toker 2000: 158).

20 One particular reference that Leona Toker made to Varlam Shalamov's stories appears to be of importance here. She is aware that his stories cross the border between fiction and factography and defines this violation as follows: "Even if a collocation of two events is a product of sieving through the random flow of reality and not of a deliberate recombination, we must read the story as a semiotically rich account of an actual day in the camp *yet also* inquire into the moral and allegorical significance of its collocations, repetitions, elisions, and recurrences. In other words, we must read the story as testimony – yet analyze it as a work of fiction." (Toker 2000: 154) This analytical discrepancy is typical of Yugoslav camp literature, too.

21 Miroslav Popović (1926–1985) spent seven years as a prisoner on Goli Otok. He did not live to see his book published. Like most memoirs, his was first serialized in a supplement of the weekly *NIN* and only later (1988) published as a book.

memories, is so intensely affective that it does not allow for any reflexive or systematizing intention on the part of the author. In these circumstances it appears that a neutral position (ideologically or emotionally), that of external focalizer, is unfeasible.

The best example of how the catalogue cannot be tamed and controlled, how it is impossible to keep a distance from the narrated events if the narrator is himself a participant, is the chapter "Illnesses." Popović sets out to compile a list of the most common illnesses on Goli Otok. He chooses a multi-level strategy. First, he draws a comparison: "Our illnesses, for example, were always worse than the equivalents outside the prison and all of them were to some extent contagious. Those that were actually contagious and those that did not spread from man to man anywhere else in the world." (Popović 1988: 134) Second, he compiles a list of these illnesses. This corresponds to a transition from general to particular. Differentiation is still the ground principle of organization:

> Dystrophy as shown on television [...] is not the same as ours. They sit there and their legs are thin as sticks.
> Ours were thick as an elephant's. They swelled from the knee down. An ankle would level with the part above it and become undistinguishable. When one pressed his thumb on that barrel which his lower leg had transformed into, a hollow remained, like in dough or an overripe melon. Quite a lot of time had to pass before it was refilled. (Popović 1988: 135)

A search for objectivity does not exclude differentiation. Moreover, it is one of the central issues in the construction of discourse that tends to be scientifically verified. But Popović is not able to stop at a dispassionate, "objective" comparison. He is led by emotions and his story drifts in the direction of fictional, or at least creative, literature:

> But one had to urinate. The dystrophic – especially often.
> In the working area it happened very quickly. Just one step aside and you are done. If you are chased, the chaser would stop to do the same. You just had to be careful not to be turned towards the guards, even if they were a hundred meters away. They could interpret what you were doing in the wrong way.
> But in the circle urinating was an enterprise preceded by long postponement, hesitation, even something like an inner discussion in that deaf, lone basement into which the man was transformed. (Popović 1988: 137–138)

The last step in this transformation of neutral general discourse into one charged with affect is accomplished. Description is transformed into a rhetorically charged story about a concrete experience of an individual in the world of the camp. Science took a step back and Popović's text became, *nolens volens*, a creative one.

It should be noted that Popović is writing along the same lines as another Serbian author who was a victim of communist terror – Borislav Pekić.[22] But there is one important distinction. Pekić was convicted and served his sentence in jail, not in a camp. Therefore, his voluminous book belongs to prison literature rather than camp literature. Nonetheless, his work may be seen as an important, yet marginal, contribution to this genre in the Yugoslavian context.

Popović shows an affinity towards Dragoslav Mihailović, who was actually the editor of *Batter the Gang*. Mihailović was imprisoned on Goli Otok and subsequently dealt with the personal trauma that obviously greatly influenced him in *When Pumpkins Blossomed*. Yet that was not all. A few years later he started to collect prisoners' memories and edited them into volumes. Five volumes have been published since 1990, containing approximately three thousand pages of testimony. The book is conceived as a testimony of ten people, whom the author, as he says, trusted. It is supplemented by a collection of documents – letters, minutes, lists – that are integrated into the main corpus. It appears that the highest principle of objectivity is not only postulated but achieved, too. Still, there are some doubts about the book's professed objectivity. First of all, the selection of witnesses appears to be purposeful, at least to some extent. Why did Mihailović choose exactly those people and not others? How did he take his pick? Second: why did he not consider the written testimonies that were already available? Did he think them in some way inferior to those he had collected? Or did he consider *skaz*, the technique he so masterly developed in his fiction, superior to any kind of conventionally written prose? Finally, why did he not write down his own testimony about his imprisonment on Goli Otok? Considering his penmanship, and his status as one of the most important contemporary Serbian authors, it is not inconceivable that he could have become the Shalamov of Yugoslav Gulag. This, however, must be left open and we will probably never have an answer. Be that as it may, the fact is that Yugoslav national literatures have not produced an author whose status in this genre might be compared with that of the Soviet "stars."

To conclude, let me summarize my main points about concentration camp literature. From a diachronic perspective I presented the first phase of discourse about the camps as the practice of the ineffable. This disguise strategy was

---

22 Pekić's three-volume book *Godine koje su pojeli skakavci* ("The years eaten by grasshoppers") is a mixture of scientific, or anthropological, exploration of the prison system that contains individual stories as well as memoirs describing his experience during a court trial and imprisonment in Yugoslavia in the 1940s. He was jailed not as a communist, but as a liberal democrat. Therefore, his bitterness has a completely different tenor than that of the prisoners on Goli Otok.

assumed for political reasons, but the art itself did not suffer from it. The second phase, which began in the 1980s after Tito's death, was characterized by first experiments in writing about Goli Otok using direct speech. This literature oscillated between a modernist and a neorealist approach; the latter prevailed and led to an abundance of testimonies and memoirs written directly by the witnesses. This final phase is still ongoing but not to the same degree as in the late 1980s and early 1990s. What remains to be seen is the response of the social sciences in general. Apart from historical representations, we still lack some sort of theoretical approach that would explore the extremely intricate construction of camps and their role in Yugoslav society in general. Therefore, my long introduction to this chapter should be understood in this sense – as an attempt to connect some dispersed facts into an at least partially meaningful unity.

Works cited

Agamben, Giorgio (1997) *Homo Sacer: Sovereign Power and Bare Life*, trans. Daniel Heller-Roazen (Stanford: Stanford University Press).
Agamben, Giorgio (1999) *The Remnants of Auschwitz: The Witness and the Archive*, trans. Daniel Heller-Roazen (NY: Zone Books).
Arendt, Hannah (1986) *The Origins of Totalitarianism* (London: André Deutsch).
Borovnik, Silvija (2004) "Razvoj dramatike Dušana Jovanovića" [The development of Dušan Jovanović's dramaturgy], *Jezik in slovstvo* 49, 49–66.
Đilas, Milovan (1982) *Tito* (Wien: Moewig).
Đilas, Milovan (1983) *Jahre der Macht: Kraftspiele hinter dem Eisernen Vorhang: Memoiren 1945–1966* [Rise and fall], (München: Molden – S. Seewald).
Hodel, Robert (1992) *Betrachtungen zum "skaz" bei N. S. Leskov und Dragoslav Mihailović* [Observations on "skaz" in N. S. Leskov and Dragoslav Mihailović], (Bern: Peter Lang).
Hofman, Branko (1984) *Noč do jutra* [Night till morning], (Ljubljana: Mladinska knjiga).
Isaković, Antonije (1982) *Tren 2: Kazivanja Čeperku* [The moment II: Narrating to Čeperko], (Beograd: Prosveta).
Jezernik, Božidar (2012) *Non Cogito Ergo Sum. Eseji o Golom otoku* [Non Cogito Ergo Sum. Essays on Naked Island], trans. Igor Smailagić (Novi Sad: Mediterran Publishing).
Jovanović, Dušan (1981) *Osvoboditev Skopja in druge gledališke igre* [The Liberation of Skopje and other plays], (Ljubljana: Mladinska knjiga).
LaCapra, Dominick (1998) *History and Memory after Auschwitz* (London: Cornell University Press).
Lampe, John R. (2000) *Yugoslavia as a History: Twice There Was a Country* (Cambridge: Cambridge University Press).
Levi, Primo (1966) *If This is a Man*, trans. Stuart Joseph Woolf (London: Bodley Held).
Levi, Primo (2013) *The Drowned and the Saved*, trans. Raymond Rosenthal (London: Abacus).
Mihailović, Dragoslav (1968) *Kad su cvetale tikve* (Novi Sad: Matica srpska), trans. Drenka Willen (1971) *When Pumpkins Blossomed* (New York: Harcourt Brace Jovanovich).

Pekić, Borislav (1991) *Godine koje su pojeli skakavci I-III: Uspomene iz zatvora ili antropopeja (1948–1954)* [The years eaten by grasshoppers I-III. Memories from the prison or anthropopee 1948–1954], (Beograd: Jedinstvo and BIGZ).

Petranović, Branko (1981) *Istorija Jugoslavije 1918–1978* [The history of Yugoslavia 1918–1978], (Beograd: Nolit).

Popović, Miroslav (1988) *Udri bandu* [Batter the gang], (Beograd: Filip Višnjić).

Sundhaussen, Holm (2012) *Jugoslawien und seine Nachfolgestaaten: Eine ungewöhnliche Geschichte des Gewöhnlichen* [Yugoslavia and its successive states. An unusual history of the usual], (Wien: Böhlau).

Titunik, Irwin R. (1977) "Das Problem des 'skaz'. Kritik und Theorie" [The problem of "skaz." Criticism and theory], *Erzählforschung 2*, ed. Wolfgang Haubrichs (Göttingen: Vandenhoeck & Ruprecht), 114–140.

Toker, Leona (2000) *Return from the Archipelago: Narratives of the Gulag Survivors* (Bloomington: Indiana University Press).

Anne-Berenike Rothstein
Presence through Absence: The Aesthetics of Blank Space in French Holocaust Literature and Film

1 "There's nothing left to say"

"Another planet," "a world of its own," "there" – finding an appropriate language for that which defies visualization and representation – the camp experiences during the Second World War – is a task for writers and filmmakers who confront the Holocaust. Railway tracks, watchtowers, barbed wire fences – these are just a few signs that induce the spectator to associate and imagine the concentration camp universe. But even this, so to speak, iconography of terror cannot express the unspeakable.

It is not only the unspeakable that is difficult to represent, but also the problem of absence – absence of referentiality, absence of most of the victims, absence of any sort of explainability. One way to tackle the issue of absence is to use blank space. This chapter focuses on the aspect of the non-spoken, of the omitted, the blank space, gap text. Blank space is actually determined in the present work as "blanks" and the goal is to define and categorize the blank spaces on the basis of contentwise criteria. Therefore, this chapter highlights spatial-semantic representations of blanks in literature (through a topographic setting) and in film (for example, through architectural composition or through a point-of-view shot or commentary). The works discussed, two novels and two documentaries, were chosen in particular to exemplify different forms of blank spaces; I will categorize them in my analysis as follows: blank space as a representation of the unspeakable/the traumatic; blank space as a representation of (lost) space; blank space as a representation of the space of memory and remembrance; and blank space as a representation of the narrative space and the space of reflection. The use of blanks in film and literature is a topic that shows how the "unspeakable" is facilitated and I will ask whether there exists a specific culture of remembrance of blank spaces.[1]

---

[1] This chapter follows in part my earlier work (Binder 2008, 2011), enhancing it by focusing on the topic of blank spaces. The chapter title is a quote from *Night and Fog* by Alain Resnais (1956).

https://doi.org/10.1515/9783110631135-008

2 Dealing with traumatic experiences: Charlotte Delbo, Soazig Aaron, Alain Resnais, and Claude Lanzmann

Charlotte Delbo's trilogy *Auschwitz and After* (1995)[2] merges several literary forms to reflect on and discuss the everyday camp life, the painful memory, and the everyday life after Auschwitz. Her search of appropriate or even new figures of speech and word combinations manifests itself in an artificial language, replete with montages and unusual lexical constructs, and also reflected in how the text appears on the page. She describes Auschwitz as another planet and recreates the time and space structure of the camp by means of several narration strategies and narrative techniques. On a visual level, on the basis of lexical, semantic, syntactical, and typographical determinants, the text reveals a specific form of space and an additional interpretation of the represented. At this point, a symbiotic relationship between form and content takes place where the text imitates, interprets, and illustrates the incidents. The difficulties involved in representing a historical trauma are therefore also transparent in the structure and spatiality of the text – a blank space becomes for Delbo another way of communicating an atrocity.

Soazig Aaron places a special emphasis on the description of life after Auschwitz in *Refusal* (2008). In narration in the form of a diary, she traces a painful return of an Auschwitz survivor, Klara, who communicates her memories in fragments and little bits of narrative, and who cannot overcome the discrepancy between her experiences of the past and her present everyday life. This relationship of mutual tension is mediated through the structure of the diary: Klara's narrations of Auschwitz alternate with accounts from everyday life in post-war Paris that are recorded by her sister-in-law, Angelika, whose diary we are reading.

The vanishing of historical events from our lived experiences is the topic of Resnais's personal documentary,[3] *Nuit et Brouillard* (*Night and Fog*; 1956). He presents the different levels of the extermination process of human beings

---

[2] The trilogy consists of the following volumes: *None of Us Will Return*, *Useless Knowledge* and *The Measure of Our Days*; for brevity, the works will be hereinafter abbreviated as *Auschwitz I*, *Auschwitz II* and *Auschwitz III*, respectively.
[3] See Insdorf: "Particularly when dealing with the overwhelming and still palpable realities of the Holocaust, certain filmmakers have been able to transform the documentary into a personal genre, closer to the memoir or journal. [...] Films like *Night and Fog*, *Sighet, Sighet*, and *Shadow of Doubt* use 'documentary' footage such as newsreels and interviews, but are in fact

inside a pseudo-factory of a concentration camp.[4] On the basis of a rather detailed description of *univers concentrationnaire* (concentration camp universe), Cayrol and Resnais attempt to demonstrate the mechanisms of evil and show the inhumane treatment of victims, at the same time formulating a moral obligation or appeal to posterity to remember the Holocaust and to prevent its recurrence. The film's effect lies in a skillful and coherent overall concept: the images come from British military film reels and originally served as documentation of historical events (Roumette 1961: 37). To reach a large(r) audience and to combine the educational purpose with an emotional component, Resnais integrated his idea with the text and commentary by Jean Caryol. The film works as an entity in which none of the elements dominate: the commentary is based on eyewitnesses' reports,[5] whereas the structure of the film is consistent with a book by Wormser and Michel, *Tragédie de la déportation 1940–1945. Témoignages de survivants des camps de concentration allemands* ("The tragedy of the deportations 1940–1945. Witness accounts of survivors of German concentration camps"),[6] and there is a dialogical cross-linking of the book's and the film's endings.[7] Whereas Wormser and Michel focused on the documentation itself (Wormser and Michel 1955: 10), Resnais emphasizes historical remembrance.[8] Blanks or voids exist at all levels: text, camera/image, narrative voice, commentary and musical score.

---

as formally rich as the best of 'fiction' films: they contain a narrative spine, poetic sinews, an edited pulse, and a profoundly personal voice." (2003: 199).
4 Introduction (edification of the camps and deportation); selection process and humiliation (life in the camp); extermination process (killing on an industrial scale; gas chamber, crematorium, etc.); conclusion (arrival of the allies; appeal for action and remembrance).
5 See Wormser and Michel (1955). Olga Wormser and Henri Michel were members of the Comité d'Histoire de la Seconde Guerre Mondiale, which was the consignor of the documentary, and both participated in the production of the film.
6 I. The convoys; II. The arrival at the camp and the quarantine; III. Everyday life; IV. Work in the concentration camps; V. Social categories in concentration camps; VI. The man's permanence; Spiritual life and resistance; VII. The territory: antichamber and death; VIII. Death: the last stop; IX. Evacuation and liberation of the camps.
7 "Wormser's and Michel's hope, that the screaming of the victims will one day break down the walls of indifference and oblivion corresponds with the statement at the end of the film, that no one is listening to the incessant screaming." (van der Knaap 2002: 75).
8 For André Bazin *Nuit et Brouillard* is a parable about humanity: "If I weren't worried about appearing paradoxical and causing misunderstandings, I would say openly that *Nuit et Brouillard* is a film about softness and tenderness, a film about pity at any rate, and not about hatred and anger [...] but *Nuit et Brouillard* is, above all, a glimpse of love and faith in mankind, the affirmation of hope beyond hopelessness. The grass did not stop growing under Attila's feet: the grass started to grow again, timidly, short and rare, among the ruins of the crematorium,

Claude Lanzmann's *Shoah* (1974–1985)[9] is at the heart of how the media approaches the Holocaust in French film. In a rather radical manner, the film espouses the prohibition of fictionalization of the Holocaust and additionally constantly renounces any kind of archive footage. The documentation tries at the same time to evoke the "gap" Holocaust and is composed of two components: place and word – as indicated by Lanzmann's working title for his documentary, *Le lieu et la parole* ("The place and the word"). The film gives voice primarily to the victims of the Holocaust, but also the perpetrators and bystanders, and is therefore a compilation of testimonies that illustrate the remembrance work. Additionally, *Shoah* returns to places of atrocity, showing what they look like and what effect they still have on individuals several decades later. Finally, Lanzmann joins those two components by bringing the survivors back to the places of atrocity, and making them repeat the movements and tasks that they had engaged in back then. Lanzmann wanted his interviewees to relive the past in the present, to be authentic, to tell (their) story and not *history*, because "Geschichte erzählt sich nicht von selbst [History doesn't tell itself]." (Baer 2000: 19) Lanzmann argues for the primacy of the word, also of witnessing by words, and hence *Shoah* is "a film made exclusively of testimonies." (Felman 2000: 104)

3 Different forms of blank spaces

"A blank space can be defined as a hidden or openly displayed absence" (Dotzler 1999: 121). The blank space is a "gap" that can and must be filled. It is an empty space and the reader's task is to extract certain information that is not explicitly mentioned (but rather, it is implied, adressed or contained in the text) (Eco 1990: 5, 63); the "unspoken that is constitutive for the meaning of the text" (Iser 1994: 283). In Holocaust literature and film in particular, it is impossible to represent and describe the events explicitly, which points to the difficulty of representability. This issue is a constituent in dealing with the Holocaust. The events are dominated by absence – absence of most of the victims, absence of sense, absence of explainability. This absence is taken up by

---

just enough to maintain that life is stronger than nothingness. [...] The truthfulness of *Nuit et Brouillard* that's the soft glow of humanity." (Bazin 1987: 139).

9 The film premiered in 1985 in France and in 1986 in Germany. Lanzmann spent 11 years shooting in eight countries and filmed over 350 hours of material. The film lasts 9 hours and 43 minutes and 47 survivors have the opportunity to tell their stories.

blank spaces that reveal different meanings. The reader's task is to fill the blank spaces (Iser 1984: 284–315) and the reader of Holocaust literature in particular is an informed reader who fills the blank space not only with context, but also with his or her (previous) historical knowledge. The reader is asked to actively decipher the unspoken message: "'Un-spoken' means that it does not manifest itself on the surface, on the level of expression; it is the 'un-spoken' that has to be updated on the actualization level of content. Therefore, the text requires – more than any other sort of message – the active and consciously cooperative steps of" (Eco 1990: 62) an "implied reader" (Iser 1978). This "cooperation" is used by the authors to establish a kind of dialogue with the reader. A dynamic interaction between the text and the recipient emerges, and the reader develops "phantom chapters" (Eco 1990: 260). Therefore, the blank space becomes accessible to the reader because of the rest of the text, because of the reader's "mental inter-textual encyclopaedia and due to his level of expectations."[10] "The blank spaces of a literary text are by no means [...] a shortcoming, they constitute a fundamental starting point for its effect. [...] It is the blank spaces that grant the reader his role in the construction of sense." (Iser 1970: 15)

3.1 Blank space as a representation of the unspeakable/traumatic

"It is also in the heart of our recent history whether we want to see it or not. For Cayrol, who write the film's script, [gas chambers] are at the foundation of postwar literature." (Colombat 1993: 125) The most impressive example of the unspeakable or the traumatic is death in concentration camps. Thanks to the blank space as a form of the unspeakable, the event is preserved in its literality, free from association and therefore "[...] knowing and not knowing are entangled in the language of trauma and in the stories associated with it" (Caruth 1995: 4).

Especially in the first and second part of her trilogy, Delbo stresses single words, phrases or sentences by arranging them typographically on the page, so they appear as verses; the language seems petrified (Langer 1978: 206). "Là-bas" is often offset, for emphasizing the particularity and inexplicability of Auschwitz:

---

[10] Reif (2005: 87). In her dissertation, Danielle Reif focuses on blank spaces in Raymond Federman's novel *La Fourrure de ma tante Rachel*.

> [...]
> I'm still there
> dying there;
> [...]
> because
> I learned
> over there
> that you cannot speak to others. (Delbo 1995: 224, 228)

Gas chambers represent the phantasmagoric centre of Auschwitz and are the embodiment of atrocity and non-representation. Neither in film nor in literature is the agony represented; instead there are glimpses of humanity in accompanying a dying friend or a beloved.[11]

In *Nuit et Brouillard* the change between the present and the past, between the space today and the space then, is less and less clear-cut, meaning that past prevails over present (and underlining its central importance in the present). The confrontation between the images in black and white and the images in colour demonstrates the necessity to remember. Shots of the gas chamber in the centre of the concentration camp are the climax of the documentary, where the image and sound merge.

> This is a shot whose function is to bring the audience into a collective recollection of a past which is in danger of being forgotten or replaced by the audience's own present. Here, with more intensity than anywhere else in this documentary, the spectators have to imagine and interpret what they see and hear. (Colombat 1993: 138)

Initially, the crematory is shown in colour – today it is a tourist attraction, as the commentator bitterly notices. The last shot in colour shows the chimney and signifies therefore that superficial remembrance will not be tolerated by the documentary. The images of ovens, today empty, are defined by the montage of black-and-white film frames. As Resnais has already used this "reanimation" or "definition" (of images in colour) by showing railway tracks, now overgrown (combined through montage with historical newsreel), the spectator is accustomed to his technique of suggesting a renewed purpose of the crematory. The black-and-white images show masses of displaced individuals, images of deportees, death, selection, liquidation, and precede Resnais's images of the present, which try to describe the last moments before death in the gas chamber. The camera moves in the gas chamber, explores the room ("What looked like a shower room welcomed

---

[11] In *L'Écriture ou la Vie*, Jorge Semprún accompanies his dying professor Maurice Halbwachs by reciting verses from Baudelaire (Semprún 1994: 60).

the arrivals"),[12] shows a close-up shot of a water pipe. Then it moves on slowly and concludes with an image (a cut of the doors) and text description; here the perpetrators' perspective is provided ("The doors were closed. A watch was kept"). In this scene the blank is primarily on the level of the text; only the sound of a flute becomes more important again – this space between life and death cannot be shown on film as there are no survivors or witnesses: "Gas chambers constitute a terribly palpable purgatory between life and death, the most concrete reality to ever approach the transcendence of death." (Avisar 1988: 10) Consequently, Resnais does not attempt to show atrocity, but uses a sign to reveal an incredible pain: the camera then pans out to the ceiling, where the scratch marks left by the dying people are traces of their agony: "The only sign, but you have to know, is this ceiling scored by finger-nails. Even the concrete was torn."[13] Cayrol does not explain the sign, for it is, in George Steiner's words, "the kind of thing under which language breaks" (1984: 166). The scratch marks could also be read as a sign that the Nazis could not erase the memory of their victims. The camera movement itself becomes more expressive; it seems to be searching for something, it tries to trace the immeasurable pain by slowly showing the ceiling, and finally, it dwells on a corner – Resnais consciously sets a short break to give the spectator the time to handle the scene.

In contrast to Resnais's usage of archive material to fill in, as it were, the blanks of memory, Lanzmann rejects any kind of archive material[14] when showing his moral and ethical recognition of the brutality of the Shoah and the suffering of those affected:

> Above all, the Holocaust is unique in that it surrounds itself with a circle of flames, a border that mustn't be crossed, because a certain level of atrocity, that is total atrocity, is not transferable: those who do so are guilty of the worst transgression. Fiction is a sort of transgression and I am firmly convinced that any kind of portrayal is forbidden. (Lanzmann 2000: 135)

---

12 See the reporting of Mordechai Podchlebnik's in Lanzmann's *Shoah*: the tracking shot also tries to trace the process of gasification and Lanzmann works (as does Resnais) with *mise en scène*, editing, and montage in order to visualize remembrance and non-representationability.
13 In direct contrast to this technique of blank space is the gas chamber scene in *Schindler's List* (1993), a film by Steven Spielberg. First, it seems that Spielberg breaks a taboo in showing the prisoners afraid of being gassed; the spectator also expects this ending. But in fact, the characters are in a shower (see the critical explanation by Kramer 1999: 9–14).
14 "If an unknown document were to fall into my hands, a film, that – secretly – since filming was strictly forbidden – had been made by an SS man and that would show how three thousand Jews, men, women and children, died together, suffocating in a gas chamber of the crematory in Auschwitz – if I had found such a film, I not only would not show it, I would destroy it. I am incapable of telling why. It is self-explanatory." (Lanzmann 2000: 138).

He differentiates between the groups of witnesses and adopts an uncompromising position: Lanzmann wants the victims to overcome their trauma.

3.2 Blank space as representation of (lost) space

> Within society, the concentration camp was a closed universe. Nowhere is the theory of the closed social system more pertinent than in the case of the concentration camp. Its boundaries could not be crossed; its inmates were isolated and locked into a world of terror in which the camp personnel enjoyed a free reign. [...] For them, the camp was a colony of terror at the far extremity of the social world. (Sofksy 1997: 14)

This "colony of terror" is hard to imagine, even though the spaces of atrocity are still there. Photographed scenes are not able to convey memory, just silence without life (Young 1988: 124). This problematic aspect is approached in different ways. As described above, Resnais uses the technique of "reanimation" of present spaces with archival material. In *Nuit et Brouillard* remembering itself is visualized and staged: starting with a walk in present-day Auschwitz, a search for traces of the past begins; the camera moves along the scene, searching. Here a mental world is traced whose movement (from the origin of the concentration camp universe until its destruction) becomes visible in a complete overview. The past is the black-and-white material, which explains the searching tracking shots, and was evoked by images in the present. This archaeological study can be viewed as an analysis not only of the (then recent) past, but also an appeal to the audience, a thorough investigation of the different regions of our selective collective memory.

Lanzmann, however, tries with the help of montage of "*le lieu et la parole*," and therefore past and present, to evoke "the blank" Holocaust. For his interview technique, this means that he faces the survivors with old places of horror, lets them sing the songs of the past again and again, uses gestures for "shifting the barrier of silence" (Lanzmann 2000: 108). An example of this is a well-known scene with barber Abraham Bomba, who recreates – in his hair salon, under Lanzmann's guidance – the act of cutting hair before extermination in the gas chamber: "Now I carry back his mind to this particular situation back then." (Lanzmann 2000: 108) Lanzmann asks Bomba to cut a man's hair just as he had done in the gas chamber immediately before the gasification of countless victims. Abraham Bomba relives – through pressing questions – the situation of then. An immediate authenticity is made credible by the presentation and staging of survivors. Representing various other scenes in the film, an interview with the barber embodies this overwhelming immediacy, a survivor who is deeply shaken by an eruption of realization. The mere survival is to be overcome, enabling a return to (real) life that also signifies "living pain. [...] [*Shoah*] is the story of the liberation of the testimony through its desacralization." (Felman 2000: 118, 119)

Charlotte Delbo's poetic language of images also manifests itself in its visual arrangement. Nicole Thatcher sees Delbo's poetic prose and her use of free verse, especially her awareness of spatiality, corporeality, and seeing, as deriving from her experience in the fields of drama and directing, having been assistant to French director Louis Jouvet (Thatcher 2000: 119). An example of how rhetorical tools and the resulting sense of theatre space are connected is the representation of arrival and departure at the beginning of *None of Us Will Return*: paragraphs that are offset typographically are separated by blank spaces. Through omitted punctuation marks, the narrator shows her uncertainty when choosing the "right" language to tell. The first and sixth paragraphs are connected by the repetition of *il y a* (at the beginning of certain lines); whereas the many *il y a* of the first section present *les gens* (an anonymous mass), the *il y a* of the sixth section are followed by explanatory details of the masses of travelers of different nationalities, countries and in various situations. Thus, two scenes are composed in symmetry and complementarity in relation to each other. The repetition of *il y a* in connection with the frequent use of *ils* (stressed by typography, indented, and mostly without punctuation) suggests an indescribable mass of people and invokes a large place where people arrive and depart from. Thus, Delbo succeeds in visualizing (by near-cinematic means) the forced gathering of Jews in Auschwitz. A number of visual structures reflect in its antithesis violence that precedes death. The second to fifth sections describe a chaotic arrival, while the seventh to ninth sections already give an insight into the everyday hierarchical and organized death ("They [...] walk neatly five by five" (*Auschwitz I*: 6)): "This antithetic parallelism creates a spatialised narrative in a way similar to the various settings or lighting structures on stage." (Thatcher 2000: 133) This scene reminds us of the deportation scenes in *Nuit et Brouillard*. The spatial dimension again evokes the main message:

> together with their children, their wives and their aged parents
> with family mementoes and family papers
> They do not know there is no arriving at this station. (Delbo 1995: 4)

Spatiality is also expressed through connections between words and phrases: "In the morning [...] In the evening [...] At night [...] With the coming of daylight [...] In winter [...] In summer" (Delbo 1995: 4.). These expressions are indented at the beginning of a line and require closer attention from the reader who has to structure the arduous journey and comprehend the fast movement of the train, arrival, and departure; at the same time they suggest temporality that mirrors the overall organization of the process of extermination. For Thatcher this spatiality reminds us again of the theatre: "Although the words on the page have a spatial relationship, in this case one of symmetry and contrast, their semantic aspect also connects them to the temporal dimension, common to narrative prose and theatre." (Thatcher 2000: 134)

3.3 Blank space as a representation of the space of memory and remembrance

Memory is fragmentary. Blanks in memory processes that naturally result from the passing of time or the act of remembering (when some thoughts are rejected and some remembered more accurately) are incorporated into the blank space as representations of the space of memory and remembrance.

Amidst the gruesome camp environment in *Auschwitz and After*, the narrator remembers springtime in Paris – this memory is in total contrast to the reality of the camp and yet the blue sky does not have a soothing effect on the narrator, but only reinforces the reality of the barbed wire fence. The last three phrases demonstrate the reality emphatically: without punctuation, negatives are juxtaposed in the same sentence structure and show that there is no life (*vert, végétal, vivant*) possible, and therefore the typography reflects, through alliteration and statement, the dreary and desolate landscape.

> In the spring, we walk across the Luxembourg gardens [...]. In the spring, the blackbird in the acacia tree beneath my window wakes before dawn. [...] Why am I the only one left with the ability to remember? [...]. The sky was very blue, a blue so blue above the white cement pylons and the white barbed wire, a blue so blue that the web of electric wiring seemed whiter, more implacable
>
>   here nothing is green
>   there is no vegetation
>   here nothing is alive.
>
> Far beyond the barbed wire, spring is flitting, spring is rustling, spring is singing. (Delbo 1995: 111)

A blank page can also illustrate the helplessness of the narrator who cannot put into words the loss of a loved one; therefore, a blank page could be read as an epigraph. For example, one page contains only these lines at the top:

> And you Viva
> and I Charlotte
> who have nothing to love left
> shall soon be dead. (Delbo 1995: 146)

The following lines are also full of perplexity:

> I do not know
> if you can still
> make something of me
> If you have the courage to try... (Delbo 1995: 352)

Elsewhere – in the same typographical style – we read about the narrator's husband:

> My heart dried up
> From love and pain
> From pain and love
> day in day out
> it withered
> slain. (Delbo 1995: 128)

Blank space can also appear between the lines of text on a page: epitomizing topography (cf. *Auschwitz I*: 14), desolation, and emptiness, but also to give a very personal testimonial:

> My mother
> she was hands, a face
> They made our mothers strip in front of us
> Here mothers are no longer mothers to their children. (Delbo 1995: 12)

The blank space gives emphasis to the last line, giving the mother and her emotional and physical relationship to her children a central position. This line not only introduces a broader perspective (from "my mother" to "our mothers" and "mothers"), but the blank space seems to symbolize the narrator preparing herself to conclude her reflection with a more general sentence.

In the fictional realization blank spaces (marked by ellipses) are often used in Aaron's *Refusal* to signify flashback: "She finally perches on the edge of an armchair, (...) 'Whoops, Klara!' She used to leap, legs flying, into any armchair" (Aaron 2008: 18). This blank space ("...") stands for a double return to the past (22): initially, the diarist goes through a change of tenses in the presence of the narrative, then she takes a step further back in time, to before Auschwitz. Horrific memories from the camp are distinguished by ellipses but nevertheless an informative, emotionally charged image of the camp arises ("Women on all fours, licking up some soup that had been split on the ground (...) a woman who'd fallen down and was beeing torn to pieces by a dog, urged on by his SS minder (...) and what Klara had said about the camp where the gipsies were kept, and the gipsy children (...)" (97)). Klara's cruellest decision in Paris seems to be a refusal to see her daughter ("Inside, I'm dead, I taste of death, I reek of it, and shall do for a long time, perhaps for ever (...)" (155)). "[...] I'm not rejecting my daughter. It's myself I'm rejecting, casting myself out of her life for the sake of her life (...)." (155) Finally, Klara reveals the real reason for rejecting motherhood "(...) Back there I had a child, a little boy (...)" (157), but the boy, Ulli, died. When Klara recounts his story, the reader feels the tension of her audience (Angelika and her husband and finally us, readers) through blank spaces that illustrate stunned horror and knowledge how the story ends (158). Each line contains only one or two sentences. Single words are displayed at the beginning of a line and illustrate the strained, chilling atmosphere:

> I had a lump in my throat. Of course we knew what was coming.
> But it had to be said.
> Klara didn't move. She looked beautiful; her features were softened.
> She was calm. We got up to have a drink of water.
> In silence.
> We moved cautiously, almost ceremoniously, Alban and I.
> Klara's eyes followed us. She was waiting.
> We knew what the end would be. We were already
> performing
> the ritual. (Aaron 2008: 160)

In his documentary, Lanzmann creates in the present spaces of memory and remembrance by staging past events through re-living (see Abraham Bomba). *Shoah* illustrates a social upheaval of generations, as the production phase lasted from the mid-1970s to 1980s. This social upheaval is a phase in the memory concept of Aleida and Jan Assmann, in which the content of communicative memory is transmitted in cultural memory: "Thus, collective memory operates simultaneously in two directions: backwards and forwards. It not only reconstructs the past but it also organizes the experience of the present and the future." (Assmann 2011: 28) The challenge lies in the non-experienceable, in non-experienced, the impossibility of a post-experience, an after-feeling of events that exist only medially mediated. *Shoah* is both backward-looking, in that it turns directly to primary witnesses and makes them the essence of the film, and directed towards the present and even towards the future, trying to imply a renewed experience. Just as the film succeeds in merging the gap between the witnesses' past and present, it builds a bridge between temporal fractures.

Today, Auschwitz is a "place of remembrance that marks the space where something meaningful once happened," but at the same time it is a "scene or site of crime that captures the indication of a crime, a person, a life for subsequent witnesses" (Assmann 1994: 17). The creative work of Resnais combines two directions: *témoigner* (to present a historical reality objectively; this is supported by the use of black-and-white material) and *méditer* (Resnais invites the viewer to go beyond this stage, in order to teach them a more general point of view; this is supported by the use of colour sequences) (Pinel 1987: 145).

3.4 Blank space as a representation of narrative space and space of reflection

All survivors had one primary goal, one *désir frénétique* (Robert Antelme): to tell their story to posterity (see Parrau 1995: 13). The blank spaces therefore stand for narration itself, for the process of telling an individual story and history at the same time. All texts and films dealing with the Holocaust try to launch an appeal and/or create a form of dialogue with readers and spectators. In this context, the audience becomes even more important and achieves the status of a co-producer of the text (Barthes 2009).

At the ending of *Nuit et Brouillard*, Resnais uses direct appeals (after several blanks/pauses in the commentary) to the audience ("'I am not responsible' [the *kapo* says]. 'I am not responsible' [the officer says]. 'I am not responsible ...'") and explicitly demands that posterity takes responsibility. The "So who is responsible?" asked over the images of corpses aims directly at the viewer.

The blank space or ellipsis[15] defines narrative sequences and conveys in a visual way the difficulty of representation in Delbo's trilogy. The sentence "None of us will return" on the penultimate page of the first volume (Delbo 1995: 113) corresponds with the "None of us was meant to return" on the last page, not only through sentence structure (the future is transmitted into a conjunctive) and as a continuation or interpretation, but also through arrangement on the page: "None of us will return" is slightly offset to the top running text and is clearly once more referencing the book's title. At the same height on the next page is a commentary to this sentence and to the book as a whole, a conclusion, or a disillusioning general comment. A combination of free lines, isolation and blank spaces is seen, for example, in a direct address to the reader: "Try to look. Just try and see" (Delbo 1995: 84), a sentence that

---

15 From the temporal point of view, the analysis of ellipses comes down to considering the story time elided, and here the first question is whether that duration is indicated (definite ellipses) or not indicated (indefinite ellipses) (Genette 1980: 106).

will be repeated on several following pages. The use of a single line within the prose can be seen particularly in the first part of the trilogy. The offset lines begin a quarter of the page in, putting a spotlight on some gruesome scenes from the camp: a cadaver whose left eye was eaten by a rat; a man being bitten by a dog; a completely exhausted Jewish woman who is dragged to the extermination chamber. Descriptions are short and intense, working on the reader's imagination:

> [...] Blood stains the stripes on his trousers. It seeps from the inside, a stain spreading as though upon a blotter.
> The man goes on walking with the dog's fangs in his flesh.
> Try to look. Just try and see. (Delbo 1995: 85)

And another excerpt:

> A flayed frog. [...] She is howling. Her knees are lacerated by the gravel.
> Try to look. Just try and see. (Delbo 1995: 86)

The offset line is aimed now explicitly at the reader who should not only see, but also understand. Thus, the text and the visible relationship between words on the page show the most horrible experience and deep emotions.

In *Refusal*, Klara's world (forever profoundly affected by her Auschwitz past) is incompatible with the post-war world of the narrator. Klara cannot return to Angelika's world, nor can Angelika put herself in Klara's Auschwitz experience. The two sides, confronted, are also visually illustrated in the text: in the structured form of a diary, Angelika explains and reflects on events, always looking for appropriate and correct language. Klara, however, speaks in fragments about Auschwitz. Elsewhere in the narrative the text imitates the events: the first conversation will take place in a café and the text reflects the confrontation between the two women ("I said," "She said," "I said" etc. get only one line; Aaron 2008: 9), as openness with each other is not yet possible. It seems that Klara wants to assure herself "I have returned." Angelika also tells herself again and again "Klara has returned," a sentence that is offset by the surrounding text and could therefore be read as an independent reflection (Aaron 2008: 25). While Klara reports about her friends and their cruel death (57), Angelika and Alban act only as a background for Klara's notes. This is reflected in the text by two features. Firstly, Angelika and Alban ask very short questions, but on the other hand – marked in each case by a paragraph – Angelika's growing horror becomes visible in the text. Silence and disbelief characterize these insertions; these blank spaces are spaces of reflection and at the same time mirror the immensity of horror that cannot be expressed.

We must have looked puzzled.

KLARA: – In Polish it means the woman in charge of a female block of prisoners – the chief (*blockova*). [...] A good chief is rare. My friend from Prague was like your colleague.
I: – Where is she now?
SHE: – Dead.
Silence.
I: – What about your other friends? [...]
SHE: – Yes a midwife. She killed several children.
We fell silent. [...]
KLARA: – She gave them injections when she could; otherwise, she strangled them... to save the mother... [...] In the winter of '44.

We were silent again. Later:

– What about the one from Linz? – I asked.
– The little one, the youngest, she was only twenty. She died in the winter of '44 too. It was the typhus that killed her as well. The typhus and I.
We were still silent, just looking at her.
[...]
Silence from us. Then, because one had to go through with it. (Aaron 2008: 57–58)

Testimony is always linked with the act of seeing. In *Shoah* there are three groups of witnesses: the victims, the perpetrators, and the bystanders. The only thing they have in common is that each group does not see certain things, they differ in their particular positions of not seeing, "not simply as witnesses, but as witnesses who *do not witness*" (Felman 1992: 211). They take a look at a reference object, the Holocaust, that is not present – a blank space, a "[...] blank space that can't be filled. A testimony of the inside [...] still isn't possible" (Lange 1999: 144). This blank space is in the centre of the documentation and all witnesses try to approach this centre. By telling their personal stories the witnesses also tell history: "One cannot know, what one cannot imagine" (Lanzmann 2010: 148). The primacy lies with the witnesses, their efforts to remember and to tell. The factual historical knowledge becomes then a strategy, an instrument for the witnesses to give testimony and pass on knowledge. Additionally, "witness statements ... aren't monologues" (Laub 2000: 80). An essential aspect of the testimony, besides the act of seeing, is speech – because the narrative arises in listening and in being heard. Listeners are essential for creating a testimony, so they have a particular responsibility towards the survivors, a *secondary testimony*. Listening thus becomes a tightrope walk between sensitivity and stimulation: "And this is exactly the strength of films like *Shoah* – they work solely with imagination." (Lanzmann in Corell 1990: 121) Witnesses are often shown in a "talking heads" television show format. It is noticeable that the camera zooms closer when witnesses' stories are personal and emotional, to come close to the witness. Lanzmann often asks for detailed descriptions and minute details, and does not allow an escape or a non-answer. Hence the frequent criticism that Lanzmann applies pressure and violence towards the witnesses. He sets the survivors in the scene ("it was necessary to transform the people into actors" (Lanzmann in Corell 1990: 123)), he stages their memory. His intention is to overcome stereotypical factual knowledge towards an actual reliving, to a "realization of the past, an incarnation and forming of memory" (Lanzmann 2010: 150).

4 *Zachor*! Blank spaces enabling remembrance

> "Literature was not ready for such procedures [the events of the Second World War] and hasn't developped any methods/means [of describing] them."[16]

The use of blank spaces tackles this fundamental problem on different levels. Blank spaces are on the one hand an admission that it is impossible to actually represent the Holocaust. On the other hand, the use of blank spaces – assuming an active reader – is a literary-esthetic means of conveying various implications, as I have tried to demonstrate in this chapter.

Both texts and films attempt to evoke the "blank space" Holocaust by literary and cinematic means and therefore negate an explicit description of the incidents in order to formulate a direct appeal to posterity: *zachor!* (remember!) is the basic message of the texts and films discussed here and of the blank spaces they contain. The reader and the audience are instructed to assume responsibility.

For a further pursuit of this subject it would be interesting to look at the second generation, the children of Holocaust victims, for example George Perec and Raymond Federman, who use blank spaces (or even blank pages) to explain whole (personal and historical) correlations: persecution, extermination, but also oblivion, displacement and the non-spoken and very personal concerns (Federman 1979, Perec 2003). A comparison of first-, second- and third-generation survivor texts and films would be an enrichment of present studies.

---

[16] Bertolt Brecht, cited in Klein (1992: 11).

Works cited

Aaron, Soazig (2008) *Refusal* (London: Vintage).
Assmann, Aleida (1994) "Das Gedächtnis der Orte" [The memory of places], *DVjs* 68, Special issue, 17–35.
Assmann, Jan (2011) *Cultural Memory and Early Civilization: Writing, Remembrance, and Political Imagination* (Cambridge: Cambridge University Press).
Avisar, Ilan (1988) *Screening the Holocaust. Cinema's Images of the Unimaginable* (Indiana: Indiana University Press).
Baer, Ulrich (ed) (2000) *Niemand zeugt für den Zeugen. Erinnerungskultur und historische Verantwortung nach der Shoa* [Nobody testifies for the witness. Memorial culture and historical responsibility after the Holocaust], (Frankfurt am Main: Suhrkamp).
Barthes, Roland (2009) "The Death of the Author," in *Image, Music, Text*, trans. Steven Heath (New York: Hill and Wang), 142–148.
Bazin, André (1987) "Nuit et Brouillard," in *Nuit et Brouillard by Alain Resnais. On the Making, Reception and Functions of a Major Documentary Film*, ed. Richard Raskin (Aarhus: Aarhus University Press), 139.
Binder, Anne-Berenike (2008) *"Mon ombre est restée là-bas." – Literarische und mediale Formen des Erinnerns in Raum und Zeit* [Literary and medial forms of remembering in time and space], (Tübingen: Niemeyer and Romania Judaica), 8.
Binder, Anne-Berenike (2011) "'Les ruines d'Auschwitz' – Stadtentwürfe in der französischen Nachkriegsliteratur" ["Les ruines d'Auschwitz' – Visions of cities in French literature after the war], in *Literarische Stadtutopien zwischen totalitärer Gewalt und Ästhetisierung*, ed. Barbara Ventarola (München: Martin Meidenbauer Verlag), 267–293.
Caruth, Cathy (ed) (1995) *Trauma. Explorations in Memory* (Baltimore: Johns Hopkins University Press).
Colombat, André Pierre (1993) *The Holocaust in French Film* (Metuchen: Scarecrow Press).
Corell, C. (2009) *Der Holocaust als Herausforderung für den Film. Formen des filmischen Umgangs mit der Shoah seit 1945. Eine Wirkungstypologie* [The challenges of the Holocaust. Representations of the Holocaust in film since 1945], (Bielefeld: Transcript).
Delbo, Charlotte (1995) *Auschwitz and After* (New Heaven: Yale University Press).
Dotzler, Bernhard J. (1999) "Leerstellen" [Blank spaces], in *Literaturwissenschaft. Einführung in ein Sprachspiel*, ed. Heinrich Bosse and Ursula Renner (Freiburg: Rombach), 211–229.
Eco, Umberto (1990) *Lector in fabula. Die Mitarbeit der Interpretation in erzählenden Texten* [Lector in fabula], (München: Hanser).
Federman, Raymond (1979) *The Voice in the Closet* (Madison, WI: Coda Press).
Felman, Shoshana (2000) "The Return of the Voice: Claude Lanzmann's *Shoah*," *Yale French Studies* 97, 103–150.
Felman, Shoshana and Dori Laub (eds) (1992) *Testimony: Crises of Witnessing in Literature, Psychoanalysis and History* (New York: Routledge).
Genette, Gérard (1980) *Narrative Discourse: An Essay in Method* (Ithaca: Cornell University Press).
Insdorf, Annette (2003) *Indelible Shadows. Film and the Holocaust*, 3rd edn (Cambridge: Cambridge University Press).
Iser, Wolfgang (1970) *Die Appellstruktur der Texte* [Appelative structure of texts], (Konstanz: Universitätsverlag).

Iser, Wolfgang (1978) *The Act of Reading. A Theory of Aesthetic Response* (Baltimore and London: The Johns Hopkins University Press).
Iser, Wolfgang (1984) *Der Akt des Lesens. Theorie ästhetischer Wirkung* [The act of reading. Theories of aesthetic effect], 2nd edn (München: Fink).
Iser, Wolfgang (1994) *Der Akt des Lesens* [The act of reading], 4th edn (München: Fink).
Klein, Judith (1992) *Literatur und Genozid. Darstellungen der nationalsozialistischen Massenvernichtung in der französischen Literatur* [Literature and genocide. Representations of national socialist mass extermination in French literature], (Wien, Köln and Weimar: Böhlau).
Kramer, Sven (1999) *Auschwitz im Widerstreit. Zur Darstellung der Shoa in Film, Philosophie und Literatur* [Auschwitz in contradiction. Representations of the Holocaust in film, philosophy, and literature], (Wiesbaden: Deutscher Universitäts-Verlag).
Lange, Sigrid (1999) *Authentisches Medium. Faschismus und Holocaust in ästhetischen Darstellungen der Gegenwart* [Authentic media. Fascism and the Holocaust in contemporary aesthetic representations], (Bielefeld: Aisthesis-Verlag).
Langer, Lawrence (1978) *The Age of Atrocity. Death in Modern Literature* (Boston: Beacon Press).
Lanzmann, Claude (2000) "Der Ort und das Wort" [The place and the word], in *"Niemand zeugt für den Zeugen." Erinnerungskultur und historische Verantwortung nach der Shoah*, ed. Ulrich Baer (Frankfurt am Main: Suhrkamp), 101–118.
Lanzmann, Claude (2010) "Der Tod ist ein Skandal: Gespräch mit Claude Lanzmann" [Death is a scandal: a conversation with Claude Lanzmann], *Spiegel* 36, 147–150.
Laub, Dori (2000) "Zeugnis ablegen oder Die Schwierigkeiten des Zuhörens" [Testifying or the difficulty of listening], in *"Niemand zeugt für den Zeugen." Erinnerungskultur und historische Verantwortung nach der Shoah*, ed. Ulrich Baer (Frankfurt am Main: Suhrkamp), 68–83.
Night and Fog (1956) Dir. Alain Resnais. Narr. Michel Bouquet (Argos Films).
Parrau, Alain (1995) *Écrire les camps* [Writing the camps], (Paris: Éditions Belin).
Perec, Georges (2003) *W, or the Memory of Childhood* (Boston: Verba Mundi Books).
Pinel, Vincent (1987) "'Nuit et Brouillard.' Institut des Hautes Etudes Cinématographiques. Fiche Filmographique (No 163)," in *Nuit et Brouillard by Alain Resnais. On the Making, Reception and Functions of a Major Documentary Film*, ed. Richard Raskin (Aarhus: Aarhus University Press), 142–146.
Reif, Danielle (2005) *Die Ästhetik der Leerstelle. Raymond Federmans Roman "La Fourrure de ma tante Rachel"* [The aesthetics of blank spaces. Raymond Federman's novel "La Fourrure de ma tante Rachel"], (Würzburg: Königshausen & Neumann).
Roumette, Sylvain (1961) "Alain Resnais à la question" [Questioning Alain Resnais], *Premier plan* 18, 36–54.
Semprún, Jorge (1994) *L'Écriture ou la Vie* [Writing or living], (Paris: Gallimard).
Shoah (1985) Dir. Claude Lanzmann (New Yorker Films).
Sofsky, Wolfgang (1997) *The Order of Terror: The Concentration Camp* (Princeton: Princeton University Press).
Steiner, George (1984) *A Reader* (New York: Oxford University Press).
Thatcher, Nicole (2000) *A Literary Analysis of Charlotte Delbo's Concentration Camp Re-presentation* (New York: Edwin Mellen Press).
van der Knaap, Ewout (2002) "Monument des Gedächtnisses: Der Beitrag von 'Nacht und Nebel' zum Holocaust-Diskurs" [Monuments of memory: the contribution of 'Night and

Fog' to the Holocaust discourse], in *Geschichte im Film. Mediale Inszenierungen des Holocaust und kulturelles Gedächtnis*, ed. Waltraud "Wara" Wende (Stuttgart: Metzler), 67–75.

Wormser, Olga and Henri Michel (eds) (1955) *Tragédie de la déportation 1940–1945: Témoignages de survivants des camps de concentration allemands* [The tragedy of the deportations 1940–1945: Witness accounts of survivors of German concentration camps], (Paris: Hachette).

Young, James Edward (1988) *Writing and Rewriting the Holocaust. Narrative and the Consequences of Interpretation* (Bloomington: Indiana University Press).

Arkadiusz Morawiec
Konzentrationslager in Polish Literature: From Metaphorization to Metaphor

1 Concentration camp as a "literature-genic" place

Tadeusz Szymański, a former prisoner of Auschwitz, who later worked in the Auschwitz-Birkenau State Museum as curator for the collection of works of art created in the concentration camp, once stated: "There is no other place that would be as 'literature-genic' as this camp" (Kąkolewski 1976: 317). It is, of course, possible to extend this observation to all, not necessarily Nazi, death camps, concentration camps, and forced labor camps. Writing, both inside and outside the camps, was motivated by a desire to bear witness, to denounce the people who were responsible for these crimes, to leave a warning for posterity, to attempt to explain and understand this phenomenon, and to develop a defense mechanism that would protect the writer against the nightmare of the camp, and help them escape it. These factors correspond to the following functions of camp literature: documentary, ethical, and therapeutic.

What gave rise to Polish *Lager* literature, i.e. literature about Nazi camps and literature written in these camps (Soviet camps are the domain of Gulag literature), was, rather surprisingly, the concern of Hitler's regime about its own image. In 1936 Jerzy Rogowicz wrote a feature about the Dachau concentration camp and published it in a Polish daily, *Kurier Warszawski* (Rogowicz 1936). Rogowicz was probably the first and only Polish journalist who was given an opportunity to see a concentration camp from the perspective of a non-prisoner. At the Munich Political Police Department he was given a pass that allowed him to enter the camp as an observer. In his article Rogowicz admits he was aware that, being shown around by SS men, he participated in a staged farce. Thus, he is scathing about those who built the camp and camp officers. He condemns them and is often alarmed. Still, his article draws a veil of silence over the extreme terror that can be found in later, war and post-war accounts. The reason why Rogowicz's article appears not to be informed by a desire to unmask the truth might be the fact that from 26 January 1934 Poland and Germany were bound by a non-aggression pact. In this declaration both parties agreed on the issue of "moral disarmament," which was supposed to prevent anti-German and anti-Polish propaganda in the press, radio, cinema, and theatre. It was not until Hitler abrogated the non-aggression pact on

28 April 1939 and Germany embarked on an anti-Polish campaign that the abuses of Hitler's regime were openly denounced. One example of this change in attitude is a reportage-style article entitled *W niemieckich obozach koncentracyjnych* ("In German concentration camps"; 1939), which was printed before the outbreak of the Second World War, or Władysław Wójcik's memoir of his internment in the Buchenwald concentration camp, where he spent several months, entitled *Byłem w piekle...* ("I was in hell..."; Wójcik 1939).[1] It is also crucial to mention Stanisław Nogaj's articles, collected in two volumes, which described life "behind the bars and barbed wires" of the Third Reich on the basis of the accounts by former prisoners (Nogaj 1937, 1939). In 1940, in German-occupied Poland, Nogaj was arrested by the Gestapo and sent to the Gusen concentration camp. He wrote about his experience in a book entitled *Gusen*, published soon after the war had ended (Nogaj 1945–1946). Let us, however, focus on the Second World War.

Polish *Lager* literature was mostly created by the numerous writers who had been imprisoned in Nazi camps. The second group of authors were those who started writing in the camps or, more often, after their release (they often authored only one book). The third group were writers who did not have any first-hand experience of Nazi camps (in fact, it is more adequate to classify their texts as literature *about* the *Lager*) (Morawiec 2009: 29–129). Rogowicz, who visited a concentration camp voluntarily, is an exception in this respect. Writers who had already debuted before being arrested, and who survived a Nazi concentration camp, are, among others: Tadeusz Borowski, Kornel Filipowicz, Zofia Kossak, Gustaw Morcinek, Tadeusz Nowakowski, Marian Pankowski, Zofia Romanowiczowa, Seweryna Szmaglewska, and Henryk Vogler. Other writers, such as Janusz Krasiński and Andrzej Kuśniewicz, debuted after they had left the camp. The majority of the writers who survived left written accounts of their concentration camp experiences. Some started writing already in the camps. Thus, even before testimonies of concentration camp survivors were published, the reality of the *Konzentrationslager* [2] had been preserved in literature written in these camps.

Poetry was the dominant form of *Lager* literature, created in extreme conditions. This is because of the obstacles to composing longer works, such as prose or dramatic texts. These obstacles were, for instance, related to certain practicalities – pencils and paper were scarce in Nazi camps (possessing writing materials was forbidden and could lead to various forms of punishment and repression,

---

[1] The last installment of the memoir was published on the day of the outbreak of the Second World War.
[2] German: concentration camp.

including death). Furthermore, short texts could be stored in a considerably easy (and safe) way – also in one's memory.

Polish concentration camp poetry was very traditional rather than innovative or outstanding. On the one hand, there were writers who used it to escape from the terrible reality of a concentration camp into a fictional world – they expressed longing for their native country, home, family or nature, or sought consolation in memories of the past. On the other hand, apart from these examples of "pure poetry," there were more numerous texts that centered on all aspects of life in a concentration camp: roll calls, labor, hunger, torture, death, and unusual events (e.g. escapes or public executions).

The very few authors who were released from Nazi camps brought back literary texts, mostly poems, which were usually inscribed in their memory. The underground resistance movement in Auschwitz was interested in prisoners' poetry and considered it documentary evidence: this status was, for instance, given to Krystyna Żywulska's poem *List niewysłany* ("A letter never sent;" Lebda-Wyborna 1975: 12–13). Making his escape from Auschwitz, Konstanty Jagiełło, member of the resistance movement, took with him not only photographic plates and documents, but also a poem entitled *Oświęcim* ("Auschwitz"), which alludes to the practice of burning piles of bodies at Birkenau (Lebda-Wyborna 1975: 24). Manuscripts were secretly passed on to the outside world in the Janowska concentration camp in Lwów (Lemberg and Lviv; Borwicz 1946: 25). The few poems smuggled from Nazi camps were printed in underground anthologies *Krwawe i zielone* ("Bloody and green;" Staich 1943) and *Z otchłani* ("From the abyss;" Wajdelota 1944). (Once the war had ended, a great number of works created in concentration camps came to light.[3]) These texts served as a source of inspiration for other literary works. They were sources of information about Nazi camps, yet not the most significant ones. Much more could be learnt from the accounts given by civilian employees of German companies that provided various services in Nazi camps, from prisoners' letters smuggled outside, from oral and written reports and accounts of those who escaped or were released from the camps, and – above all – from the articles, brochures, and books that were secretly printed in occupied Poland or published in exile, mostly in Great Britain, the United States, the Middle East, and the Soviet Union.[4] Materials that were distributed abroad often used Polish sources or even contained full reprints of Polish underground publications.

---

3 See, for example, Hołuj (1945), Lurczyński (1945), Borwicz (1947).
4 See, for example, Z. B. (1941), *Wyzwolenie przychodzi ze śmiercią (Relacja z Oświęcimia)* ("Liberation comes with death (A report from Auschwitz);" 1942), Bielecki (1944).

An underground publication that should be mentioned in this context is the first brochure on Auschwitz entitled *Oświęcim: Pamiętnik więźnia* ("Auschwitz: Diary of a Prisoner;" Krahelska 1942). Printed in 1942 and edited by the novelist Halina Krahelska, the brochure was based on reports of former Auschwitz prisoners, mainly on the oral account given by Władysław Bartoszewski. *Oświęcim* has a considerable documentary value but of equal importance are its ideological overtones. The brochure aptly combines demythologization with the (more important) propagandist, didactic, and hortative functions ("the nation will survive and Poland will rise!"). Hence, according to the "diary," Polish society's treatment of all prisoners

> [...] as national heroes and attributing to them some kind of superhuman dedication, patriotism, bravery, valor, etc. is at odds with the objective truth that the inmates are ordinary, today very unhappy, people; they are forced to endure terrible conditions, which in some awaken heroic potential and in others arouse basest instincts, but in most cases their self-preservation instinct leads them to find ways to survive. (Krahelska 1985: 29)

2 The "appropriateness" of fiction

One may expect that, having faced the reality of concentration camps, Polish literature should be dominated by documentary texts. Articles, reports, and memoirs were already being published before the outbreak of the Second World War, and the latter two continued to be published during the war (Trepiński 1943; Wiernik 1944). These works include pieces of great literary value,[5] many of which lean towards literary fiction (for instance, some elements of fiction are present in Krahelska's *Diary of a Prisoner*, which was fashioned to resemble a death-bed confession). Concentration camp reality serves in these works as a pretext for philosophical, moral, and social reflection.

Written in 1942 (published in 1945) and frequently read at secret literary meetings, Jerzy Andrzejewski's short story entitled *Apel* ("Roll call") is one of the earliest, and best, strictly literary (fiction) works that depict a concentration camp. The story is allegedly based on facts. However, Andrzejewski treats the camp more like a tool (or a background) than a historical place. He focuses mostly on axiological issues. The characters, who participate in a roll call that takes place at night, are forced to make dramatic existential choices. *Apel* is an example of psychological and moralistic fiction. The concentration camp is

---

[5] See Kossak (1942), particularly the chapter "Normalny obozowy dzień" ("An ordinary day in the camp"), and Zarembina (1942).

depicted as a crucible in which fear, loneliness, and suffering are distilled. These feelings either give ultimate meaning to one's life or they evaporate, and the only thing that remains is senseless pain. Virtue eventually prevails, and so does the writer's belief that it is possible to remain human regardless of the circumstances. Anthropocentric humanism – solidarity, dignity, love, and compassion – serves in the story as the absolute measure of values. Another work from that period that deserves our attention, albeit itself of little literary value, is the anonymous *Obóz w Oświęcimiu* ("The camp in Oświęcim"). Presented in 1942 in an underground magazine *Wojsko i Niepodległość*, it was probably the first purely literary text published in Polish that addressed the issue of concentration camps. Another, more successful short story is *Biała noc* ("White Night") by Juliusz Kydryński. It was written in 1942, after Kydryński had been released from Auschwitz, and printed in 1943 in an underground monthly, *Miesięcznik Literacki* (Kydryński 1943). Like in Andrzejewski's *Apel*, the concentration camp, with all its terror, serves in *Biała noc* as a glass retort in which the characters' humanity – seemingly irrecoverable – is distilled.

A crucial change in the way in which *Konzentrationslagers* and death camps were presented took place after the Red Army had entered the abandoned Majdanek concentration camp (on 23 July 1944) and later discovered the sites of former death camps (e.g. Treblinka), and after other Nazi camps, including Auschwitz, had been liberated. Numerous war crime testimonies, reports from liberated camps (e.g. by Jerzy Putrament, 1944) and eyewitness testimonies, including texts of literary value, such as, for instance, Seweryna Szmaglewska's *Dymy nad Birkenau* (*Smoke over Birkenau*, 1945),[6] appeared in official publications. They were distributed to the community in exile and on the territory of present-day Poland, which was then still occupied by the Soviet Army. In a collection of short stories (which read like reportage) entitled *Medaliony* (*Medallions*), written in the spring and summer of 1945 and published a year later, Zofia Nałkowska states: "We are learning new details from prisoners returning now to Poland from the German camps, from Dachau and Oranienburg, and this information augments our knowledge of the facts." (2000: 46)

People soon realized that this "literature-genic place," to borrow Szymański's term, which Polish readers gradually began discovering in more detail, could inspire texts that approach this subject matter in an inadequate or even inappropriate way. One example of what was then considered inappropriate was the "cynical" attitude of Tadeusz Borowski, who in 1947 reviewed Zofia Kossak's memoirs of Birkenau, entitled *Z otchłani* (*From the Abyss: Memories from*

---

[6] The book was entered as evidence in the records of the Nuremberg Trials.

the Camp). He criticized Kossak's martyrological perspective and her perception of the concentration camp, which accentuated the suffering and solidarity of the victims. Borowski, who survived Auschwitz, believed that a writer had a duty to examine their own conscience: one could survive imprisonment in such an inhumane place only at the expense of others (Borowski 1947). This is what he shows in his bold short stories published in collections *Pożegnanie z Marią* (*Farewell to Maria*) and *Kamienny świat* (*World of Stone*; Borowski 1948a, 1948b).[7]

Writers also faced other objections. In 1946, Ewa Korzeniewska wrote:

> It would be inappropriate to transform the story of German oppression into a crime novel – it seems improper to bring individual experience to the fore. Finally, we are appalled by what does not do justice to history – using events that took place during the occupation [of Poland – ed.] as arguments to support the author's theses, or as tools which help to convey the inner complexity of literary characters. (Korzeniewska 1946: 7)

Many years later, Andrzej Werner maintained that in Andrzejewski's *Apel* the concentration camp plays a secondary role and serves to expose an old moral problem. He added: "However, one can also thus interpret works based on personal experience" (1971: 18). Korzeniewska, a Marxist critic, was troubled by a psychological approach (an image of reality filtered through subjective lens), which she considered inappropriate. Undoubtedly, however, the pretextual quality referred to by both Werner and Korzeniewska is integral to the concentration camp, because on the one hand, we do not have at our disposal the kind of language that would describe the unique (specific) reality of a *Konzentrationslager*, and on the other hand, the concentration camp tends to be perceived as a sort of model of the world.

Tadeusz Hołuj, writer and concentration camp prisoner, declared that the truth about Auschwitz is simple: "Human life in a concentration camp [...] did not differ in any significant way from normal life, if we disconnect it from the specific temporal context. It contained all the basic elements of normal life – they were only extremely concentrated and intensified." (1947: 139)

Krystyna Żywulska approaches this issue in a similar way: "It is impossible to see a naked human being anywhere else. In any kind of civilized conditions, human beings always mask themselves. Here, they have to show their real selves." (1946: 150) What corresponds to this perception of a Nazi camp as a concentrated, heightened or naked reality which exemplifies a universalizing attitude, is a tendency to inscribe this reality into a long line of events such as

---

[7] The first short stories about Nazi camps by Borowski were published in a literary magazine *Twórczość* in 1946, no. 4.

the tragic fate of those who built the pyramids of Egypt, the human sacrifices of the Aztecs, or slavery.

Adopting a perspective which seeks to find a point of reference is often treated as indicative of relativism. One should, however, ask whether a tendency to treat Nazi death camps and the present times in general as particularly cruel is not an exaggeration, the result of historical distance between us and the past with its own crimes. Mass murders occurred throughout human history. In the seventeenth century nearly all Native Americans of Virginia were slayed. In the nineteenth and at the beginning of the twentieth century mass crimes were committed in Africa (Morawiec 2017: 225–239). At the turn of the twentieth century, the German colonial army methodically exterminated the Herero and Nama tribes in Namibia. Herero survivors were imprisoned in concentration camps: inmates were registered, forced to perform hard labor and subjected to medical experiments (Wojnar 2005: 36–41). Yet these crimes, like other cases of genocide, were not as shocking to the public as Nazi camps and the Holocaust have been. The trauma that shaped the social and cultural beliefs of the West and that resulted from the uncovering of Nazi crimes (thanks to the growth of mass media), as well as the use of new tools and technologies in genocide, were the reasons that concentration camps, death camps and the Holocaust have been depicted as unprecedented, monstrous, and unique events in the history of mankind. This gives rise to a certain prohibition. Michał Głowiński cautions: "These events should not be trivialized or domesticated by making references to anything else." (Grupińska 2001: 15) Still, is it possible to avoid this alleged or actual trivialization? Is there a language that does not domesticate this reality? After all, the very act of writing narratives that attempt to capture concentration camp reality entails obscuring its uniqueness.

3 In search of a new language

Analyzing literary works written in Nazi camps, Michał Borwicz accentuates the difference between the experience of an extreme reality and the way this experience is conveyed by language. In response to the "surreal" categories of thinking typical of the concentration camp environment, writers tended to use clear wording, simple syntax, and trivial concepts. They attempted to reconstruct the traditional links between words and objects (Borwicz 1946: 53). Commenting on Borwicz's arguments, Czesław Miłosz maintains that extreme experiences were usually passed on in a conventional, inherited language: language could not keep up with the experience and therefore retreated and took recourse to familiar motifs and formulas (Miłosz 1986: 164). This situation concerned not only people who started writing in response to an extreme situation, but also experienced writers. The motifs and metaphors most often used to represent the world of *Konzentrationslagers* in both reports and fiction were: the Last Judgment (Borowski's *The people who were walking* ["Ludzie, którzy szli"]), the Passion (Ernst Wiechert's *Forest of the Dead*), "an awry world" (Jorge Semprún's *The Long Voyage*), and *theatrum mundi*, which was a response to the unreal aspects of life in a concentration camp (Primo Levi's *If This is a Man*). Above all, the most common motif was that of hell, which was frequently juxtaposed with the recurrent theme of paradise/Arcadia (Zofia Posmysz's *Wakacje nad Adriatykiem* ("Holidays by the Adriatic Sea")).

A prisoner of Buchenwald ironically writes in a letter to his wife: "I've just started Dante's *Divine Comedy*. It is a difficult but fully satisfying book" (quoted in Czarnecki and Zonik 1969: 391). Still, in mid-twentieth century, Dante's vision of hell became outdated and was replaced by "planet Auschwitz" (Pankowski 2000: 30). "Hell" was perceived as the domain of "literature" (Posmysz 1962: 38). As an Auschwitz *Sonderkommando* member comments, "this is a totally different world – this world, if you wish, is simply hell; Dante's vision, when compared with this real hell, is incomparably ridiculous" (Herman 1971: 179).

Thus, regardless of moral or ideological reservations, the most common motif in *Lager* literature begins to emerge. The concentration camp becomes a symbol, a literary device. It enters the world of archetypes and becomes universalized. Thus, the words of Alvin Rosenfeld, who professed that one of the most significant characteristics of Holocaust literature and its most important rule is that there are no metaphors for Auschwitz, just as Auschwitz is not a metaphor for anything else (2003: 41), can only be considered as a proposition (and a prohibition). By contrast, Imre Kertész states that in European consciousness Auschwitz has become a timeless parable that bears the stigma of immortality (2004: 33), while the Serbian writer Marija Knežević, in an essay about the recent war in former Yugoslavia, considers a concentration camp as the key metaphor of the twentieth century (1997: 16). Hence, the problem consists not so much in the universalization, as in the misuse of the theme of Nazi camps.

4 Concentration camp as a metaphor

In general and simple terms, one may say that literature created by prisoners and former inmates of concentration camps used a broadly conceived metaphor to describe life in the camp, whereas authors who did not have any direct concentration camp experience often used the camp (the concentration camp reality) as a metaphor that served to describe their own, contemporary reality. At the same time, increasingly often concentration camps become an argument in ideological debates or a tool of provocation. One may say that, placed between these two ends of the spectrum (which can also be presented diachronically: from the metaphorization of a *Konzentrationslager* to the *Konzentrationslager* as a metaphor), concentration camp serves as a theme that offers a pretext for philosophical, historiosophical, social and moral reflections, and which is often explored in an intentionally sensationalist plot.

One example of this phenomenon of using a concentration camp as, above all, a literary theme is a tendency to focus on "the other side" of a *Konzentrationslager*, which emerged in Polish literature of the 1960s. Numerous works published at that time show an image of the oppressor – a camp officer. We find him in the following novels: Zofia Posmysz's *Pasażerka* ("The woman passenger"), Stanisław Grochowiak's *Trismus*, Kornel Filipowicz's *Ogród pana Nietschke* ("Mr Nietschke's garden"), and Jan Dobraczyński's *Doścignięty* ("Captured"). This tendency was shaped by, for instance: the publication of the memoirs of Rudolf Höss (1956), Auschwitz commandant, the trial of Adolf Eichmann in 1961 and the no less spectacular Frankfurt Trial of Auschwitz personnel, held in 1963–1965. These events brought awareness to contemporary society that mass crimes were also committed and overseen by ordinary people, and that the evil of these crimes was, to use Hannah Arendt's words, banal. Thus, the theme of banal evil was (also for writers) no less fascinating than the idea of "demonic" evil, explored, for instance, in Alexander Czerski's novel *Nieśmiertelni* ("The immortal").

In recent years, and particularly since censorship (particularly severe in the case of writings that made historical references) in Poland was abolished in 1990, memoirs of Nazi camp survivors are still being published. The documentary function is also performed by texts that are classed as literature, for instance, Henryk Grynberg's and Ida Fink's short stories or Irit Amiel's poetry.[8] These writers do not intend to use the Nazi camp as a tool. They approach the concentration camp reality in a direct, literal manner, though usually from the perspective of another (that of the eye witness and participant in the events) or from a temporal distance (all these authors encountered the Holocaust when they were young, but avoided deportation to a concentration camp). The situation is different, for

---

8 See *Ja jestem z Oświęcimia* ("I am from Auschwitz") and *Szkic węgierski* ("A Hungarian sketch") in Grynberg (1997); *Dłoń* ("The hand"), *Nocne wariacje na temat* ("Nocturnal variations on a theme") and *Zmartwychwstanie piekarza* ("The baker's ongoing resurrection") in Fink (1996); and Amiel (1994, 1998, 2002).

instance, in the case of Ewa Lipska, who was born right after the war. In her poem *Sklepy zoologiczne* ("Pet shops"), published at the turn of the twenty-first century, Auschwitz becomes a tool of a peculiar discourse: the world and social life are compared to a concentration camp. Lipska composed an emotionally motivated, poetic enthymeme – pet shops with enslaved animals, which she saw in her childhood, depress her. She recalls "Verdun mousetraps / and so on until Auschwitz," and concludes with an existential punch line: "I'd no idea how it would end / when I signed up for life. / As a volunteer." (2002: 37)

Rosenfeld notes that the problem of metaphorization is most conspicuous in poetry, where the motif of ghettos and camps is frequently used not so much as a means of expressing the pain of history,[9] but as a way to describe personal suffering. This tendency can make poetry more powerful, but it may also breed pathology: concentration camp as a hyperbole is an exemplar of history being dominated by hysteria (Rosenfeld 2003: 232–233, 240). Such a hyperbolic and hysterical depiction of reality is not unique to poetry. Artist Jerzy Nowosielski (born 1923), for instance, declared: "All nature, all evolution and all life are one great Auschwitz." (Podgórzec 1993: 20) These words may remind one of Czesław Miłosz's poem *Przyrodzie – pogróżka* ("A threat to nature"). Written in 1944, it contains this disturbing verse: "Dachau of grasshoppers! Ants' Auschwitz!" (Miłosz 2011: 289) It is also conspicuous that anti-abortion campaigners speak of the "holocaust of babies," while animal rights activists use the term "animal Auschwitz" (Hartmann 1994: 15).[10] The latter metaphor inspired some episodes in an allegorical, socially engaged and accusatory novel by Bogdan Loebl (born 1932), *Dymek mesjasz zwierząt* ("Smoky, the animals' Messiah"). The eponymous character is a dog that is badly treated by humans. In this context, it is useful to quote an excerpt that conveys the message of the novel particularly well:

> This is one of countless death camps for animals – said Smoky. – Recently people have shed oceans of anniversary tears over the victims of death camps for humans, but they do not weep over the death of animals, which have been murdered and are still being

---

[9] In Polish poetry an expression of the pain of history can, for instance, be found in the works of writers who experienced the war and German occupation – in Jerzy Ficowski's poems, Wisława Szymborska's *Obóz głodowy pod Jasłem* ("Hunger camp at Jaslo"), Julian Przyboś's *Oświęcim* ("Auschwitz") and in numerous poems by Tadeusz Różewicz, such as *Masakra chłopców* ("Massacre of the boys").

[10] In J.M. Coetzee's essay *Elizabeth Costello* (2003), which pretends to be a novel, the eponymous writer, who is a vegetarian, speaks of a "holocaust" in an academic lecture which centers on human violence towards animals, making a reference to Treblinka and concentration camps.

murdered every day. In the full majesty of human law, they build new camps and improve the methods of killing our brethren. (Loebl 2008: 49)

In this novel the characters, who are animals, use such expressions as "death camps for chickens," "death camps for chinchillas."[11]

What informs the poem *Plakat* ("Poster") by Filip Zawada (born 1983) is undoubtedly (hyper) sensitivity and the Polish model of education and culture, which still shapes young people's imagination by recalling the events of the Second World War. In the poem the use of the word "camp" – which once evoked "so many beautiful associations" (Kossak 1946: 1), especially with scouting and scout camps – is truly surprising:

> It was already dark when on the poster
> the fluorescent process
> proceeded slowly
> CAMPS FOR CHILDREN
> with a German language course. (Zawada 1999: 50)

If we consider this poem as an expression or indication of a Polish memory discourse, in which Nazi crimes occupy a special place, then *Absolutna amnezja* ("Absolute amnesia"; 1995), a novel by Izabela Filipiak (born 1961), serves as an example of an ideologically charged use of a Nazi camp, a peculiar displacement of Nazi camp reality. What motivates this approach? For Rosenfeld, concentration camps are an example of extreme human cruelty and therefore cannot serve as a background to other social problems (Rosenfeld 2003: 224). However, Filipiak's feminist novel avers that most people did not pay any attention to the fact that "the architects of the Third Reich were all men" (Chicago 1993: 5). The line of thinking that informs such a "discovery" verges on creating a reality in which patriarchal oppression is depicted as a *Konzentrationslager*.

Literary works that center on the Holocaust or concentration camps, or any other topic which is equally crucial in historical, social, moral and ideological terms, often draw criticism. Readers, for instance, disapproved of Paul Celan's poem *Fugue of Death*, Borowski's short stories, Sylvia Plath's poems *Daddy* and *Lady Lazarus*, William Styron's novel *Sophie's Choice* and Jonathan Littell's book, *The Kindly Ones*. These and many other authors were accused of lacking historical accuracy and especially of using a tragic theme to sensationalize the plot, to attract readers, and to provoke strong emotional reactions. Undoubtedly, literary

---

[11] See *Chicken Run* (2000; dir. Nick Park & Peter Lord), an animated comedy/drama about chickens living on a farm that resembles a concentration camp.

texts which explore the issue of genocide, and the Holocaust in particular, are approached in a certain way. Most often, readers assume the roles of moralist and guardian of collective memory (Ezrahi 1989: 77–97).

An increasing number of both literary and non-literary works show that the Holocaust is becoming not only an attractive topic (the *Konzentrationslager* has been such a topic for a long time),[12] but also an object of artistic manipulation. Since the generation who witnessed the extermination is gradually passing away, this process will escalate, making the Holocaust (and concentration camps) one event out of many. Therefore, as Michał Głowiński maintains, although those who know the Holocaust from their own or from their relatives' experience may find it difficult to come to terms with its "metamorphosis" (and possibly trivialization),

> Like all other historical tragedies – massacres perpetrated by the crusaders, the extermination of the Albigensians, the slaughter of Native American tribes, [...] the death of 1.5 million Armenians who were killed by the Turks – Nazi extermination becomes a theme among many. (Głowiński 2002: 210–211)

Głowiński suggests that in the case of Holocaust literature it is impossible to formulate any general rules as to what is proper and fits the decorum, understood as being faithful to facts and in particular respecting certain moral principles and rules of propriety. As those who had pre-condemned Roberto Benigni's tragicomic movie *Life is Beautiful* were made to realize, it is individual stories that matter. Critics often treat the classical category of propriety as a universal criterion (although it is always to some extent subjective) that indicates what "seems to be properly used and what seems to be in the right place" (Głowiński 2002: 210–211) in aesthetic, moral, and ideological terms. Still, one may expect that in time artists will break other taboos and search for new, more daring (at one time considered inappropriate) means to express the "sacred" (Des Pres 1988: 217) theme of the Holocaust (and Nazi camps) and, as a consequence, these norms will become less stringent.

In this context, it should be remembered that already in 1946 Polish critic and writer Henryk Vogler suggested that a full and faithful representation of

> [...] the horrors of concentration camps, gas chambers, crematories, serial, mechanized murderers, and human bestiality, which – equipped with highly advanced technology

---

[12] Examples include Ryszard Kozielewski's short story *Trzeba głęboko oddychać...* ("You need to breathe deeply..."; 1961), and plays with sensationalist and/or provocative plots: Ireneusz Iredyński's *Jasełka-moderne* ("Nativity play-moderne"; 1962), Tadeusz Hołuj's *Puste pole* ("An empty field"; 1963), Krzysztof Choiński's *Alarm* (1966).

– have almost reached the limits of madness [...] can only be possible if one takes recourse to a dark, fantastic and grotesque style which will resemble that of Poe, E.T.A. Hoffmann or Meyrink. (Korzeniewska 1946: 7)

5 The relationship between literature and experience in the context of a concentration camp

Before I reach my conclusion, I would like to look at the relationship between concentration camp experience and literature, and at the existence and functioning of *Lager* literature in an intertextual context. The evidence of intertextual mediation of (the experience of) a Nazi camp already in the lager is not limited to Dantesque hell. Describing his first day in a concentration camp in Ellrich, Adolf Gawalewicz confesses: "I thought I had truly *reached the end of the night*" (1968: 103 [emphasis mine]). Describing hunger in Auschwitz, Filip Friedman alludes to Knut Hamsun's *Hunger* (Friedman 1945: 44).

Non-*lager* literature is also useful for critics – it helps them to name the phenomena that recur in *Lager* literature. Referring to Szmaglewska's *Smoke over Birkenau*, Wanda Kragen, for instance, states: "Only here do we step into the deepest abyss, the deepest *heart of darkness*" (1946: 5 [emphasis mine]). Obviously, without literature (culture) it is impossible to capture Nazi camp reality. The motif of hell is the most evident example supporting this observation. However, one may, and perhaps should, approach the textual aspects of experience and the intertextual aspects of *Lager* literature from yet another perspective.

According to Jorge Luis Borges, "The fact is that every writer *creates* his own precursors. His work modifies our conception of the past, as it will modify the future." (1964: 201 [emphasis mine]) Hence, we may argue that the world of concentration camps, and, by extension, *Lager* literature, "created" the works of Sade, Poe's *The Pit and the Pendulum*, Dostoevsky's *The House of the Dead*, Conrad's *Heart of Darkness*, Musil's *The Confusions of Young Törless*, Kafka's *In the Penal Colony*, Huxley's *Brave New World*, and Céline's *Journey to the End of the Night*, and it certainly re-created them – it imposed on these and many other texts a peculiar, updated interpretation. This kind of interpretation can be described as metaphorical, "prophetic" or prefigurative. This imposition often takes place automatically and is frequently misconceived; for instance, I have come across a student analysis of Józef Czechowicz's poem *Śmierć* ("Death") as an allegory of the Holocaust (the proposed reading was a result of ignorance; the poem talks of cows destined for slaughter and loaded into cattle wagons at a train station). The students-allegorists were not aware of the fact that the poem was published in 1930!

Twentieth-century totalitarian systems have changed the perception of Plato (who, following Karl R. Popper, is now often seen as the founder of totalitarianism) and, similarly, have endowed some literary works with a predictive (as in the case of Plato's *Republic*) or even prophetic quality. In either case, they tend to be read as preconfiguring concentration camps. Although such interpretations may be seen as far-fetched, they certainly encourage reflection. Józef Szajna suggests that "Aeschylus' tragedies and Dante's *Inferno* needed concentration camps so that they could be experienced and described" (quoted in: Oleksy 1995: 91), while Głowiński asks: "And how would *Inferno* look like if Dante wrote it today?" (1998: 57) What remains most relevant for academic research is the extent to which these suppositions, statements, questions and interpretations make sense and are valid.

In order to resolve this issue, it is helpful to combine the competencies of a literary scholar with those of a historian and to approach concentration camp reality (both Nazi and Soviet) and the Holocaust from a distance – to consider them as events that are *not entirely* unique in the history of the world (I shall leave this issue for further consideration). Such attempts, or rather suggestions, can be found in the few statements that were made by Polish writers and critics. In his essay *Podobny do bogów* ("Similar to gods"), Mieczysław Jastrun, for instance, argues that a sober analysis of Homer's epic poems would uncover in these ancient works the germs of all contemporary crimes, described in poetic fashion. Jastrun also encourages his readers to closely look at the works of Thucydides, which are equally informative. He implores: "One should read this insightful, objective history of the Peloponnesian War in order to find in it a Mediterranean miniature version of every form of madness, betrayal and finally genocide of our times." (1962: 13–14)

Jastrun considers the quarry that was transformed by Syracusans into a harsh prison for Athenian prisoners of war as "the first concentration camp," which would have made Lord Herbert Kitchener[13] or even Himmler himself proud (Jastrun 1962: 13–14). In his commentary to Dostoevsky's *The House of the Dead*, Ryszard Przybylski compares penal servitude in Russian *katorga* to Nazi concentration camps, depicting the former as "a mechanism that was still imperfect" and highlighting the fact that writers such as Borowski and Aleksandr Solzhenitsyn, "bearing witness to the events they had experienced,

---

[13] A British general who became infamous for his cruelty during the wars with the Mahdists and the Boers.

[wrote] a peculiar sequel to Dostoevsky's observations about *katorga*" (Przybylski 1964: 158). The idea that there is continuity between Dostoevsky's penal servitude in a Russian labor camp, *katorga* ("the dead house"), and Soviet camps can also be found in Gustaw Herling-Grudziński's *A World Apart* (1951).

Andrzej Werner likewise argues that some literary diagnoses by Dostoevsky, Musil, Kafka, or Huxley: "[...] preceded the historical fulfillment of the threat. [...] Certain prerequisites were there and some people were able to predict their consequences. [...] It was even possible to refer to some facts that in a way anticipated Nazi camps and were their prototypes." (Werner 1971: 221)

Michał Głowiński concludes that in *In the Penal Colony*, Kafka "foresaw the institutions of organized crime which came into being a dozen or so years after the short story was written" (1998). Last but not least, Eugeniusz Czaplejewicz maintains that Conrad's *Heart of Darkness* describes a "concentration camp, a prototype of a [Soviet] camp" (1992: 19). Of course, it would be useful to provide more justification for these statements, which are often treated as misinterpretations. We may naturally assume that Dostoevsky, Kafka or Conrad intuitively sensed the direction in which our civilization was heading. Still, one may argue that we have an increasing amount of evidence at our disposal (let us consider the growing number of publications about various acts of genocide and the roots of twentieth-century totalitarian systems[14]) to support the idea that these conclusions were drawn on the basis of facts the writers had observed or events they had experienced. I suppose that the above-mentioned lack of broad perspective, the blurring of our memory, or even a failure to access our (Western) consciousness, and the erasure of older or more distant events than those associated with Nazi camps, Soviet camps or the Shoah, from this consciousness (both due to the shock that the Second World War had inflicted and the guilty conscience of the colonizers) make us perceive the three writers as "prophets" at best (Morawiec 2018). As Bernard Bruneteau, who is a historian and expert on totalitarianism and genocide, surmises,

> Twentieth-century violence had been prepared in advance. It has [...] its "roots," which are not so much direct "causes" of violence as various elements which crystalized to become its integral parts. We can find these roots throughout the history of the nineteenth century. The terror of genocide reveals its own past – imperialism and "total war." The period of imperialism, when new racist ideas served as a justification for bloody colonial expansion, marks the beginning of "administrative massacres." The 1914–1918 war, which combined the animalization of the enemy, extreme violence and mass death, led to the

---

[14] See, for instance: Stannard (1992), Hochschild (1998), Plumelle-Uribe (2001), Traverso (2002), Gellately and Kiernan (2003), Midlarsky (2005), Goldhagen (2009), Olusoga and Erichsen (2010).

brutalization of European societies. These elements created the intellectual, social and political foundation for the later careless negation of human rights. (Bruneteau 2005: 29)

It is also telling and heuristically important that Karol Zimmerring, a Belgian Jew imprisoned in Auschwitz, compared *Konzentrationslager* to the system of slavery created by the European colonizers in the Belgian Congo. Before the war, he had often traveled to this African country (Kubiak 1981: 122).[15] Another visitor to the Belgian Congo, in 1890, was Józef Korzeniowski, better known as Joseph Conrad. Set in the Belgian Congo, *Heart of Darkness*, which was published at the turn of the twentieth century, is one of the most insightful works of world literature. If it is true that the world that contributed to the creation of Auschwitz is still our world (Nancy 2005: 46), then it needs to be stressed that this world has very long and deep roots. As Conrad concludes in *Heart of Darkness*, "All Europe contributed to the making of Kurtz." (1999: 77)

Translated by Katarzyna Ojrzyńska

Works cited

Amiel, Irit (1994) *Egzamin z Zagłady* [A Holocaust exam], (Łódź: Oficyna Bibliofilów).
Amiel, Irit (1998) *Nie zdążyłam* [Delayed], (Łódź: Oficyna Bibliofilów).
Amiel, Irit (2002) *Wdychać głęboko* [Breathe deeply], (Izabelin: Świat Literacki).
[Andrzejewski, Jerzy] (1945) *Apel* [Roll call], (London: Światowy Związek Polaków zza Granicy).
Bielecki, Wacław (1944) *Obozy śmierci* [Camps of death], (Moskva: Związek Patriotów Polskich w ZSRR).
Borges, Jorge Luis (1964) "Kafka and His Precursors," in *Labyrinths: Selected Stories & Other Writings*, trans. James E. Irby (New York: New Direction Publishing Corporation), 199–201.
Borowski, Tadeusz (1947) "Alicja w krainie czarów" [Alice in Wonderland], *Pokolenie* 1, 9.
Borowski, Tadeusz (1948a) *Kamienny świat: Opowiadanie w dwudziestu obrazach* [World of stone: the twenty-scenes story], (Warszawa: Czytelnik).
Borowski, Tadeusz (1948b) *Pożegnanie z Marią: Opowiadania* [Farewell to Maria: Stories], (Warszawa: Wiedza).
Borwicz [Boruchowicz], Michał Maksymilian (1946) *Literatura w obozie* [Literature in the concentration camp], (Kraków: Wojewódzka Żydowska Komisja Historyczna).
Borwicz, Michał M. (ed) (1947) *Pieśń ujdzie cało...: Antologia wierszy o Żydach pod okupacją niemiecką* [The song will survive...: An anthology of poetry about Jews under the German occupation], (Warszawa: Centralna Żydowska Komisja Historyczna).
Bruneteau, Bernard (2005) *Wiek ludobójstwa* [The age of genocide], trans. Beata Spieralska (Warszawa: Oficyna Wydawnicza "Mówią wieki").
Chicago, Judy (1993) *Holocaust Project: From Darkness into Light* (New York: Penguin Books).

---

15 A former Mauthausen-Gusen prisoner states that concentration camps were "caricatured and deformed colonial countries in a 'test tube'." Quoted in: Wesełucha (1970: 242).

Choiński, Krzysztof (1966) "Alarm: Sztuka w 2 aktach" [Alarm: A play in two acts], *Dialog* 6, 5–24.
Coetzee, J. M. (2003) *Elizabeth Costello* (New York: Viking).
Conrad, Joseph (1999) "Heart of Darkness," in *Heart of Darkness & Other Stories* introd. and notes Gene M. Moore (London: Wordsworth Editions), 29–106.
Czaplejewicz, Eugeniusz (1992) *Polska literatura łagrowa* [Polish Gulag literature], (Warszawa: PWN).
Czarnecki, Wacław and Zygmunt Zonik (1969) *Walczący obóz Buchenwald* [Buchenwald: A fighting camp], (Warszawa: Książka i Wiedza).
Des Pres, Terrence (1988) "Holocaust laughter?" in *Writing and the Holocaust*, ed. Berel Lang (New York: Holmes & Meier), 216–233.
Ezrahi, Sidra DeKoven (1989) "The Holocaust and the shifting boundaries of art and history," *History and Memory* 2, 77–97.
Filipiak, Izabela (1995) *Absolutna amnezja* [Absolute amnesia], (Poznań: Obserwator).
Fink, Ida (1996) *Ślady* [Traces], (Warszawa: W.A.B.).
Friedman, Filip (1945) *To jest Oświęcim!* [This is Auschwitz!], (Warszawa: Państwowe Wydawnictwo Literatury Politycznej).
Gawalewicz, Adolf (1968) *Refleksje z poczekalni do gazu: Ze wspomnień muzułmana* [Reflections in a gas chamber's waiting room: From the memoirs of a muselmann], (Kraków: Wydawnictwo Literackie).
Gellately, Robert and Ben Kiernan (eds) (2003) *The Specter of Genocide: Mass Murder in Historical Perspective* (Cambridge: Cambridge University Press).
Głowiński, Michał (1998) "Windą – do piekła" [By elevator – to hell], in *Przywidzenia i figury: Małe szkice 1977–1997* (Kraków: Wydawnictwo Literackie), 57.
Głowiński, Michał (2002) "Wielkie zderzenie" [A big clash], *Teksty Drugie* 3, 199–211.
Goldhagen, Daniel Jonah (2009) *Worse than War: Genocide, Eliminationism, and the Ongoing Assault on Humanity* (New York: Public Affairs).
Grupińska, Anna (2001) "Zapisywanie Zagłady: Z Michałem Głowińskim rozmawia Anka Grupińska" [Recording the Holocaust: Anka Grupińska talks with Michał Głowiński], *Tygodnik Powszechny*, supplement *Kontrapunkt* 1.2, 14–15.
Grynberg, Henryk (1997) *Drohobycz, Drohobycz* (Warszawa: W.A.B.).
Hartmann, Geoffrey H. (ed) (1994) "Introduction: darkness visible," in *Holocaust Remembrance: The Shapes of Memory* ed. Geoffrey H. Hartmann (Oxford and Cambridge: Blackwell), 1–22.
Herman, Chaim (1971) [Letter to the Family], in *Rękopisy członków Sonderkommando*, trans. Zofia Cierniak, ed. Jadwiga Bezwińska and Danuta Czech (Oświęcim: Państwowe Muzeum w Oświęcimiu), 175–184.
Herling, Gustav (1951) *A World Apart*, trans. Joseph Marek (London: Heinemann).
Hochschild, Adam (1998) *King Leopold's Ghosts: A Story of Greed, Terror, and Heroism in Colonial Africa* (Boston: Houghton Mifflin).
Hołuj, Tadeusz (1945) *Wiersze z obozu* [Poems from the camp], (Łódź: Książka).
Hołuj, Tadeusz (1947) "Temat Oświęcim" [Theme: Auschwitz], *Twórczość* 2, 138–142.
Hołuj, Tadeusz (1963) "Puste pole: Sztuka w 3 aktach" [An empty field: A Play in three acts], *Dialog* 4, 5–33.
Iredyński, Ireneusz (1962) "Jasełka-moderne" [Nativity play-moderne], *Dialog* 11, 15–36.
Jastrun, Mieczysław (1962) "Podobny do bogów" [Like gods], in *Mit śródziemnomorski* (Warszawa: PIW), 5–21.

Kąkolewski, Krzysztof (1976) "Sianokosy w Brzezince" [Haymaking in Birkenau], in *Baśnie udokumentowane* (Warszawa: Iskry), 307–321.
Kertész, Imre (2004) *Język na wygnaniu* [Language in exile], trans. Elżbieta Sobolewska (Warszawa: W.A.B.).
Knežević, Marija (1997) "Obóz jako metafora" [Camp as a metaphor], trans. Dorota Jovanka Ćirlić, *Tygiel Kultury* 10.12, 15–18.
Korzeniewska, Ewa (1946) "Prozaicy i okupacja" [Writers and occupation], *Kuźnica* 23, 7–8.
[Kossak, Zofia] [1942] *W piekle* [In hell], (Warszawa: Front Odrodzenia Polski).
Kossak, Zofia (1946) *Z otchłani: Wspomnienia z lagru* [From the abyss: Memories from the camp], (Poznań: Wł. Nagłowski).
Kozielewski, Ryszard (1961) "Trzeba głęboko oddychać..." [You need to breathe deeply...], *Twórczość* 7, 10–48.
Kragen, Wanda (1946) "Książka o obozie śmierci" [A book about a death camp], *Robotnik* 83, 5.
[Krahelska, Halina] [1942] *Oświęcim: Pamiętnik więźnia* [Auschwitz: diary of a prisoner], (Warszawa: (KOPR)).
[Krahelska, Halina] (1985) "Oświęcim: Pamiętnik więźnia" [Auschwitz: diary of a prisoner], *Więź* 1.3, 5–41.
Kubiak, Michał (1981) *Tacy byliśmy: Wspomnienia więźnia nr 15262 z KL Auschwitz* [The way we were: memories of Auschwitz prisoner no. 15262], (Warszawa: MON).
[Kydryński, Juliusz] (1943) "Biała noc" [White night], *Miesięcznik Literacki* [Kraków] 3, 11–17.
Lebda-Wyborna, Anna (1975) "Poezja powstała w KL Auschwitz" [Poetry created in KL Auschwitz], *Zeszyty Oświęcimskie* 16, 5–69.
Lipska, Ewa (2002) "Pet Shops," in *Pet Shops and Other Poems*, trans. Barbara Bogoczek and Tony Howard (Todmorden: Arc Publications), 37.
Loebl, Bogdan (2008) *Dymek mesjasz zwierząt* [Smoky, the animals' messiah], (Warszawa: Nowy Świat).
Lurczyński, Mieczysław (1945) *Caracho-Weg* (Hanover: Polski Związek Wychodźctwa Przymusowego).
Midlarsky, Manus I. (2005) *The Killing Trap: Genocide in the Twentieth Century* (Cambridge: Cambridge University Press).
Miłosz, Czesław (1986) "Niemoralność sztuki" [The immorality of art], in *Ogród nauk* (Lublin: RW KUL), 160–167.
Miłosz, Czesław (2011) "A threat to nature," in *The Auschwitz Poems*, ed. Adam Zych (Oświęcim: Państwowe Muzeum Auschwitz-Birkenau), 289.
Morawiec, Arkadiusz (2009) *Literatura w lagrze, lager w literaturze: Fakt – temat – metafora* [Literature in concentration camps, concentration camps in literature: fact – theme - metaphor], (Łódź: Wydawnictwo Akademii Humanistyczno-Ekonomicznej).
Morawiec, Arkadiusz (2017) "The Holocausts," *Poznańskie Studia Slawistyczne* 12, 225–239.
Morawiec, Arkadiusz (2018) *Literatura polska wobec ludobójstwa: Rekonesans* [Polish literature towards genocide: reconnaissance], (Łódź: Wydawnictwo Uniwersytetu Łódzkiego).
Nałkowska, Zofia (2000) *Medallions*, trans. and introd. Diana Kuprel (Evanston: Northwestern University Press).
Nancy, Jean-Luc (2005) *The Ground of the Image*, trans. Jeff Fort (New York: Fordham University Press).
Nogaj, Stanisław (1937) *Za kratami i drutami Trzeciej Rzeszy (Reportaże)* [Behind the bars and barbed wires of the Third Reich: reporting], (Katowice: Polonia).

Nogaj, Stanisław (1939) *Za kratami i drutami Trzeciej Rzeszy: Reportaże* [Behind the bars and barbed wires of the Third Reich: reporting], (Katowice: Stanisław Szarłata), vol. II.

Nogaj, Stanisław (1945–1946) *Gusen: Pamiętnik dziennikarza* [Gusen: a journalist's memoir], 3 vols (Katowice, Chorzów: Komitet b. więźniów obozu koncentracyjnego Gusen).

"Obóz w Oświęcimiu (fragment opowiadania)" [The camp in Oświęcim (excerpt)], (1942) *Wojsko i Niepodległość* [Warszawa] 1 March.

Oleksy, Krystyna (ed) (1995) *Świat Józefa Szajny* [Józef Szajna's world], (Kraków: Państwowe Muzeum Oświęcim-Brzezinka).

Olusoga, David and Casper W. Erichsen (2010) *The Kaiser's Holocaust: Germany's Forgotten Genocide and the Colonial Roots of Nazism* (London: Faber and Faber).

Pankowski, Marian (2000) *Z Auszwicu do Belsen: Przygody* [From Auschwitz to Belsen: adventures], (Warszawa: Czytelnik).

Plumelle-Uribe, Rosa Amelia (2001) *La férocité blanche: Des non-Blancs aux non-Aryens, génocides occultés de 1492 à nos jours* [White savagery: from non-Whites to non-Aryans: hidden genocide from 1492 to today], (Paris: Albin Michel).

Podgórzec, Zbigniew (1993) *Mój Chrystus: Rozmowy z Jerzym Nowosielskim* [My Christ: conversations with Jerzy Nowosielski], (Białystok: Łuk).

Posmysz, Zofia (1962) *Pasażerka* [The woman passenger], (Warszawa: Czytelnik).

Przybylski, Ryszard (1964) *Dostojewski i "przeklęte problemy": Od "Biednych ludzi" do "Zbrodni i kary"* [Dostoevsky and "accursed problems": from the "Poor Folk" to "Crime and Punishment"], (Warszawa: PIW).

Putrament, Jerzy (1944) "Fabryka śmierci w Majdanku" [The death factory in Majdanek], *Rzeczpospolita* [Lublin] 3.3, 4, 3.

Rogowicz, Jerzy (1936) "W obozie koncentracyjnym" [In the concentration camp], *Kurier Warszawski*, No. 255 (evening edition), p. 2–3; No. 256 (evening edition), p. 2–3; No. 258, p. 6; No. 260 (evening edition), p. 2–3; No. 308 (evening edition), p. 2; No. 314, p. 5; No. 321, p. 7–8.

Rosenfeld, Alvin H. (2003) *Podwójna śmierć: Rozważania o literaturze Holocaustu* [A double dying: reflections on Holocaust literature], trans. Barbara Krawcowicz (Warszawa: Cyklady).

Staich, Tadeusz (ed) (1943) *Krwawe i zielone: Antologia poezji polskiej 1939–1943* [Bloody and green: the anthology of Polish poetry 1939–1943], (Kraków: Biblioteka "Watry").

Stannard, David E. (1992) *American Holocaust: The Conquest of the New World* (New York: Oxford University Press).

Szmaglewska, Seweryna (1945) *Dymy nad Birkenau* [Smoke over Birkenau], (Warszawa: Czytelnik).

Traverso, Enzo (2002) *La Violence nazie, une généalogie européenne* [The origins of Nazi violence], (Paris: La Fabrique).

[Trepiński, Antoni] [1943] *Trzy tygodnie w Majdanku* [Three weeks in Majdanek], (Warszawa: Front Odrodzenia Polski).

Vogler, Henryk (1946) "Liryka i piekło" [Poetry and hell], *Dziennik Polski* 69, 7.

Wajdelota, Jan [Sarnecki, Tadeusz] (ed.) (1944) *Z otchłani: Poezje* [From the abyss: poems], (Warszawa: ŻKN [Żydowski Komitet Narodowy]).

Werner, Andrzej (1971) *Zwyczajna apokalipsa: Tadeusz Borowski i jego wizja świata obozów* [An ordinary apocalypse: Tadeusz Borowski and his vision of the world of concentration camps], (Warszawa: Czytelnik).

Wesełucha, Piotr (1970) "Obóz jako eksperyment psychiatryczny" [The camp as a psychiatric experiment], *Przegląd Lekarski* 1, 242–246.

[Wiernik, Jankiel] (1944) *Rok w Treblince* [A year in Treblinka], (Warszawa: [Żydowska] Komisja Koordynacyjna).

"W niemieckich obozach koncentracyjnych" [In German concentration camps], (1939) *Przewodnik Katolicki* 27, 439–440.

Wojnar, Waldemar (2005) "Zanim powstały łagry i kacety" [Before the Soviet camps and KZs were built], *Mówią wieki* 4, 36–41.

Wójcik, Władysław (1939) "Byłem w piekle... Lublinianin w niemieckim obozie koncentracyjnym w Buchenwaldzie" [I was in hell: a citizen of Lublin in a German concentration camp in Buchenwald], *Głos Lubelski*, No. 225, p. 5; No. 226, p. 5; No. 227, p. 7; No. 229, p. 5; No. 230, p. 6; No. 231, p. 5; No. 232, p. 5; No. 233, p. 5; No. 234, p. 6; No. 236, p. 5; No. 237, p. 5; No. 238, p 5; No. 239, p. 5.

"Wyzwolenie przychodzi ze śmiercią (Relacja z Oświęcimia)" [Liberation comes with death (a report from Auschwitz)], (1942) *Dziennik Żołnierza* [Glasgow] 136, 2.

Z.B. (1941) "Niemcy wojny nie wygrają (Opowiadanie Polaka, zbiegłego z niemieckiego obozu koncentracyjnego)" [Germans will not win the war (the story of a Pole who escaped from a German concentration camp], *Gazeta Polska* [Jerusalem] 39, 4.

[Zarembina, Natalia] (1942) *Obóz śmierci* [The camp of death], ([Warszawa]: WRN [Wolność – Równość – Niepodległość]).

Zawada, Filip (1999) "Plakat" [Poster], in *Bóg Aldehyd* (Kraków: Zielona Sowa), 50.

Żywulska, Krystyna (1946) *Przeżyłam Oświęcim* [I came back], (Warszawa: Wiedza).

III: Witnessing and Remembering Camp Experiences: Comparative Case Studies

Silke Segler-Messner
The Grey Zones of Witnessing: Levi, Améry, Shalamov

1 Entangled memories

Since the publication of *Testimony: Crisis of Witnessing in Literature, Psychoanalysis and History* by Shoshana Felman and Dori Laub (1992), the act of witnessing, and especially the testimony as a privileged form of communication, has become an area of research not only in cultural and literary studies, but also in history and philosophy. The survivors of the Shoah seem to embody a certain knowledge, presumably suppressed until the 1980s, when Claude Lanzmann convinced some members of the *Sonderkommando* to re-enact their experiences at the historical sites in Poland (Lanzmann 1985). They are to be situated in the center of all debates about the historical, political, and ethical consequences of death camps. Besides the discourse of Lévinas, Ricœur, Derrida or Agamben, who – instead of giving a definition of testimony – insist on the aporetic structure of witnessing, the philosopher Sibylle Schmidt has been trying to synthesize in a series of studies the epistemic and ethical dimensions of bearing witness into a concept of testimony as a social practice of knowledge (Schmidt 2009, 2015; Krämer 2011). Her aim is to shift the philosophical focus from the theoretical to the more practical impact of the act of witnessing, which not only transmits sheer facts or pieces of information, but also offers the possibility of interpersonal exchange, or at least of acknowledging the pain of the other (Schmidt 2015: 16–17). Even though she emphasizes the universal character of her studies, the only historical event she cites is the Shoah, since it assumes the function of an undisputed authority for her philosophical interest in witnessing as a mode of knowledge. In this context she misses the chance of widening her perspective and of getting over the dominant position of the Shoah in the global discussion of memory culture.

The fact that the Shoah dominates the public and critical discourses of Western Europe and the United States seems to smother other memories of repressions, such as the Gulag or the decolonization of Africa, as well as more general questions, for example the research for a phenomenology of camp narratives in the West and in Eastern Europe. On the occasion of the commemoration of the end of the Second World War in 2005 all journals and commentators talked of the "divided memory" and the "split past," relating to the different processes of coming to terms with the two main ideologies of the twentieth century – National

Socialism and Communism, closely associated with the Shoah and the Gulag (Troebst 2005). It was Jorge Semprún in his memorial address at Buchenwald concentration camp who articulated the wish that in 2015 the *Kolyma Tales* of Varlam Shalamov would be integrated in the (European) canon of camp literature and that the experience of the Gulag would become part of the collective memory of Europe (Semprún 2005: 52). Indeed, in the past decade a number of articles and analyses of different aspects of the *Kolyma Tales* have been published, a sign of a nascent critical discussion of an avant-garde author, who had been ignored by European critics for a long time.[1] In his article Ulrich Schmid outlines the European reception of the *Kolyma Tales*, which had been translated already in the 1960s, but passed more or less unnoticed in the wake of the publication of *The Gulag Archipelago* (Schmid 2007: 87–90). As Schmid points out, the 1970s were influenced by the Cold War and Solzhenitsyn provided the European public with a powerful narrative of living and surviving in the Gulag, whereas *Kolyma Tales* are stories of different length in non-chronological order and do not offer a coherent story of Shalamov's experiences. Trying to avoid all moral judgment and all sort of dramatization, they keep the reader at a distance, not wanting him to become a moral or emotional accomplice in the narration. This difficult access is perhaps one of the main reasons for their belated reception in Europe as well as in Russia.

Lack of attention of a wider audience is a phenomenon that concerns not only the *Kolyma Tales*, but also the first editions of the survival stories of Primo Levi and Robert Antelme. European post-war societies were not able to face the atrocities of the (death) camps and to admit their tacit complicity with the Nazi regime in the persecution and deportation of the Jews, while they were busy rebuilding their democratic systems. Another example of a French writer unjustly ignored is Georges Hyvernaud, who told his experience as a prisoner of war in Germany in a way similar to Shalamov's, that is to say in a laconic, subjectless prose, which re-enacts the physical effects of dehumanization (he titles his first work *La Peau et les Os* (Hyvernaud 1997; published in English as *Skin and Bones*, 1994) and denounces all attempts to idealize the war, the Resistance, or survival. Unlike Shalamov, Hyvernaud decided to abandon writing definitively when his second book, *Wagon à vaches* (1953; Engl. *The Cattle Car*, 1994), did not achieve critical success either (Lecarme 2009).

---

[1] One of the first to analyze the *Kolyma Tales* was Leona Toker (1989, 2000). It is also worth mentioning a special edition of the *Osteuropa* journal (2007, 57.6), entitled *Das Lager schreiben. Varlam Šalamov und die Aufarbeitung des Gulag* ("Writing about the lager. Varlam Shalamov and the coming to terms with the Gulag").

All these examples show that a survivor who wants to tell his or her experiences needs an audience willing to listen and to understand, as well as a historical and cultural context in which his testimony is recognized not only as a source of knowledge, but as an expression of (literary) resistance to the oppressing system, no matter if it is the German enemy (in the case of Hyvernaud), the Stalinist regime or the National Socialist government under Hitler. Resistance in this respect is not to be compared with political commitment, but rather with the need to put the unspeakable or the unbelievable into a verbal form. Storytelling assumes the function of reconstructing the wounded, traumatized self, and of facilitating the return from the dead in the presence of an audience.

Neither Primo Levi nor Varlam Shalamov or Jean Améry used their testimonies as tools of direct political protest, although they do have a critical dimension, inasmuch as they are putting the victim and the missing social and historical acceptance in the center of their considerations. They share not only the traumatic memory of the camp, but also the permanent self-questioning in their respective roles as (intellectual) witnesses of Auschwitz and the Gulag. They all felt a responsibility to remind the public of its repressed memories, even if they were aware of the futility of their efforts. As far as literary techniques are concerned, they experimented with open and new forms of life-telling or bearing witness. Whereas Levi and Améry chose the essay form, which allows intertwining their personal memories with philosophical, historical, or ethical perspectives, Shalamov created an innovative narrative: the "lived document," in opposition to the humanistic novels of the nineteenth century. Like Levi and Améry, he not only transferred his experience of the Gulag into radicalized prose, but also reviewed his writing in several essays and letters. In his essay *On Prose* (2014), he declares that the question of the camp is a topic even more important than the war, which is functioning as a psychological screen for the publicly organized mass murder of citizens.

In this chapter I present a reading of *The Drowned and the Saved* (Levi 2013), *At the Mind's Limits. Contemplations by a Survivor on Auschwitz and Its Realities* (Améry 1980) and *Kolyma Tales* (Shalamov 1994) as entangled memories, in which the actualization and transmission of the camp experience is the main subject. Since the limits between form and content in the texts are fluid, the act of witnessing is located in a "grey zone," that is to say, in an area in which all clear-cut distinctions and oppositions are suspended. The author, the narrator, the traumatized survivor, and the intellectual who reflects and comments on the events he has lived through are equivalent instances, and it is often impossible to decide exactly who is speaking. This confusion upsets the reader, who is confronted with a perspective that does not answer to his need of a clear statement about the past. Levi, Améry, and Shalamov do not convey messages or a moral. Therefore, I will discuss in the next section the authors' choice of the essay and of the "lived document" as a "grey zone" of witnessing in the sense of a paradoxical? process of narrative justification of victimhood and the indissoluble traumatic loss associated with it.

The most threatening knowledge articulated by Levi, Améry, and Shalamov is perhaps the awareness of the persistence of mass violence and of the possibility of the victims' collaboration with their oppressors. In the second essay from the collection *The Drowned and the Saved*, Primo Levi introduces the concept of a "grey zone" as a sphere where the opposition between victims and perpetrators dissolves. The most striking example is that of members of the *Sonderkommando*, who were forced to put women, men, and children into the crematories. The contamination of the deportees with the will of the SS to systematically and ultimately destroy the other as a human being leads to the decomposition of solidarity among the victims, a phenomenon also noted by Shalamov in the *Kolyma Tales*, although in a different way. In this context I will also focus upon the situation of the intellectual in the camp, who is trying to discern causalities and regularities of camp life and has to recognize the replacement of the body–mind dualism by an approximation of humans to animals, thus creating a new zone of indistinguishability. This approach is echoed in Levi, Améry, and Shalamov, and even if Levi seems to criticize Améry in his essay *The Intellectual at Auschwitz* (Levi 2013) his confession of faith in the vital forces of life remains questionable when one considers his supposed suicide one year after the publication of *The Drowned and The Saved*. All education loses its cultural function in the camp, a belief shared especially by Améry and Shalamov. The violence suffered in the camp belies the pretended superiority of the intellect and puts the vulnerability of mankind in the forefront.

2 The grey zone of witnessing

The second volume of Georges Didi-Huberman's series "L'œil de l'histoire," *Remontages du temps subi* [Montage of times gone] (Didi-Huberman 2010), opens with a description of remembrance ceremonies of the 60th anniversary of the Holocaust. As happens every year, certain films are shown over a few weeks, certain books are reprinted, survivors are interviewed, and some magazine covers show horrible shots of the camps and their cadaverous survivors. Yet, despite the omnipresence of "Auschwitz" in the public media, Didi-Huberman is wondering whether this remembrance spectacle keeps the memory alive or rather, whether it freezes the remembrance of Auschwitz by simply repeating a well-known set of commonplaces and by unwittingly encouraging the impression of having already "seen it all" (Didi-Huberman 2010: 11). He cites Annette Wieviorka, who talks about "*mémoire saturée*" (saturated memory), and who presents a number of doubts concerning all current attempts at working through "Auschwitz" (Wieviorka 2005: 9). Wieviorka concludes that Auschwitz has become an abstract concept of evil beyond historical knowledge. Stressing the necessity to re-read historical events such as Auschwitz because of their impact on our present, Didi-Huberman argues in support of montage as one of the few practices to "(re-) open the eyes" and to "(re-)open the mind" to the historical reality of the camps (2010: 144–145). His examples of a new legibility of the past, including a vital critique of violence, are the films of Harun Farocki, which work like an essay, creating a montage of different types of media that does not tell a story but exposes the story before the public.

The noun "essay" comes from the Latin noun *exagium*, which means "weight" and in a figurative sense the process of pondering the facts and circumstances. One of the first European writers who revealed the potential of the essay as a way of self-questioning that yields more questions than it does answers was Michel de Montaigne. Having lost his only friend, and in light of his approaching death, he gave up all public charges and retired in 1571 to a famous tower he owned (Starobinski 2001: 64). The starting point for his deliberations was his experience and awareness as a human being, with all his moral and physical defects. In permanent dialogue with the Greek and Latin classics, he discussed modern topics such as the question of good education, the Europeans dealing with the "savages," and last but not least, the anthropological aspects of human nature being like the affinity to vanity or the ambition of glory. In a circular process of reasoning, which often starts form general observations, Montaigne places his own experience in opposition to the works of Aristotle, Plato, or Cicero, and finally turns back to subjective perception, presenting the image of a weak modern subject, who depends on his physical body and is delivered onto life in the consciousness of certain death.

If both Primo Levi and Jean Améry have chosen the essay form for standing up publicly as survivors of Auschwitz, they deliberately put themselves at a distance from the corpus of documentary survivor tales and intertwined their traumatic memories and general considerations. Referring to the hypothesis of Adorno, Didi-Huberman emphasizes the composite character of the essay, which combines exegesis and criticism by creating a sphere of experimentation and interpretation that transgresses the traditional idea of truth. "The Essay, however, does not let its domain be prescribed for it," writes Adorno. And further,

> [...] Its concepts are not derived from a first principle, nor do they fill out to become ultimate principles. Its interpretations are not philologically definitive and conscientious; in principle they are over-interpretations – according to the mechanized verdict of the vigilant intellect that hires out to stupidity as a watchdog against the mind. (Adorno 1991: 4)

The central point of reference for essayistic writing is the opposition between experience and thinking in certitudes and facts. According to Adorno, the essay is signed by the "consciousness of the non-identity of presentation and subject matter" (1991: 18). Even if in his essays Améry appears to congenially illustrate Adorno's thesis (Lorenz 1991; Hofmann 2003: 41), a most striking difference becomes apparent in the bodily presence of the trauma of dehumanization. All writing of Jean Améry ends in the certainty that someone who has been tortured remains tortured for the rest of his life. This corporal knowledge overwrites all attempts at dealing with the traumatic past, so that the non-finite character of the essay is to be situated in a tension to the physical limits of a (possible) visualization.

Unlike Primo Levi, who wrote the first account of his camp experience directly after the liberation of Auschwitz and shortly afterwards wrote his testimony *If This is a Man* (Levi 1959), Jean Améry presents himself for the first time as a persecuted German Jew in the collection of essays, *At the Mind's Limits. Contemplations by a Survivor on Auschwitz and its Realities*, from 1966. As he reveals in the preface to the first edition, the Auschwitz trials in Frankfurt coincided with the writing of his first text concerning his experiences in the Third Reich. At first, he discussed the condition of being an intellectual in Auschwitz, with no plans of continuation; but afterwards he became aware of the need to find an answer to the general question of how he got into the death camp, he who was at no time a practicing Jew and, what is more, an expert on German literature. Despite his wish to keep an objective and distanced view, he realizes that it is impossible for him to reject his "I" and his experiences: "If in the first lines of the Auschwitz essay I had still believed that I could remain circumspect and distant and face the reader with refined objectivity, I now saw that this was simply impossible. Where the word 'I' was to have been avoided completely, it proved to be the single useful starting point." (Améry 1980: XIII) Améry's aim is to attempt a "phenomenological description of the existence of the victim" (XIII), and having elucidated the non-historical, but chronological order of his five essays, he revises the expression of "Nazi victim," to him all too general: "[...] only when I reached the end and pondered on the necessity and impossibility of being a Jew, did I discover myself in the image of the *Jewish* victim." (XIV) This displacement from the general to the particular, from an objective description of victimhood to a self-reflection in the image of the Jewish victim, marks the schism between object and subject that Améry tries to overcome in his essays, knowing at the same time that it is impossible. Imre Kertész dedicates his essay "The Holocaust as Culture" to Améry and argues for the necessity of the victim to liberate himself from the degradation suffered by assuming the right to objectify and therefore to reconstruct his negated subjectivity as the common ground of his writing (Kertész 1999: 54).

The essay "Torture," which opens with a detailed description of Fort Breendonk, the site where Améry was tortured, is undoubtedly of particular importance from a tourist's point of view. It ends with a repeated declaration: "Whoever has succumbed to torture can no longer feel at home in the world." (Améry 1980: 40) In the exposition the narrative voice, which seems to be familiar with the evoked site, guides the reader like a tourist, from the outside into the present-day Belgian national museum. After a short scene in the first paragraph, in which the first-person narrator reveals his limited knowledge concerning the history of Fort Breendonk from the First World War onwards, the voice switches to an impersonal mode of presentation, until the reader-tourist enters a windowless arch inside the fortress. At the end of the third paragraph the narrative voice announces not only the subject of the essay, but also, rather unexpectedly, the object: "From there no scream penetrated to the outside. There I experienced it: torture." (Améry 1980: 22) As Christian Poetini points out, the repetition of the adverb of place "there" (Ger. *dort*) draws the reader's attention to syntactical inversion, which stresses the importance of the indirect object (Ger. *mir*) that stands in a direct relation to the postponed subject, "(the) torture" (Poetini 2014: 67). Since the second sentence is written in the passive voice, a special emphasis is placed on the act of the narrator's suffering. A colon marks the gap between the object and the subject – "There I experienced it: torture." (Améry 1980: 22) – as well as the distance between the narrator and the reader, who is only a visitor to the site and does not know what it means to be tortured. As torture reduces the "I" to his body and confronts the victim with his own death, the passive voice indicates it is a chronic condition rather than a singular event.

All the essays in *At the Mind's Limits* revolve around the loss of home (land), the negation as a human being worth living, self-alienation, and otherness. All of Jean Améry's reasoning is based on the inscription of physical violence in his body during the extreme situation of torture: "At the first blow [...] this trust in the world breaks down. The other person, opposite whom I exist physically in the world and with whom I can exist only as long as he does not touch my skin surface as border, forces his own corporeality on me with the first blow." (Améry 1980: 28) The experience of being overpowered by a fellow human being constitutes the focal point of the second part of the German title of the collection: *Bewältigungsversuche eines Überwältigten*. Already the use of the past participle (*überwältigt*) reveals that neither the temporal distance nor the act of witnessing has changed or suspended his condition as a victim of the Nazis. With every essay Améry tries to embody the event in its temporality that had made of him a Jewish victim (Didi-Huberman 2010: 28). And even if he knows that his essays do not answer the questions he raises, he continues to protest publicly against the closure of the past by a present that falsifies the reality of the camps by prematurely placing communism on equal terms with the Nazi ideology of annihilation and by displaying a general indifference towards the victims. The growing anti-Semitism of the European left refers to an absent confrontation with Auschwitz and reflects the actuality of the last of Améry's essays, in which he is dealing with the "necessity and impossibility of being a Jew" (Améry 1980: 82–101).

At this point, Améry's exposed position in the preface to the second edition overlaps with the preliminary remarks of Primo Levi's in *The Drowned and The Saved*. More than forty years after the liberation of Nazi concentration camps, and more than forty years after witnessing the process of dehumanization for the first time, Primo Levi submits his memories of Auschwitz to a critical review. There are at least two reasons for his need of bearing witness once again. On the one hand, unfolding the truth of the camps by historians and in victims' testimonies bore no consequences at all for global politics (Levi 2013: 11–13). Yet for Levi the question of whether the camp really disappeared as a historical phenomenon or just returned in different forms, like in the crimes of Hiroshima and Nagasaki, of Vietnam, Argentina, and Cambodia, and last but not least, in the gulags of the Soviet Union, is fundamental. On the other hand, already in the foreword a certain moral unease can be noticed, which concerns Levi's position as a witness and survivor. Having discussed the restricted view of the memories of former camp inmates, Levi finds that most of the testimonies have been written by those who had been privileged in the camp:

> At a distance of years, one can today definitely affirm that the history of the Lagers has been written almost exclusively by those who, like myself, never fathomed them to the bottom. Those who did so did not return, or their capacity for observation was paralyzed by suffering and incomprehension. (Levi 2013: 9)

In the following essays Levi repeats this argument several times; it forms the title of the essay collection and already appeared for the first time in *If This Is a Man*, where it had formed the middle axis of this testimony and represented a sort of conclusion to Levi's camp experience. The will to come to a generalizable judgment reflects Levi's scientific mind and underlines his intention to understand the idea of this incredible experiment with mankind. In the opening paragraph of the chapter "The Drowned and the Saved," he confronts the Nazi project of total annihilation of the European Jews with his conviction that there is no human experience devoid of sense and unworthy to be remembered. He concludes: "We would also like to consider that the *Lager* was pre-eminently a gigantic biological and social experience." (Levi 1959: 99) and creates a new paradigm, extrapolated from his experiences and reflections about the camp. All tentative attempts to divide the mankind into good *versus* bad or courageous *versus* cowardly become less important and at least less visible in the camp, because there really is only one fundamental opposition: "[...] there comes to light the existence of two particularly well differentiated categories among men – the saved and the drowned" (Levi 1959: 100). For Levi the "drowned" are synonymous with *Muselmann*, that is to say with those prisoners who have lost all will to live, vegetating, already in a place where they neither suffer nor think. As they died quickly and left no stories to tell, Levi feels himself haunted by "their faceless presences" (103). But the more threatening aspect is the position of the narrator himself, who becomes privileged by getting a job in a chemical laboratory because of his background in chemistry. How can Levi justify his survival?

This question seems to return forty years later in correlation with a changing public discourse, which undermines the authority of the survivors and offends the memory of the "drowned." In the first essay of the collection *The Drowned and the Saved*, dedicated to "The memory of the Offense," Levi refers to an article by the French revisionist Louis Darquier de Pellepoix (*L'Express*, 28.10.1978), which provoked a debate about the existence of gas chambers, culminating in the philosophical contradiction by Jean-François Lyotard in *Le Différend*.[2] Even if the subject of this essay suggests a re-examination of his own traumatic memories, Levi keeps a distanced, nearly objective perspective, giving the impression of having worked through his traumatic memories, of not being involved:

> I intend to examine here the memories of extreme experiences, of injuries suffered or inflicted. In this case, all or almost all the factors that can obliterate or deform the mnemonic record are at work. The memory of a trauma suffered or inflicted is itself traumatic because recalling it is painful or at least disturbing: a person who was wounded tends to block out the memory so as not to renew the pain; the person who has inflicted the wound pushes the memory deep down, to be rid of it, to alleviate the feeling of guilt. (Levi 2013: 16–17)

In the next paragraph he emphasizes the irremediable character of the offense suffered, but instead of proving this assertion by his own example he remembers Jean Améry and cites the conclusion of the essay "Torture": "Whoever was

---

[2] Published in English as *The Differend: Phrases in Dispute* (1999; trans. Georges Van den Abbeele, Minneapolis: University of Minnesota Press) [Ed.].

tortured, stays tortured." (Améry 1980: 34) As this is the only quotation that appears in this essay (Levi's first), Améry's testimony assumes particular significance. The German philosopher, who like Primo Levi was an active member of the Resistance (Belgian) and also a Jew, not only becomes the preferred addressee of Levi's inner dialogue, but also the voice of the suffered offense, of the physical dimension of the camp experience that Levi never describes directly. However, another aspect is hidden behind the reference to Améry. In the exposition of the first chapter of *If This Is a Man* Levi points out that he identified himself as an Italian Jew during the first interrogation by the Italian militia, fearing he would be tortured or even killed if he had confessed his part in the Resistance (Levi 1959: 4). Taking into account, the decision to betray his political commitment in order to save his life, unlike Améry, who accepted the torture because of his role in the Resistance, Levi seems to grant a certain moral superiority to his intellectual companion and at the same time dissociates himself from him, as we will see in the context of the later discussion of the role of the intellectual in Auschwitz.

The confrontation with Améry in *The Drowned and the Saved* reveals a different thematic priority, which puts the main stress on moral or ethical dilemmas and especially on the survivors' guilt and shame. The first three essays in the collection all deal with a belated justification of Primo Levi's survival by dissecting his traumatic memories one more time, oscillating between a scientific-dispassionate and a nearly self-destructive mode, between an impartial and a personal-intimate presentation. "I felt innocent, yes," writes Levi in "Shame," "but enrolled among the saved and therefore in permanent search for a justification in my own eyes and in the eyes of others. The worst survived – that is, the fittest; the best all died" (Levi 2013: 87–88). The dramatic culmination of the fundamental gap between the saved and the drowned, identified with the worst and the best respectively, cannot be bridged and threatens to sap the act of witnessing itself, which at least serves to reopen the wound and reactivate the pain, as Levi writes in "The Memory of the Offence". But there is another threat that Levi is writing against by giving his voice to the collective of survivors: the risk to be forgotten and to have survived for nothing. In the conclusion to his collection of essays he reflects on the difficult dialogue with the younger generation, for whom the survival testimonies are only stories of the past without relevance to their personal life:

> For us to speak with the young becomes ever more difficult. We see it as a duty, and at the same time as a risk: the risk of appearing anachronistic, of not being listened to. We must be listened to: above and beyond our personal experience, we have collectively been the witnesses of a fundamental, unexpected event, fundamental precisely because unexpected, not foreseen by anyone. (Levi 2013: 230)

If there is no audience ready to listen, bearing witness loses its epistemic and ethical foundation. The repetition of the need to be heard in relation to an event that is two times designated as fundamental illustrates the growing concern of a witness who has to recognize a change in the global perception of the Holocaust. The series of catastrophes that Levi refers to show not only the persistence of mass violence, but also a process of relativization undermining the singularity of the Holocaust, which Levi, and also Améry, try to defend.

If Levi justifies his testimony ethically as witnessing in the name of *Muselmänner*, who normally never returned from Auschwitz, Varlam Shalamov highlights especially the *dochodjaga* ("goners") or as Wolfgang Kissel writes, the condition of a minimal life completely reduced to an instinctive, physical languishing comparable to that of an animal (Kissel 2009: 163–164). After nearly eighteen years as prisoner of the Gulag, fourteen in the Kolyma region, he began to write in the 1950s (Thun-Hohenstein 2007). The starting point for his project to create a completely new sort of narrative is to bear witness to the exhaustion and dehumanization suffered in an almost physical sense. The distance between the suffering body and (in retrospective) the act of writing is to be suspended, so that the author himself becomes the object of literary investigation, as Luba Jurgenson observes (2007: 171). Therefore, all witnessing of the Gulag as an experience of an extreme situation reveals a paradox: on the one hand, Shalamov tries to inscribe his physical trauma in the text (Siguan 2014), but on the other hand, precisely the act of writing implies a growing distance to the past. The gulf between the bodily experience, still present, and the written testimony cannot be bridged, so that the *Kolyma Tales* aim not only at visualizing the nuances of this minimal life, but also at the literary process of translation. The opening episode of the *Kolyma Tales* illustrates perfectly the crucial importance of the reader as an addressee and accomplice of the narration, who has to assume the role of a secondary witness and must realize the testimony by deciphering the (re-)constructed marks of the physical pain that are all exposed to the danger of getting lost and forgotten.

The *Kolyma Tales* cycle opens with a description of a group of men plowing through a pristine, snow-covered surface. This scene can neither be located in space or time, nor can it be associated directly with the experience of the Gulag. The narrator first asks, "How is a road beaten down through the virgin snow?" (Shalamov 1994: 3), as if he is referring to a writing exercise, and then shows a picture of a group of men walking through the deep snow and creating a first track. He does not give us their names or details of their appearance, but focuses on their physical effort, that is to say on the use of their sheer physical force, manifest in their breath and sweat. The creation of a path in the white surface can be read as a reference to the process of writing, a theory that is confirmed with the last sentence of the story: "Later will come tractors and horses driven by readers, instead of authors and poets." (Shalamov 1994: 4) If the writer does not come on horseback, nor by tractor, he is to be found among or near the walking men, whereas the position of the reader is characterized by a fundamental temporal difference and distance. He only arrives on the scene after the work has been done and as he stands outside the setting, he has to visualize the related event. The writer, in turn, is not only close to the nameless characters that can be identified as all those who died in the Gulag, but becomes himself like a living dead described in the last story of the second volume, "The Sentence." Here the first-person narrator is in a condition of advanced consumption, having lost all contact with the outside world and getting more and more closed up within himself. In a painful process of self-dissection, he notes the transformation of his body into a rag of skin and bones and the subsequent severing of all emotions. All that remains is bitterness. In this story, as well as in the first episode of "Through the Snow," bearing witness to a primarily physical experience is seen as a paradoxical process of appropriation and loss of self. The body becomes a vehicle of suffering that cannot be expressed directly. The survivor and writer has to transfer the traces of his pain and troubles to the text, which assumes the status of a supplement to memory.[3]

As Shalamov explains in his essay "On Prose," the Gulag as well as the Auschwitz experiences necessitate a different kind of writing and an uncommon aesthetics experimenting with the traditional opposition of literature *versus* document, memory *versus* history and life *versus* art. He characterizes his texts by a set of negations. They are neither tales nor literature. They are not linked to the Russian canon, because they break with all humanistic ideals. Briefly speaking, they can be defined as scenic visualizations of situations, encounters, and observations. One of the most disturbing insights consists in the definition of humanity by boundless physical resilience: in the short story "Rain" the narrator notices that horses die before prisoners in the Gulag. This awareness of his physical strength is, the narrator confesses, the only thing that prevents him from dying by suicide. Besides the domination of the body over the mind as one of the main characteristics of mankind, in several stories Shalamov hints at the possibility of returning from the (near) dead to the living. In contrast to the presentation of the *Muselmann* by Primo Levi and in contrast to Agamben, who situates the *Muselmann* on the edge of death and life,

---

[3] For Luba Jurgenson the memory assumes the function of "prosthesis" (Jurgenson 2007: 179–182).

Shalamov presents the Gulag prisoner as a participant in a never-ending cycle of passing away and returning back to life.

The experience of the Gulag as an extreme situation demands a radicalized writing style, reduced to a minimalist aesthetic without moral judgment and without the possibility of identification with the characters. Therefore, Shalamov generates a fragmented narrative that, like the essay, creates a montage of scenes in a nearly identical setting, but with changing narrative voices and protagonists. Sometimes, the narrator can be identified with the communal voice, sometimes it is the autodiegetic narrative instance that reports an event, and sometimes the narrator seems to be entirely absent from the story, focusing on the life stories of his camp inmates.[4] Iteration as a narrative strategy reinforces the impression of an eternal recurrence of the same, that is to say, of living and dying in the Gulag (Kissel 2009: 166).

Levi, Améry, and Shalamov all deal with the question of bearing witness by reflecting on forms of transmission and comprehension beyond the mere facts. Choosing between the essay and a new prose form documents the emphasis on the question of transfer and on the communication with the reader, confronting him with a poetics of writing based on the visualization of the indignities suffered. Even if the loss of identity and physical integrity cannot be bridged, witnessing remains the only form of self-reassurance and of re-integration into a world after Auschwitz and the Gulag.

3 The intellectual and the grey zone of collaboration

Primo Levi's reflections on the grey zone are directly associated with the general observation that humans need precise directions to understand history. The process of understanding often corresponds to the simplification of complex situations; thus, after a catastrophe everyone wants to restore, as quickly as possible, the vision of an ideal world in which the question of responsibility can be answered without hesitation. But the reality, and the facts of life, cannot only be categorized in simple binary oppositions – good or bad, guilty or innocent, winner or loser. Even in the world of concentration camps the distinction between victims and perpetrators is not as obvious as it may seem at first sight. The most terrible shock for Primo Levi was the arrival at the camp, because his humanistic

---

4 For a discussion of the different effects that are produced by different narrative voices in the *Kolyma Tales*, see Golden (2004).

belief in solidarity among the oppressed and in the spirit of charity was completely destroyed. Instead, arrival in the *Lager* was indeed a shock because of the surprise it entailed:

> The world in which one was precipitated was terrible, yes, but also indecipherable: it did not conform to any model, the enemy was all around but also inside, the "we" lost its limits, the contenders were not two, one could not discern a single frontier but rather many confused, perhaps innumerable frontiers, which stretched between each of us. One entered hoping at least for the solidarity of one's companions in misfortune, but the hoped-for allies, except in special cases, were not there; there were instead a thousand sealed-off monads, and in between them a desperate hidden and continuous struggle. The brusque revelation, which became manifest from the very first hours of imprisonment, often in the instant form of a concentric aggression on the part of those in whom one hoped to find future allies, was so harsh [as] to cause the immediate collapse of one's capacity to resist. For many it was lethal, indirectly or even directly: it is difficult to defend oneself against a blow for which one is not prepared. (Levi 2013: 33–34)

This excerpt documents the traumatic effects of entering into a cosmos in which evil seems to be everywhere and in which the deportee is promptly involved in a struggle for survival. Jean Améry has noted that the first blow destroys not only any idea of self-determination, but also confidence in a world in which the Jews are expelled from human community. In this context the camp is not only an area of detention but also a sphere of relentless aggression against humanity and at the same time of continuous resistance against the negation of being human. What Levi describes is the breakdown of modern European civilization as the necessary condition for the creation of grey zones. In this regard his critical view of the supposed supremacy of the human being seems to converge with the position of Varlam Shalamov, for whom the humanist literature of the nineteenth century, with all its convictions, bears some blame for the twentieth-century catastrophes of Auschwitz and the Gulag.

Besides the entry ritual that involves kicks and blows, screamed orders, stripping of clothes until complete nakedness and the shaving of the hair, the destruction of solidarity among the victims in the concentration camp was furthermore promoted by according privileges to those who were inclined to collaborate with the Nazis. As Primo Levi observes, the system of totalitarian oppression does not only want to humiliate the deportees, but tries to make them resemble their own oppressors by giving them the power to discipline and punish their comrades. The introduction of a system of privileges blurs the dividing lines between victims and perpetrators and encourages the creation of a grey zone, an area of complicity and collaboration between the privileged prisoners and the SS guards, "with ill-defined outlines which both separate and join the two camps of masters and servants" (Levi 2013: 38).

Therefore, Levi insists on the fact that the area between victims and perpetrators has to be explored, because neither in Nazi *Lagers*, nor in Soviet camps, are the respective spheres well defined. The harsher the oppression, the more the oppressed is willing to collaborate with the oppressor. The motives of collaboration with the Nazis are various and Levi cites the following: "[...] terror, ideological seduction, servile imitation of the victor, myopic desire for any power whatsoever, even though ridiculously circumscribed in space and time, cowardice, and finally, cold calculation aimed at eluding the orders and the imposed order." He concludes: "All these motives, on their own or combined, have been at work in creating the grey zone, whose components were held together by the wish to preserve and consolidate their privilege vis-à-vis those without privilege." (Levi 2013: 40)

In this regard Levi defines the *Lager* as an excellent "laboratory" of complicity between victims and perpetrators. For Giorgio Agamben, Primo Levi is the first to sketch the frame for a new ethic after Auschwitz, with the grey zone in its center. In *Remnants of Auschwitz* the grey zone becomes an emblematic area that is "independent of every establishment of responsibility" or is "a zone of irresponsibility" (Agamben 1999: 21), because it is an area in which "victims become executioners and executioners become victims" (17). The Italian philosopher suggests that in the grey zone the positions of victim and oppressor are reversible or interchangeable, a statement that does not correspond to the position taken by Levi.[5] Far from generalizing the change of roles and the question of guilt, Levi gives priority to the responsibility of "the very structure of the totalitarian state" (Levi 2013: 40). Even if it is impossible to judge the different forms of collaboration, he rejects the idea of extending the grey zone to an anthropological state. Opting most of the time for an impersonal modus of presentation signaling distance and objectivity, the narrative voice changes the moment he cites Liliana Cavani, declaring in an interview: "We are all victims or murderers, and we accept these roles voluntarily." (Levi 2013: 46) For Levi the question of responsibility is not to be confused with psychoanalytical interpretations or identifications. The truth of the camp is clear to see: at a collective level the totalitarian state organized the annihilation of millions of victims, whereas at a personal level Primo Levi definitely highlights his victimhood:

> I am not an expert of the unconscious and the mind's depth, but I do know that few people are experts in this sphere, and that these few are the most cautious; I do not know, and it does not much interest me to know, whether in my depths there lurks a murderer, but I do know that I was a guiltless victim and I was not a murderer. I know that the

---

[5] For a critical analysis of the position of Agamben, see Leys (2007).

> murderers existed, not only in Germany, and still exist, retired or on active duty, and that to confuse them with their victims is a moral disease or an aesthetic affectation or a sinister sign of complicity; above all, it is precious service rendered (intentionally or not) to the negators of truth. (Levi 2013: 46)

Through the anaphoric repetition of the "I" Levi emphasizes his personal experience as a source of knowledge. In the essay collection *The Drowned and the Saved* there are only a few paragraphs in which he refers in such a direct and unequivocal way to his authority as a moral witness. His statement can be read as an intervention against the illegitimate appropriation of Auschwitz by a public discourse that ignores the differences among the group of victims and the nuances of guilt in a concentrationary system. That leads Levi to develop a sort of hierarchy of guilt, with the exponents of the Nazi regime at the top, followed by camp functionaries – the *kapos* and barracks chiefs. Those individuals did not just carry out SS orders, they also agreed to chastise and torture their companions, hoping to thus save their own lives, or sometimes also enjoying the pain of others. Even though Levi indicates possible motives of collaboration and identifies the totalitarian state as the original cause of oppression, he condemns all kind of violence executed by the oppressed against the oppressed (Brown 2013).

As far as this point, there is an overlap between Levi's and Shalamov's positions. In the last chapter of the first volume of the *Kolyma Tales*, Shalamov sums up his experience in the different camps by enumerating what he had seen and what he had learnt. Previously, in the ninth tale, "Marching Rations," the narrator affirms his refusal to become a brigadier, because he never wants to impose his will on others. Although he has lost all his empathy in the Gulag and has become a man reduced to obeying his instincts and living for the next moment, he is proud that he has never been responsible for the death of a comrade, as he writes in the last chapter. He adds that he never betrayed any of his companions in misfortune. Concerning the formation of the grey zone, the differences between prisoners and executioners seem to be even more flexible in the Gulag, because the Stalinist system of arbitrary arrests and detentions without trial is based on a variegated image of the enemy. All prisoners with dominant positions can quickly lose their privileges because of betrayal and changing alliances. The entire Russian people were subjected to reprisals, no social class was excluded, and in each village, factory or family there was a neighbor or a relative who suddenly found himself/ herself confronted with some unfounded accusation. The Kolyma region thus constitutes a microcosm in which the totalitarian organization of the Soviet state is reflected.

Unlike Primo Levi, who categorizes the population of the camp in *If this is a Man* by distinguishing the drowned from the saved, Shalamov considers the mass of prisoners "without a biography, without a past and without a future," including himself not in his role as outstanding, observing writer but as a participant of the drama of life. Whereas Levi explores all nuances of grey in the camp, presenting the Special Squads and Chaim Rumkowski, the president of the Łódź ghetto in Poland, as two cases of extreme collaboration, Shalamov does not seek to enter into the moral ambiguities of collaboration. In general, he distinguishes three groups of people: ordinary prisoners, prisoners in a commanding position, and crooks or gangsters, who inhabit a world of their own and who will not hesitate to sell out or kill their companions for a privilege. These are the most dangerous people in the Gulag, because their immorality corrodes the last remnants of solidarity between the oppressed.

In a camp the intellectual occupies a special position, being on the one hand an object of ridicule and mockery, as Shalamov shows in several of his stories, and on the other hand suffering more than the mass of ordinary prisoners because of his analytic mind. As already mentioned, Shalamov leaves no doubt about the disempowerment of intellect in the camp in the face of basic physical needs. The real grey zone in the *Kolyma Tales* does not refer to complicity with the oppressing system of the Gulag, but to the floating transitions between humans and animals. The intellectual can react in two ways: he can either accept the breakdown of civilization and use his mental fortitude in the (biological) struggle for life, or he can continue to believe in the superiority of his intellect, so that his mental strength becomes another source of moral suffering. Shalamov adopts the first attitude. It enables him to endure the physical suffering and the reduction to a sort of primitive, instinctive reasoning concentrated on the satisfaction of essential needs. He rejects the idea of intellectual heroism and stresses the impossibility of escaping from an extreme situation.

Jean Améry, too, states that the victim cannot repress the pain, which remains embedded in the body for the rest of his life. Thus, a single act of torture forever destroys the physical and mental identity of the victim: "Twenty-two years later I am still dangling above the ground by dislocated arms, panting, and accusing myself. In such an instance there is no 'repression.'" (Améry 1980: 36) Classical education becomes pointless in confrontation with the absolute willingness to annihilate the Jews as part of humankind. Intellectual arrogance gets lost in light of an extreme situation such as Auschwitz, in which dying and death are omnipresent and determine the condition of everyday life. The immediate reality of the camp supplants the philosophical idealism and corrodes the aesthetic concept of death presented by Novalis, Arthur Schopenhauer, Richard Wagner, and Thomas Mann. For Améry the consequences that this recognition entails are to be located on a collective and individual level. At the end of his first essay, "At the Mind's Limits," he cites the famous statement that Karl Kraus delivered at the beginning of the Third Reich: "The word fell into sleep, when that world awoke." (Améry 1980: 20) Although Kraus announces the end of the metaphysical dimension of language, he obviously rests convinced of the transcending potential of words. With his discovery that no word can transcend the reality of the camp, Améry puts the futility of culture, and ultimately the worthlessness of the experience he suffered, in the foreground. If there is something to learn about Auschwitz, it is a deep skepticism towards all culture and all idea of humanism.

Neither Améry nor Shalamov envision ethical consequences for writing after Auschwitz and the Gulag (Siguan 2014: 206–207). Whereas Améry, in his essay "On the Necessity and Impossibility of Being a Jew," confesses that the camp experience disabled him for metaphysical speculation, Shalamov, to the contrary, radicalizes the camp as a complete negative experience corrupting everybody who gets in contact with it – including bystanders and readers. In his notes he explains his motivation to write in three points. First, he insists that literature has no moral function and no power to reform humanity. Then he points out that literary texts cannot save mankind from the repetition of history. After having realized the impasse into which he has maneuvered himself by these two negations, he nevertheless expresses hope that the reader of his new prose may be inspired to do something positive in his own life. In spite of all the disillusionment he has suffered, he implicitly indicates in this context an ethical founding of his bearing witness addressed to the other, who in the *Kolyma Tales* is confronted with the truth banished from the official discourse in the Soviet Union and who himself is inclined to forget his troublesome memories and the traumatic events that befell him.

In contrast to Améry and Shalamov, Primo Levi endeavors to show the positive effects of a classical education and cultural knowledge in his essay about the exceptional position of the intellectual in Auschwitz. Levi compares his camp experience to Améry's essay "At the Mind's Limits" that in his view reflects bitterness and emotional coldness, and he indicates perhaps one fundamental difference: whereas Améry entered the camp world as an intellectual, Levi became one only afterwards. His relationship to Améry remains deeply ambivalent, describing him as "companion and antagonist" at the same time. On the one hand, he asserts his affinity by validating the conclusions drawn by Améry. He stresses the similarities of their perceptions and uses the communal voice. On the other hand, he feels the need to present himself as different, be it regarding his definition of the term "intellectual" or referring to his survival philosophy in the camp, which was based on the conservation of his vital energies and at no time on considerations about possible forms of death, which Améry exposes:

> On this point, my experience and my recollections diverge from Améry's. Perhaps because I was younger, perhaps because I was more ignorant than he, or less marked, or less conscious, I almost never had the time to devote to death; I had many other things to keep me busy – find a bit of bread, exhausting work, patch my shoes, steal a broom, or interpret the signs and faces around me. The aims of life are the best defence against death: and not only in the camp. (Levi 2013: 167)

Even if Levi appears to idealize the "aims of life" and his ability to preserve the faith in life within a world of utter negation, he cannot leave the grey zone of guilt and shame and feels himself persecuted by the drowned, as he repeatedly admits. His pretended differences from Améry cannot abolish their common Jewish background that marks them both, although in different ways. Whereas Améry, as an Austrian philosopher, is aware of being expelled from the German culture and regards himself homeless, Levi not only finds in his cultural knowledge a source of survival, but he can also return home to a country that in the past had defended him against the attacks of the Germans and the Austrians (Segre 2003). If he lacks Améry's political education, he becomes more and more political in *The Drowned and the Saved*, where he emphasizes the persistence of mass violence and insists on the collective responsibility of the German people for crimes against humanity perpetrated by the Nazis. Bearing witness for him, as for Améry and Shalamov, becomes in this context an act of self-assertion and at the same time a performative display of his physical and mental vulnerability.

Works cited

Adorno, Theodor W. (1991) "The essay as form," in *Notes to Literature* ed. Rolf Tiedemann, trans. Shierry Weber Nicholson (New York: Columbia University Press), vol. I, 3–23.
Agamben, Giorgio (1999) *Remnants of Auschwitz. The Witness and the Archive* (New York: Zone books).
Améry, Jean (1980) *At the Mind's Limits. Contemplations by a Survivor on Auschwitz and its Realities* (Bloomington: Indiana University Press).
Brown, Adam (2013) *Judging "Privileged Jews." Holocaust Ethics, Representation and the "Grey Zone"* (New York and Oxford: Berghahn).
Didi-Huberman, Georges (2010) *Remontages du temps subi. L'œil de l'Histoire, 2* [The eye of history], (Paris: Minuit).
Felman, Shoshana and Dori Laub (1992) *Testimony: Crisis of Witnessing in Literature, Psychoanalysis and History* (New York: Routledge).

Golden, Nathanel (2004) *Varlam Shalamov's "Kolyma Tales." A Formalist Analysis* (Amsterdam and New York: Rodopi).
Hofmann, Michael (2003) *Literaturgeschichte der Shoah* [Literary history of the Holocaust], (Münster: Aschendorff Verlag).
Hyvernaud, Georges (1997) *La Peau et les Os* [Skin and bones], (Paris: Le Dilettante).
Hyvernaud, Georges (1994) *Skin and Bones* (Evanston: Marlboro Press).
Hyvernaud, Georges (1997) *Wagon à vaches* [The cattle car], (Paris: Le Dilettante).
Hyvernaud, Geores (1997) *The Cattle Car* (Evanston: Marlboro Press).
Jurgenson, Luba (2007) "Spur, Dokument, Prothese. Varlam Shalamovs *Erzählungen aus Kolyma*" [Trace, document, prosthesis. Varlam Shalamov's *Tales from Kolyma*], *Osteuropa* 57.6, 169–182.
Kertész, Imre (1999) *Eine Gedankenlänge Stille, während das Erschießungskommando neu lädt. Essays* [For the duration of a thought. Silence while the killing squad is reloading. Essays], (Reinbek bei Hamburg: Rowohlt).
Kissel, Wolfgang Stephan (2009) "Überlebenswissen in Varlam Shalamovs *Erzählungen aus Kolyma*. Zur Epistemologie der *Vita minima*" [Knowledge for survival. Varlam Shalamov's *Tales from Kolyma*. The epistemology of the *Vita minima*], *Poetica. Zeitschrift für Sprach- und Literaturwissenschaft* 41, 161–187.
Krämer, Sybille, Sibylle Schmidt and Ramon Voges (eds) (2011) *Politik der Zeugenschaft. Zur Kritik einer Wissenspraxis* [Politics of witnessing. Towards a critique of knowledge], (Bielefeld: Transcript).
Lanzmann, Claude (1985) *Shoah* (film). New Yorker Films.
Lecarme, Jacques (2009) "Georges Hyvernaud (1902–1983)," in *Mémoires du roman. La revue littéraire des romanciers oubliés. Domains francais – XXe siècle*, ed. Bruno Curatolo and Paul Renard (Besançon: Presses Universitaires de Franche-Comté), 93–105.
Leys, Ruth (2007) *From Guilt to Shame. Auschwitz and After* (Princeton: Princeton University Press), 157–179.
Levi, Primo (1959) *If This is a Man* (New York: Orion Press).
Levi, Primo (2013) *The Drowned and the Saved* (London: Abacus).
Lorenz, Dagmar (1991) *Scheitern als Ereignis. Der Autor Jean Améry im Kontext europäischer Kulturkritik* [Failing as event. Jean Améry in the context of European traditions of cultural critique], (Frankfurt am Main: Peter Lang), 94–125.
Poetini, Christian (2014) *Weiterüberleben. Jean Améry und Imre Kertész* [Continue to survive. Jean Améry und Imre Kertész], (Bielefeld: Aisthesis).
Schmidt, Sibylle (2009) *Zeugenschaft. Ethische und politische Dimensionen* [Testimonies. Ethical and political dimensions], (Frankfurt am Main: Peter Lang).
Schmidt, Sibylle (2015) *Ethik und Episteme der Zeugenschaft* [Ethics and epistemology of witnessing], (Kontanz: University Press).
Schmid, Ulrich (2007) "Nicht-Literatur ohne Moral. Warum Varlam Shalamov nicht gelesen wurde" [Non-literature without moral constraints. Why Varlam Shalamov has not been read], *Osteuropa* 57.6, 87–105.
Segre, Cesare (2003) "Un dissenso istruttivo: Primo Levi e Jean Améry" [Intuitive disagreement: Primov Levi and Jean Améry], in *I sommersi e I salvati* [The Drowned and the Saved], ed. Primo Levi (Torino: Einaudi), 203–213.
Semprún, Jorge (2005) "Niemand wird mehr sagen können: 'Ja, so war es'" [Nobody will be able to say: Yes, that's how it was], *Die Zeit* 16, 14 April, 52.
Shalamov, Varlam (1994) *Kolyma Tales* (London: Penguin).

Shalamov, Varlam (2014) "On prose," trans. Brian R. Johnson, in *Late and Post-Soviet Russian Literature: A Reader*, book II: Thaw and Stagnation, ed. Mark Lipovetsky and Lisa Ryoko Wakamiya (Brighton: Academic Studies Press), 111–126.

Siguan, Marisa (2014) *Schreiben an den Grenzen der Sprache. Studien zu Améry, Kertész, Semprún, Schalamow, Herta Müller und Aub* [Writing on the borders of language. Studies on Améry, Kertész, Semprún, Shalamov, and Herta Müller], (Berlin: De Gruyter).

Starobinski, Jean (2001) *Montaigne. Denken und Existenz* [Montaigne. Thoughts and existence], (Frankfurt am Main: Fischer).

Thun-Hohenstein, Franziska (2007) "Poetik der Unerbittlichkeit. Varlam Shalamov: Leben und Werk" [Poetics of implacability. Varlam Shalamov: Life and work], *Osteuropa* 57.6, 35–51.

Toker, Leona (1989) "Stories from Kolyma: the sense of history," in *Hebrew University Studies in Literature and the Arts* XVII, (Hebrew University of Jerusalem, Institute of Languages, Literatures and Arts), 188–221.

Toker, Leona (2000) *Return from the Archipelago. Narratives of Gulag Survivors* (Bloomington: Indiana University Press).

Troebst, Stefan (2005) "Jalta versus Stalingrad, GULag versus Holocaust. Konfligierende Erinnerungskulturen im größeren Europa" [Conflicting memorial cultures in a greater Euorpe], *Berliner Journal für Soziologie* 15.3, 381–400.

Wieviorka, Annette (2005) *Auschwitz, 60 ans après* [Auschwitz, 60 years later], (Paris: Laffont).

Irina Sandomirskaja
The Ghetto of Leningrad, the Siege of Theresienstadt: A Comparative Reading of Enforced Communities

1 How to compare the incomparable?

In this chapter I will summarize two research projects – one about the siege of Leningrad, the other about the SS concentration camp/Jewish ghetto of Theresienstadt. I have been working on these projects for a long time, but until now I never considered them from a common perspective. This chapter contains only a small part of what I think would be needed in order to create a relevant comparative study. The reader will certainly note one highly relevant aspect of the comparison I am not touching upon, for lack of space: the intensive cultural production in Theresienstadt and in Leningrad, a factor that creates the strongest affinity between those contexts and at the same time marks them out as absolutely unique. These stories will have to be left for another occasion. In what follows, I have had to restrict myself to just a sketch of Theresienstadt and Leningrad as comparable *dispositifs*. My purpose is not even a comparative study in the proper sense of the term: comparativity itself is a way of thinking about and representing concepts and ideas that requires a separate critical discussion. What I am trying to do is listen to the voices of Leningrad and Theresienstadt as if they were talking in a chorus, or rather singing a motet: never in unison, each one leading its own individual melody and theme, but complementing and enriching each other, each voice sometimes questioning, and sometimes supporting the other.

For the purpose of this study, one of these voices belongs to Lydia Ginzburg, the author of a piercing analysis of the catastrophe of Leningrad during the 900 days of its besiegement in 1941–1944.[1] The other is that of Hans Günther Adler, historian and sociologist of another catastrophe, that of the town and fortress of Terezin, and its Jewish ghetto / concentration camp of Theresienstadt during the five years it existed (1941–1945) (Adler 2005).[2] I will try to

---

[1] On Ginzburg's biography and her critique of culture, see Ginzburg (2011: 501–557), as well as Van Baskirk and Zorin (2012).
[2] Adler (2005, 2017). On Adler's days and works, see Adler (200: 71–100) and Franklin (2011); a more recent and rich collection of essays about Adler covering his biography, scholarly and literary work is Finch and Wolff (2014). It was G. W. Sebald who (re)discovered Adler for the

compare these two contexts and corpora by looking at the similarities of the respective spatiotemporal structures, the organization of systems of violence, and the resulting subjectivities. I will attempt to reconstruct these two historical episodes and the two projects of writing about them, as disparate as they are, as if reflecting (on) each other and illuminating each other's darkness. Quite simply speaking, this work is an attempt to analyze a siege as a form of ghettoization, and a ghetto as a form of besiegement.[3]

2 Siege and ghetto: Reciprocality of forms of oppression

Both Leningrad and Theresienstadt were material and symbolic *loci* governed by the rule of the state of exception.[4] This term can be understood twofold, and this is just one ambiguity that we are going to confront in the co-reading of Theresienstadt and Leningrad. On the one hand, it is the state of exception as suggested by Giorgio Agamben (2005). Both contexts can be considered special cases of community, brought together, constituted and maintained through the force of organized coercion (or *Zwangsgemeinschaften*, a term devised by H. G. Adler), ruled by the military order, by the law of the state of war, with the suspension of all legal forms of power as well as division of power. On the other hand, the state of exception can be understood metaphorically, as related to the extremely uncertain conditions of the person who is subject to it, excluded from ordinary life and forced to lead an existence that in every respect represents an exception from the norms of humanity. Both Leningrad in besiegement and Theresienstadt controlled by the SS became places of extreme social experimentation, where technologies of power were invented, sometimes *ad hoc*, and applied without

---

broad reading public by including a reflection on his book about Theresienstadt in his internationally acclaimed novel *Austerlitz*.
3 I am indebted to Franziska Thun-Hohenstein who first suggested the idea of such a reciprocal transformation in her approach to Ginzburg as a phenomenon of camp civilization (Thun-Hohenstein 2007: 41–86).
4 First proposed by Carl Schmitt, the concept of the state of exception was preceded by other terms ("dictatorship" and "the state of siege"), or according to Schmitt, a system that "seems to subtract itself from any consideration of law." For a critique of Schmitt's political-theological understanding of the state of exception, as well as the relevance of the "subtraction of law" for present-day political orders, see Agamben (2005: 1–40); the quotation from Schmitt in Agamben (2005: 32–33).

any reservations to manipulate human life to the brink of extermination.⁵ Ghetto and besiegement have organizational, political, and existential structures that allow us to consider both, after Walter Benjamin, as places in which emergency and exception became the only norm.⁶ This may explain why the stories of both stand somewhat apart within each of their grand narratives, that of the Great Patriotic War and that of the Holocaust, respectively. While these narratives are memorialized and cultivated as epics of heroism and martyrdom, both contexts in question, each in its own way, conceal complexities that the standard narratives cannot account for.

Hundreds of thousands of civilians were locked inside the Leningrad siege without a way out and subjected to unrelenting and unspeakably cruel extermination by artillery and air raid attacks, hunger, disease, slave labor, police repressions, and all possible forms of humiliation. Since the end of the siege, this story has been told in many ways, but never free from ideological control and political speculation (Dzeniskevich 1998). As often happens, especially when the history of the event is written by a repressive regime like that of post-war Stalinism, the survivors of the siege were mostly silent, or presented their personal experience in a way that would confirm the official narrative of heroism and self-sacrifice.⁷ In Soviet historiography, the catastrophe of the civil population was only an episode in the military history of Leningrad, in which the massive destruction inside the city – through hunger and disease more than through bombing and shelling – could be written off as collateral damage (which, incidentally, has not yet been fully assessed, not even statistically).⁸ At the same time, the images and narratives about the heroic people of the city of Lenin and the crucible of the Russian

---

5 Emil Utitz, a philosopher and survivor of Theresienstadt, in his 1948 study of Theresienstadt's psychology, ironically defined it as an experiment: "Theresienstadt war ja ein 'Experiment', wie es vielleicht noch niemals da war und hoffentlich nie wieder sein wird." [Theresienstadt was an "experiment," one that had not existed before and hopefully will never exist again] (Mehring 2015: 38). H.G. Adler also considered concentration camps to be used by the SS as "a field for experimentation in evil" (Adler 2013: 57) and ascribed the idea of political technologies and experimentation in history to "mechanical materialism" (2013: 130), which, he believed, underlay the Nazi philosophy and the SS practice in concentration camps.
6 "The tradition of the oppressed teaches us that the 'state of emergency' in which we live is not the exception but the rule." (Benjamin 2003: 392).
7 On the moral condition and behavior during the most devastating period of the siege, see Iarov (2012). The concept of *blokadnyi styd* (the shame of the siege), the predominant attitude among the survivors towards their own experiences in besiegement, is discussed by the poet and historian of the siege, Polina Barskova, for instance in Barskova and Sandomirskaja (2012).
8 See, for instance, Cherepenina (2005: 28–70).

revolution, dying but not surrendering to the overwhelming force of the Nazi invasion, were actively used by Soviet authorities in the propaganda abroad and in negotiations with the Allies on the division of Europe after the defeat of the Nazis.

In another episode of besiegement, that of the Jewish prisoners in the former fortress of Theresienstadt – a little township that, according to the Nazi propaganda, was Hitler's personal gift to the Jews and a "paradise" of a concentration camp[9]– the Jews appeared *as if* they have found an oasis of relative peacefulness, *as if* they were not under threat of immediate destruction, and to themselves their doom appeared *as if* to be suspended and delayed. I will presently return to the deadly significance of this pregnant operator of metaphorization, the marker of imaginary and falsified reality, the *as if* of Theresienstadt and Leningrad. This suspension was the central moment that set Theresienstadt apart from an "ordinary" concentration camp and from Auschwitz, where Adler also spent several months after his deportation from Theresienstadt in 1944. The Satanic misrepresentation of a concentration camp as a paradise was created and promoted by the Nazis with a dual purpose of disinformation both inside the Reich and in the wider world or, towards the end of the war, of persuading international Jewish communities to pay for the release of their compatriots. The demand that the prisoners uphold the pretense of a happy Jewish life at the price of a hope of survival was extremely ambiguous and morally destructive.[10] Theresienstadt thus became a locus of terrible ambiguities, which needed to be resolved on a daily basis at the very heart of the miserable existence inside the walls of that "paradise," in a place where, in a temporary suspension of physical destruction but subject to the horrors of hunger, disease, death on a massive scale, slavery, and perpetual waiting for one's turn to be sent to the gas chambers – man's moral and symbolic annihilation achieved an unresolvable complexity.

Both Theresienstadt as seen by Adler and Leningrad as seen by Ginzburg appear as phenomena of in-betweenness, as if located neither here nor there, instances of destruction cruelly suspended and deferred – distinct from extermination in death camps, where no *différance* was possible at all and the

---

9 In a little dictionary of Theresienstadt language, Adler explains the notion of "paradise ghetto: "The SS-officer said in 1942 to the 'Judenältester': 'You don't know how well you will be here. We will turn Theresienstadt into a paradise ghetto.'" (2005: XLVII) Later, he continues: "In order to create this paradise 17,500 persons had to disappear in Auschwitz." (151).
10 Adler called Theresienstadt's efforts to look like a paradise "the most spectacular ring dance of ghosts in the history of the persecution of the Jews" (2005: 151). Benjamin Murmelstein, the last Jewish elder of Theresienstadt, compared the ghetto with Sheherezade, whose life and safety depended on her ability to tell fairy tales and thus to defer her execution, night after night (The United States Holocaust Memorial Museum, 7 October 2015).

victims were slaughtered immediately after their transports arrived. Theresienstadt and Leningrad had structures of violence and destruction that were quite distinct, representing a parenthesis in the totality of annihilation, for whatever life was possible inside to continue at the expense of the contradictions of the regimens that regulated and decided over it, a life that was extremely fragile and constantly on the verge of termination. This interim world produced a subject that was, too, an instance of contradictory in-betweenness, a human being suspended from history. Ginzburg calls this subject "an unrequested man" (*neponadobivshiisia chelovek*), he (she) whom

> [t]he siege allows [...] to keep [...] busy by preserving his own life. [...] He has not as yet been called forth by the Leviathan and is therefore doomed to idleness that is probably the punishment of sinners in hell. He is in the middle of everything, everyone is next to him; passively, he experiences everything, but himself, he does not participate in anything. (Ginzburg 2011: 432)[11]

In the case of Theresienstadt, suspension from history was even more complicated. Locked in the "paradise ghetto," the prisoners appeared to be saved, to be unjustly privileged amidst the total annihilation that was the common destiny of European Jewry; an ambiguous and inexplicable favor from the executioner that did indeed save life, but also saved the image of the SS in the eyes of the observers abroad and increased the chances for the SS to avoid retribution after defeat.[12] The way the SS advertised Hitler's "gift" served directly to even further increase antisemitism in Germany, already full of hatred, frustrated and suffering from the privations of the final year of the war. The antisemitic propaganda established by the SS in Theresienstadt portrayed the prisoners as happy holidaymakers celebrating in the middle of Germany's disaster, and the Jews, moreover, were forced to produce these images themselves.[13] This situation can be compared to the malicious rumors about the alleged well-being of the prisoners of

---

[11] All translations from Russian are mine.

[12] This became particularly evident in connection with the Danish and International Red Cross inspections in Theresienstadt in 1944. In preparation for the visits, the ghetto was thoroughly rebuilt, sanitized, and decorated to look like a "Jewish settlement." Prisoners were forced to participate in a humiliating performance by acting like happy settlers. A detailed history is available in Adler (2005: 150–184).

[13] Adler describes the story of two film projects in Theresienstadt in which the prisoners were forced to play the "Jewish types" living a happy life in a model paradise (2005: especially 180–184). See also Karel Margry (1992, 1999). Extensive visual materials and documentation were shown in Terezín in 2014, in an exhibition called *Truth and Lies: Filming in the Terezín Ghetto, 1942–1945* (see also a DVD of the same title produced by the Jewish Museum in Prague). In September 2014, Natascha Drubek-Meyer organized a conference *Films from Ghettos and*

the Leningrad siege that circulated outside the city, especially in the Kremlin, convinced that the Leningrad authorities were covering up a mass sabotage of Stalin's war efforts. As if punished for their suspension from everybody else's history of heroism and martyrdom, the almost extinct populations of Leningrad and Theresienstadt, each in their own way, became convinced (persuaded by the respective regimes) that this ambiguous enforced in-betweenness was their own shame and personal guilt.[14]

Both Ginzburg and Adler were aware that the complexity of each set of circumstances would negatively affect the memory of their victims.[15] Long after the war, the authors fought their own struggles to make their work public and both were resigned to the fact that even long afterwards their writing was but partially acceptable. Indeed, recognition came to Ginzburg only too late in life, and to Adler, in fact, posthumously. They fought on because they were convinced that their voice was vitally important for the understanding of post-war realities, both in Western European democracies and in the post-Stalinist USSR.

Similarities between Leningrad and Theresienstadt appear in their respective topologies, temporalities, and subjectivities. Both were organized, supported, and made effective by means of multiple technologies of power. In Theresienstadt, it was violence of the SS, combined with a system of policing inside (the German *Ordnungspolizei* and the Czech *gendarmes*) and with administrative bureaucracy of the camp's "self-administration" (the Jewish Council, which organized slave workforce to produce cheap goods for the SS and decided, among other things, who to send to the gas chambers),[16] and still further

---

Camps: Propaganda – Clandestine Messages – Historical Source, where these problems were discussed.

14 Of the daily sacrifices among the dying friends and relatives, Ginzburg says: "Writhing with pity or cursing, people would share their bread. They cursed and shared; they shared, and died. Those who had left the city also left such domestic sacrifices to those who stayed behind. And the insufficiency of sacrifices (if you survived, that means you hadn't sacrificed enough), and the remorse, together with the insufficiency." (2011: 314).

15 Adler's novel *The Wall* (first published in 1989) is about the SS Jewish Museum in Prague and is dedicated to the problem of de-memorializing the falsified collective memory produced by the ideological effort of the killers. On apparatuses of representation and falsification in Adler's novels, see Sandomirskaja (2016).

16 The painful topic of "Selbstverwaltung" ("self-administration"; by Adler given always in quotation marks) by the Jewish Council in the ghetto and its responsibility has been debated ever since Hannah Arendt made her statement about the negative role played by Jewish councils in ghettoes and by Jewish communities in the Third Reich. To a great extent, Arendt's criticism was based on Adler's analysis of "self-administration" in Theresienstadt. "Self-administration" contributed to the ambiguity and in-betweenness of the subject in the ghetto discussed in this chapter.

complicated by symbolic violence involved in the SS propaganda efforts abroad. The last was particularly ambiguous, marking Theresienstadt's (and its prisoners') unique position in the universe of Nazi concentration camps. Being forced to take part in the fabrication of lies about themselves, the Jewish victims were exposed to profound (self-)humiliation that proved terribly morally destructive – even though it was robbing them of their dignity, their participation effectively delayed their physical destruction, for as long as the propaganda needed them more or less alive and "happy" for its own purposes. One remarkable period of suspended destruction is remembered by all survivors in their memoirs, and Adler dedicated many pages to it in his own account about Theresienstadt as well as in his novel *Eine Reise* (1962, Engl. *The Journey*, 2008). It coincided with the SS campaign of *Verschönerung* (embellishment), a bizarre, absurd, and extremely cruel project of camouflaging Theresienstadt's misery (including its half-dead population) in preparation for a visit of the International Red Cross. The idea was to present the concentration camp as a happy and modern Jewish settlement. Even during that relatively "vegetarian time" (Anna Akhmatova) of *Verschönerungwahnsinn* (the craze to embellish the camp), 7500 prisoners were transported to Auschwitz (Adler 2005: 180).

In Leningrad, destruction was no less complex in terms of its forces, and as manifold in structure. Apart from military violence by the Nazis and their allies surrounding the city, the quickly diminishing remainder of life inside it was totally dominated by political terror at the hands of the NKVD pursuing imaginary treason and revolt among the civilians, locked inside and dying every day by the thousands, decimated by the combined effects of shooting, bombing, hunger, disease, suicide, and cannibalism. There was also another kind of violence – the power of discipline, when city authorities used policing to mobilize even the terminally ill to perform public work. No less damaging was the administrative rule by an arbitrary power of decree of the city bureaucracy, in the distribution of food coupons, medical help, childcare, and other support. Bread rations, for instance, were distributed according to the person's "usefulness"; this administrative violence in the giving out (or withdrawal) of vital resources controlled by the bureaucracy predictably led to another type of pressure: uncontrollable economic violence by an invisible hand of the criminalized, and an even more vigorous black market that re-distributed the scanty resources through a system of privileges and/or pure banditry.[17] Like

---

[17] Lomagin (2005) writes about political control and monitoring of public attitudes in besieged Leningrad, and has also published documents on how the authorities were policing and criminalizing the practices of economic exchange, including extreme cases of banditry and cannibalism (Lomagin 2000: 142–290).

Theresienstadt, Leningrad was actively used by the propaganda and the information war that the USSR waged against both its enemies and its allies, which gave Leningrad citizens hope of survival, even at the expense of considerable moral sacrifices. Ginzburg, for instance, survived because she was employed by Leningrad's Radio Committee, the very heart of the Soviet propaganda in and outside Leningrad. To the outside world it broadcast a brutally falsified, heroized image of the city of death, but to the city itself it delivered a mere appearance of communication and coherence, for the most part serving the purposes of disinformation and mobilization.[18]

The in-betweenness from which their writing sprung also seemed to cast a shadow over the authors themselves. Ginzburg's privileged (even though insignificantly so) position inside the propaganda system saved her during the war, but resulted in an ambiguity and doubt around her testimony that are still present in reader responses today. Adler's history of Theresienstadt was highly appreciated by the progressive intellectuals after the war (Hanna Arendt, Theodor Adorno, and Elias Canetti among them), but rejected as evidence at the Eichmann trial in 1961, apparently for political reasons.[19] Adler's fiction – a corpus of unpublished prose and poetry, including a three-volume set of novels in which he reflected upon his wartime experiences – was rejected as not good literature during his lifetime and only published posthumously, in the 2000s, when all of a sudden he was discovered as a genius author, "compared by critics to Kafka and Joyce [...] one of the towering figures of twentieth-century's fiction," as proclaimed in a blurb on the back cover of the first American edition, in 2015, of his 1989 novel *The Wall*. At the same time Adler's literary prose was criticized, Ginzburg was struggling to have her notes from the siege published; Leningrad publishing houses invariably rejected them as of insufficient literary and generally aesthetic qualities (Van Buskirk and Zorin 2011: 545–556).

3 An enforced community

As already mentioned, I am reading these two events outside of their "natural" classificatory nomenclatures, as if they were reflections in each other's mirrors:

---

18 Communication in the city in the absence of any media or other reliable information is discussed by Piankevich (2014).
19 On the difficult relations between Adler and Adorno, and Adler's critique of Adorno's thesis about the impossibility of writing poetry after Auschwitz, see Adler (2000: 71–100).

Leningrad as a case of ghettoization, Theresienstadt as a case of besiegement. Their structural similarities, outlined above, account both for the complexity of power relations and for the ambiguities of their respective subjectivities. Adler worked hard to elaborate his historical and sociological models of modern subjectivities, both in his book on Theresienstadt and in a later treatise on *Verwaltung* (administration): a modern technique of power that he researched when writing a history of Jewish deportations in the Third Reich.[20] Adler's "administered man" (*der verwaltete Mensch*) is a twin of Ginzburg's own character summing up subjectivity in besiegement, a "siege man" (*blokadnyi chelovek*). To account for both of these, I will use Adler's concept of *Zwangsgemeinschaft* – an enforced community: a community of coercion, a community imposed on its subjects by force and violence. What is the structure of such a community? Let us see how this is approached by Lydia Ginzburg.

Leningrad's besiegement is generally imagined as a circle produced by just one force of coercion and violence: the catastrophe of the civil population is explained as being entirely a consequence of military actions by the Nazis. Similarly, in the collective memory of concentration camps, it is the violence of the SS and the Gestapo that appears to have created the isolation of the state of exception inside. I contend that the structure of power was more complicated and the administration inside the walls, holding the siege/ghetto in place, was no less coercive or violent and no less destructive towards the citizens/inmates, even though in different ways, through different means and with different goals. Both Ginzburg in her anthropology of besieged Leningrad and Adler in his history and sociology of Theresienstadt identify a significant moment of a reduplication of the circle of besiegement. From the outside, military violence isolates it from the outer world, to prevent the town from exploding and the inmates from spilling out into the free world. From the inside, administrative violence enforces draconian rules to prevent it from implosion and collapse. Ginzburg describes the reduplication of coercion in her characteristic language of understatement, as originating from two terribly anonymous, omnipotent and evil sources: "these" and "those" (Ginzburg 2011: 432). "Those" are the Nazis, with their artillery attacks and air raids, leaving thousands of dead bodies lying around in destroyed apartments and in the streets. "These" are the NKVD, with their night searches and arrests, when people disappear without a trace and without anyone asking about their fate. Both "these" and "those" appear with certain regularity, at fixed times during the daytime and/or at night.

---

[20] *Der verwaltete Mensch* is discussed in Adler (1974) and a shorter version is included in Adler (2013: 189–238).

Intervals in between their appearances are more or less peaceful and constitute the order of a daily cycle, fear of death retreating for some time to come back later, at the scheduled hour of an air raid alarm or, also scheduled, a ring at the door at night. Ginzburg thus suggests that death and destruction seized Leningraders both from within and from without, in rhythmic cycles, as if time were coiling into a pattern of repetitions, into a vicious circularity that seemed to reproduce the circular topology of the besieged city. The temporality and spatiality of the siege appeared to be mimicking each other, both locked onto themselves and moving no further, like two tautologies. Just like the urban space turned into a closed circle without an exit, so time was going on but moving nowhere, towards no purpose or aim.

This double encirclement in a tautological time and a tautological space produced the ambiguity of besiegement, since its second – internal circle was meant to resist the first – external one, by means of an indefinitely prolonged struggle, making it impossible for the enemy to take the city and making the civilians' suffering even more unbearable. The city was being saved from surrender by sacrificing the civilian population on the altar of defense. Leningrad's self-administration therefore was difficult to differentiate from self-immolation: the survival of the city was ensured by a radical reduction of the collective body of its citizens. Surrounded by the circle of advancing Nazi troops and their allies, Leningrad was allowing, willingly or involuntarily, a massive loss of human life drowning in an abyss of famine, cold, darkness, and illness. The external forces of encirclement exerted physical violence trying to break up the ring from the outside. Inside the circle, the city defending itself inflicted violence on its civil population, trying to eradicate any seed of possible revolt that could explode the siege from within.[21]

However, this task could not be achieved by pure repression: through a dense network of informers and denouncers, "these" were scanning the city for the minutest manifestations of "negative attitudes," but political repression could not stop growing entropy. As a matter of security, life in the city needed to be policed, but also organized and selectively supported, fed and sanitized: the administration of daily life, evacuating those who could be made useful elsewhere, mobilizing whatever workforce was available for the management of the city and its defense facilities, and the administration of the remaining, the already unusable ones, including the dying and the dead. The result was that the

---

[21] Nikita Lomagin's research on the policing and management of the Leningrad population (Lomagin 2000, 2005) is an extremely useful source for the understanding of the logic of "these" not only cleansing the city, but gaining more and more power over all other authorities.

majority (still not fully accounted for in the statistics) died of hunger and diseases that the inadequate city administration was incapable of (or just did not consider worthwhile) preventing. "A pretty well-organized famine," was Ginzburg's laconic and highly ambiguous description of the situation (Ginzburg 2002: 646). The terrible ambiguity of besiegement is that one cannot give a definite answer to the question of whether city bureaucracy was the factor that actually saved life, or did it rather work as a macabre ministry of death whose "pretty well organized" malfunction actually contributed to the appalling mortality rates among the civilians, the figures so shocking that they were deleted even from top secret statistics of the time (Cherepenina 2005). Masses of people perished not only in direct extermination by war or terror, but also as a result of daily life administration, "pretty well organized" – in practice, either not prioritized or intentionally torpedoed by the military authorities (in one case) and camp administration (in the other).

4 Bureaucracy and the act of writing as complicit in oppression

In *Theresienstadt 1941–1945*, Adler provides a complete outline of the administration of the population in the ghetto: a full nomenclature on seventeen pages in very small type painting a monumental picture of the internal regimen of Theresienstadt, the order of the inner circle of its tautological chronotope: the draconic discipline of regulations and institutions imposed over the everyday reality of very difficult and conflicted survival (Adler 2005: 223–240). The list is, indeed, a faithful representation of *Verwaltung* as, in Adler's view, an organized insanity expressing itself in a hyper-systematic nomenclature of terrifying euphemisms. Adler explains their actual meaning in a mini-lexicon of Theresienstadt terms and concepts attached to the tome (e.g. *Transportabteilung* – the management of deportations, *Matratzenreferat* – privileges gained by some prisoners to the detriment of others) (Adler 2005: XXI–LIX). In a terrifyingly monotonous way, in an incessant flow of very long, hardly readable and almost incomprehensible substantive nouns, in a typical Nazi version of German bureaucratic language, Adler lists all of the bureaucratic institutions in the ghetto, its executive bodies, councils, departments, divisions, subdivisions, groups responsible for performing occasional functions, including policing, finance, food, housing, cleaning and hygiene, medical services, the rationing of work and free time, family, old age, childcare, culture and entertaining – in short, the full regimen of an evil Utopia, an ironic macabre of state order, a perversion and parody of all allegorical cities of the European tradition, including Plato's *politeia*, Campanella's *Sun City* and Moore's *Utopia*. There is a ghostly visibility of order ruling over the reality of a spectral, semi-extinct life, a "pseudo-order of Chaos, a specter of order"[22] (Adler 2005: 240–241).

By defining the Theresienstadt ghetto as a *Zwangsgemeinschaft* (enforced community), Adler followed the Weberian discrimination between force and power, between governing by open violence or by the coercion of *die Zwangsapparate* (apparatus of force), with their administrative regulations. Such is also the nature of coercion in the *Zwangsgemeinschaft* of Theresienstadt as Adler construes it: officially, the apparatus of coercion is called "*Selbstverwaltung*." The re-thinking, in the reality of terror in Theresienstadt, of Weber's concept of *Verwaltung* and the human problems involved in this technique of modern power – its politics, economics, and ethics – became Adler's most important contribution to the understanding of the Holocaust as a specifically modern historical phenomenon. Concentration camps in the Third Reich were ruled by a division of the SS responsible for SS's economic activities, the *SS-Wirtschafts-Verwaltungshauptamt*. That is, the connection between the administration of human bodies and the economic considerations and interests that drove the process forward was evident even in the nomenclature.

Adler introduced his theory of administration by postulating the uniquely modern character of *Verwaltung* as a form of executive power (or violence, *Gewalt*) that did not appear in the European state until the early 1800s and since then has radically changed the reality of the state as such (2005: 189–190).[23] He described the Nazi bureaucracy of annihilation as abused or abnormal administration, in an opposition to some imaginary normal one, while at the same time considering administration in itself – even of the "normal" kind – an abuse of the human being, a way of transforming living humans into objects, and life and death into a question of bookkeeping.

Adler's analysis of the biopolitics of *Verwaltung*, however, has an important symbolic dimension. Administration – initially, a subsidiary technique of record-making and keeping track of economic transactions, or the bookkeeping of power in a modern state, according to Adler – primarily amounts to the practice of writing. Its purpose as writing is to produce representation of social

---

[22] Germ. "Scheinordnung des Chaotischen, eine Gespentenordnung."
[23] Regrettably, neither Ginzburg's nor Adler's voice has been heard so far in the discussion of bureaucracy after Weber, e.g. by Hannah Arendt and the Frankfurt School. Another interesting comparative context would be Michel Foucault's biopolitics, the development of pastoral power into administrative surveillance and regulation, and the gradual overpowering of law in modern society by administrative regimes. Hopefully, such comparative reading will emerge in the near future.

events that it seeks to administer over. However, writing – any writing in general – commands a share of autonomy and thus claims considerable power. Administrative writing *preserves* objects, processes, and human lives in its archives of protocols, acts, doctor's reports, and other documents; however, it would be more precise to say that administrative writing *produces* things, processes, and human lives as something preservable and further manipulable. There is no bureaucracy without production and exchange of written instructions and reports; the production of written records of its own activities is in fact *the* activity of administration: it is a body of institutions that acts by incessantly telling (writing) the stories of their own activities. *Verwaltung* is therefore first and foremost a symbolic medium, a universe of discourse seeking to impose control on life by accumulating detailed administrative archives in which reality is produced as consisting of *a priori* manipulable entities.

Now, in an "abnormal" situation, such as the deportation and extermination of the Jews in Nazi Germany, state violence is exercised by military command (*Befehlsgewalt*), by an uncontrollable ruler that abolishes the division of power into its legislative, executive and judicial domains and replaces it with the rule of the state of exception (Adler 2005: 232–234; see Agamben 2005). Thus, administration substitutes its own procedures and protocols for the procedures of legitimate power and takes over those tasks that in a normal situation constitute the tasks of governing and enforcement. A combination of bureaucracy with its uninterrupted production of papers on the one hand, and uncontrollable rule by military command on the other was the mechanism by which mass deportations and exterminations were implemented, when the internal logic and the instrumental order of the bureaucratic *Verwaltung* imposed its symbolic order over anomy in a society subjected to rule by military order. The total rule of *Befehlsgewalt* and the limitless potential of administration re-writing life into manipulable archives combine in a reality in which life finds itself completely overtaken by the writerly routines of the *Schreibtischtäter* ("desk perpetrators"). Here, the symbolic orders of writing and representation played a crucial role. When left to its own devices in the anonymity of the anomy of the total rule, administration tends to grow its records of social life to a critical extent, and representation – a record of a life event – tends to be a substitute for the life event as such, reduplicating reality and producing a counter-world and an alternative reality that replaces with its own images the actual reality of the human beings.[24]

---

[24] Representation that betrays life and literally takes over its place is a recurrent motif in Adler's novels (Sandomirskaja 2016).

While Adler explains the logic and genesis of *Verwaltung*, Ginzburg makes comparable reflections in the form of laconic, realistic sketches, quasi-anecdotes from the everyday life of the besieged city. As if playing myth to Adler's logos, her observations in the physiology of the dying Leningrad appear to have been written specifically to complement Adler's speculations. What Adler analyzes by revealing its logic, Ginzburg demonstrates in allegories and fables. Such is her study of various types of petty secretaries, doctors, and other rank-and-file functionaries in the *Zwangsgemeinschaft* of Leningrad, the regime's human puppets, concrete embodiments of the fundamental principle of coercion in besiegement by segregating people into those to be supported and those left to die (Ginzburg 2011: 300–301).

In an image of a well-fed and completely dehumanized secretary, a female *Schreibtischtäter*, the reader confronts an Adlerian situation: an act of administration – by definition, an act of registering, signifying, and thus representing life – seeks to become an instance of life itself, to become a social being (*gesellschaftliches Dasein*, Adler 2005: 236), at the expense of the death of a living being (*Dasein*) confronting the secretary face to face and begging, in vain, to be saved. Representation – the *als ob* (as if) of life – exterminates the object of representation, life itself.

This absolute domination of the bureaucratic *als ob* over the reality of human annihilation is represented by Ginzburg in an allegory of the distrophic human body. When the "pretty well organized famine" becomes an instrument of government, what happens is primarily a catastrophe of language, the de-metaphorization of all meaning, the reduction of the symbolic universe to a small number of primordial and primitive direct meanings, to bare references. It is a profound impoverishment of all modalities and connotations, in fact, a collapse of all meaning, memory, and culture.[25] This symbolic implosion seems to reproduce the process of decay in a body dying of hunger and disease. It atrophies because it nourishes on the proteins of its own muscle tissues (Magaeva 2005: 123–159). In other words, the survival of the body – just like the survival of the community – depends on its consumption of itself, on the extermination of the self by the self: a tautology that in its circularity reproduced the spatiotemporal circularity of besiegement and ghettoization. It is a tautological logic of (self-)extermination that Ginzburg allegorized in the image of a dying, distrophic body, and Adler in the analysis of "self-administration" (once again, invariably in

---

[25] On the de-metaphorization of the world in besiegement, as a symbolic and bodily symptom of hunger, with its subsequent re-metaphorization in the process of the subject's social and physical recuperation, see Sandomirskaja (2013: 230–241).

quotation marks) – the circulation, without an exit, of the ever narrowing circles of destruction around a community that seems to be able to preserve and organize itself only by destroying itself, by consuming its own members, by sacrificing its constitutive parts, by decimating itself and nourishing on the death of a share of its members for the sake of the survival of another share.

One can discern the echoes of Kafka's voice in the political theory produced by Adler, a German-speaking Jew from Prague. But even more audible is the voice of Theresienstadt itself. The famous cabaret song that became, in the eyes of the prisoners, the most adequate summary of the absurd and murderous reality of the ghetto described Theresienstadt as a domain of a total power of metaphor, *Die Stadt Als Ob*. Theresienstadt – an *as if* town – consists of spectral *as if* objects and is populated by *as if* people who belong to an *as if* race and live an *as if* life full of *as if* truths, who bear their heavy lot "as if it were not that heavy and speak of a better future as if there could be any tomorrow whatsoever" (*Art against Death*, in Blodig 2002: 215). The *Als Ob* in the song totally denudes human life, not only by driving it to death in an unending torture of violence, hunger, and disease, but also seeking to eliminate any vestige of value and dignity in the subject. This is exactly the effect of "self-administration" in Adler's theory, a metaphor caught up in the complexities of its own counter-world building by purely symbolic acts of reduplicating the living world in its labyrinthine *Als Obs*, dehumanizing – and thus making literally expendable, and easily destructible – millions and millions of thus administered human beings. They were destroyed, Adler specifically underlines, by *Sprachregelungen* (2013: 233), the rules of language usage: a "thanatopolitics of language," to play on a term by Giorgio Agamben; the use of language exclusively towards death.

This system of the "*Selbstverwaltung*" of death, Adler says, as insane as it appeared but in fact designed in all its perfection to serve order by counteracting life, was effective in the formation of a community in Theresienstadt: an unwilling togetherness of men, women, and children, brought together by lawlessness and brutal force. The ghetto's spectral order – the order of its bureaucratic language – indeed cemented the community of prisoners by a mixture of active insanity, passive obsession, and SS violence (Adler 2005: 240). The insanity of Theresienstadt's spectral order resulted from a profound, truly infernal ambiguity in the very foundation of its organization. "Cemented" by the total violence of the total power of the SS, the prisoners lived in an environment that was radically different from the much more understandable reality of a concentration camp, and Adler insists on pointing out the difference again and again. Theresienstadt killed, but not in the same way as the concentration camp did. Ambiguity was the fundamental law and the constructive force creating and reproducing the peculiar *Zwangsgemeinschaft* in which Theresienstadt's Jews were not only imprisoned, but also manipulated and forced to perform a spectacle of the "self-administration" of their own extermination. The prisoner remained cruelly torn into pieces between the violently imposed, murderous discipline of the centripetal forces represented by the institutions of "*Selbstverwaltung*," and the centrifugal forces inherent in the individual, with his life instincts, vitality, and the economic interests of survival.

"*Selbstverwaltung*" was a social invention of Nazi terror, a set of institutions that claimed to support life and order, but in the final analysis saved some life inside itself by destroying the life of the other part, also inside itself. Under the control of the SS, who did not even care to interfere otherwise than by direct violence in exceptional cases, the *Zwangsgemeinschaft* was supposed to itself decide whom from its midst to send to Auschwitz, and when. It was also supposed to come forward with rationalization of such ghastly decisions, and on a regular basis, as a matter of everyday bureaucratic routine. The administration of death in the efforts of preserving life was the unsolvable paradox of Theresienstadt's reality. As for Ginzburg, she seemed to summarize the very essence of Adler's "*Selbstverwaltung*" when she identified "the sign of our time" not in terror or cruelty – that, Ginzburg said, always happened throughout man's history – but in "the all-pervading betrayal that no one ever eluded" (Ginzburg 2002: 308).[26] This, she insists, is the "main feature" of "our time," the whole of the twentieth century that started in 1914, both inside and outside Stalin's empire of hunger, the century that perfected modern power technologies at the expense of millions of deaths, in its various forms of besiegement and ghettoization.

5 Survivors as participants in the theoretical discourse

There is a prejudiced opinion maintaining that survivors are only rarely capable of theorizing their experience. This is most often explained by psychological arguments of traumatization or by phenomenological arguments that any account coming from a survivor would necessary be an incomplete testimony. At best, the survivor can witness partially, that is, supply the audience with some facts, not necessarily correctly narrated or true. At any event, she is not believed to be fully in power to take a critical distance from her own experiences that is necessary for analysis and theoretical generalization.[27] It would appear that there

---

[26] On Ginzburg's analysis of betrayal, see Sandomirskaja (2013: 213–230).
[27] On the impossibility of complete witnessing, see Agamben (2002: 15–40).

exists a division of labor between the survivor and the historian or the political theorist. Survivors live their lives, suffer their sufferings and experience their experience, but because their horizon is limited by the reality of living, they cannot step outside of it to make sense of their own existence. As opposed to that, historians/theorists do not partake of the survivor's living process but has a position outside and therefore an excess of vision that allows them to comprehend and theoretically reflect on what the survivor experiences immediately.

When applied to Holocaust memoirs, such a hegemonic approach tends to reduce the experience of survival to pathology and produce a theoretical discourse as if it were the professional talk of medical doctors deciding on the patient's fate over her body. It fully ignores the theoretical value of experience because it concedes experience only a secondary role in the understanding of history. In my view, the survivor claims the right for himself/herself to speak not only in terms of "what," "when," "where," and "who," but also, importantly, in terms of "why" and "how." My purpose in writing this chapter was to support this claim: individual experience gained under the immediate threat of extermination must be given its due, primarily as a source of theoretical reflection, as a lesson in critical thinking. One survivor made it his mission to provide an understanding of Theresienstadt by constructing a theory from the inside of his inferno. The other made it her choice to suggest a theory from the inside of another one. When read today, these two disparate voices start talking in a chorus, both confirming and enriching each other's insights. Our task in comparative reading is to let them talk to each other and to make audible the very concern that drove them forward in their obstinate struggle to make their testimony public: the concern about the present-day reality which has inherited and re-applied the structures of besiegement and ghettoization, as well as the social inventions that serve to support them, but make them hardly recognizable. Theory from the center of hell could help us recognize their persistence and continued presence when the walls that once surrounded the inferno are no longer standing.

Works cited

Adler, H. G. (1974) *Der verwaltete Mensch: Studien zur Deportation der Juden aus Deutschland* [The administered man: studies of the deportation of the Jews from Germany], (Tübingen: Mohr).
Adler, H. G. (2005) *Theresienstadt 1941–1945: Das Antlitz einer Zwangsgemeinschaft* [Theresienstadt 1941–1945: the face of an enforced community], (Göttingen: Wallstein Verlag).
Adler, H. G. (2008) *The Journey: A Novel*, trans. Peter Filkins (New York: Random House).

Adler, H. G. (2013) *Nach der Befreiung: Ausgewählte Essays zur Geschichte und Soziologie* [After liberation: selected essays in history and sociology], (Konstanz: Konstanz University Press).
Adler, Jeremy (2000) "Good against Evil? H. G. Adler, T. W. Adorno, and the Representation of the Holocaust," in *Social Theory after the Holocaust*, ed. Robert Fine and Charles Turner (Liverpool: Liverpool University Press), 71–100.
Agamben, Giorgio (2002) *Remnants of Auschwitz: The Witness and the Archive* (New York: Zone Books).
Agamben, Giorgio (2005) *The State of Exception* (Chicago and London: University of Chicago Press).
Barskova, Polina and Irina Sandomirskaja (2012) *Postchelovecheskoe sostoianie chekoveka* [The post-human condition of man], <http://os.colta.ru/literature/events/details/37070/page2/> (accessed 6 October 2018).
Benjamin, Walter (2003) "On the concept of history," in *Selected Writingsii*, vol. IV: 1938–1940, ed. Howard Eiland and Michael W. Jennings (Cambridge: The Belknap Press of Harvard University Press), 389–400.
Blodig, Vojtěch (ed) (2002) *Art Against Death: Permanent Exhibitions of the Terezin Memorial in the Former Magdeburg Barracks* (Praha: OSWALD).
Cherepenina, Nadezhda (2005) "Assessing the scale of famine and death in the besieged city," in *Life and Death in Besieged Leningrad, 1941–44*, ed. John Barber and Andrei Dzeniskevich (Chippenham and Eastbourne: Palgrave Macmillan), 28–70.
Dzeniskevich, A.R. (1998) *Blokada i politika: Oborona Leningrada v politicheskoi kon'iunkture* [The blockade and politics: the defense of Leningrad in a political situation], (Sankt-Peterburg: Nestor).
Franklin, Ruth (2011) "The long view: a rediscovered master of Holocaust writing," *New Yorker* 31 January, 74–79.
Finch, Helen and Lynn L. Wolff, (eds) (2014) *Witnessing, Memory, Poetics: H. G. Adler and W. G. Sebald* (Rochester: Camden House)
Ginzburg, Lydia (2002) *Zapisnye knizhki. Vospominaniia. Esse* [Notebooks. Memoirs. Essays], (Sankt-Peterburg: Iskusstvo-SPb).
Ginzburg, Lydia (2011) *Prokhodiashchie kharaktery: Proza voennykh let. Zapiski blokadnogo cheloveka* [Passing characters: prose from the years of war. Notes of the blockade person], (Moskva: Novoe izdatel'stvo).
Iarov, Sergei (2012) *Blokadnaia etika: Predstavleniia o morali v Leningrade v 1941–1942 gg* [Blockade ethics: principles of morality in Leningrad in 1941–1942], (Moskva and Sankt-Peterburg: Tsentrpoligraf).
Lomagin, N.A. (2000) *V tiskakh goloda: blokada Leningrada v dokumentakh germanskikh specsluzhb i NKVD* [In the grip of famine: the siege of Leningrad in the documents of German special forces and the NKVD], (Sankt-Peterburg: Evropeiskii dom).
Lomagin, Nikita (2005) *Leningrad v blockade* [Leningrad under siege], (Moskva: EKSMO Iauza).
Magaeva, Svetlana (2005) "Physiological and psychosomatic prerequisites for survival and recovery," in *Life and Death in Besieged Leningrad, 1941–44*, ed. John Barber and Andrei Dzeniskevich (Chippenham and Eastbourne: Palgrave Macmillan), 123–159.
Margry, Karel (1992) "'Theresienstadt' (1944–1945): the Nazi propaganda film depicting the concentration camp as paradise," *Historical Journal of Film, Radio and Television* 12.2, 145–162.

Margry, Karel (1999) "The first Theresienstadt film (1942)," *Historical Journal of Film, Radio and Television* **19**.3, 309–337.

Mehring, Reinhard (2015) *Ethik nach Theresienstadt: Späte Texte des Prager Philosophen Emil Utitz (1883–1956)* [Ethics after Theresienstadt: late texts of the Prague philosopher Emil Utitz (1883–1956)], (Würzburg: Königshausen & Neumann).

Piankevich, V.L. (2014) *Liudi zhili slukhami: Neformal'noe kommunikativnoe prostranstvo blokadnogo Leningrada* [People lived by rumors: the informal communicative space in besieged Leningrad], (Sankt-Peterburg: Vladimir Dal').

Sandomirskaja, Irina (2013) *Blokada v slove: ocherki kriticheskoi teorii i biopolitki iazyka* [Besiegement in language: essays in the critical theory and biopolitics of language], (Moskva: NLO).

Sandomirskaja, Irina (2016) "Welcome to Panorama Theresienstadt: cinematography and extermination in the town called 'as if' (reading H.G. Adler)," *Apparatus*. <http://www.apparatusjournal.net/index.php/apparatus> (accessed 14 December 2018).

Thun-Hochenstein, Franziska (2007) *Gebrochene Linien: Autobiographisches Schreiben und Lagerzivilisation* [The broken line: autobiographic writing and camp civilization], (Berlin: Kulturverlag Kadmos).

Van Baskirk, Emili and Andrei Zorin (2011) "'Zapiski blokadnogo cheloveka:' istoriia teksta" ["Notes of a blockade person": the history of the text], in *Prokhodiashchie kharaktery: Proza voennykh let. Zapiski blokadnogo cheloveka*, ed. Lydia Ginzburg (Moskva: Novoe izdatel'stvo), 545–556.

Van Buskirk, Emily and Andrei Zorin (eds) (2012) *Lydia Ginzburg's Alternative Literary Identities: A Collection of Articles and New Translations* (Oxford: Peter Lang).

The United States Holocaust Memorial Museum, the Stephen Spielberg Film and Video Archive. The Claude Lanzmann Shoah Collection, Interview with Benjamin Murmelstein (September 2009 to October 2010), transcript [in English]. <http://data.ushmm.org/intermedia/film_video/spielberg_archive/transcript/RG60_5009/09E79F04-7CD0-4BFB-8265-3A01A0AC703A.pdf> (accessed 7 October 2015).

Doerte Bischoff
Uncanny Contingencies: Translation, Comparison, and Compassion in Herta Müller's *The Hunger Angel*

1 In search of a new language: The camp experience in literary discourse

If camp experiences, as has often been postulated, are formative of the twentieth century,[1] this implies that common traits may be discerned in different forms of totalitarian rule, suppression and violence. In *The Origins of Totalitarianism*, Hannah Arendt considers concentration camps, instruments of terror established both by National Socialism and Stalinism, "laboratories in the experiment of total domination" (Arendt 1973: 436). One of the main characteristics she describes is the effort, manifesting itself in the institution of the camp, to create a space sealed off from the rest of society, even totalitarian society, in which common ideas of guilt, legal punishment or individual responsibility are fundamentally broken. Entering the "concentrationary universe" – to use a term coined by David Rousset, himself a survivor of Neuengamme and Buchenwald[2] – thus means to be confronted with a reality that resists understanding and therefore narrative accounts able to explain the events and the logic of the camp to the outside world.

In Primo Levi's *If This is a Man*, the autodiegetic narrator soon after arriving in Auschwitz-Monowitz notes: "we feel outside this world" (Levi 1996: 23). In a similar way, many camp narratives describe the fundamental break between the world outside and the world inside, which, however, cannot be understood as such because it remains related to the outside precisely by this cut and discrepancy.[3] Levi's narrator asks a guard about reasons for the seemingly absurd regulations and events in the camp: "'*Warum?*' I asked him in my poor German.

---

[1] See, for example Bauman (2001: 266), Kotek and Rigoulot (2000), Shalamov (2007: 194).
[2] After 1945 Rousset was a driving force in Western investigations into the Stalinist Gulag system; he founded the International Commission Against Concentrationist Regimes in 1949.
[3] In his much discussed observations on camps, Giorgio Agamben has stated that the "camp is the space which is opened when the state of exception begins to become the rule. In the camp, the state of exception [...] is now given a permanent spatial arrangement, which as such nevertheless remains outside the normal order" (1998: 168–169).

'*Hier ist kein warum*' (There is no why here)." (Levi 1996: 29)[4] The limits of understanding, accentuated in the text by the appearance of a foreign language as language of the perpetrators, are also reflected in the anticipation that readers will most likely not comprehend what it means to be completely stripped of any personal possessions and signs of individuality. The need to tell and to remember is thus confronted with the problem of translation, which exceeds the idea of different languages, codes or value systems by touching the abyss of an attempt at total destruction of human expression and dignity.

Hannah Arendt, who consents that eye witness accounts and recollections tend to be repetitive and "uncommunicative," in that many merely record the horror without being able to interpret or explain it, expresses a deep skepticism towards the idea that a lesson can be learned from the experience of the camps, nor has it, in her view, proved to be able to serve as a basis for political consciousness or action (Arendt 1973: 441). Instead, she asserts that only the fear of concentration camps can relate and preserve the idea of a threat of totalitarianism, which has unmasked the fragility of civilization in the twentieth century and needs to be acknowledged and remembered as such. This twist is certainly surprising in the analysis by a political thinker; however, it underscores the concern of the text to develop perspectives for modes of narration and memory that answer the challenges of the camps. While critical research on the history, phases, and different functions of various camp systems has by now provided a differentiated picture that alerts us to the fact that the term "camp" has actually been used to denote very different institutions and phenomena,[5] there is also a tendency in philosophy and cultural studies to embrace the term anew as signifying life under extreme conditions,[6] at the "absolute point zero of the political as well as the private" (Schwarte 2007: 168)[7] – even if brought about by different contexts and with different aims in mind.

Having analyzed the differences between Nazi concentration camps and the Gulag, Anne Applebaum contends that when reading accounts of survivors "one is struck more by the differences between the victims' experiences than by the differences between the two camp systems." (2003: 39) With the focus on the singularity of each life story the perspective changes, from the functions and effects of the system, as well as from attempts to systematize camp experiences according to the respective context, towards the experience as such. If

---

4 German words in the English translation appear as such in the Italian original as well.
5 See for instance Applebaum (2003: 36–39), Ganzenmüller (2014).
6 The term "extreme conditions" is used frequently when attempting to describe life in the camps (e.g. Suderland 2013).
7 Unless otherwise indicated, translations from the German are mine (D.B.).

this is typically not expressed in conventional terms and narratives – which is also indicated by the monotony and abundance of stereotyped speech Arendt notices in survivors' stories – it can be found in the narrative modes of repetition, mimicry, and ellipsis that exceed the order and the constraints of stereotyped thinking (*Lagerdenken*). Svetlana Boym, who has identified these narrative modes as typical of Varlam Shalamov's *Kolyma Tales*, has read them in connection with a concept of imagination developed by Arendt. To use imagination "to confront what might seem unimaginable" in her view means to employ strategies "that can move outside the box of the temporal and spatial limitation of the present moment" (Boym 2008: 362–363) and thus disrupt the logic of confinement formative for the camp discourse. Thus, a specific "new form of imaginative documentary prose that doesn't describe but cocreates the experience" (2008: 362) can be discerned, which also lends itself to literary accounts of camp experiences that do not only bear witness to a specific historical situation and ideological framework, but that tend to transgress spatial and temporal confinement. This also implies that beyond the documentary impetus these texts expose an unprecedented experience, which cannot be described in traditional modes, nor with reference to the categories made up by the political systems that rely on camps as ultimate means of subjugation and control. By being inherently non-systematic and what may be called hyper-representational, they refute being reduced to, respectively, linguistic or literary accounts of a camp or the camp system – which have typically been aimed at subduing any human expression going beyond its immediate realm – but rather imply a claim to a testimony of the camp experience in a broader sense. In this perspective, with its focus on the unsystematic and the poetic, different forms of camps appear to coincide with regard to the experiences and the difficulties articulating and translating them.

Interestingly, Boym's approach to Shalamov's camp narratives reveals a similar train of thought as that expressed in the programmatic title of a book on the camp as a paradigm of the modern conception of space, which came out at around the same time. The book, *Auszug aus dem Lager* ("Exodus from the camp"), denotes a polyvalence by hinting, firstly, at a time after the camps were abandoned – which is the precondition for writing about them – and secondly, at the idea that because of this departure from the camps the possibility of a new kind of thinking about space, topography, power, and human expression opens up (Schwarte 2007: 165). *Auszug* here also means extract, combining therefore the notion of temporal distance with that of a condensed or fragmented substance, which can be grasped only tentatively and which is not revealed by attempts to point out systematic similarities between different types of camps. In recent studies cultural concepts of space have increasingly been associated with negotiations of cultural multiplicity and difference, thus highlighting strategies of signification and a mode of translation that subvert the attempts at enforcing hegemonic or colonial power. Bringing together a comparative study of camps and a perspective on processes of cultural mimicry and translation still largely remains a desideratum. The following observations, regarding a particularly intriguing postmemorial camp novel, are intended as a contribution to opening up this field.

2 The text as a witness

In 2009, in temporal proximity to the texts and trends described above, Herta Müller published her book on camp experience, *Atemschaukel* (*The Hunger Angel*), which received a lot of attention, especially after Müller was awarded the Nobel Prize for Literature in the same year. The text describes the camp experience of a young man from German-speaking Transylvania, deported to a Russian camp in Ukraine shortly after the Second World War. The narrative is based on interviews with former inmates of similar camps, among them Müller's mother, and on a close collaboration with her friend and fellow writer Oskar Pastior, whose experience of internment was a starting point for the joint writing project that the two had originally planned, until Pastior unexpectedly died in 2006. In her afterword, Müller explains that after a first shock and perplexity as to how to carry on with the project, she resorted to employing a (male) first-person narrator, thereby indicating closeness and empathy with an eye witness whose testimony is thus interlaced with an act of memory, which transforms the eye witness into a literary figure (called Leopold Auberg in the novel). The afterword also gives a brief historical background concerning a wave of deportations of the German-speaking population, which was associated with Romania's fascist past and the attempt to shift the blame on to the German minority, who in fact had often sympathized and openly collaborated with the national socialists (Herta Müller's father was a member of the Waffen-SS). Not surprisingly, Müller's mother's fate as a deportee was a taboo in the family; this aspect of life in Soviet-occupied Romania had no place in the Banat-Swabian community in communist Romania. The biographic constellation that the mother is deported as a young woman while the father, who until his death continues to bawl Nazi-songs at village fetes (Müller 2011),[8] is not, in a certain

---

8 "I often thought that my mother had to go to the Russian labor camp because of the collective guilt, meaning because of my father's war. How absurd is this reflection of history as guilt

way is reflected in the novel as well, where the focus is on young people whose deportation stands in no relation to any personal deed or guilt (Spiridon 2013: 143).[9] Gender obviously plays an important, albeit undeclared, role when it comes to stabilization of power and victimization, as will be discussed later in greater detail.

In earlier accounts of deportations of Romanian Germans found in a number of Müller's texts,[10] interest and sympathy clearly lie with those who suddenly find themselves made liable for things alien to them and who resist the categorization that labels and convicts them (Müller 1992: 65).[11] Thus, the mechanisms used to construct homogeneous groups by assigning a collective guilt to those declared enemies are unmasked as such. In the transition or conflict of the (totalitarian) political systems and ideologies, guilt and suffering are not brought to the fore and settled; rather, the enforcement of new categories again subjects individuals to alienating classifications. The fatal dilemma exposed in those texts, particularly in the fate of *The Hunger Angel*'s protagonist Leo Auberg, is created by the overlapping and entanglement of suppressive systems, which highlights the fact that there really is no before or beyond the alienating experience to rely on for identification and the projection of alternative individual or collective life. Auberg, who as an adolescent suffers from a suffocating and threatening atmosphere within a post-Nazi, homophobic social environment, at first projects vague expectations on the other space to which he is bound to be deported.[12] However, of course, life in the camp reveals another, more extreme form of suppression and estrangement.

---

and punishment in a single married couple, how unjustly it is distributed among my two parents." (Müller 2014: 38).
9 Historical accounts hold that in fact it was mostly "the wrong persons" who were subject to retribution and deportation: "…women, older men and adolescents, sometimes even children. Many of those who were guilty among the Germans of Romania – who had been active agents of the national socialists […] were not within reach any more. They had long fled the scene together with the retreating German troops." (Sienerth 2009: 336).
10 Spiridon remarks that the theme of deportation (to Russia) runs like a golden thread through Müller's work (2010: 380). See also Müller: "For forty-five years I have thought that one should write a whole book on the deportation, and then I always shrank back from it and wrote another book. For in my head the threat of the topic of deportation has never ceased." (2014: 199).
11 The essay *Eine warme Kartoffel ist ein warmes Bett* ("A warm potato is a warm bed") (Müller 1992) begins with a memory of a survivor of the deportation who is characterized as "one of the few Romanian Germans who during the Second World War were not in the SS."
12 "I wanted to escape from my family, to a camp if need be." (Müller 2012: 4).

By narrating the story of deportations of Romanian Germans to Stalinist camps Herta Müller contributes to the memory of a group that did not have a voice in the official Romanian narratives of history, from which the German minority, as Dieter Schlesak observed, simply disappeared – together with the memory of Romanian collaboration with Hitler (Spiridon 2010: 369). The novel, as well as Müller's earlier works, does not give a voice to the minority as a collective, but explores the fate and suffering of those who lack any recourse to a community, any "we" that could orientate and reaffirm their individual needs, wishes, and hopes. This also implies that language, particularly the mother tongue, cannot only be used to express one's inner thoughts and feelings; instead, the deep estrangement manifests itself through language as well. Even before his time in the camp (*Lagerzeit*) Leo Auberg is not only haunted by words like *Rassenschande* ("racial shame"; Müller 2012: 4)[13] when thinking of his intimate life, but seemingly ordinary words also appear to acquire a life of their own, when they come "out of nowhere" and catch him, instead of him being able to employ them to articulate his wishes and concerns. Neologistic word creations, like *Atemschaukel* (breath-swing), *Herzschaufel* (heart-shovel) or *Hungerengel* (hunger angel), which epitomize the novel's strife to open up traditional language to an otherwise inexpressible experience, reflect the poetic commitment to break up spatial, ideological, and linguistic confinements to give voice to a singularity beyond forceful constructions of collectivity and masterhood. By evoking similar word compositions as those known from texts by Paul Celan (*Atemwende*) or Primo Levi (*Atempause*), *Atemschaukel* (*The Hunger Angel*) also establishes a connection with a number of intertexts witnessing Nazi concentration camps and the Shoah. Müller's texts repeatedly reference Paul Celan, Primo Levi, Jean Améry, Jorge Semprún, George-Arthur Goldschmidt or Ruth Klüger, sometimes in connection with her own complicated heritage as a child of a Nazi father and a mother who only three years before her birth had come back from a five-year internment in a Russian camp (Müller 1996: 21–24, 40; 2014: 38).[14]

In the afterword of *The Hunger Angel* Müller explains her impulse to write about the deportation of Romanian Germans as having been triggered by

---

[13] German in the English version.
[14] See also the early literary account of a visit to Maramuresh, a region in Romania (formerly Hungary) from which the Jewish population was deported to Auschwitz and Birkenau. Here the autodiegetic narrator, who visits Jewish cemeteries, reflects: "If I were to die now my hair would not be a brush, my bones would not be flour. My death would be German like my father's. He was in the SS, after the war he returned to the village, got married and fathered me." (Müller 1987: 105).

experiences she had had as a child when overhearing furtive hints and sensing a still vivid anxiety. Thus, the novel might also be viewed as a document of writing in the second generation, which in a certain way is affected by transgenerational transmission of subdued feelings and memories that now call for expression and treatment (Bannasch 2011: 125–126). By drawing on the form of autobiographical camp narrative *The Hunger Angel* cites the blurring of factography and fiction characteristic of this genre (Taterka 1999: 184–185; Toker 2000: 123–140). However, the novel has also rightly been regarded as a phenomenon of transition, since it bears marks of a fictionalized account of a personal experience while at the same time clearly breaking the factographic pact by reflecting on itself as post-testimonial.[15] Thus it draws attention to the fact that there is no testimony "as such" without narrative modes of mediation and intertextual traces and that the generations coming after the eye witnesses have to develop their own literary forms of remembrance, lest camp experiences be forgotten.

As a poetic and a comparatively belated account, this treatment of camps does, of course, already rely on a number of literary intertexts that have addressed the Gulag, especially Varlam Shalamov's *Kolyma Tales*, written between 1954 and 1973 and first published in German between 2007 and 2010, but also Aleksandr Solzhenizyn's *The Gulag Archipelago* or *One Day in the Life of Ivan Denisovich*, or Eugenia Ginzburg's autobiographical works (Eke 2011: 56; Opitz 2012).[16] However, having been written in German, the novel is also more closely bound to the context of German history and memory than can be said of texts that are exclusively focused on the Gulag system as a symptom of Stalinist totalitarianism. Thus it can also be viewed as being part of a larger, until recently little acclaimed, field of German literature in Romania in which the general taboo concerning deportations to Russia had in fact constantly been broken (Spiridon 2010: 371).[17] Furthermore, some of the rare accounts of the Gulag experience in Kazakhstan and the Kolyma region in German come to mind as possible intertexts: Angela Rohr's (alias Helene Golnipa) *Im Angesicht der Todesengel Stalins* ("In the face of Stalin's death angels") and *Lager* ("Camp") as well as Margarete Buber-Neumann's *Under Two Dictators: Prisoner of Stalin and Hitler*, which actually testifies to camp experience on both "sides": having been handed over to the Nazis in 1940, communist Buber-Neumann was imprisoned in Ravensbrück (Toker 2000: 40–42).

---

15 See, for instance, Braun (2011: 48), where the novel is called "postmemorial heterofiction."
16 Müller herself mostly refers to "literature about the camps of the Gulag" that she read during her research (Müller 2014: 207).
17 For intertexts see also Maurer (2013: 39).

The Hunger Angel certainly does not engage in explicit comparisons between the two systems' ideologies and systems of mass murder. However, by evoking the memories and narratives referring to different types of camps, and especially by focusing on a character who in a certain way is affected by the dehumanizing violence of both systems, it can be seen as a contribution to the more recent debate on camps and mass violence as a general phenomenon of the time (Etkind 2004; Snyder 2010). It can also be viewed as increasing our awareness of the interrelatedness of memories and the limitations revealed in any national or group-oriented memory when contrasted or brought together with conflicting narratives. The perspective of Leo Auberg who is the focalizer of the entire narrative is far too limited to actually be suitable for a well-informed and distanced comparative account: he is 17 when he is deported and has had no higher education or job experience. However, he is an acute observer and some of his reflections reveal not only parallels but also entanglements of the two repressive orders. Thus, through his perspective, which is the non-sovereign position of someone who refutes the dominant discourses of identity while not having recourse to an alternative collective or memorial narrative, a multidirectionality of memory is highlighted in the sense espoused by Michael Rothberg (2009). Instead of being the architect of a picture and interpretation of two (or more) competing systems and memories, the character of Leo Auberg is positioned at the point where they intersect and reveal uncanny contiguities without, however, being systematically set in relation to each other. Thus, what is at stake here stands in clear contrast to the striving to compare, which initiated the historians' debate in Germany in the 1980s (Katz 1993: 18). Instead of leveling the differences between Nazi camps and the Gulag by establishing a teleology or moral hierarchy, but also instead of setting them as absolute, thus implicitly affirming ideological claims to internal homogeneity and clear distinctions, the text stays with the non-sovereign position and thus with the effort to witness an experience that does not testify to the Gulag system only – and that does not simply witness a coherent system at all.

3 Body image, masculinity, and homosexuality in the Soviet and Nazi ideology

In the chapter "Exciting times," Auberg's experiences as camp prisoner are intertwined with memories of the fascist home from which he has seemingly escaped through his deportation. Like other forced laborers, he can sometimes leave the camp and go to the nearby Russian village to trade coal and other items for food. A gramophone reminds him of a radio at home, which his father had bought in 1936 to follow the Berlin Olympics, staged as a triumphant event reflecting the supposed historical superiority of Nazi Germany. The radio also broadcast exercise classes, which his parents took at home every day, thus linking "great" history and the private realm, which appear similarly permeated by propaganda, with the radio as its medium. This also affects Leo, who as a child is made to go to an exercise class called "gymnastics for cripples" (Müller 2012: 45) because his parents want him to be "more soldierly" – that is, more in compliance with the normative idea of the perfect male body propagated by National Socialism. That this also implies a specific concept of a "healthy" racial corpus (*Volkskörper*) is reflected in the fact that the class is associated with "cripples," a category that ultimately signifies the limits of even forced compliance and co-ordination that aimed at relinquishing individuality and difference. "Cripples" were regarded as "worthless life" in the Nazi ideology and were subject to euthanasia programs set up to exterminate "unhealthy elements." Influenced by this ideology, the child Leo perceives himself as an outcast, as somehow not in order. When in an "act of disobedience" he decides to skip a class called *völkischer Donnerstag* ("national-socialist Thursday"), where children are engaged in a military drill, this only "reinforces [his] sense of being crippled" (Müller 2012: 46). Disobedience does not strengthen the child's sense of the self as autonomous but rather reenacts the internalized racist order, leaving him torn between affirmation and resistance – a non-sovereign position, which in its description nevertheless reveals a lot about the totalitarian politics and the phantasm of a "healthy" body.

In the very dense description of the transformations at home indicating its infiltration by Nazi ideology, Leo as narrator also links his father's interest in "girl gymnasts and Transylvanian Saxon girls in folk costume," whom he likes to photograph – another medium combining official racial ideology and personal desire – with his new interest in hunting. Photo shooting the young German girls' bodies and shooting hares is thus presented as connected. An aggressive (male) desire to fix a certain ideal coincides with the killing of animals whose skin is removed: "the hares looked like the Saxon gymnast girls at the barre. The hares were eaten." (Müller 2012: 47) For a while a Jewish character, Herr Fränkel, is associated with the hares' skin – and therefore with their violent death – as every six months Fränkel comes to pick up the furs. Until he stops coming: "No one wanted to know anything more. He was Jewish, reddish-blond, tall, and nearly as slender as a hare." (2012: 47) The comparison alludes to the fact that Jews were not regarded as human anymore. Prior to extermination they are associated with animals that are condemned to be chased.

The fact that "[n]eighbours and relatives and teachers went off to fight for the Romanian Fascists or for Hitler" (Müller 2012: 47) is mentioned alongside the stories about gymnasts, the photo shooting and hunting, creating a dense network of textual clues and contiguities that show any expression of private or everyday life as pervaded by and interwoven with Nazi ideology and the developments on the German scene. At the same time the novel interweaves these glimpses of Fascism in the Romanian German community, presented as the narrator's childhood memories, with his present experiences in a Russian camp. The word "cripples" induces the narrator to switch to a recent event in the camp when an outside officer lectures about "peace and FUSSKULTUR" (Müller 2012: 45). The strange word that disrupts the reading process – marked by capital letters in the original – turns out to be a mistranslation. As is explained by a bilingual fellow inmate, the Russian speaker had originally intended to talk about the importance of physical training to "steel" people for the establishment of the Soviet Union. By trying to use a German equivalent of the Russian term *fiscultura* (physical culture) he had produced the non-existing *Fusskultur*, which to German speakers sounds like "culture of the feet," and made the plea to engage in bodily enhancement that directly results in a strengthening of the heart and thus "the heart of the Soviet Socialist Republics" (Müller 2012: 45) even more absurd. The propagated idea of bodily unity and centrality signified by the heart metaphor is decentered by the shift to one single body part, the one most "down to earth." The mistranslated word stands out and blocks the transmission of an ideological message. As something not understandable in the present context, it prompts the narrator to refer to contexts better known to him:

> I knew all about FUSSKULTUR from the cripple gymnastics and from our *Volk* course [*völkischer Donnerstag*] in high school [...]. We were drilled in the schoolyard: lie down, stand up, climb the fence, squat, lie down, push up, stand up. [...] Wotan, Vikings, Germanic ballads. (Müller 2012: 46)

On the one hand the episode with the lecture on physical culture accentuates the differences between Nazi ideology (and camps) and Soviet propaganda, which is shown to be based on the idea of reeducation and betterment,[18] while the Nazi ideology upholds the notion of an (uneducable) foreign body that has to be eliminated to strengthen the body of the people (*Volkskörper*). On the other hand, however, parallels and similarities come to the fore in the seizure of the body and concepts of community, which eliminate individuality and

---

18 For this central ideology underlying Soviet camps, see Maurer (2013: 37).

difference. The narrator is associated with a moment in which the performance of one ideology – in an attempt to reach and subject even those who speak a different language and come from another country, in an attempt, that is, to translate and universalize it – is interrupted, displaced, and affected by difference.[19] His sudden memory of "cripple gymnastics" inserts a foreign element into the observed context of the camp, which itself is presented as a space sealed off from any contrasting or conflicting notion of reality. However, an attempt to ideologically justify this space by performance and translation reveals two aspects of untranslatability. First, clashes are shown between the Soviet discourse of betterment and the Nazi discourse of elimination, which is part of the heritage these particular inmates came to the camp with and which affects their understanding of the situation. Thus, total control over humans, over bodies and meaning, which is to be implemented by the institution of the camp, is subverted. The second aspect of untranslatability can be seen in the fact that the act of (mis-)translation brings out the similarities of the propagated system and the system of its proclaimed enemy. Instead of being reeducated according to communist ideas these inmates, who have officially been sent to the camp because of their involvement with the enemy, German Fascism, can bring out the uncanny similarity of the two systems and their entanglements.

The narrator in particular occupies a position "between" the camps; his appears to be "an outsider's existence" (Spiridon 2013: 136). As a homosexual he would have been doomed to persecution, internment, and possibly even extermination in a Nazi-controlled world, which still haunts life in the Banat-Swabian land of his childhood. However, it is very clear that in the Soviet camp any open expression of homosexual desire would equal death, too (Müller 2012: 3). Both systems or ideologies are largely characterized by male dominance and a tendency to idealize a certain image of the body as well as a tendency to eliminate differences (also in terms of gender differences). They share homophobic tendencies and regard any crossing of boundaries, including articulations of intimacy, as threat to their control. Homophobia in Nazi Germany was actually ambivalent, since homosexuality was partly regarded as curable, which resulted in manifold efforts to influence and "reeducate" homosexual people in order to bring them back to the norm of male sexuality (including the obligation to procreation).

---

[19] Here textual strategies resemble those described by Homi Bhabha, who has observed that the "migrant culture of the 'in-between,' the minority position, dramatizes the activity of culture's untranslatability; and in so doing, it moves the question of culture's appropriation beyond the assimilationist's dream, or the racist's nightmare, of a 'full transmissal of subject-matter;' and towards an encounter with the ambivalent process of splitting and hybridity that marks the identification with culture's difference." (Bhabha 1994: 224).

Individuals who were regarded as biologically inclined and therefore hopeless and incurable, however, were subject to the logic of elimination. The term "cripple gymnastics," which apparently is not an official term but rather a vernacular saying, reflects this ambivalence: the "real" people with disabilities would not be in the class, since they would have been singled out as hopeless cases. However, as a closeted homosexual who apparently does not meet the body norms of the hegemonic community, Leo Auberg is always in danger of being exposed and singled out – that he who has never been "part of any war" (Müller 2012: 36) is sent off to the camp almost appears as a fulfillment of this possibility. Thus, in more than one way, the narrator's homosexuality, for which he himself has hardly any explicit words, brings out uncanny contingencies between the systems.

4 Rifts in the Gulag system: Race and disability

Indicative of such contiguities is also the figure of Tur Prikulitsch, a sadistic, narcissistic, and corrupt camp warden. He is introduced as *kapo* – a term that, in German, is firmly associated with Nazi concentration camps, where it signified a prisoner with privileges who was supposed to support the brutal camp order; in the context of the Gulag the term is usually not used. Arthur (Tur) Prikulitsch is introduced as a native of the Carpathian Ukraine, which explains his Russian–German bilingualism. This double affiliation is indicated by his name, which combines a traditional German first name with a surname with a Slavic ending, which evokes a mythical figure from Transylvanian folk tales impersonating evil (Maurer 2013: 41). As a translator, he has access to both sides and obscures the possibility of drawing clear lines between Russians and Germans, victims and perpetrators. The fact that there is a Jewish prisoner among the inmates is remarkable here because he is said to have been arrested as one of the Germans accused of Hitler's crimes (Müller 2012: 36). This happened after "Zither Lommer" (so nicknamed because he plays the zither) had his tailor shop expropriated and left his family behind in the Bucovina[20] to make a living as an itinerant craftsman. Even if officially he is not interned for being Jewish, as he would have been under Nazi rule, his case still speaks of the coarseness of the supposedly political categories of the Gulag logic, which is blind to differences and questions of justice. He seems to be just another collateral damage, which cannot confute the rightness of the system as a whole. He remains in the camp for three-and-a-half

---

[20] In the English version translated as "Moldavia."

years and is then released, an event quite unthinkable in Nazi camps (Thun-Hohenstein 2007: 194).²¹ In a (non-equal) conversation between Tur Prikulitsch, the camp barber shaving him and Leo, who is standing by, the apparently highly charged question about the fate of David Lommer is raised. The barber, who is from the same region as Prikulitsch, has the courage to ask him why Lommer was sent to Odessa (which is far from his home town). Prikulitsch does not give a straightforward answer: "Lommer had no business being here, and from Odessa he can go wherever he wants" (Müller 2012: 37). What sounds like freedom of choice and mobility is only obscuring the fact that Lommer had lost everything. Leo comments: "But where is he supposed to go. There's no one left for him at home." So another interpretation of his "release" arises: he was released in order to be rid of him, not only from the camp community, which officially is supposed to be part of the wider community, but which first has to undergo a process of improvement through forced labor, but also from the Soviet Union (Odessa being a port city and a place of transit). He is the only person in the book whose earlier release from the camp is recounted. This is remarkable in view of the reality of Russian camps in general, where there used to be a lot of movement, either because of general fluctuation or because of transports to other camps, a fact described in many memoirs (Toker 2000: 84–85).

Having finished, the barber finally asks Prikulitsch whether he is satisfied. This question is ambiguous, as is Prikulitsch's answer, when he says: "With my nose, yes" (Müller 2012: 37). The whole scene is so charged and very subtly allusive that reading it one can easily miss the possible implications. Is the *kapo* responding not only to the question concerning his treatment in the barber shop but also to the underlying question about his anti-Semitism (including concepts of body normativity and deviance) and his potential complicity with the Nazis? Does the fact that he deliberately limits the scope of meaning of his being satisfied to the treatment of his nose indicate that he tries to fend off any allegations concerning his responsibility for Lommer's fate, that of his family and of other Jews? How much does the barber, who potentially has known Prikulitsch from before the camps, know about his involvement in the genocide of the Jews in Eastern Europe? Is the fact that this potential Nazi serves as a mediator between German inmates and Russian camp authorities a hint at manifold transferences and relations between Nazism and Stalinism? To this last, very far-reaching and rather abstract question, *The Hunger Angel* definitely has no answer, nor does it really justify it. The novel widely refrains from explicit

---

21 The impossibility of release or return for Jews in the Nazi camp system is described as a central marker of difference between the camp systems.

political statements, but rather scrutinizes the microphysics of human behavior and relations in the context of totalitarian power. However, what can be seen in this episode is that this micro-perspective reveals not only similar phenomena, like the ambivalent figure of the *kapo*, who, although a prisoner, acts as a henchman of the system of repression. It also sheds light on the fluid and porous boundaries of the two systems and thus undermines their ideological rhetoric of distinction. If distinctions are implied by the text, it appears that they cannot simply be attributed to the different ideologies or to the fact that one system is less atrocious or inhuman than the other. Rather, it is the specific situation among the camp inmates and their behavior that actually enables us to see these differences.

To demonstrate this, let us look at yet another person in the camp, Katharina Seidel, called Planton-Kati, who has obviously gotten there "by mistake." This is at least what the narrator, in a somewhat naive fashion, assumes because she has a mental disability and is clearly "not suited to any type of work" (Müller 2012: 91). She is like a foreign body inside the world of a labor camp: she "didn't understand what a quota was, or a command, or a punishment" (2012: 91). Since she obviously cannot have been sent to the camp for the usual reasons, justifying the official version of the aim and meaning of camps, the narrator ponders over her being there – she had to replace someone on the list who paid to be exempted or was put on the list by a sadistic crook. Those considerations do not yield a clear answer but they alert the reader to this case, which obviously cannot easily be explained by reference to the official narrative of the Gulag. A mentally disabled person in a camp, however, evokes Nazi narratives and practices concerning "unworthy" life. Considering the fact that Lommer, a Jew, may have been sent to the camp not by accident, but because of the anti-Semitism of those in charge, it may also be speculated whether Kati had got there for similar reasons, because someone sympathized with fascist ideas. In any case, the fact that she is there shows that the ideological reasoning for the existence of the camps on the Russian side is not consistent or rather is much more complex in practice than it is on paper. That Kati survives five years of camp life is only indirectly attributed to the fact that this camp is not explicitly a death camp and that she is not in a group of people deliberately brought there to die. When at some point the Russian camp inspector calls her "fascist" because of her apparent stubbornness, therefore attributing to her a political category, it is clear that she is in immediate danger. If Kati survives, it is because her complete ignorance and helplessness together with her involuntary resistance to the camp order stirs the remaining vestiges of compassion in the other inmates. In her they can defend the rest of their own humanity: "we treat her as something that belongs to all of us. We make up for what we do to one another by standing up for her. We're capable of many things, but as long as she is living among us, there's a limit to how far we actually go." (Müller 2012: 112) Remarkably, this impulse is not explained with reference to an abstract humanist ideal – which is utterly foreign to the camp: the protagonist has long transformed the books he brought with him into sheets of paper useful in everyday life in the camp. Rather, Kati is regarded as a kind of cherished possession in which each of the inmates sees what he himself needs most under the actual conditions: not reason and rationality, but her way of performing "the most basic tasks without thinking" (Müller 2012: 94) and her way of adjusting to the conditions without succumbing to the logic of its rules.

5 Camp memories: The impossibility of sharing

The fact that the story of the disappearance of a Jewish inmate is related in a chapter titled "A motley crew," referring to the ragtag society of inmates as the barber sees it, is surely no coincidence. Thus the idea of the inmates as some kind of (counter-)community is refuted here on two counts: first, because one member is excluded (or at least exempted) and second, naturally, because it appears absurd in conditions that destroy both communal and moral behavior. "Inside the camp, the we-form is singular" (Müller 2012: 251) is one of the quasi-conclusions of the narrator sharing his insights about the camp. In its abbreviated form it seems like a completely self-evident statement of utmost clarity, but for the reader it remains somewhat cryptic. Obviously, the common notions of individual and collective identity are disrupted here; the equation of "we" and the singular points at the breakdown of the individual, which in the plural can form a group or society. This also implies a confusion concerning the grammatical rules and conventions: singular and plural do not serve as linguistic classifications any more; as they collapse, the conventional possibilities of systematization, distinction and orientation appear fundamentally disrupted. The narrator demonstrates this when he points to the different conditions that privileged prisoners such as the barber live in compared with ordinary inmates. It infuriates him that the barber compares the camp to a hotel where people from different places come together. In an evocation of the camp as a gathering place for people of different origin and language there might be an implicit reference to Primo Levi's comparison of the Buna tower in Auschwitz with the Babel tower and the confusion of languages after its fall (Levi 1996: 36, 81).[22]

---

[22] See also Toker (2000: 98).

This underlines the notion that in the camp any idea of communal identity in light of the totalitarian grip on people aimed at an effacement of their histories and particularities appears highly problematic. Neither can it rightfully become the point of reference for conceptions of another, morally justified, transnational community. Here Arendt's skepticism with respect to thinking of camp inmates as a community of victims to which moral or political ideas could be attributed comes to mind.

Thus, the cited chapter, with its faint intertextual references that do not work as concrete comparisons (with the heteroglossia of the Jews in Auschwitz coming together there in the immediacy of genocide), could be read as a commentary on the limits to which camp inmates as a group can be represented in any positive sense. Considering the large number of Gulag texts, and especially their reception by the samizdat, the exile communities and the West, critical of the Soviets, which in various ways have propagated a better counter-society with reference to the moral authority of camp survivors, Herta Müller's *The Hunger Angel* consequently defies attempts at such instrumentalizations of the victims. The text focuses on the question of what happens to the individual when confined in the concentration camp universe. Since he loses any hold on the systems of meaning and the certainty to think of himself as a member of the human race, any conception of a better world that is constructed in reference to his experience fails to take precisely this loss of faith in meaning (in both a religious and a secular sense) into account. After his return, Leo Auberg encounters a former fellow inmate, Trudi Pelikan, in the street of their hometown. Although they notice each other, they pretend not to and proceed without any sign of recognition: "For our own sakes we preferred to act as though we didn't know each other. There's nothing to understand about that." (Müller 2012: 267) That this limit of meaning and understanding is no sign of rudeness or indifference is made clear in the following comment, where Leo assures the reader: "how gladly I would have put my arms around her and had let her know that I agreed with her." (Müller 2012: 267) By not doing this he protects both Trudi and himself from being overpowered by traumatic memories, which cannot be dealt with and which – as clearly shown here – cannot be a basis for a community of victims or those who identify with them. This means that, likewise, they cannot be a reference point for a community of (shared) experience.

In fact, the term experience, which has so far also guided the deliberations in this chapter, is marked as problematic in the text. In one chapter ("Homesickness. That's the last thing I need") the narrator, then still a prisoner, singles it out as one of the words that "have me as a target, that seem created solely for my re-deportation" (Müller 2012: 221). Like several other words in the text, it is spelled out in capital letters, marking its status as a foreign body that blocks reference rather than denoting something outside language. If EXPERIENCE is nothing that the camp survivor can easily relate to but that, on the contrary, implies the danger of an actualization of his suffering, it should be handled with great care (the same holds true for MEMORY, also spelled in capitals). This is a premise especially for those who try to remember camp experience as a central and at the same time unrelatable reality of this time. Like Primo Levi, Jean Améry or Varlam Shalamov, Herta Müller demonstrates in *The Hunger Angel* that there is nothing positive to be drawn from life in the camps. By not ending with the protagonist's liberation, the novel departs from the pattern most camp novels are structured around (Toker 2000: 93). The six chapters that deal with a period after the liberation, already hinted at in some proleptic episodes, show the narrator as distanced from the events, which in some cases span at least sixty years. The reality of the camp, however, has not receded into the past; rather, as a traumatic caesura, it persists in the present and haunts the narrator. When he talks about his marriage (which he had ended after eleven years) and the lack of steady relationships afterwards – "Wild animal crossings, nothing more" (2012: 279) – his words conjure up an association of his (homosexual) desire and sexual activity with the animal world, implying expulsion and exclusion from the normative human realm as he has experienced it from early on. Words evoke the story discussed earlier, where a hare doomed to be chased is compared with human beings subject to totalitarian hold – in fact, the hare is a central signifier that reappears in different contexts in the novel, thus marking its diffusion and a permanent possibility of its sudden (traumatic) reappearance. Long after the end of Nazi rule and the decline of the Soviet system the narrator's attempts to talk about himself are still deeply pervaded by foreign words and concepts estranging him from feelings, memories, and experiences that could consciously be reflected as his own. From this it follows that if there is a collective memory that can grow from this kind of EXPERIENCE and can preserve it for future generations, it has to find ways not to forget the insistence of what cannot be settled in representational modes of speaking.

In *The Hunger Angel* the protagonist, after first being upset about the camp being referred to as a "hotel," for a while comes to even embrace the idea, which so completely contradicts the reality of the camp that clinging to it in his (individual) phantasies can temporarily be understood as an act of mental resistance, at least near the beginning of his stay. Eventually, though, it becomes a "cursed word we couldn't inhabit," like so many others that have a meaning only within a world from which the inmates are radically cut off. The camp is not a transitory place, unlike a hotel, which in spatial or temporal terms can still be seen as an approximation of a "home." However, even after the release, it is insinuated at this early moment in the novel, there will be no return home. Here, the momentous insight the narrator has about the fate of his Jewish fellow prisoner can also be read as a cue of what the camp experience will do to the narrator himself. While his own fate is quite different, in that after the release he can actually return to his home town and his family, it also bears similarities to the experience of the Jewish prisoner who cannot return because his home has been destroyed and his family murdered. The years of violence, starvation, and humiliation have left their indelible marks on him and in his family, there is no place for him any more: they had given up on him, not expecting he would be coming back. Thus, the birth of his baby brother appears to him like an act of replacement that only continues the processes of effacement of individuality and singularity, which characterized camp life.

In the text there is no question mark after his remark about David Lommer: "But where is he supposed to go." Syntactically, it is a question and at the same time it is not a question, since it is neither really directed at someone, meant to elicit an answer or communication in general, nor is it opening up a potential of meanings. The text does not take on the perspective of its Jewish character. It speaks for him without assuming or trying to identify with his position, and it points to parallels without erasing the differences.

In one of the last chapters Leo Auberg, after returning home and having been confronted with the incommunicability of his experiences "at home," buys a notebook in order to write down his memories. The first sentence is: "Will you understand me, question mark." (Müller 2012: 269) Here, the question mark, which is missing throughout the book, finally appears not as a conventional punctuation mark, but written out in words. The "you" is supposed to be the book, the narrator informs us. Where communication is interrupted, resorting to words as substitutes for punctuation that would form meaningful sentences appears as a possibility. In fact, words in the text often replace meaningful structures, or rather the abyss of meaninglessness, which revokes representation. In the extreme, this is visible even in the text's typeface, which at times dissolves into mere lists of words rupturing any syntactical coherence (e.g. Müller 2012: 146–147). "All you can do is lists" (Müller 2012: 81) is also one of the insights on the camp from the protagonist. On the one hand, making a list is a practice that reflects the tendency of totalitarian systems to transform individuals into items or pure numbers, thus subjecting them to the bureaucratic logic of exchangeability and control. Thus, by learning this lesson, the inmate-narrator has adapted to this logic, which is bound to estrange him from other ways of relating to the world. On the other hand, however, his lists appear as highly idiosyncratic inventories of words, phrases, and things, which cannot be subsumed to any order other than that of the poetic text.

Lists obviously hold at bay the "point zero," which is repeatedly described as the limit of representation: "Absolute zero is that which cannot be expressed" (Müller 2012: 271). At the same time it marks it as a void by foregrounding the disconnectedness of things, the impossibility of recollecting the meaning that words and things had for Leo Auberg as a prisoner in the camp. The gap between the two worlds – repeatedly the camp is described as a world in itself, with rules, significances and words of its own – cannot be bridged because the man who has experienced it is not identical with the man who is now trying to tell us about it: "The only way you can talk about something is by again becoming the person you're talking about." (Müller 2012: 258)

Memory is described here not as a process of recollection of past events, conditions, and sensations but as a practice of selecting, discarding, and repeating, which manifests itself in Leo's attempts at writing. Thus, he muses over something that his former camp inmates said about him during their long journey home: "Look how he's bawling, he's falling apart" (Müller 2012: 270).[23] The apparently intense feeling indicated by tears can only be noted by others; when Leo later tries to write his memoirs he cannot recall what he felt back then, but he remembers those (external) words that obviously describe and miss him at the same time. Trying to come to terms with this feeling of being torn between inadequate words of others and the void inside himself – later he speaks about "[m]y steep-sided hollowness [...] I fall apart by going inward" (Müller 2012: 283). His writing process resembles Freudian fort-da game, since it repeatedly alternates self-assertion with symbolization and rejection: "I thought about that sentence a lot. Then I wrote it down on an empty page. And the next day I scratched it out. The day after that I wrote it down again underneath. Scratched it out again, wrote it down again. When the page was full I tore it out." (Müller 2012: 270)

Writing a memoir appears difficult if not impossible not only because nobody asks and nobody wants to know, but because the split between the worlds has affected and will always have affected the narrating "I." This dilemma has been articulated in several canonical texts of camp literature, the best known probably in the foreword of Robert Antelme's *The Human Race*, where the author/narrator speaks of his "frantic desire to describe it such as it had been" (Antelme 1998: 3). And of the immediate insight "that it was impossible": "No sooner would we begin to tell our story that we would be choking over it. [...] even to us, what we had to tell, seemed *unimaginable*" (3). In the "narration-dream" in Primo Levi's *If This is a Man* the protagonist envisions a situation where he is back home telling the story about his life in the camp to his family.

---

23 In German: "Schau, wie der heult, dem läuft was über."

When he sees that they are not interested and do not listen, he is seized by intense pain. Afterwards, he realizes that this nightmarish dream does not express individual anxiety but is dreamt repeatedly by many of his fellow prisoners as well (Levi 1996: 58). Herta Müller's "heterofiction," which in the end describes the narrator as struggling with words and pages of notes that he continuously writes and rejects, evokes this nightmare while at the same time shifting the focus to the ways words and concepts connected to a totalitarian seizure of the individual are repeated and translated into different contexts in which they reveal their power, but can also be placed at a distance by poetic strategies. Here, these two strands of text meet: by focusing on a position "between the camps," which is affected by different hegemonic and totalitarian discourses, incidences of translation appear to reveal breaks and fissures in the respective ideologies, thus opening spaces of their poetic reflection and transformation. By employing a postmemorial, post-factual heterofiction, the topoi and genre characteristics of factographic and autobiographical camp narratives witnessing different historical and political contexts are cited and translated into a realm of cultural memory, thus registering a break with the ideas of community, tradition, collective identity, and communicable individual experience in a poetic form.

Works cited

Agamben, Giorgio (1998) *Homo Sacer. Sovereign Power and Bare Life*, trans. Daniel Heller-Roazen (Stanford: Stanford University Press).
Antelme, Robert (1998) *The Human Race*, trans. Jeffrey Haight and Annie Mahler (Evanston: Marlboro Press).
Applebaum, Anne (2003) *Gulag. A History* (New York: Doubleday).
Arendt, Hannah (1973) *The Origins of Totalitarianism* (Orlando: Harcourt).
Bannasch, Bettina (2011) "Zero – a gaping mouth: the discourse of the camps in Herta Müller's *Atemschaukel* between literary theory and political philosophy," in *Other People's Pain. Narratives of Trauma and the Question of Ethics*, ed. Martin Modlinger and Philipp Sonntag (Oxford: Peter Lang), 115–144.
Bauman, Zygmunt (2001) "A century of camps?," in *The Bauman Reader*, ed. Peter Beilharz (Oxford: Blackwell), 266–278.
Bhabha, Homi (1994) *The Location of Culture* (London and New York: Routledge).
Boym, Svetlana (2008) "'Banality of evil,' mimicry, and the Soviet subject: Varlam Shalamov and Hannah Arendt," *Slavic Review* 7.2, 342–363.
Braun, Michael (2011) "Die Erfindung der Erinnerung: Herta Müller's *Atemschaukel*" [The invention of remembrance: Herta Müller's "Atemschaukel"], *Gegenwartsliteratur* 10, 33–53.
Buber-Neumann, Margarete (2008) *Under Two Dictators. Prisoner of Stalin and Hitler* (London: Random House).

Eke, Norbert Otto (2011) "'Gelber Mais, keine Zeit.' Herta Müller's Nach-Schrift *Atemschaukel. Roman*" [Herta Müller's After-script Hunger Angel. Novel], *Gegenwartsliteratur* 10, 54–74.

Etkind, Alexander (2004) "Hard and soft in cultural memory: political mourning in Russia and Germany," *Grey Room* 16, 37–59.

Ganzenmüller, Jörg (2014) "Gulag und Konzentrationslager: Sowjetische und deutsche Lagersysteme im Vergleich" [Gulag and concentration camp: Soviet and German camp systems in comparison], in *Gulag: Texte und Dokumente*, ed. Julia Landau, Irina Scherbakowa (Göttingen: Wallstein), 50–59.

Golnipa, Helene (1989) *Im Angesicht der Todesengel Stalins* [In the face of Stalin's death angels], ed. Isabella Ackerl (Mattersburg-Katzelsdorf: Edition Tau).

Golnipa, Helene (2015) *Lager. Autobiographischer Roman* [Camp. An autobiographical novel], ed. Gesine Bey (Berlin: Aufbau).

Katz, Steven T. (1993) *The Holocaust and Comparative History* (Leo Baeck Memorial Lecture 37) (New York: Leo Baeck Institute).

Kotek, Joël and Pierre Rigoulot (2000) *Le siècle des camps: Détention, concentration, extermination: cent ans de mal radical* [The age of camps: confinement, concentration, extermination: hundred years of radical evil], (Paris: Lattès).

Levi, Primo (1996) *Survival in Auschwitz. The Nazi Assault on Humanity* (New York: Touchstone).

Maurer, Maria (2013) "*Atemschaukel* im Lagerdiskurs: Systemimmanente Gewalt in Herta Müllers Roman" [The Hunger Angel in camp discourse: Systemic violence in Herta Müller's novel], *Spiegelungen: Zeitschrift für die deutsche Kultur und Geschichte Südosteuropas* 8.1, 35–46.

Müller, Herta (1987) *Barfüßiger Februar* [Barefoot February], (Berlin: Rotbuch).

Müller, Herta (1992) "Eine warme Kartoffel ist ein warmes Bett" [A warm potato is a warm bed], in *Eine warme Kartoffel ist ein warmes Bett* (Hamburg: Europäische Verlagsanstalt), 65–68.

Müller, Herta (1996) *In der Falle* [Trapped] (Göttingen: Wallstein).

Müller, Herta (2009) *Atemschaukel* [Hunger Angel] (München: Hanser).

Müller, Herta (2011) "Die Anwendung der dünnen Straßen" [The application of thin streets], in *Immer derselbe Schnee und immer derselbe Onkel* (München: Hanser), 110–124.

Müller, Herta (2012) *The Hunger Angel*, trans. Philip Boehm (London: Portobello).

Müller, Herta (2014) *Mein Vaterland war ein Apfelkorn. Ein Gespräch mit Angelika Klammer* [My fatherland was an apple-seed. A conversation with Angelika Klammer], (München: Hanser).

Opitz, Antonia (2012) "Literarische Orte menschlicher Bewährung: Aleksandr Solzhenitzyns 'Ein Tag des Iwan Denissowitsch' und Herta Müllers 'Atemschaukel'" [Literary spaces of human integrity: Aleksandr Solzhenitsyn's "One day in the life of Ivan Denisovich" and Herta Müller's "Hunger Angel"], in *Interkulturelle Begegnungen. Leben, Schreiben und Lernen in zwei Kulturen*, ed. Andrea Benedek, Renata Alice Crisan and Szabolcs János (Frankfurt am Main: Peter Lang), 359–372.

Rothberg, Michael (2009) *Multidirectional Memory. Remembering the Holocaust in the Age of Decolonization* (Stanford: Stanford University Press).

Shalamov, Varlam (2007) "Über Prosa" [On prose], *Osteuropa* 57.6, 183–194.

Schwarte, Ludger (2007) "Auszug aus dem Lager" [Exodus from the camp], in *Auszug aus dem Lager: Zur Überwindung des modernen Raumparadigmas*, ed. Ludger Schwarte (Bielefeld: Transcript), 162–179.

Sienerth, Stefan (2009) "Bilder der Deportation: ausdrucksstark und präzise" [Images of deportations: expressive and precise], *Spiegelungen: Zeitschrift für deutsche Kultur und Geschichte Südosteuropas* 4.58, 333–337.

Snyder, Timothy (2010) *Bloodlands. Europe between Hitler and Stalin* (New York: Basic Books).

Spiridon, Olivia (2010) "Herta Müllers *Atemschaukel* im Kontext der literarischen Erinnerungen an die 'Russlanddeportation'" [Herta Müller's "Hunger Angel" in the context of remembering deportations to Russia], in *Gedächtnis der Literatur: Erinnerungskulturen in den südosteuropäischen Ländern nach 1989. Rumänien im Blickfeld*, ed. Edda Binder-Iijima and Romanița Constaninescu (Ludwigsburg: Pop Verlag), 367–397.

Spiridon, Olivia (2013) "From fact to fiction. Herta Müller's *Atemschaukel*," in *Herta Müller. Politics and Aesthetics*, ed. Bettina Brandt and Valentina Glajar (Lincoln: University of Nebraska Press), 130–152.

Suderland, Maja (2013) *Inside Concentration Camps. Social Life at the Extremes*, trans. Jessica Spengler (Cambridge: Polity).

Taterka, Thomas (1999) *Dante Deutsch. Studien zur Lagerliteratur* [Dante in German. Studies on camp literature], (Berlin: Erich Schmidt Verlag).

Thun-Hohenstein, Franziska (2007) "Auszug aus der 'Lagerzivilisation': Russische Lagerliteratur im europäischen Kontext" [Exodus from the camp civilization: Russian camp literature in a European context], in *Auszug aus dem Lager: Zur Überwindung des modernen Raumparadigmas*, ed. Ludger Schwarte (Bielefeld: Transcript), 180–200.

Toker, Leona (2000) *Return from the Archipelago: Narratives of Gulag Survivors* (Bloomington: Indiana University Press).

Anna Artwińska
A Communist Woman in the Gulag: Gender, Ideology, and Limit-Experience in Ginzburg and Budzyńska

1 Introduction

In Anne Applebaum's *Gulag*, the chapter on women (and children) begins:

> They met the same work norms and they ate the same watery soup. They lived in the same sort of barracks and travelled in the same cattle train. Their clothes were almost identical, their shoes equally inadequate. They were treated no differently under interrogation. And yet – men's and women's camp experiences are not quite the same. (Applebaum 2003: 284)

Fifteen years have passed since the publication of Applebaum's book: in the meantime, many new studies have appeared on feminist issues within the context of limit-experiences, as well as on the unique experiences of women in the gulags (see, among others, Stark 2003; Czerska 2011). Nevertheless, Applebaum's judgement still holds true. Meanwhile, the question of differences between female and male experiences of gulag imprisonment has been one of the leitmotifs of the "camp and Gulag literature" from the beginning – the first notes from "a world apart"[1] informed about the suffering of imprisoned women by virtue of their gender, but also about the different treatment they received from other prisoners and the guards (Kamm 2009). We might conclude that, similarly to the studies of Nazi labour camps' survivor literature,[2] in Gulag literature gender is also an indispensable analytical category, affording a better understanding of such texts and the experiences they articulate. In analyzing the phenomenon of Soviet gulags, a gendered approach is useful both on the sociological level, enabling a study of the day-to-day in the gulag (from administrative to existential aspects) through the lens of gener, and in reference to narrative practices and memoir-writing conventions.

---

[1] A book by Gustaw Herling-Grudziński of the same title (*Inny świat. Zapiski sowieckie*), first published in English in 1953 as *A World Apart: A Memoir of the Gulag*. A chapter entitled "Hunting by night" brings up sexual violence experienced by imprisoned women (Herling-Grudziński 2007).
[2] See, among others, Petö et al. (2015), Karwowska (2009).

In this chapter, I focus on one type of female Gulag stories: memoirs by women associated with the communist movement,[3] both at the time of arrest and while serving their time in the Gulag, and finally – albeit to a different degree – after release. Based on *Krutoj marshrut: chronika vremen kul'ta lichnosti* (*Whirlwind*; 1967)[4] by Eugenia Ginzburg and *Strzępy rodzinnej sagi* ("Shreds of a family saga"; 1997) by Celina Budzyńska, I will consider how the female perspective blends in with the ideological perspective and whether it is possible to distinguish formal features and thematic motifs in memoirs written by communist women, former prisoners of Soviet gulags. My next point of interest is the role that time spent in the Gulag played in the two narratives and the significance it was assigned by the authors in the process of shaping their communist identities. The chapter comprises three parts. First, I will examine the works from the perspective of the genre, approaching them as examples of testimonial memoirs, relating Gulag experiences from a female point of view. Next, I will ask to what extent it is justified to read them not only in the context of "Gulag" poetics, but also as a discourse whose modal framework is delimited by a need to understand one's own biography, especially one's communist past and its retrospective assessment. I am concerned with the question which arguments which rhetorical and aesthetic strategies both authors use to write about their paths to communism and how they present the very fact of being a communist: during incarceration in the gulag and after release. I will focus on two central categories here – that of autobiography and that of generation. In the final part of the chapter, I will consider the value of comparing the experiences of these two prisoner authors who, albeit hailing from the same generation of pre-war communists of Jewish descent, were, after all, shaped by different historical, cultural, and – last but not least – gender contexts. In other words, I am interested to which extent the issue of gender and ideology may be deemed universal in the context of limit-experiences, and to what extent it is determined by particular contexts.

---

[3] "Communist movement" is used as a technical term here and I am aware of the simplifications it implies. Yet a thorough analysis of the various factions of the communist movement would go beyond the scope of this work.

[4] The English edition was published in two volumes: *Journey into the Whirlwind: The Critically Acclaimed Memoir of Stalin's Reign of Terror* and *Within the Whirlwind*. From here on, I use the abbreviated title *Whirlwind* in reference to the entire text.

2 *Shreds of a Family Saga* and *Whirlwind*: Testimony and gender

The texts I am exploring in this article are of varying literary value and belong to different genres. *Whirlwind* is a seminal work in the canon of Gulag literature, one of the first testimonies of Soviet crimes as well as a text that delineates and determines the poetics of "gulag memoir"[5] as a genre (Thun-Hohenstein 2014: 87–88). Literature of the subject places *Whirlwind* alongside books by Aleksandr Solzhenitsyn, Varlam Shalamov, József Czapski or Gustaw Herling-Grudziński, as masterpieces of testimonial narratives on life in "the Gulag Archipelago" (Cooke 2005: 3). Budzyńska does not (yet?)[6] belong to this canon; *Shreds of a Family Saga* is read first and foremost as an autobiographical novel or, as suggested by its title, a family saga, in which centre stage is taken by the problem of understanding one's own biography, approached as a model biography of a certain generation. Even though the most voluminous chapter is entitled "Gulag," and although it contains all the motifs and topoi characteristic of Gulag literature (a description of an arrest, investigation, moments of reprieve, gulag as a zone, narrative that follows subsequent "stages" (Toker 2000: 82–94; Burska 1992)), it is rarely cited within the context of narratives on twentieth-century limit-experiences. The acclaim it has received cannot compare with Ginzburg's – *Shreds of a Family Saga* was published in a small print run in Poland and is practically unknown to foreign readers. These facts, however, speak not so much of the value of the text itself, but rather of the political and cultural circumstances in which it was written.

Both works conform to the theoretical and methodological premises regarding the poetics of testimony and the position of eyewitness in literature (see, among others, Krämer et al. 2011). Their value does not lie in providing tangible evidence of verifiable information on limit-experiences, but rather in combining a subjective perspective with information[7] (Weigel 2000), as well as in feeding

---

5 I concur with Tadeusz Sucharski that employing the term "gulag literature" to refer to accounts from soviet camps "as opposed to "GULag" shifts the attention "from a criminal system onto its victims" (Sucharski 2007: 97).

6 However, Feliks Tych includes Budzyńska's memoirs amongst "the greatest works of Gulag literature" (Tych 1997, 6).

7 At this point, I would like to point to one similarity between the two texts. In the epilogue to her memoirs, Ginzburg emphasized that she had written "the truth and nothing but the truth." These words reveal the need to emphasize the reliability of her own memories, as – though they cannot serve as a basis for reconstruction of what the Soviet gulags were really like – the category of truth relates mainly to the situation of the lyrical subject, who tries to describe her

an individual experience into a broader historical, political, and sociocultural context. The need to give testimony arises from the belief in one's moral obligation to testify, that is to tell others of one's experience and fate. As noted by Leona Toker, this is about "[...] 1) tension between the *ethical* drive and *aesthetic* impulse, closely associated with the bi-functionality of Gulag narratives as acts of witness-bearing and as works of art, 2) interconnection of *individual* and *communal* concerns" (Toker 2000: 74).[8] Giving testimony is at the same time a strategy that legitimizes autobiographical reflection, allowing an individual to understand their own position in the aftermath of a catastrophe (Thun-Hohenstein 2014: 90). To both authors, the process of writing a memoir fulfils a quasi-therapeutic role, allowing them a space to express their own experiences. The narration on time spent in the gulag seamlessly morphs into a narration on the meanders of life and on the attitude of the lyrical subject toward communism, a topic I will explore later on in the chapter.

Giving testimony invariably assumes the presence of a listener, who is the addressee of the story. Thus, a virtual addressee is a constant presence in these texts, making them immanently dialogical. Testimonial memoirs are often stories addressed first and foremost to family and friends and only second to a broader readership: "The sense of one's obligation to testify on behalf of the collective is often intertwined with a specific personal motivation for telling the story" (Toker 2000: 76). Both texts feed into this convention. The first addressee of Ginzburg's story was her teenage son Vasiliy Aksyonov, whom she told what she had been through before writing the memoir, while in exile. Budzyńska reconstructed her story in response to questions from her children and grandchildren, curious about her life. Thus, in both cases giving testimony was harnessed into the service of transgenerational dialogue. The tales were meant to bridge a generational gap, to fill an abyss that stemmed from radical differences between the horizons of their experiences. At the same time, the story-testimony addressed to family members was a tale that allowed for other listeners – especially, those whose biographies had a similar trajectory and those to whom the authors felt obliged to testify, clarify, and explain.

In their memoirs both authors operate with an essentialist definition of femininity. They weave their narratives as communist activists, but also as wives

---

own experience as honestly as possible. For Budzyńska, the need to clarify her own motives also comes to the fore, as well as the desire to tell of her fate in a way that may be understandable to future generations.

8 Next, Toker enumerates the following features of the genre: "3) inclusion of specific topoi as morphological variables, and 4) a modal scheme that can be described in terms of *Lent*" (Toker 2000: 74).

and mothers, who even in the gulag try to fulfil the expectations associated with these roles. They devote quite a lot of attention to the issues of the body, corporeality, personal hygiene, and looks. They closely register problems connected with human physiology, lamenting the loss of femininity in the camp. They express solidarity with women who suffer sexual violence.[9] They also write about their feelings towards their husbands and children (motherhood plays a significant role in both texts, although it does not exhaust the identity of a female communist). And they believed women to be stronger than man oder their feelings were stronger. According to Budzyńska, "men let themselves go faster. [...] they were unkept, unshaved. They degraded quickly. They were tremendously lonely" (Torańska 2004: 30). It would be difficult to find in these texts any subversive potential aiming to undermine the cultural gender order. To the contrary, both authors draw concrete conclusions from the fact of being female prisoners. Their belief that female identity cannot be separated from the identity of an activist is, in my opinion, an important distinctive feature of both memoirs, determining their uniqueness. Plus their allegiance to the communist movement result in certain obligations, which often overlaps with humanistic ideals; even in the gulag they try to make the world a better place. Yet, this is not about grand, heroic feats, but rather about normal, everyday actions (Kolchevska 1998: 153–154).[10] When remembering the time spent in the gulag, Budzyńska writes at length about the solidarity of women and the strength of female bonds, which made imprisonment more bearable. One of her first reflections after the arrest is that after months of paralysis caused by her husband's detention, in the camp she finally could "get back to life" and feel "a member of community of these unfortunate women" (Budzyńska 1997: 298). And so, for example, when describing the nightmare of the first time she went into the prison bathhouse: "Clouds of steam, pools of filthy water, slippery stone floor. And this feeling of humiliation, when naked, drenched women take their clothes reeking of disinfection back from the hands of grinning guards," she adds habitually: "Yet, in this chaos, I retained enough clarity of thoughts to

---

9 At the same time, both texts relate with disgust and revulsion the non-normative sexual acts that women in the gulag engage in and – typical for narratives of that time – representations of limit-experiences, such as mass rapes, concerning others, but not the authors themselves: "I describe what I saw and what I went through, perhaps I was very lucky, because I did not experience any such thing" (Budzyńska 1997: 413).
10 Kolchevska cites Barbara Heldt who, writing about (also gender-determined) differences in the attitudes of Solzhenitsyn and Ginzburg, stressed: "Ginzburg while describing the most abject inhumanities, also seeks and finds the human spirit: this is her 'great aim', but it is performed rather than stated, her continual forging of links with other human beings... gave life to others and surviving strength to herself" (Kolchevska 1998: 149).

take care of Stefa, hand in and take back her things, bring [her] water. I even tried to decipher the writings etched on the wall, names, sentence numbers." (Budzyńska 1997: 299)[11] When writing about female energy, strength, and wisdom, Budzyńska refers mostly to female communists and activists. Thus, this is not solidarity built exclusively upon a shared female experience, but above all, solidarity stemming from the experience of a shared political fate and a common cause.[12] Her fellow female inmates sometimes experience moments of crisis or doubt, but even in the most challenging moments they never neglect thinking about education, self-improvement, and character building. Unlike male activists, busy with lofty ideas, female communists had their minds set on changes on the micro level. We can see a similar attitude in the memoirs of the Russian author:

> [...] by far the greater number actively clung to life. We still took pleasure in the fugitive mists of morning, the violet sunsets that blazed over us as we returned from the quarry, the proximity of ocean-going ships which we felt by some sixth sense – and in poetry, which we still repeated to one another at night. [...] It was by preserving all these treasures in our minds that we should resist the onslaught of the horrors around us. (Ginzburg 1995: 343)

Both Budzyńska and Ginzburg recall group book readings and attempts at organizing an ersatz of a cultural life in the barracks. In *Shreds of a Family Saga* we read: "Perhaps Solzhenitsyn [...] would be appalled by the fact that the wives of husbands shot to death, mothers of children wretched by orphanhood, were having fun with poetry, dance, crippled self-education. But I think [...] that all this expressed our striving to salvage our humanity [...]" (Budzyńska 1997: 346). Both authors devote a lot of attention to the need for education, even in the camp. Ginzburg relates, for example, her attempts to raise gulag children, whom she tried to encourage to talk about themselves, which failed altogether, because hardly any of the children knew such words as "mother" or "family," and they were unable to tell that a building that the narrator had drawn on a piece of

---

11 A similar motif appears in Ginzburg's memoirs. In the chapter "A bathhouse! Just an ordinary bathhouse!" in which she recounts her time in prison before the gulag, she describes meeting other women in the bathhouse, preceded by a long period of isolation: "In a way that is all too rare in life, we in that bathhouse felt true love for one another. We were not yet affected by the corrosive jungle law of the camps, which in later years – it is no use trying to hide the fact – degraded more than one of us... At present, purified by our sufferings and full of the joy of meeting other human beings after two years of solitude, we felt like sisters in the noblest sense of the word" (Ginzburg 1995: 264).

12 I would like to thank Agnieszka Mrozik for bringing this problem to my attention, as well as for all her comments, to which this chapter owes a great deal.

paper was meant to be a house. This failure only strengthened Ginzburg's belief in the need to continue the work, understood as striving to improve not just the living conditions of children in the barracks, but also their education. This attitude was accompanied by a belief that the upbringing of next generations is, in a way, a natural duty of a woman, and especially a communist woman, who believes that the world may be made better. Ideology and world-view eased the horrors of the gulag (Stark 2003: 459–461). Celina Budzyńska writes that gulag years instilled in her a "respect for women" and that she did not see similar solidarity among male prisoners. Interestingly, to support this thesis, she refers to Ginzburg's "beautiful memories," which to her emphatically attest to the phenomenon of female solidarity (Budzyńska 1997: 435). This focus on the motif of female solidarity, as well as stressing the heroic attitude of women prisoners, does not mean that the authors diminished the meaning of the Gulag as a system of violence – their tales are still tales of limit, inhumane experiences: of hunger, excruciatingly hard labour, physical and mental abuse, disease, and, ultimately, death by exhaustion. In these memoirs, stories of women who hold philosophical debates after returning from forest logging appear alongside stories of Gulag *Muselmänner*, sadistic guards, and waves of prisoner deaths.

3 "Gulags did not open people's eyes, not always and not everywhere": Biographical truth and generational logic

Celina Budzyńska was born in 1907 in Warsaw to a family of assimilated Polish Jews with a rich revolutionary and communist tradition.[13] Since 1923 she had been active in the Young Communist League, where she met her first (and later her third) husband, Zygmunt Trawiński, also a long-term Gulag prisoner. Her second husband was Stanisław Budzyński, with whom she had two daughters. In 1927, in order to avoid repressions and potential arrests for her communist activities, illegal in Poland at the time, Budzyńska left to study in the USSR, where she

---

13 Celina Budzyńska was a niece of Julian Bruno, a well-known socialist-democrat and a communist activist, writer, and publicist. Her aunt was Helena Bobińska, children's and young people's author, translator, and activist. Budzyńska's mother, a painter, had been politically involved with the communist movement for years. The first part of *Shreds of a Family Saga* recounts memories of conspiracy work and revolutionary activities of the milieu in which the author grew up.

graduated from the Communist University of National Minorities of the West. She also studied in Leningrad (now Saint Petersburg). In July 1937, Budzyńska was arrested in Moscow by NKVD and sentenced to eight years in the Gulag as "a family member of traitors of the motherland"; she arrived in the camp after two years in jail. In 1937, during the purges of Polish communists by NKVD, Stanisław Budzyński was executed. Celina was at first held in the Temnikov Gulag in the Mordovian Autonomous Soviet Socialist Republic, and later in the Talagi Camp in the Arkhangelsk Oblast. Freed after an intervention by Bolesław Bierut, in 1945 she returned to Poland. After her return, she was prohibited from mentioning either the arrests or the Gulag in her official biography. She retained close links with the Communist Party, where she held important political and cultural functions. Budzyńska was, among other things, principal of the Central Party School in Łódź, an educator, and a pedagogue. The anti-Semitic purge of 1968 shook her confidence in the communist ideology, and it was only the introduction of martial law in Poland in 1981 that finally alienated her from the party. In the 1980s, Budzyńska was active in the anti-communist opposition. She began writing her memoirs in the 1960s, continuously adding to and adapting them in subsequent decades. They were finally published in 1997 as *Strzępy rodzinnej sagi*. In the 1990s, Budzyńska gave an in-depth interview to Teresa Torańska, a distinguished Polish journalist, who included it in a new edition of *Oni* ("Them;" Torańska 2004: 11–67), a collection of interviews with the most prominent Polish communists. Budzyńska died in 1993 after a serious illness, before her memoirs were published.[14]

Eugenia Ginzburg also belonged to a generation of pre-war communists. Author, lecturer, literary historian at Kazan University and editor of a local Communist Party newspaper, she was born in 1904 in Moscow to a pharmacist family of assimilated Jews.[15] In 1909, her family moved to Kazan. Following her studies at Kazan State University and the Pedagogical Institute, in the 1920s Ginzburg commenced her academic career and became involved with the communist movement. Around this time, she married Pavel Aksyonov, a high-ranking official and also a communist activist; the couple had two sons. In 1937 Ginzburg was expelled from the Party and arrested for counter-revolutionary Trotskyist agitation. After two years in the Yaroslavl prison, she spent the next decade in the gulags of Kolyma. Upon her release in 1947, like many other former prisoners, she was sentenced to many years in exile. The place of her

---

14 This section is based on a biographical note written by Feliks Tych for Budzyńska's memoirs (Tych 1997) and on the author's own accounts (Budzyńska 1997; Torańska 2004).
15 The section on Ginzburg's biography is based on Kasack (1986: 224) and Klein (1992: 378–379).

banishment was Magadan, the main city in the Kolyma region. The Gehenna of the gulag was soon made worse by another arrest in 1949 – this time she spent a month in prison. Ginzburg was finally released from exile after Stalin's death, and fully rehabilitated in 1955. After the rehabilitation, Ginzburg and her second husband Anton Walter, a doctor whom she had met in the gulag, moved to Lvov, and following his death in the 1960s, Ginzburg relocated to Moscow, where she worked as a journalist and author. She wrote mostly on pedagogics and autobiographical texts about the Soviet Union in the 1920s (see, among others, Ginzburg 1963). She was invited to re-join the Party, an offer that could not be refused. At that time, as will be explored later, her attitude to communism was not thoroughly negative – it was at best ambivalent (Klein 1992: 379, 382). Ginzburg was only able to start working on her memoirs of the Gulag in 1959, even though she had felt the need to testify to what she had been through from early camp days. *Whirlwind* was officially accepted for print in the Soviet Union in 1988,[16] but it had been available (and popular) in the *samizdat* from the 1960s. The Soviet edition was preceded by Western ones: the first in 1967 in Milan. The first volume of Ginzburg's memoirs was published simultaneously in Russian and Italian. Ginzburg died in Moscow in 1977.

The memoirs of Eugenia Ginzburg and Celina Budzyńska may be read not only as testimonials on limit-experiences in Soviet gulags, but also as commentaries criticizing the system that gave rise to these camps – as "chronicle[s] of the period of the cult of the individual"[17] and as sociological analyses. In their assessments of Stalinism and, broader, communism, both authors attempt to understand the role they played in this system. The question of "what was Stalinism/communism" is intertwined with the question of how they became its active participants and the consequences that this collaboration had brought. What their considerations have in common is a sense of tremendous, almost eschatological guilt, and the need to redeem themselves. "Increasingly often I think that even eighteen years of hell on earth would not be enough to redeem my guilt" – we read in *Whirlwind*. In both texts, the question of perpetration comes to the fore: the two female prisoners of the Gulag feel that they are not only victims of the Stalinist system, but also its co-authors. Perhaps it is because of this that they write not only about their suffering, but also about the

---

16 What impressed Russian readers was not only the content of these memoirs (as they had already been partially known), but the fact that they could finally be published. This had a significant influence on the situation of personal documentaries in Russian literature (Paperno 2009: 2).

17 "Chronika vremen kul'ta ličnosti," the Russian subtitle of *Whirlwind*, which does not appear in the English translation.

fact that they did nothing to prevent that suffering. Thus, *Shreds of a Family Saga* and *Whirlwind* are interesting also in that they provide a perspective of actors of the communist revolution. This is the perspective of perpetrators who, up until a certain moment, actively shaped that system, unaware of the fact that their vision of the Party was based on false premises, or that they did not know the truth about the system they helped create. Thus, the social role of the perpetrator and the role of the victim overlap.

Both authors reconstruct in their memoirs the drama of their own lives, whose breakthrough moments came in the tragic decades of the 1930s and 1940s. What is interesting here is not just their admonition of Stalinism – it should be remembered that both authors began writing their memoirs after Stalin's death, when such criticism was already possible and practised – but rather their shared attempt at answering when, for the first time, they realized that joining the communist movement may have been a mistake. Celina Budzyńska claims that, even though she was forced to review her world-view when in exile, it was not until after the war, long after her return from the gulag, that she began to comprehend that her political choices were based on false premises and that she had been mistaken in her judgments. Speaking to Teresa Torańska, Budzyńska makes a striking comment: "Gulags did not open people's eyes, not always and not everywhere" (Torańska 2004: 44), thus effectively admitting that time spent in Soviet gulags did not undermine her faith in the communist system or that it could be "reform[ed] ... from within" (Adler 2012: 127). In her memoirs, she often emphasized that she saw her experiences in Soviet Russia and in the gulags as a high, yet necessary, price for the revolution, which did not undermine the idea itself:

> I have lived through my worst years in the Soviet Union – collectivization, trials, arrests of my nearest and dearest, prison, camp. My husband was murdered, my mother led to death, my friends killed. I saw violence, lawlessness, a tragedy of a nation. At the same time, I was not quite as blind as were many others. [...] Well – then, and for many years to come, I still deeply believed that the idea itself was right and that what had happened in the Soviet Union were mere deformations stemming from the fact that the revolution had won in such a backwards country that did not know democracy. [...] I was certain it would be different in Poland [...]. (Budzyńska 1997: 458)

This distinction between the varieties of communism also comes up in Ginzburg's memoirs: it was the fact that Stalinism had been overcome in the USSR that made Ginzburg faithful to communist ideas despite her experiences in the gulag. Unlike Budzyńska, however, Ginzburg in retrospect presented herself as someone who quickly realized the dangers associated with the politics of the 1930s, and especially with Stalin. In one of the first chapters of her memoirs, regarding the period from before her arrest (!), she offers the following reflection:

> Evidently some sixth sense told me that this man [Stalin – A.A.] was to be the evil genius in my life and that of my children. [...] The naive monarchistic notion of the kindly ruler ignorant of the abuses perpetrated by his officials was not one which I felt sympathy for even at that early stage of my long and steep road. (Ginzburg 1995: 26)

In literary studies, writing that grapples with the issue of departing from communism is referred to as "literature of disillusionment: the writings of former Communists in response to Stalinist terror" (Toker 2000: 52). It comprises a group of autobiographical texts written from the perspective of "former communists," recounting their road to communism (and away from it) in categories of ideological enslavement, mistake, and error. The breakthrough moment in these biographies is often the arrest, followed by investigation and deportation to the gulag. On the other end of the spectrum are the writings of communists who, despite repressions or many years in exile, remained faithful to the Party and its ideals, although the degree of this loyalty, as well as the motives behind it, are very much varied.[18] In the two analyzed memoirs, feelings of guilt and disillusionment as well as the need to confess one's "sins" are very strong – even so, I still do not think that they are typical only of literature of disillusionment. In *Whirlwind* communism is not presented in an exclusively negative light; and this is certainly not only because Ginzburg had been a Party member. Writing her memoirs in the 1960s, Ginzburg asserts that the great "Leninist truth" ultimately claimed victory over terror and repressions; she is also certain that, at some point in the future, "honest people and true communists" will be able to understand her life choices. This supports the theory of Pavel Kolář on the complex process of transformation of communist identity after Stalinism: to the majority of ideological Party members, awareness of Stalinist crimes did not automatically imply a break with communism; it was rather an impulse to shift their own position. Khrushchev's speech on the personality cult became an opportunity to return to the roots of the movement:

> To be communist in the twentieth century meant to believe that there was no other meaningful way of life but being communist, for the development towards communist society

---

18 Adler's typology (concerning the USSR) entails the following models: (1) faith-like belief in communism; (2) psychological defense mechanism; (3) cognitive dissonance; (4) functionalism; (5) traumatic bond (Adler 2012: 12–22). For more about communist autobiographies (as regards Spanish communists), see also Herrmann (2009).

was assumed to be irreversible. In this understanding, human life made sense only as long as it evolved in concert with the objective course of history. (Kolář 2012: 403)

Ginzburg's declaration on remaining with the communist movement *after* gulags and *despite* gulags does not stem from the need to consolidate her identity or to find a symbolic closure for her biography. To the contrary: the author strongly emphasized the transformation of her personality, distancing herself from the previous embodiment of a "naive communist."[19] Her memoirs were constructed so as to distance her from the old "naive self" on the one hand and to provide a framework where this past self could be expressed on the other. Thus, her declaration of loyalty to the communist movement after and despite the Gulag should rather be seen in the context of her belief that the communist system remains the only feasible alternative. When recounting the first months following her arrest, Ginzburg easily moves on from criticizing Stalin to gratitude toward the revolution: "Even now – we asked ourselves – after all that happened to us, would we vote for any other than the Soviet system? [...] Everything I had in the world [...] all this had been given me by the Soviet system, and the revolution, which had transformed my world while I was still a child." (Giznburg 1995: 227)[20]

The autobiographical narration also disintegrates into two voices in Budzyńska, but this disintegration is not a metonymy of a personality breakdown. Unlike Ginzburg, the Polish author does not view her old self as "the other" or "a stranger." One significant example:

> My grandchildren and my young friends ask me: "How could you, after everything you'd lived through and everything you'd seen, return to 'building socialism,' and in your own country at that?" It is hard to respond to this question when asked by others but it is especially hard to answer to myself. I cannot get away [...] with saying that it was not me, that it was someone completely different. No, it was me, with all my thoughts which somehow co-existed alongside a deep faith in socialism, with the ideas of justice etc. Funny, but not all that much, and this is not about beating my chest, it is about figuring out how this could have happened. (Budzyńska 1997: 453)

Despite narrative gestures that articulate the need for expiation, and despite Budzyńska's involvement in anti-communist opposition, *Shreds of a Family*

---

[19] Franziska Thun-Hohenstein observes that Ginzburg does not dwell on the reasons of her own naivety. Unlike Budzyńska, she dismisses the influence of her Jewish background, her family home and early youth on her political choices (Thun-Hohenstein 2014: 99).

[20] In an interview with Torańska, Budzyńska said: "It was the party that pulled us out of this swamp [the gulags – A.A.]. Never mind who did it personally, it was the party" (Torańska 2004: 40).

Saga does not, in my opinion, fully belong to literature of disillusionment either. The author wants nothing in common with Stalinism in its Russian or Polish variety, yet she does not reject the idea itself. Her narrative oscillates between the need for rhetorical "redemption of guilt," all the stronger considering when it was written, and the need to do justice by all those who had joined the communist movement for idealistic reasons and whose attitudes did not render themselves to interpretation based on mental clichés produced by anti-communist discourse.

It is noteworthy that both Ginzburg and Budzyńska view their political decisions not only on an individual level, but also as choices characteristic of a certain group of people born around the same time and shaped by a similar worldview. The category of generation,[21] also applied by the authors, may be helpful in describing this issue. By adopting a collective perspective, both works become as much autobiographical as biographical, attempting to grasp the dynamics, values and mentality of a certain generation. In the case of Budzyńska, it is the generation of Polish and Polish-Jewish pre-war communists, born in the early twentieth century and growing up in interwar Poland. Their association with the communist movement grew out of a deep belief in the need to reform the world and to abolish class differences, anti-Semitism, and illiteracy, improve the conditions of the working class and the rural population, and restrict the influence of the Catholic Church.[22] Joining Polish Communists and, consequently, contacts with Soviet Russia were for that generation logical consequences of these beliefs. This is the context provided by Celina Budzyńska for her deliberations, as she positioned herself as a representative of a larger group, for whom communism became a real opportunity to change the world they lived in. Party membership was not for them strategically motivated; it was not so much about career as about service:

---

21 Research regarding the topic of generation is enormous and still growing. In this work I am mostly influenced by Parnes et al. (2008).
22 Both in the case of Budzyńska and Ginzburg, I restrict myself to reconstructing their own visions of themselves and of the world-view of their generation. The way the motivation of this generation is described in research is a different matter and does not fall within the scope of this chapter. As a side note, it is worth mentioning that pre-war communists are not perceived as a "real" generation in Polish historical discourses of twentieth-century generations, as this term is reserved for groups associated with resistance, conspiracy and opposition against Fascism and Communism. What this fact reveals is the problematic nature of "generation" as an analytical category on the one hand, and on the other hand, the stigmatization that results from treating communist movements as foreign to Polish culture. See Artwińska et al. (2015: 347–367).

> We were all young, ideologically driven, enthusiastic, under the profound influence of the October Revolution. Many [...] had travelled a long and winding road from patriotic-legionary or Christian ideology to Marxism or communism. The first years of independence gave us plenty of reasons for disappointment and bitterness. Abject poverty, unemployment, incredible inflation, lack of perspectives, indolence of the constantly changing government, acts of lawlessness – all this pushed ideological and thinking youth to search for new paths. We came from different backgrounds, there were a manyworkers, youth from intelligentsia or petit bourgeois families, from poor Jewish houses, but there was no lack of sons and daughters of wealthy bourgeoisie either. [...] The common idea gave rise to a feeling of fraternity, deepened by political repressions [...]. We shared an ideology [...]. There were no symptoms of cult of the leaders. (Budzyńska 1997: 439)

Anti-communist discourse, already present in Polish culture before the war and particularly strong after 1989, does not do justice to Celina Budzyńska's generation, placing an equality mark between communism as an ideology and its worst perversions. In notes to her memoirs, as will be discussed in the next part of this chapter, Budzyńska herself adopts the arguments of this discourse, discrediting her own life choices. These notes become, to some extent, errata to her earlier works. Her growing anti-communism affects her assessment of the past, leading, for example, to idealization of the generation of her mother, her aunts and uncles, the first generation of Polish communist ideologues, which is pitted against her own "lost generation" of "Stalinist" communists.

A generational perspective is also characteristic in Ginzburg's writing. Leona Toker proposes the term "priviligentsia" (Toker 2000: 53) to describe Ginzburg's generation, emphasizing its privileged position in the Soviet social system and its (perhaps slightly paradoxical) connections with the ethos of Russian intelligentsia. In her memoirs Ginzburg paints a portrait of a group that believed in progress, education, and modernity and that severed its ties with its "bourgeois" roots – the author writes how difficult it was for her to accept her own non-proletarian background. It cannot be denied that this generation enjoyed certain privileges (Ginzburg does not gloss over them either), but they did not define its generational identity. More important seemed to be the belief in the possibility of creating a better world, in overcoming social injustice, almost organically intertwined with Russia's history. Party membership and compliance with its directives was to this generation proof that they understood the overarching idea and how to turn it into reality. Owing to the subsequent schism between theory and practice, the balance of life turned out particularly unfavorably for this generation: "For the old generation who were committed to the Party, who considered themselves to be the 'builders of socialism' even while in camp, a disconfirmation of their original ideology could raise unsettling questions about how they (mis)spent their lives" (Adler 2012: 23).

Reminiscing about her early days in the Party, Ginzburg will later say with irony that "we didn't possess the truth in its final form" (Ginzburg 1995: 22), at the same time confessing that none of her later suffering in the camps could compare with the torment of hearing the first accusations against her (Ginzburg 1995: 16). These were so painful to her because they put a question mark over everything she had considered had given meaning to her life. The absolute belief that the October Revolution marked a total breakthrough moment in the history of the world and that the Communist Party was infallible was shared by many communists of her generation. It was the cornerstone of the generational community and of the readiness to make even the greatest sacrifices in the name of an idea.

4 Gulags, communism, gender: The rules of memory

Researchers interested in the theory of memory and the processes of remembrance/forgetting, such as Maurice Halbwachs and Jan and Aleida Assmann, have argued that individual memory depends on social frameworks: that what we remember as actors is determined by the memory of our environment, and so by particular memories of our group, family, generation, society, or culture. Biographical memory of the individual depends on collective memory, which often acts as a censor, in a way forcing one to filter their memories to align them with the official version of the past. At the same time, collective memory cannot be treated as a monolith – many collective memories coexist within a single community, which becomes obvious if memories of various groups or generations are juxtaposed (Giesen 2009: 200). It is worth keeping these concepts in mind when reading the memoirs of Ginzburg and Budzyńska. For instance, the final structure of *Shreds of a Family Saga* was certainly affected by the memory of discourses that emerged in the 1960s, especially those that contributed to the revision of Stalinist past and the anti-communist memory promoted by Polish opposition in the 1980s. Although they do not explain the feeling of guilt that consumes the author or her disillusionment with communism, they help to understand her ever-present need to justify her past life choices and to "confess her sins" in public. In line with the rules of anti-communist discourse, joining the communist movement cannot be either logically explained or understood – thus, the reasons must remain inexplicable, a mystery or a riddle. In a note added to her memoirs in 1990 (composed when she was already ill), Budzyńska explains:

> Shedding your old skin is very painful, especially when it is accompanied by a feeling that your whole life was devoid of sense, that the prisons, camps, renouncing your personal happiness were futile [...]. This awareness, the awareness of being part responsible, remained with many of my friends until their death. Well, the young generation will not understand us; it can't understand us, and it will not forgive us...
> (Budzyńska 1997: 452)

What comes to the fore in this declaration is that Budzyńska, ideologically already on the side of the opposition (after "shedding her old skin"), who edits her memories to toe the line of the discourse propagated by the Solidarity generation, still tries to speak for the generation of her youth ("*my* friends," "will not understand *us*" – emphasis mine), presented in the categories of a tragic, lost generation cheated by fate and history. In the 1990s, Budzyńska was still a member of this generation of pre-war communists. Her note, finally, confirms my earlier thesis that despite the fact that her views have evolved, her identity remained coherent and cohesive: while regretting her earlier decisions, Budzyńska does not shift responsibility onto the "other I"; acknowledging the failure of her own generation, she remains (or wants to remain) faithful to its ideals. This example clearly shows the restrictions that individual biographical memory has to contend with, overlapped by various images from the past and rituals of remembrance. As a side note, it would be futile to search for similar rhetoric of guilt in the memoirs of other female communists from this generation, published in the 1960s and 1970s. As shown by Agnieszka Mrozik, even though the majority of these authors were sent to political retirement upon Gomułka's ascent to power and were shunted from political life, not only did they not break with communist ideals, but they also did not regret their earlier commitment to Stalinism. In this respect, Budzyńska's attitude stands apart from the majority of her generation and it may be understood within the context of frameworks of memory binding in the 1990s (Mrozik 2015: 263–264).

Eugenia Ginzburg's memoirs were also influenced by contemporary discourses, and specifically the debates of the 1960s' generation, formed at times of thaw and de-Stalinization. For this reason, Ginzburg's memoirs should be analyzed in the context of opposition to the Brezhnev period, during which "a new stock figure emerged in films and literature, the martyred intellectual as tragic bearer of cultural memory" (Clark 1993: 298 in Kolchevska 2003: 162). For the 1960s' generation, the thaw presented hope for an end to the period of a cult of the individual and of Stalinist repressions. While acknowledging the crimes of Stalinism, they positioned themselves as guardians of Russian culture and its humanistic values, systematically quashed in the years of red terror. It was then that the *habitus* of the Russian intellectual-dissident was forged, combining intellectual and moral functions in reference to the values and ideals of pre-revolutionary

Russian intelligentsia (Kolchevska 2003: 148). In Ginzburg's memoirs, we observe a conflict between the need to belong to a generation of dissidents and the need for separateness, or, as it was put by Thun-Hohenstein: "[...] Eugenia Ginzburg shapes her autobiographical 'I' as part of a real community, from which she simultaneously tries to break free" (2014: 89). Her identity and biographical memory had been, after all, also influenced by values typical of the "priviligentsia": a generation of Soviet communists born in the first decade of the twentieth century who, after the revolution, busied themselves with implementing a utopia, holding important Party functions, and who then themselves fell victims to repressions in 1937. Following her rehabilitation, Ginzburg turned from an orthodox communist activist into a liberal activist, which certainly played a role in her contacts with dissidents (Orlowa and Kopelew 1989: 126–127); yet she never drew a line between herself and communism. In this sense, despite many obvious historical, political, and cultural differences between Poland and Russia, the circumstances that accompanied the writing of *Whirlwind* may be compared with those experienced by Budzyńska; for both authors a marked tension is present between the various types of memory and ways of remembering, as well as attempts to situate one's own narration in the context of a potential reader's world-view. As much as Budzyńska stresses the difficulties associated with justifying her choices, Ginzburg structures her own narration as a coming-of-age story, emphasizing the evolution of her own views and her transformation:

> Whatever happens, I consider it my duty to finish the book. Not so much because I want to record the facts about my later years in camp and exile as to reveal to the reader the heroine's spiritual evolution, the gradual transformation of a naive young Communist idealist into someone who had tasted unforgettably the fruits of the tree of the knowledge of good and evil, a human being who amid all her setbacks and suffering also had moments (however brief) of fresh insight in her search for truth. It is this cruel journey of the soul and not just the chronology of my suffering I want to bring home to the reader. (Ginzburg 1989: 423)

According to Dariusz Tołczyk, the motif of transformation is of key significance in understanding, on the one hand, Ginzburg's position on the map of accounts of the Gulag, and on the other hand, the fact that *Whirlwind* intertwines the Gulag narrative with discourses and contexts related to the thaw (Tołczyk 2005a: 53–70). In the post-Stalinist period, Gulag was used by the Party to legitimize its own position: it could now present itself as a victim of Stalin's politics as well as forcing through the claim that "true communists" had come out victorious from the trials of the Gulag. It was, as shown by Tołczyk, one of the versions of the tale of transformation that takes place as a result of the limit-experience of being deprived of one's liberty and imprisoned. This tale, deeply ingrained not only in

Russian culture, may emerge in the version hailing the death of the "old man" and the birth of a "new man," or to the contrary, it may stress the need to preserve one's own identity in the face of coercion (Tołczyk 2005a: 55–59). While during Stalinism the dominant version was the former, where gulags were fashioned as sites of transformation of the "class unconscious" into people of the Party (*perekovka* – the reforging of men), during the thaw Gulag began to be presented as a litmus test for "true communists."[23] Tołczyk argues that Ginzburg refers to the paradigm present in the official discourse intentionally – by writing of her evolution and return to "Leninist truth," as this is the only way she can relate what she had been through. This reference, then, is a type of game with the rules of discourse. Was it a game, as Tołczyk believes, or a manoeuver that was to distract the reader from the fact that in reality Ginzburg does not return to her old identity, but to the contrary: presents herself as reborn? In my opinion, it is indeed impossible to overestimate the role of internal censorship and the pressure of the official politics of remembrance. Yet, as I have stated earlier, I believe that the process of shedding the illusions about Stalinism and of the attendant evolution of her own identity was not tantamount to Ginzburg rejecting communism as an idea. *Whirlwind*, similarly to Budzyńska's *Shreds of a Family Saga*, is interesting also because it shows with acuteness that to one generation communism was the only conceivable vision of the world – against the gulags and despite the gulags. Both authors regret their short-sightedness regarding a specific social practice and feel guilty for not having foreseen its distortions. For this reason, they transform their identity and write about this transformation. Nevertheless, the transformation takes place within communism, not outside of it.

Budzyńska and Ginzburg wrote their memoirs at times of poorly developed gender consciousness, when the position of men was in a way "naturally" perceived as more privileged than that of women. Both authors, more or less consciously, challenged in their work the authority of Solzhenitsyn, whose unquestionable position as a moral and literary beacon was partially predicated on his gender. Budzyńska and Ginzburg, while internalizing the belief of "natural" differences between women and men, created a gender hierarchy in their works: they attributed a greater role to the female experience than to the male

---

[23] "So, in the thaw, the Stalinist paradigm of perekovka, which portrayed the GULag as a locus of the death of the old man and the birth of the new one, was replaced in the official Soviet discourse by a new paradigm presenting spiritual ascent in the GULag as a result of the resistance of 'true Communists' to forced transformation. According to this discourse, the GULag and the purges did not change the 'true Communists.' On the contrary, these experiences made them (and their party) even more what they had been before their arrest" (Tołczyk 2005a: 61).

experience. While speaking for themselves, both authors also spoke on behalf of other imprisoned women, thus forming a female collective subject of sorts, onto which they projected their own experiences and thoughts. This collective subject are women activists, well educated, conscious of their social position, and involved with the Party from early youth. Regardless of how much the authors themselves were convinced of equality of the sexes, or in fact of female superiority in some sense, their memoirs must be read as texts shaped by cultures with prevalent patriarchal models. Besides Jewish background and a shared world-view, it was the authors' gender that determined both their writing and later reception of their works both in Russia and in Poland.

Works cited

Adler, Nancy (2012) *Keeping Faith with the Party. Communist Believers Return from the Gulag* (Bloomington: Indiana University Press).
Artwińska, Anna, Małgorzata Fidelis, Agnieszka Mrozik, and Anna Zawadzka (2016) "Pożytki z 'pokolenia': Dyskusja o 'pokoleniu' jako kategorii analitycznej" [The usefulness of 'generation'. Discussing 'generation' as analytical category], *Teksty Drugie* 1, 347–366.
Applebaum, Anne (2003) *Gulag. A History of the Soviet Camps* (London: Penguin Books).
Budzyńska, Celina (1997) *Strzępy rodzinnej sagi* [Shreds of a family saga], (Warszawa: Żydowski Instytut Historyczny).
Burska, Lidia (1992) "Obozowa literatura" [Camp literature], in *Słownik literatury polskiej XX wieku*, ed. Alina Brodzka (Wrocław: Ossolineum), 740–746.
Clark, Katerina (1993) "Changing Historical Paradigms in Soviet Culture", *Late Soviet Culture from Perestroika to Novostroika*, eds. Thomas Lahusen and Gene Kuperman, (Durham: Duke University Press), 289–306.
Cooke, Olga (2005) "Introduction," *Canadian-American Slavic Studies* 39.1, 1–6.
Czerska, Tatiana (2011) "Kobiety w łagrach" [Women in camps], *Annales Neophilologiarum* 5, 59–74.
Ginzburg, Eugenia (1963) *Tak načinalos. Zapiski učitelnicy* [How it began. Notes of a teacher], (Kazan).
Ginzburg, Eugenia (1977) *Krutoj maršrut. Chronika vremen kul'ta ličnosti* [Whirlwind], (Moskva: FTM).
Ginzburg, Eugenia (1995) *Journey Into The Whirlwind. The Critically Acclaimed Memoir of Stalin's Reign of Terror*, trans. Paul Stevenson and Max Hayward (New York: Hartcourt).
Ginzburg Eugenia (1989) *Within the Whirlwind*, trans. Ian Boland (London: Collins Harvill).
Giesen, Bernhard (2009) "Ungleichzeitigkeit, Erfahrung und der Begriff der Generation" [Non-simultaneity, experience and the concept of generation], in *Generationen: Erfahrung – Erzählung – Identität*, ed. Andreas Kraft and Mark Weißhaupt (Konstanz: UVK Verl.-Ges), 191–215.
Thun-Hohenstein, Franziska (2014) "Narrative Gesten der Nähe. Evgenija Ginzburg" [Narrative gestures of intimacy. Eugenia Ginzburg], in *Gebrochene Linien. Autobiographisches Schreiben und Lagerzivilisation* (Berlin: Kadmos), 87–137.

Herling-Grudziński, Gustaw (2007) *Inny świat. Zapiski sowieckie* [Worlds Apart. Soviet Notes], (Kraków: Wydawnictwo Literackie).
Herrmann, Gina (2009) *Written in Red: The Communist Memoir in Spain* (Bloomington: University of Illinois Press).
Kamm, Nina (ed) (2009) *Weggesperrt. Frauen im Gulag* [Imprisoned. Women in the Gulag], (Berlin: Karl Dietz Verlag).
Kasack, Wolfgang (1986) *Lexikon der russischen Literatur ab 1917* [Handbook of Russian literature since 1917], (Stuttgart: Kröner), 224.
Karwowska, Bożena (2009) *Ciało. Seksualność. Obozy Zagłady* [Body. Sexuality. Holocaust camps], (Kraków: Universitas).
Klein, Joachim (1992) "Lagerprosa: Evgenija Ginzburgs 'Gratwanderung'" [Camp prose: Eugenia Ginzburg], *Zeitschrift für Slawistik* 37.3, 378–389.
Kolář, Pavel (2012) "The party as a new utopia: reshaping communist identity after Stalinism," *Social History* 37.4, 402–424.
Kolchevska, Natasha (1998) "A difficult journey: Evgeniia Ginzburg and women's writing of camp memoirs," in *Women and Russian Culture. Projection and Self-Perceptions* ed. Rosalind Marsh (New York and Oxford: Berghahn Books), 148–163.
Kolchevska, Natasha (2003) "The art of memory. Cultural reverence as political critique in Evgeniia Ginzburg's writing of the Gulag," in *The Russian Memoir: History and Literature*, ed. Beth Holmgren (Evanston: Nortwestern University Press), 145–166.
Mrozik, Agnieszka (2015) "Porządki (po)rewolucyjnej rzeczywistości: Konstruowanie historii lewicy we wspomnieniach polskich komunistek w latach sześćdziesiątych XX wieku" [Spinners of the post-revolutionary reality: Constructing history of the left in the 1960s memoirs Polish female communists], in *Rok 1966 – PRL na zakręcie*, ed. Katarzyna Chmielewska, Grzegorz Wołowiec and Tomasz Żukowski (Warszawa: IBL), 255–299.
Orlowa, Raissa and Lew Kopelew (1989) "Am Ende der Gratwanderung: Jewgenija Ginsburg" [At the end of the journey into the whirlwind: Eugenia Ginzburg], in *Zeitgenossen. Meister. Freunde*, trans. Eva Rönnau and Marianne Wiebe (München: Albrecht Knaus), 121–170.
Paperno, Irina (2009) *Stories of the Soviet Experience: Memoirs, Diaries, Dreams* (Ithaca and London: Cornell University Press).
Parnes, Ohad, Ulrike Vedder and Stefan Willer (2008) *Das Konzept der Generation. Eine Wissenschafts- und Kulturgeschichte* [The concept of generation. A cultural history], (Frankfurt am Main: Suhrkamp).
Petö, Andrea, Louise Hecht and Karolina Krasuska (eds) (2015) *Women and the Holocaust: New Perspectives and Challenges* (Warszawa: IBL).
Schmidt, Sibylle, Sybille Krämer and Ramon Voges (eds) (2011) Politik der Zeugenschaft. Zur Kritik einer Wissenspraxis [Politics of witnessing. Towards a critique of knowledge], (Bielefeld: Transcript).
Stark, Meinhard (2003) *Frauen im Gulag. Alltag und Überleben 1936–1956* [Women in the gulag. Everyday life and survival 1936–1956], (München: Hanser).
Sucharski, Tadeusz (2007) "Literatura Holocaustu i literatura Gułagu? Literatura doświadczenia totalitarnego!" [Literature of the Holocaust and literature of the Gulag? Literature of a totalitarian experience!], *Słupskie Prace Filologiczne* (Seria Filologia Polska) 5, 93–118.
Tołczyk, Dariusz (2005a) "The Politics of resurrection: Evgeniia Ginzburg, the romantic prison, and the Soviet rhetoric of the Gulag," *Canadian-American Slavic Studies* 39.1, 53–70.

Tołczyk, Dariusz (2005b) "The uses of vulnerability: literature and ideology in Evgeniia Ginzburg's memoir of the Gulag," *Literature and History* 14.1, 56–74.
Toker, Leona (2000) *Return from the Archipelago: Narratives of Gulags Survivors* (Bloomington: Indiana University Press).
Torańska, Teresa (2004) "Celina Budzyńska" [interview], in *Oni* (Warszawa: Iskry), 11–67.
Tych, Feliks (1997) "Słowo wstępne" [Introduction], in *Strzępy rodzinnej sagi*, Celina Budzyńska (Warszawa: Żydowski Instytut Historyczny), 5–8.
Weigel, Sigrid (2000) "Zeugnis und Zeugenschaft, Klage und Anklage. Die Geste des Bezeugens in der Differenz von identity politics, juristischem und historiographischem Diskurs" [Witness accounts and witnessing, lament and complaint. The gesture of testifying with regard to identity politics, legal and historical discourse], in *Zeugnis und Zeugenschaft: Jahrbuch des Einstein Forums 1999* (Berlin: Akademie-Verlag), 111–135.

Alexander Kratochvil
Trauma Narration as Adventure Fiction: Ivan Bahrianyj's Novel *The Hunters and the Hunted*

> [...] literary texts can be about trauma, in the sense that they can depict perpetration of violence against characters who are traumatized by the violence and then successfully or unsuccessfully witness their trauma. But texts can also "perform" trauma, in the sense that they can "fail" to tell the story, by eliding, repeating, and fragmenting components of the story. (Kacandes 1999: 56)

1 Trauma *versus* literary narration: Overcoming contradictions

The title of this study, juxtaposing trauma narrative and adventure story, indicates a certain tension. It is tension between a rather unusual combination of two different modes of narration: trauma narration and storytelling within the popular literary genre of adventure fiction. Problems on the performative and mimetical levels of literary accounts in general and of certain genres in particular have already been addressed in research on literature about the Shoah. On the background of that research, and without overgeneralizing, one can state that the representations of inhumanity and traumatic circumstances can be shaped not only by testimony or testimonial literature, but by other forms of narration as well.[1] In our case the form of narration is typical of adventure fiction. It does not describe or explain trauma as an object, nor does it perform trauma on the level of the text by "eliding, repeating, and fragmenting components," as Kacandes' quote indicates. So the question arises, why should I present a story as trauma narrative when it seems to be at first glance merely adventure fiction?

---

[1] This view is to be found in general terms in J. E. Young's book *Writing and Rewriting the Holocaust. Narrative and the Consequences of Interpretation*: "The aim here, is to understand the manner in which historical actuality and the forms in which it is delivered to us may be intertwined; it is to know what happened and how it is represented." (1988: 5) The point Young made for literature and the Shoah was addressed by Leona Toker (2000), who studied the complexity of literature and the Gulag and the relationship of facts, history, memory, and testimony too as fiction.

https://doi.org/10.1515/9783110631135-014

During the process of reading I felt somehow a contradiction opening up between the genre, its fast-paced plot, motifs, language, and the content of the narrative. Above all, I am familiar with the author's biography and his sociocultural and political background. For that reason it seems that apart from what is being said on the surface of the novel, something else is being conveyed, which not only differs from the content of the narrative, but creates another reality. Kacandes' quote implies that a failed performance of trauma narration can nonetheless convey trauma. It is not unusual that popular literary genres sometimes offer multi-layered reading for different audiences, depending on their backgrounds and perspectives from which they approach the text. This leads to the question of how the narrative of this adventure novel is linked with a narrative of trauma and memory.

Memory is a selective process, a conscious recollection of past events and their meaningful assembling into sociocultural relations and contexts. Trauma, on the other hand, as it is understood in psychology, social science, and cultural studies, can arise as a result of a wide variety of events, which share a few common aspects. There is frequently a violation of the person's entrenched ideas about the world and of their human rights, putting them in a state of extreme confusion and insecurity. This is also seen when individuals or institutions that people depend on for survival violate, betray, or disillusion the person in some unforeseen way. Traumatic events in general involve a threat of death to oneself or to someone else, or a threat to one's own or someone else's physical, sexual, or psychological integrity, overwhelming the individual's ability to cope.[2] These aspects apply to the Stalinist rule in Ukraine, owing not only to the annihilation of human life but also to the disintegration and loss of national and cultural beliefs and values, which can be considered as collective and cultural trauma in the sense conceptualized by Jeffrey C. Alexander.[3] I use

---

[2] While conscious remembering is identified with a meaningful narrative, trauma subverts the order created in the remembering narrative. According to van der Kolk, traumatic "memories" (as the effects of trauma are frequently presented) do not occur "in the distorted form of normal recall," but "as affective states, bodily sensations or imagined images (as nightmares, for example, or flashback experiences)" (Kolk 1994: 26). Sturken makes a similar point: "Traumatic memory is depicted as 'prenarrative,' or, one could argue, prerepresentational. [...] The term 'traumatic memory' is thus a kind of oxymoron; the traumatic event is not initially remembered or represented but is held at bay by dissociation and reenacted without remembering. It is narrative integration that produces the memory of the traumatic event" (1999: 235). The issue is also discussed by Peters (2007: 563–564).

[3] Alexander's "cultural trauma" approach is constructivist and stresses the fact that not every horrendous event will turn into a trauma for the collective that encounters it. He explains: "cultural trauma occurs when members of a collectivity feel they have been subjected to a

the term traumatic experience as a category for literary studies and it has of course basic resemblance to the meaning above, especially in that a traumatic event destabilizes the sense of reality and challenges the model of the perceived world and the modes of comprehending it. This is the case of trauma literature, which has to handle a contradictory situation in order to speak about experience, which already means a conflict with the signifying power of language. It implies the problem of conscious recall of a traumatizing event and the difficulties of integrating that event into a meaningful order. Bahrianyj's novel recreates a meaningful order in a particular way. The literary exploration and representation of the horror of the traumatic experience and its impact are transformed into a success story despite, or even because of, all the implicit tragedy of the narration.[4] I am aware of a tendency towards a possible "overinterpretation" by using the trauma concept in an essentialist way, that is as a somehow free and variable parameter for the unsayable, and thus ignoring or oversimplifying psychotraumatological research about the more complex relationship between trauma, memory, and language. Or, on the other hand, of using the concept of trauma as metaphor for a universal human experience, which denies the uniqueness of experiencing trauma and severing the connection to associated circumstances. Bearing this in mind, I shall explore Bahrianyj's *The Hunter and the Hunted* as an innovative attempt (within the context of the Gulag stories) to represent the unspeakable and to construct a meaningful narrative through the medium of a popular genre, the adventure novel. Such a reading is possible because one can identify traumatic experience on the level of the author and the protagonist. Bahrianyj himself wrote extensively in his essay *The Birth of a Book* about the conditions and function of the writing process for his inner self:

> The awareness of having to finish something important (moreover, something that someone needed, because this "someone" also had to escape from depression and was in need of life-saving optimism) created the will to finish it, the need to finish it came from inside. To became a book my manuscript had to be revised. I did not consider it a book. For me it was not a book but something more than a book. It was my life-jacket. It kept me miraculously on the surface… on the surface of faith. On the surface of life. […] I didn't just write, I lived! […] living again and anew, I bypassed the horror. The horror then ceased

---

horrendous event that leaves indelible marks upon their group consciousness, marking their memories forever and changing their future identity in fundamental and irrevocable ways." (2004: 1).

4 Regarding the modes of writing in the face of extreme and liminal experience and the attempts of self-saving and bearing witness by writing testimonies, see Sturken (1999), Thaidigsmann (2009: 4–16) and Toker (2000: 123–140).

to exist, because death was then ridiculous and pitiful. [...] I wanted to laugh at it, to mock it, to ban it from my life before it would ban me and destroy my life. (Bahriany 1956)

The quote shows an important role of the narrative at the bottom of the adventure story: it is a metaphor for the struggle to survive. The Ukrainian title of the novel – *Tiger Hunters*, refers to this basic will to survive. Bahrianyj wrote the novel in a state of life-threatening uncertainty when due to his involvement with the underground he was hiding from the German occupation administration in Western Ukraine. The novel is about the survival of a traumatized person (whom Bahrianyj was at least in part) on the level of an individual and collective identity.

2 Biographical sketch

An important source of inspiration for his literary work was Bahrianyj's life. Ivan Bahrianyj, real name Ivan Lozovjahyna, was born on 2 October 1906 and died on 25 August 1963 in Germany, St. Blasien (Schwarzwald, buried in Neu Ulm). He grew up in Okhtyrka, a provincial town in eastern Ukraine, today in the Sumy region. His education was interrupted by the war, the revolutions and post-war chaos, and never completed. He entered the Kiev Institute of Art, but did not graduate.

In 1926, his poetry started to appear in newspapers and journals and in 1927 he published his first collection, soon followed by a collection of short stories. He took part in the then vibrant literary life in Soviet Ukraine. The 1920s were formative for Bahrianyj as a writer. He was linked to the groups of liberal Ukrainian writers, who were a few years later accused of "bourgeois nationalism" or labeled "enemies of the people" and in the 1950s were referred to as the "executed Renaissance" (*rozstriljane vidrodzhennja*). In 1932, he was arrested by the GPU,[5] and after spending 11 months in an isolation cell was sentenced to five years of penal servitude in concentration camps at the BAMLAG.[6] That period in Bahrianyj's life is somehow misty and puzzling, because we have

---

[5] Gosudarstvennoe politicheskoe upravlenie (State Political Directorate). Its first chief was the Cheka's former chairman, Felix Dzerzhinsky. The organization was responsible for the enforcement of measures like the agricultural collectivization (1929–1933).
[6] Baikal Amur Corrective Labor Camp, which existed during 1932–1948. In the 1930s labor camp inmates, in particular from the Bamlag, had to build various sections of railroad tracks in Siberia.

different accounts of what happened. In one version of events, in 1936 he escaped from the camp and made his way to the Ukrainian settlements in the Amur River region (the *Zelenyj Kiln*, "Green Ukraine"[7]) and lived there, married into a local Ukrainian family and had a son. Another version says he was released from the camp when his sentence ended, but was prevented from returning to Ukraine and therefore lived and married in a Ukrainian settlement in Siberia. In yet another version, he tried to escape in 1935, but was caught, had his sentence extended by three years and got transferred to another BAMLAG. Nevertheless, in 1938, he illegally made his way back to his hometown in Ukraine. There he was betrayed, probably by a neighbor, and was thrown yet gain into the NKVD prison in Kharkiv for nearly two years. When Yezhov[8] was discredited in 1939, Bahrianyj was released on the grounds of having been imprisoned "without cause." He had to live in Okhtyrka under police surveillance. During the German occupation in 1941, he moved to Kharkiv and made a living by writing for journals and newspapers. When the front moved westward in 1943, Bahrianyj moved to western Ukraine, first to Lviv and then to the Subcarpathia region. There he got involved with the resistance movement and was probably in contact with the UPA,[9] while also completing and publishing in 1944 his adventure novel, *The Hunters and the Hunted*.[10] The origin of the novel is remarkable: it took the author only two weeks to write, as he stated in his essay *The Birth of a Book*. He tells us that the book emerged from a motivation to speak about his experiences as a way of escaping from them, a deep need to find a way out of despair and depression: "Writing a book becomes more important for an author than the daily bread, because the process of writing becomes for the writer somehow a life-jacket in the stormy sea of destruction."[11] Bahriany managed to reach Slovakia, but there he was picked up and sent to Germany as an Ostarbeiter. Finally, at the end of the war, he found himself in a displaced persons camp in Fürth, Bavaria. There, in September 1945, together with other Ukrainian intellectuals, he founded The Artistic Ukrainian Movement, an artistic-literary society of Ukrainian *émigrés* in Europe. In 1946,

---

[7] Green Ukraine or literally the green gore/wedge is a historical Ukrainian name for the land in the Russian Far East area between the Amur River and the Pacific Ocean.
[8] Head of the NKVD from 1936 to 1938, during the deadliest period of Stalin's Great Purge.
[9] Ukrajinska Povstans'ka Armija (Ukrainian Insurgent Army), Ukrainian nationalist paramilitary and later partisan army that engaged in a guerrilla war during the Second World War against Nazi Germany, the Soviet Union, and both Underground and Communist Poland.
[10] In Ukrainian, *Tyhrolovy*, i.e. tiger hunters, first title *Zvirolovy*.
[11] This and all other quotes are my translations from Ukrainian, except for the quotations from *The Hunters and the Hunted* (A.K.).

Bahrianyj published a poetry collection titled *Golden Boomerang* that originated during his various episodes of imprisonment. His poetry is interesting and revealing as an act of literary creation in the sense of a manifestation of the writer's inner freedom. It contains many allusions to Taras Shevchenko's poetry written during his imprisonment. In the same vein, a few years later (1948–1950) Bahrianyj wrote two more novels reflecting on wartime chaos. He talks about the permanent threat from the Wehrmacht on the one side and the Red Army on the other side in the novel *A Man Running on the Brink of a Precipice*, whereas the traumatizing experiences of NKVD prisons are recounted in the play *Moriturite* and in the novel *Garden of Gethsemane*. In exile he wrote several pieces of prose, poetry, essays and children's literature. His essay *Why I Do Not Wish to Return to the Soviet Union* (1946b) received broad international attention. As a former prisoner of Soviet and Nazi regimes and an Ostarbeiter, Bahrianyj outlines a declaration of national dignity and human rights against the forced repatriation to the Soviet Union. He regards the USSR as a huge concentration camp, built on slavery, physical and mental torture, terror, and starvation. This text is more like a pamphlet; it was translated into several languages and was influential in bringing attention to, and decision-making on, the problematic practice of sending Ostarbeiter, prisoners of war and others back to the Soviet Union, handing them over to Stalin. Apart from that, Bahrianyj was very busy with cultural and political activities, for instance he was the main editor of the exile newspaper *Ukrajins'ke visti* (*Ukrainian News*) and founded the Ukrainian Revolutionary-Democratic Party. Its political principles are based on the ideas of the Ukrainian cultural and national rebirth in Soviet Ukraine in 1920.

We can assess two main features of his biography: first, Bahrianyj's social and political activities arise out of a nineteenth-century rebirth of European nations, mixed with socialist beliefs and an outlook towards Europe, a phenomenon common to many Ukrainian artists and intellectuals in the 1920s; and on the other hand, the traumatic experiences of war and the 1917–1921 revolutions, as well as his incarcerations in NKVD prisons and the Gulag, sentenced as bourgeois nationalist. This was a destiny Bahrianyj shared with many Ukrainian writers and intellectuals, who from 1929 are very tellingly referred to as the "executed Renaissance" – its victims were several hundred Ukrainian writers, artists, and intellectuals (Kostiuk 1960; Luckyj 1987).

I will conclude this biographical sketch with an episode from Bahrianyj's youth. It refers to the killing of his grandfather and his uncles by the Checkhists in 1920, when he was just a 14-year-old boy:

> [...] in the late afternoon some men with guns arrived. They were speaking in a foreign language. In front of me and the other grandsons they murdered my grandfather and his

son (my uncle). We kids were crying and screaming. Before they killed them, they interrogated them and beat and tortured them with ropes. At the end of the interrogation they were covered in blood. The men with the guns were mocking. Then they shot them. And blood was everywhere. I had blood in my eyes all my life.[12]

3 Trauma narration as adventure novel

3.1 Main characters

How can one reflect on these and other experiences of inhumanity, cruelty, and destruction of basic and common human values? Bahrianyj repeatedly described the writing process as an escape, as a deep-rooted need to run away from destruction. It was probably the only way for him to reflect on what had happened, because there was yet no public discussion of these events. Toni Morrison pointed out that "[t]here is necessity for remembering the horror, but of course there's necessity for remembering it in a manner in which it can be digested, in a manner in which the memory is not destructive. The act of writing the book, in a way, is a way of confronting it and making it possible to remember." (Taylor-Guthrie 1994: 247–248) What does such a book look like? What kind of narrative will one find in it? These questions lead us to *The Hunters and the Hunted*.

On the surface, we find an adventure novel with its typical elements. The plot is a journey with a series of adventures. It is interwoven with elements from other popular genres – war novels, crime novels, Robinsonade, Wild West stories, with exoticism of all kinds and from all parts of the world. Major allusions can be found in the accounts of nature, including flora and fauna, whereas the hunting scenes can be traced back to the stories from *The North* by Jack London, who was very popular in the first two decades of the twentieth century in the Russian empire and later in the Soviet Union (Danylyshyna 2006). The main feature of adventure fiction is a fast-paced plot focusing on a hero's actions within a changing setting. In *The Hunters and the Hunted* the hero is Hryhorij Mnohohrishnyj, who escapes from a heavily guarded train taking him, and many others like him, to Siberia. After his escape he is starving, wandering across the wilderness on the brink of death, experiencing severe hallucinations, but then he is rescued by a Ukrainian family of hunters, who accept him as if he were their son. The novel is set in a dangerous but scenic

---

[12] Bahrjanyj, cited in Leonid Cherevatenko (undated).

Siberia, with many hunting adventures, including tiger hunting, and some encounters with Mnohohrishnyj's Soviet pursuers. He falls in love with the family's daughter, Natalka, and as the chase closes in on him, he and Natalka heroically escape to the Far East, leaving the Soviet Union, "the great GULAG" (as it is called in the novel) behind them.

The hero is – as in nearly every classic adventure story – male. He has a revealing name: Mnohohrishnyj. His ancestor is Dem'jan Mnohohrishnyj (1631–1703), Hetman of Left-Bank Ukraine, who participated in the 1668 anti-Muscovite rebellion led by Hetman Ivan Briukhovetsky. Through betrayal, Mnohohrishnyj was arrested (in Baturyn, on 23 March 1672) and secretly taken in chains to Moscow. There he was charged with high treason, tortured, and finally sentenced to life in exile in Siberia. The destiny of his ancestors relates to Hryhorij Mnohohrishnyj's own life and fight for independent Ukraine. It fits perfectly to his background that as a very young man, Hryhorij took part in the notorious anti-Bolshevik rebellion of Kholodnyj Jar (1919–1923).[13] The following excerpt gives some idea of the stylistic devices used in the novel. After his escape from a heavily guarded train, the hero wandered for several days through the taiga and is now more dead than alive:

> He did not want to move his arms or legs, he no longer wanted to think, he only wanted to lie there on and on into eternity. [...] He heard the echoes of his childhood, tiny bells in the meadow, the roaring waters of the Vorsklo and the Dnieper, ringing girls' voices. He remembered blue flowers in the fields, the acrid smell of the thyme in the valley... [...] Suddenly he opened his eyes. "What's that? A shot!" He sat up. He felt faint and dizzy but the rebel within lifted him up. Another shot, like a blast of thunder, at the same time a terrified, inhuman yell: "Hrytsko!" It was the desperate cry of youth seized by the fangs of death: "Hrytsko!" Immediately he was on his feet. Reeling, he summoned all his strength and hurried through the undergrowth. Again a cry, this time nearer. Summoning all his strength, he broke out into the clearing. There!... A huge black bear was standing on its hind legs, trying to seize within its jaws someone who, pressed into a crack between rocks, was fighting back desperately with a gunstock.
>
> Like a madman he went straight for the beast, driven by a fierce lust to kill. His hand lunged for his knife. [...] Driven by diabolical strength, the man sank the knife into the white collar, deep into the gullet, twisting it crosswise. Triumphantly he saw the blood spurt in all directions, flooding that expanse of white, and for a fleeting moment he glimpsed the youth, dressed in the leather garment of a hunter, dash towards him. That

---

[13] Kholdnyj Yar is a famous, symbolical location in Ukrainian literature; it refers among others to literary works of Taras Shevchenko and Mykola Khvyl'ovyj. The rebellion of Kholodnyj Yar was not anti-socialist but had an outspoken anti-Bolshevik character; the rebels took part in the fight of the Ukrainian National Republic (Ukrajins'ka Narodna Respublika, 1917–1921) for Ukrainian independence.

was the last thing he saw. Everything turned black; he fell to the ground with that hairy black mass, which covered him like a blanket of night. For a few moments there still continued in his ears the far-away melody:
My beautiful mother, now I am lost for ever,
Why have you sent me away where I have never been before?
Then everything was still[14] (Bahriany 1957: 47–49)

On the one hand, this scene might portray a typical episode from any adventure novel: the main protagonist – even though totally exhausted with hunger, thirst, and the drudgery of his getaway – is still a resolute and brave man, who does not spare himself and is able to save his fellow human from mortal danger. On the other hand, there are elements in this scene that run as leitmotifs through the whole story and occur in the author's other novels as well. They concern the deep relationship with his native country ("beautiful mother" Ukraine), which becomes his spiritual home – when he is about to give up and die, he begins to sing a folk song ("My beautiful mother, now I am lost for ever"), the "mother" also Ukraine. The verses from the folk song speak about a girl who had to leave her homeland ("Why have you sent me away where I have never been before?") and have a second meaning, related to the literary heritage of the major Ukrainian poet of the nineteenth century, Taras Shevchenko.[15] He constructed the literary metaphor of Ukraine as a mistreated and occupied mother who has to give her children away, i.e. to the empire, as workers, brides, and mistresses or soldiers. Mnohohrishnyj associated this key scene ("Why have you sent me away where I have never been before?") with his own fate.

Seen against this background, the killing of a bear who is threatening a (Ukrainian) girl becomes in a sense a symbolic killing of the Bolshevik–Russian domination.[16] The saved girl is the protagonist's future beloved wife, Natalka.

Another leitmotif in this and other works by Bahrianyj is the characterization of the hero as a rebel ("He felt faint and dizzy but the rebel within lifted him up"). In this novel the rebellion is mainly directed against the Bolshevik rule. Closely tied up with the motif of rebellion is of course the hero's

---

[14] The English translation differs slightly from the original, and quotes a different stanza from the folksong, which made sense from the translator's point of view and stresses the metaphor of mother Ukraine.

[15] See Grabowicz (1982). Shevchenko's poem *Kataryna* is a good example of such an interpretation, as it was recently interpreted from a post-colonial perspective (Zborovs'ka 1999; Zabuzhko 2001).

[16] I am aware that this may be an over-interpretation, but the novel as a whole does not preclude such reading.

problematic state of mind, his rage and fierceness, close to insanity ("Like a madman he went straight for the beast, driven by a fierce lust to kill"). On the one hand it points to his own damaged humanity as a result of traumatic experiences; the hero is repeatedly described as a man under intense mental pressure and compared to wild animals. On the other hand, this rebellion and the vision of the hero as a rebel has intertextual connotations beyond the adventure novel. It refers to a whole "rebellious" generation of Ukrainian intellectuals of Kharkiv in the 1920s, their spirit of optimism and departure to new horizons. Mnohohrishnyj's profession is telling in that sense; he is an aviation engineer and pilot from Kharkiv. This generation was very quickly, at the beginning of the 1930s, ravaged by Stalinism and later became known as the "executed Renaissance." The rebellious mood of this generation is espoused especially by Mykola Khvyl'ovyj and his writings about the betrayed and lost revolution and the Bolsheviks' philistinism. In his highly controversial and disputed essays, he addresses, amongst other issues, Ukrainian messianism, a concept with roots in Asia entangling Western thoughts and culture with Asian vitality and spiritualism.[17] Bahrianyj himself often referred in his writings to Khvyl'ovyj and his literary texts, and in *The Hunters and The Hunted* offers an interpretation of that Ukrainian renaissance, rooted in Siberia, with its Ukrainian settlements and its somehow "Asian Ukrainians."

3.2 Exoticism

Whether it is a familiar place during an unfamiliar time or a contemporary tale in a faraway setting, location is more than just a scenery for the characters in this novel. One might be surprised that in the Far East we find so many Ukrainian settlers, and not just prisoners of various camps. This region, called *Zelenyj Klin* (Green Ukraine), has been inhabited by Ukrainians since 1883, when the tsarist government organized the first resettlement of Ukrainian peasants (from Chernihiv and Kiev governorates) to Vladivostok. They were followed by tens of thousands of others from elsewhere in Ukraine, and according to the studies by A.V. Chernomaz,[18] in 1914 there were more Ukrainians in that region than Russians. The villages they built in the region resembled Ukrainian farms and had Ukrainian names, and there was even a short-lived Green Ukrainian Republic after 1917. Bahrianyj wrote an article about the settlements

---

[17] For more on Khvyl'ovyj, see Kratochvil (1999).
[18] Chernomaz (2005, especially Chapter 1.1).

in the Far East titled *Ukraine at the Pacific shore* (1944) based on his own observations from a two-year stay in such a settlement.

In the 1930s the Ukrainians in the Far East were in a traditional sense more Ukrainian than Ukraine itself. In the novel this point is illustrated with many elements from folklore, names, toponyms etc. The Ukrainian family of hunters whose daughter was saved by Mnohohrishnyj and who later saved Mnohohrishnyj in return, is an old Cossack family, Sirko. They respect the Cossack traditions and follow them in their lives ("They drank and talked and feasted in Cossack style and tradition." Bahriany 1957: 111). They transform Siberia into an extraterritorial, idyllic, perfect Ukraine. It resembles the Garden of Eden. This is particularly obvious in the chapters "A meeting with the Moroz family" or "Autumn and winter in the taiga:"

> ...And even more so that resurrection, that coming again to life in this world; [...] in a world of rainbow brilliance, a world of limitless, joyful peace and happiness. (Bahriany 1957: 135)

Mnohohrishnyj is rescued by "Asian Ukrainians" after his fight with a bear, and in the course of the story he will be reborn, will fall in love with the daughter of the family, and will have the strength to leave with her the Soviet Union; he says at one point that he will leave through the East, but return from the West. This individual rebirth is mirrored on a collective scale, too. In the novel this Asian region is transformed into a spiritual Ukrainian homeland, and this spiritual homeland with traditional Ukrainian and human values, not spoiled by Bolshevik policies of the 1930s, will provide the ground for a real Ukrainian renaissance: "They are tough and hard. Ruthless hunters, cheerful but merciless trappers, athletic dictators in this green, archaic state, proud predatory conquerors [...]" (Bahrianyj 1996: 109).[19]

This is a very vitalistic depiction, inspired by the so-called romantic vitalism, a term coined by Mykola Khvyl'ovyj and other modernist and avant-garde writers of the1920s. The strong national momentum is a literary echo of the politics of Ukrainization of the 1920s.[20]

---

19 This sentence is missing from the English translation of 1957 and has been quoted from the 1996 reprint of the original. Translated by A.K.

20 Ukrainization was part of the Soviet indigenization policy of the 1920s (*korenizatsiya*). It promoted the usage of the Ukrainian language and other elements of Ukrainian culture in various spheres of public life such as education, publishing, government and religion, and was aimed to strengthen Soviet influence in Soviet Ukraine.

3.3 The psyche

At the heart of adventure stories lies the eternal battle between good and evil. This is what attracted audiences to myth, epic, or tales at any time and in any culture. We can trace adventure fiction back to antiquity, with Homer's *Ulysses* or the *Iliad*, where the protagonists experienced one adventure after another; similar plots, with a journey and a series of adventures, can be found in medieval romances. In the nineteenth century it developed into a genre not only with historical settings and themes (Walter Scott, Alexander Dumas), but with elements of exoticism (Robert Louis Stevenson, Karl May), technical progress (Jules Verne), and since the end of the nineteenth century, blending elements of different themes and locations, often entangling adventure fiction with other genres, especially love stories. This is the case with Bahrianyj's novel as well. The hero's adventures begin before he falls in love with his future partner. In the beginning, the heroine often ignores the hero and it takes some time until they become aware of their feelings towards one another (the reader of course is aware of them very early on). This development is part of the plot in Bahrianyj's novel too, and the journey through Siberia can be read on a metaphorical level as a quest for identity.

The journey or quest is of course essential to the genre, because without it there is no adventure. While this is certainly true, there is another, more important reason for such a challenge in adventure fiction: the hero is not perfect, and his deficits serve to make him seem more human and to move the story forward. In *The Hunters and the Hunted* the hero's deficits are within his inner self, and they do not make him look more human, quite the opposite. At the beginning, fury and hatred are Mnohohrishnyj's main driving forces, caused by his imprisonment, torture, psychological terror, and helplessness during the clash with the Stalinist regime.

In literary trauma narrations the main momentum is usually the problem of identity, the attempts of the self to come to terms with traumatic experiences, when every order is disintegrated, and personal security and social orientation are destroyed. The result is often a breakdown of identity, individual and social alienation. When this happens, the individual's name is an important identifier:

> "Name?" There was a brief pause and then slowly, in a deep sullen tone, "Hryhory." For a moment the Commandant of the express looked silently into the man's face; apparently reassured, he turned and went back. The eyes in the pale face now glued to the grating followed him and a voice coming from deep down, from an inferno boiling in the heart, burst through clenched teeth: "So you are guarding me; you dog."

> [...] Suddenly the man burst out in a shower of awful, uncontrollable curses against law, against the Universe, against Hell, against Heaven itself. (Bahrianyj 1957: 3)

The family name of Mnohohrishnyj (in a literal sense, a "notorious sinner"), as well as having historical and biographical dimensions, also indicates someone who is outside of normal human behavior. The NKVD major Medvyn, who is hunting Mnohohrishnyj, knows him already from his job in the NKVD prison in Kharkiv: "What didn't he do to him! [...] he had broken his ribs, twisted his joints... He no longer insisted on his confession – no, he only wanted the devil to howl and weep and to beg him as all the others had done. [...]" (Bahrianyj 1957: 30). Interestingly, the psyche of this secret service officer is depicted as severely affected by his profession as an NKVD investigator and man hunter. He hallucinates and he sees Mnohohrishnyj as his fate, because he could not break him like all the others, but quite the opposite, he is afraid of him. In is imagination Mnohohrishnyj grew into an Old Testament prophet, because he foretold him:

> The man [Mnohohrishnyj] had said so at the very beginning: I will torment you for the rest of your days. All of us who have come through here, we will all torment you and accompany you to your grave – thousands of us who have been beaten and tortured... You will go to sleep, but you will not be able to sleep; we will yell and roar in your ears. You will have a mistress – but you will not find happiness with her; you will kiss her like a thief, but will not posses her – we will yell, roar and howl... You will have children, but they will not bring you comfort; you will see us in their eyes. I shall stare at you from their eyes and you will run from your own flesh and blood, but there will be no escape. (Bahriany 1957: 31)

This prophecy came true: Major Medvyn, himself a Ukrainian, is a Stalinist executioner, and is haunted by his victims. That fits perfectly to the blueprint of adventure fiction and related genres – the bad ones, the criminals, often suffer with a crisis of conscience. Medvyn destroyed so many existences that his own psyche is seriously damaged as well:

> The devil must have cast a spell! The major remembered those suffocating sleepless nights which he alone knew. And [...] he had hallucinations. Eventually he was afraid to sleep by himself and he had got married. And having married, he used to run away, afraid to sleep at home (Bahriany 1957: 31)

The hero is called by other NKVD officials "the devil in human form"; even his fellow prisoners refer to him as "the real devil." This can be read as a significant social and individual alienation of the main protagonist and indicates his seriously injured personality. On the other hand, it is not only his desperate fury and hatred that keeps him alive. The encounter with his hate and the wounds of his psyche had changed him, and during his stay with the Ukrainian hunters he recovered and reestablished his personality and social roots, occasioned his rebirth and integration into a traditional Ukrainian family, in a sense a return into the human family, too. His love for Natalka and the integration into a Ukrainian family enables him to orientate himself to the future, to transform his traumatic experience into a family memory (even in the sense of the big Ukrainian national family) and to be healed. The last step of liberation from trauma is – according to Cossack tradition – revenge and homicide against Medvyn, when Mnohohrishnyj himself becomes the merciless hunter. The following extended quote is a scene from the end of the novel:

> Now he went forward, a rifle in hand, to meet the oncoming sleigh. Two figures who had been sitting in the sleigh covered up to their ears now threw aside the blankets and displayed a "Budenivka" and a Yezhov cap. They reached for their weapons. [...] "Stand still!" shouted Hryhory.
>
> "Drop the pistol! Up with your hands! Three paces apart! Stand there!" Hryhory walked up to them, and suddenly his heart pounded madly in his chest. His eyes sank fang-like into the one in the Yezhov cap ... and then he burst out in uproarious, frightening, joyful laughter. "Medvyn!"
>
> My God! This moment, this moment of wonder, of risible gladness. Yes, there is a God on earth and in heaven! And Medvyn, that brave hero, that terrible judge and master of the souls of "puny folks," [...] stood there and trembled... yes trembled; even his lips trembled, and the eyes betrayed the soul of a loathsome coward. Three bars on his collar – like three splashes of blood.
>
> The great chief himself? Yes... "Greetings..."
>
> "Well, that must be all, 'comrade investigator'! That's everything... the investigation is finished," and then his voice became slow and hard: "Now I shall be your tribunal!"
>
> He raised the rifle and fired. [...]
>
> For a moment Hryhory stood motionless. Wait! Nobody is responsible for my actions. He looked and then wrote over the clean expanse of snow with his finger in large letters: Judged, and the judgment executed by me – Hryhory Mnohohrishny. As to the crime – this dog knows very well. And he signed it. (Bahriany 1957: 223–224)

The killing of the NKVD agent seemed to be an ultimate act of self-liberation for Mnohohrishnyj, and on a more symbolic level, the liberation of the Ukrainian community. It has to do with the original traumatic experience at the bottom of this novel, the strong effort to gain control over one's own life and destiny and the quest for identity on the individual and the collective (Ukrainian) level. By the explicit act of writing in the snow, which allows him to regain his name, Mnohohrishnyj not only gets back control over his life: by judging Medvyn he can restore order in the world around him and his moral and ethical code.

3.4 Trauma – narration – memory

One of the main characteristics of trauma in literature is its resistance to narrative representation, while at the same time, the traumatized memory urges its own narration. For Bahrianyj, the need to write was a matter of survival, a struggle to re-establish faith and trust in human values, social and cultural. He needed to restore the flow of communication. This, however, leads to tension between the narrative, memory, and trauma. This includes the question about the reader and the reception.

It is of interest that in his essays about the origin of the book, Bahrianyj refers to a little helper, a 4-year-old boy, the son of the family who protected Bahrianyj from persecution. The boy usually came in the late afternoon and spent about an hour every day with Bahrianyj while he wrote. Bahrianyj refers to that little helper as to a future reader of his book; and this gives him the strength and confidence to continue writing; at some point, he describes his book as a product of two authors: "So we wrote the book together." When it was finished, the boy asked Bahrianyj to now write something especially for him, with pictures and drawings. And indeed, Bahriany fulfilled the boy's wish and created *A Fairy Tale about the Stork and Pavlik the Traveler* (written in 1943). Interestingly, here the author tells a story about a boy who goes to a far-away land with fantastic landscapes, and after various adventures makes his way back home to Ukraine.

Bahrianyj's adventure novel can be read as a trauma story concerning the suffering of individuals, but above all of the individual as a representative of an ethnic group, by assuming a relationship and responsibility to others beyond personal interests. It is an effective and appropriate literary mode to deal with collective trauma, because it underlines the connection between an emotional rather than a rational response to experience. Emotions are conveyed by symbolic modes of narration. They point to the linking between individual experience and cultural memory and enable the transition of an individual trauma into supra-individual, collective trauma. Jeffrey C. Alexander considers collective trauma as a construct. Literature can translate a traumatic memory into the construction of a narrative memory, illustrate it and make it accessible for others on a collective level. A literary account of a traumatic experience is influenced by temporal distance and existing or non-existing memory practices in a given historical–sociocultural situation. There must be a collective awareness and communicative memory to integrate a traumatic experience into the cultural memory. The victim is always also a witness and part of a specific historical reality (Bohleber 2000: 823). In the case of Bahrianyj, imagination and aesthetics are used as a means of bridging the gap between his individual experience and its narrative representation.

Critics of literary accounts of traumatic experiences (especially of the Shoah) have objected that fiction devices such as chronology, characterization or a self-conscious narrative voice interfere with testimony and rationalize or reinterpret traumatic events after the fact, philosophizing about death, for example, or universalizing personal experience.[21] While this is an important point, it is equally important not to overlook that any kind of aesthetic and literary account provides distance, because it is a mediated account of human experiences, and this mediation enables individuals to speak about that which is otherwise unspeakable. In order to make the traumatic impact of Bahrianyj's experiences lose some of their weight, some sort of translation into narrative memory had had to take place, and an adventure novel has served this purpose.

4 Conclusions

The Hunters and the Hunted, a novel belonging to adventure fiction, with its exotic content and Far East setting against the background of the Soviet Gulag system, can be read as an interesting piece of popular literature. This is the most common reception the novel enjoys. But there is another level, a remarkable attempt by the author to come to terms with his traumatic experiences in the Gulag. To make that experience bearable, a translation into a cultural narrative has had to take place. It is a reality-organizing narrative that arranges the world around so that the traumatized individual can rise again as an actor, not a helpless victim. It is an attempt at a cultural translation combined with a search for language and a construction of a meaningful narrative, in the case of Bahrianyj a rather traditional national narrative. The format of adventure fiction allows him to be in control of that narrative; in other words: he is remembering in order to forget, to overcome past and put it behind him. That process goes often hand in hand with the creation of an aesthetic translation that enables distance. This translation process may be considered as re-creative and the distance as necessary for re-humanizing existence in the teeth of dehumanizing violence and destruction.

---

21 See, for instance, Langer: "Writing about Holocaust literature, or even written memoirs [...] challenges the imagination through the mediation of a text, raising issues of style and form and tone and figurative language that [...] can deflect our attention from the *dreadful familiarity* of the event itself." (1993: XI-XII; emphasis in the original).

Works cited

Alexander, Jeffrey C. (2004) "Toward a theory of cultural trauma," in *Cultural Trauma and Collective Identity*, Ron Eyerman (Berkeley: University of California Press), 1–30.
Bahrianyj, Ivan (1944) "Ukrajina bilja Tychoho okeany" [*Ukraine at the Pacific shore*], *Krakivs'ki visti* 40.43, 47–49.
Bahrianyj, Ivan (1946a) *Golden Boomerang* (Novi Sad: Prometej).
Bahrianyj, Ivan (1946b) *Chomu ja ne khochu povertatysja do SRSR?* [Why I do not wish to return to the Soviet Union], (Wien: Ukrajins'kyj suchudolovyj instytut), 7.
Bahrianyj, Ivan (1947) *Moriturite* (Novi Sad: Prometej).
Bahrianyj, Ivan (1950) *The Garden of Gethsemane* (New York: Neu Ulm).
Bahrianyj, Ivan (1956) "Narodzhennja knyhy" [The birth of a book], *Ukrajinski visti* 1, 2, 3 January 1956. <http://chtyvo.org.ua/authors/Bahrianyi/Narodzhennia_knyhy/> (accessed 20 June 2015).
Bahriany, Ivan (1957) *The Hunters and the Hunted* (New York: St. Martin's Press).
Bahrianyj, Ivan (1965) *A Man Runs Over the Abyss* (New York: Neu Ulm).
Bahrianyj, Ivan (1996) *Tyhrolovy: Roman. Ohnenne kolo. Povist* [Tiger hunters. Novel. The Fiery Cycle. Novel], [1943] (Kyjiv: Ukrajins'kyj pysmennyk).
Best, Otto F. (1980) *Abenteuer. Wonnetraum aus Flucht und Ferne. Geschichte und Deutung* [Adventure: Happy dreams of escape and distant lands. History and interpretation], (Frankfurt am Main: Fischer-Taschenbuch-Verlag).
Bohleber, Werner (2000) *Psyche Sonderheft. Trauma, Gewalt und kollektives Gedächtnis* [Special Edition Psyche: Trauma, violence, and collective memory], (Stuttgart: Klett-Cotta).
Cherevatenko, Leonid (n.d.) *Ja povernusja do svojeji Vitchyzni...* [I Will Return to Vitchyzni...] <http://www.ukrlib.com.ua/krstat/printout.php?id=11> (accessed 15 June 2015).
Chernomaz, Vjacheslav A. (2005) *Ukrainskoe nacional'noe dvizhennie na Dal'nem Vostoke: 1917–1922 gg.* [The Ukrainian National Movement in the Far East, 1917–1922], (Vladivostok: Izdatel'stvo Dal'nevost).
Danylyshyna, Tetjana (2006) "Zhaha do zhyttja: Neoromantychni motyvy und tvorchosti Dzhaka Londona ta Ivana Bahrjanoho" [Thirst for life: Neoromantic motivs in the works of Jack London and Ivan Bahrjanyj], *Ukrajins'ka mova ta literatura* 41–43, 55.
Grabowicz, George (1982) *The Poet as a Mythmaker: A Study in Symbolic Meaning in Taras Shevchenko* (Cambridge: Harvard University Press).
Kacandes, Irene (1999) "Narrative witnessing as memory work: reading Gertrud Kolmar's 'A Jewish Mother'," in *Acts of Memory: Cultural Recall in the Present*, ed. Mieke Bal, Jonathan Crewe and Leo Spitzer (Hanover and London: University Press of New England), 55–71.
Kolk van der, Bessel A. (1994) "The body keeps the score: memory and the psychobiology of PTSD," *Harvard Review of Psychiatry* 1, 253–265.
Kostiuk, Hryhory (1960) *Stalinist Rule in the Ukraine: A Study of the Decade of Mass Terror (1929–1939)* (München: Institut zur Erforschung der UdSSR).
Kratochvil, Alexander (1999) *Mykola Chvyl'ovyj. Eine Studie zu Leben und Werk* [Mykola Chvyl'ovyj: A study of life and work], (München: Verlag Otto Sagner).
Langer, Lawrence (1993) *Testimonies: The Ruins of Memory* (New Haven: Yale University Press).
Luckyj, George S. N. (1987) *Keeping a Record: Literary Purges in Soviet Ukraine (1930s): A Bio-Bibliography* (Edmonton: Canadian Institute of Ukrainian Studies, University of Alberta).

Peters, Uwe Henrik (2007) *Lexikon. Psychiatrie, Psychotherapie, Medizinische Psychologie* [Lexicon: psychiatry, psychotherapy, psychological medicine], (München: Urban & Fischer Verlag).

Sturken, Marita (1999) "Narratives of recovery: repressed memory as cultural memory," in *Acts of Memory: Cultural Recall in the Present*, ed. Mieke Bal, Jonathan Crewe and Leo Spitzer (Hanover and London: University Press of New England), 231–248.

Taylor-Guthrie, Danielle (ed) (1994) *Conversations with Toni Morrison* (Jackson: University Press of Mississippi).

Thaidigsmann, Karoline (2009) *Lagererfahrung und Identität. Literarische Spiegelungen sowjetischer Lagerhaft in Texten von Varlam Salamov, Lev Konson, Naum Nim und Andrej Sinjavskij* (Heidelberg: Universitätsverlag Winter).

Toker, Leona (2000) *Return from the Archipelago. Narratives of Gulag Survivors* (Bloomington: Indiana University Press).

Young, James E. (1988) *Writing and Rewriting the Holocaust. Narrative and the Consequences of Interpretation* (Bloomington: Indiana University Press).

Zborovs'ka, Nila (1999) "Taras Shevchenko u 'zhinochykh studiiakh'" [Taras Shevchenko in "women's studies"], in *Krytyka* 3.3, 25–28.

Zabuzhko, Oksana (2001) *Shevchenkiv mif Ukrajiny. Sproba filosofs'koho analizu* [Shevchenko's myth of Ukraine: toward a philosophical verification], (Kyjiv: Abrys).

About the Authors

Anna Artwińska is Junior Professor of Slavic Literature and Culture Studies and chair of the Centre for Women´s and Gender Studies at the University of Leipzig, Germany. Her main research interests are memory of communism in Slavic literatures, post-catastrophic representation of the Shoah, Socialist Realism, auto/biographical writing as well as gender, and postcolonial studies.

Davor Beganović is Lecturer in the Slavic Department of the University of Tübingen, Germany and Adjunct Lecturer in the Slavic Department of the University of Zurich, Switzerland. His main research interests are literary theory, especially narratology, studies in cultural memory and contemporary South Slavic literatures as well as works of Danilo Kiš.

Doerte Bischoff is Professor at the Department of Germanic Literatures and chair of the Walter A. Berendsohn Research Center for German Exile Literature at the University of Hamburg, Germany. Her research interests are literature and exile, transnationality and transculturality in literature, German-Jewish literature, memory of the Holocaust, gender studies, and literature and material culture.

Ruxandra Cesereanu is Professor at the Faculty of Letters (Department of Comparative Literature) at the Babeș-Bolyai University in Cluj, Romania. She is a noted poet and prose author who has been awarded a number of literary honors. Her works have been translated into Bulgarian, English, Italian and Hungarian. She is a member of the Romanian Writers' Union, Phantasma – The Center for Imagination Studies, and the Romanian PEN Club. Her PhD thesis explored the impact of communist persecution on Romanian culture.

Alexander Kratochvil is J.E. Purkyně Postdoctoral Fellow at the Czech Academy of Sciences, Prague. His research areas include nineteenth- and twentieth-century Eastern and Western Slavic literature (in particular, Ukranian, Belorussian, Russian and Czech literature), sociolinguistics, and postmodernism in literature and film.

Eneken Laanes is Associate Professor in Comparative Literature at Tallinn University and Senior Research Fellow at the Under and Tuglas Literature Centre of the Estonian Academy of Sciences. Her research focuses on cultural memory, trauma theory, theories of subject formation, theories of autobiography and self-writing, and the historical novel.

Arkadiusz Morawiec is Associate Professor at the Department of Polish Literature of the 20th and 21st Century at the University of Łódź, Poland. His research interests are contemporary Polish literature, concentration camp writings and literature of genocide, questions of literariness, literary representation and literary axiology.

PD. Dr. phil. habil. Anne-Berenike Rothstein is Senior Lecturer and Researcher at the University of Constance/Department of Literature, Art&Media, Germany. In 2019 she was a Visiting Fellow at the University of Seychelles, in 2018 at the USC Shoah Foundation in Los Angeles. In 2013/2014 she was a Visiting Professor of French and Spanish Literature and Cultural Studies at the Humboldt University, Berlin. Her main researches are in the fields of Myth and

Hybridity, Holocaust and Genocide Studies, Literature and Aesthetics of the 19th century, Gender Studies. Numerous publications and research projects. Currently she is leading a research group on Tattoos as Memorable Palimpsest – Identification Levels and Potentials in War- and Post-War Periods and a transfer project on new digital mediation strategies for witnessing and commemorating.

Irina Sandomirskaja is Professor of Russian Culture at the School of Culture and Education at Södertörn University, Sweden. Her research focuses on cultural studies and Soviet cultural history, film, literature and theory, history of linguistics, the mother tongue theory and theory of translation, as well as liminal experiences and experiences of totalitarian violence.

Silke Segler-Messner is Professor of French and Italian Literature at the University of Hamburg, Germany. Her main research areas include trauma and memory, victims and perpetrators, testimonial literature of the Holocaust in France and Italy, French literature of the Maghreb and gender studies (Moderata Fonte, Lucrezia Marinella, Nouvelles scandaleuses).

Tadeusz Sucharski is Associate Professor in the Department of Polish Literature, Pomeranian University in Słupsk, Poland. His research interests include contemporary Polish and Russian literature, Polish–Russian literary relations, concentration-camp writings, literature of the Holocaust, as well as works of Fedor Dostoevsky.

Anja Tippner is Professor of Slavic Literatures at the University of Hamburg, Germany. Her research focuses on concepts of documentation and life-writing as well as representations of (post-)catastrophes and extreme experiences in Russian, Polish and Czech literatures, representations of the Holocaust in a comparative perspective, Jewish literature and culture in Eastern Europe (especially aspects of transnationality and cultural translation).

Leona Toker is Professor emerita in the English Department of the Hebrew University of Jerusalem, Israel. She is founder and editor of *Partial Answers: Journal of Literature and the History of Ideas*. She is also a member of several journal advisory boards (*Connotations, Nabokov Studies, Gulag Studies* and *Respectus Philologicus*). Her research focus is narratology, Nabokov, Joyce, as well as literature of the Gulag and the Holocaust.

Index of Names

Aaron, Soazig 7, 33, 128, 137, 138, 140, 141
Adler, H. G. 190–191n2, 192n5, 193n9, 193n 10, 194n12, 194n13, 195nn15–16, 196, 197n19, 198n20, 200, 201n23, 202n24, 203–205
Adler, Jeremy 197n19
Adler, Nancy 240n18, 244
Adorno, Theodor W. 173, 174, 197n19
Aeschylus 159
Agamben, Giorgio 7, 31, 40, 110, 111n7, 112, 113, 169, 180, 183n5, 191n4, 202, 204, 205n27, 209n3
Alexander, Jeffrey C. 253n3, 266
Améry, Jean 7, 171–179, 181–182, 185–187, 214, 225
Amiel, Irit 154n8
Anders, Władysław 90, 92
Andrzejewski, Jerzy 149, 150, 151
Anepaio, Terje 55
Antelme, Robert 139, 170, 227
Applebaum, Anne 31, 93n6, 210n5, 231
Arendt, Hannah 7, 31, 110, 111, 112, 154, 195n16, 197, 201n23, 209–211, 224
Aristotle 173
Artwińska, Anna 8, 34, 243n22
Assmann, Aleida 66n22, 138–139, 245
Assmann, Jan 138, 245
Augstein, Rudolf 33
Augustinčić, Anton 107n4
Avisar, Ilan 133

Baberowski, Jörg 33
Baer, Ulrich 130
Bahrianyj, Ivan [Pseudonym: Lozovjahyna, Ivan] 8, 254–258, 260–264, 266–267
Baird, Marie L. 20n15
Bakhtin, Mikhail 102–103
Bălănescu, Gabriel 73
Baldaev, Danzig 62n16, 63n17
Baltă, Nicolae 71
Bannasch, Bettina 215
Barbusse, Henri 94

Barskova, Polina 192n7
Barthes, Roland 139
Bartoszewski, Władysław 149
Baudelaire, Charles 132n11
Bauman, Zygmunt 31, 209n1
Bazin, André 129–130n8
Beganović, Davor 6–7
Bely, Andrei 122n19
Benigni, Roberto 157
Benjamin, Walter 192n6, 193n10
Beria, Lavrentii 15n5
Bettelheim, Bruno 36, 112–113
Beyle, Marie-Henri [Pseudonym: Stendhal] 82
Bhabha, Homi 219n19
Bielecki, Wacław 148n4
Binder, Anne-Berenike 127n1
Bischoff, Doerte 8
Bitov, Andrei 40
Blacker, Uilleam 64–65
Bloch, Marc 20n16
Blodig, Vojtěch 204
Bohleber, Werner 266
Bolecki, Włodzimierz 98, 100
Borges, Jorge Luis 158
Borovnik, Silvija 115n11
Borowski, Tadeusz 27, 34, 147, 150–151, 153, 156, 159
Borwicz [Boruchowicz], Michał Maksymilian 148, 152
Boym, Svetlana 42, 211
Braun, Michael 215n15
Brecht, Bertolt 142n16
Brodsky, Joseph 88n2
Brown, Adam 62, 184
Bruneteau, Bernard 160
Buber-Neumann, Margarete 3, 27, 34, 38, 215
Budzyńska, Celina 8, 232–240, 242–248
Bukovsky, Vladimir 76
Bullock, Allan 18
Bunin, Ivan 121n19

Burek, Tomasz 102
Burska, Lidia 233
Butskovsky, A. P. 14–17

Campanella, Tommaso 201
Canetti, Elias 197
Cârja, Ion 72
Caruth, Cathy 131
Caryol, Jean 129
Cavani, Liliana 183
Ceaușescu, Nicolae 4n7
Celan, Paul 156, 214
Cesereanu, Ruxandra 6, 36
Cesianu, Constantin 73
Chekhov, Anton 21–22n21, 37, 121n19
Cherepenina, Nadezhda 192n8, 200
Cherevatenko, Leonid 258n12
Chernomaz, Vyacheslav A. 261
Chicago, Judy 156
Choiński, Krzysztof 157n12
Churchill, Winston 76
Cicero 173
Clark, Katerina 246
Clendinnen, Inga 18n12
Coetzee, J. M. 155n10
Cohn, Dorrit 22n22
Colombat, André Pierre 131–132
Conrad, Joseph 158, 160, 161
Consonni, Manuela 24n26
Constante, Lena 6, 74, 83–84
Cooke, Olga 233
Cordoș, Sanda 83–84
Corell, C. 141–142
Czaplejewicz, Eugeniusz 88, 160
Czapski, Józef 90, 93, 95, 96, 98, 99, 233
Czarnecki, Wacław 153
Czechowicz, Józef 158
Czerska, Tatiana 231
Czerski, Alexander 154
Czuchnowski, Marian 91, 98, 100–101

Danilewicz-Zielińska, Marian 98
Danylyshyna, Tetjana 258
de Balzac, Honoré 82
de Cesari, Chiara 67
Defoe, Daniel 102n11

DeKoven Ezrahi, Sidra 157
Delbo, Charlotte 7, 128, 131, 135, 139
Derrida Jacques 169
Des Pres, Terrence 18n12, 157
Detienne, Marcel 20
Didi-Huberman, Georges 172–173, 176
Đilas, Milovan 107, 109n6
Dobraczyński, Jan 154
Domenach, Jean-Luc 4n8
Dostoevky, Fyodor 34, 36, 95, 102n11, 121n19, 158–160
Dotzler, Bernhard J. 130
Dumas, Alexandre 36, 263
Duncan, Martha Grace 36
Dzeniskevich, Andrei 192

Eco, Umberto 130–131
Eke, Norbert Otto 215
Eliaser, Rutt 55n5
Erichsen, Casper W. 160n14
Erll, Astrid 54
Etkind, Alexander 1n1, 32, 34, 39, 40, 64–65, 216

Fackenheim, Emil 19n14
Farocki, Harun 173
Farrell, Colin 101n9
Fassin, Didier 52, 53n3, 54, 56
Federman, Raymond 131n10, 142
Feldman, Yael S. 16n7
Felman, Shoshana 130, 135, 141, 169
Feuchtwanger, Lion 94
Ficowski, Jerzy 155n9
Figes, Orlando 43
Filipiak, Izabela 156
Filipowicz, Kornel 147, 154
Finch, Helen 190–191n2
Fink, Ida 154n8
Foucault, Michel 201n23
Fox, Michael David 2n2
France, Anatole 94
Frankl, Victor 21n20
Franklin, Ruth 190n2
Frazier, Lessie Jo 4n8
Friedman, Filip 158
Frieß, Nina 43

Ganzenmüller, Jörg 3n6, 210n5
Gawalewicz, Adolf 158
Gellately, Robert 160n14
Genette, Gérard 139n15
Georgescu, Adriana 74, 83
Ghibu, Onisifor 72
Giesen, Bernhard 245
Ginzburg, Eugenia 8, 27, 30, 34, 38–40, 215, 232–234, 235n10, 236n11, 237, 238n15, 239–241, 242n19, 244–248
Ginzburg, Lydia 190, 198
Giurescu, Constantin C. 73–74, 85
Gliksman, Jerzy 92, 98, 101
Głowiński, Michał 152, 157, 159–160
Glucksmann, André 71
Godzich, Wlad 19n14
Golden, Nathanel 117n13, 181n4, 213n10
Goldhagen, Daniel Jonah 160n14
Goldschmidt, Georges-Arthur 214
Goma, Paul 6, 72–73, 82
Grabowicz, George 260n15
Grochowiak, Stanisław 154
Grubiński, Wacław 90, 91, 98, 101, 103
Gruenwald, Oskar 3
Grupińska, Anna 152
Grynberg, Henryk 154n8

Habermas, Jürgen 33
Halbwachs, Maurice 132n11, 245
Harris, Ed 101n9
Harrison, Bernard 19n14
Hartman, Geoffrey H. 155
Hartmann, Anne 35
Heinsohn, Gunnar 19n14
Heinzig, Dieter 4
Heldt, Barbara 235n10
Herling-Grudziński, Gustaw 30, 34, 40, 41, 90, 91, 93–96, 97–100
Herman, Chaim 153
Herrmann, Gina 241n18
Hillgruber, Andreas 33
Hinrikus, Rutt 57, 58n12
Hirsch, Marianne 52, 60–61
Hitler, Adolf 16n6, 18, 19n14, 90, 101, 146–147, 171, 193–194, 214–215, 218, 220
Hobsbawm, Eric 1
Hochschild, Adam 160n14

Hodel, Robert 120n16
Hoffmann, E. T. A. 158
Hofman, Branko 7, 117–119
Hofmann, Michael 174
Holban, Ioan 74
Holban, Maxim 74
Hołuj, Tadeusz 148n48, 151, 157n12
Homer 159, 263
Höss, Rudolf 154
Hossu, Iuliu 72, 77–78
Hryciuk, Grzegorz 89
Huxley, Aldous 158, 160
Huyssen, Andreas 2n3, 52
Hyvernaud, Georges 170–171

Iarov, Sergei 192n7
Ilves, Toomas Hendrik 67n24
Insdorf, Annette 128n3
Ioanid, Ion 6, 75, 80–81
Iredyński, Ireneusz 157n12
Isaković, Antonije 7, 117, 120–122
Iser, Wolfgang 22n23, 130–131

Janion, Maria 96
Jastrun, Mieczysław 159
Jela, Doina 74
Jezernik, Božidar 107n3, 109n6, 114n10
Jinks, Rebecca 4
Jovanović, Dušan 115
Judt, Tony 33
Jurgenson, Luba 18n13, 21–22n21, 179, 180n3

Kacandes, Irene 252–253
Kafka, Franz 103, 158, 160, 197, 204
Kahane, Claire 60
Kąkolewski, Krzysztof 146
Kamm, Nina 231
Karusoo, Merle 56n8
Karwowska, Bożena 231n2
Kasack, Wolfgang 238n15
Katz, Steven T. 216
Kaugver, Raimond 56–57
Kayser, Wolfgang 103
Kershaw, Ian 18n12
Kertész, Imre 5, 13–14, 16–17, 27, 65n20, 153, 175
Khvyl'ovyj, Mykola 259n13, 261n17, 262

Kiernan, Ben 160n14
Kiik, Heino 56
Kipling, Rudyard 83
Kirss, Tiina 58n12, 59, 61n15
Kissel, Wolfgang Stephan 179
Klein, Joachim 238n15, 239
Klein, Judith 142n16
Klüger, Ruth 30, 32, 37, 38
Knežević, Marija 153
Kocka, Jürgen 19
Kolář, Pavel 241–242
Kolchevska, Natasha 235n10, 246–247
Kolk van der, Bessel A. 253n2
Kopelew, Lew 247
Koppermann, Maria 55n5
Kõresaar, Ene 58n12, 59
Korzeniewska, Ewa 151
Kossak, Zofia 97, 147, 149n5, 150–151, 156
Kostiuk, Hryhory 257
Kotek, Joël 209n1
Kott, Matthew 61n14
Kovner, Abba 16n7
Kozielewski, Ryszard 157n12
Kragen, Wanda 158
Krahelska, Halina 149
Krajačić, Stevo 107
Krakowiecki, Anatol 90, 91, 97–99, 101
Kramer, Sven 133n13
Krämer, Sybille 169, 233
Krasiński, Janusz 147
Kratochvil, Alexander 8, 261n17
Kraus, Karl 186
Kruusvall, Jaan 56n8
Kubiak, Michał 161
Kudelski, Zdzisław 95
Kurvet-Käosaar, Leena 59, 61
Kuśniewicz, Andrzej 147
Kusturica, Emir 117
Kydryński, Juliusz 150

Laanes, Eneken 5, 67–68n25
LaCapra, Dominick 42, 114n9
Lampe, John R. 106n2
Landsberg, Alison 67
Lange, Sigrid 141
Langer, Lawrence 131, 267n21

Lanzmann, Claude 7, 42, 65n20, 128, 130n9, 133n12, 134, 138, 141–142
Laub, Dori 141, 169
Lebda-Wyborna, Anna 148
Lebedev, Sergei 43
Lecarme, Jacques 170
Leskov, Nicolai 102n12, 121n19
Levi, Neil 3
Levi, Primo 3, 5, 7, 20, 23n24, 24–26, 30–31, 36, 37–38, 65n20, 93n6, 112n8, 113, 153, 170–174, 176–187, 209–210, 214, 223, 225, 227
Lévinas, Emmanuel 169
Levy, Daniel 32, 33, 38, 52
Lewin, Kurt 18
Leys, Ruth 183n5
Lipska, Ewa 155
Lipski, Leo 91, 105, 103n13
Littell, Jonathan 156
Liu, Sarah 18
Loebl, Bogdan 155–156
Lomagin, Nikita 196–197n17, 199n21
Lord, Peter 78, 156n11, 159
Lorenz, Dagmar 174
Lothe, Jakob 18n11, 18n13
Lovinescu, Monica 74, 75, 84
Luckyj, George S. N. 257
Luik, Viivi 51n1
Lurczyński, Mieczysław 148n3
Lyotard, Jean-François 177

Magaeva, Svetlana 203
Mälksoo, Maria 64
Manu, George 82
Mărgineanu, Nicolae 73, 79–80
Margolin, Julius 3, 21–22n21
Margry, Karel 194n13
Marić, Milomir 109n6
Marin, Mariana 74
Marino, Adrian 72
Markiewicz, Zygmunt 98
Martti, Helde 66
Maurer, Maria 215n17, 218n18, 220
May, Karl 263
Mayewski, Paweł 91, 101, 103
Mehring, Reinhard 192n5

Merişca, Costin 73
Merridale, Catherine 53, 54, 59
Meyrink, Gustav 158
Midlarsky, Manus I. 160n14
Mihailović, Dragoslav 7, 116n12, 117, 120n16, 124
Mihalcea, Al. 74
Mikli, Marika 56
Miller, Nancy K. 34–35, 43
Miłosz, Czesław 152, 153, 155
Molotov, Vyacheslav 89
Montaigne, Michel de 173
Morand, Bernadette 12, 18
Morawiec, Arkadiusz 7, 147, 152, 160
Morcinek, Gustaw 147
Morrison, Toni 258
Mrozik, Agnieszka 236n12, 246
Mukařovský, Jan 13n1
Müller, Herta 8, 212–213, 214n14, 215n16, 217–221
Murmelstein, Benjamin 193n10
Musil, Robert 158, 160

Naglerowa, Herminia 90, 91, 95, 96, 97, 99, 101
Nałkowska, Zofia 150
Nancy, Jean-Luc 161
Nandriş-Cudla, Aniţa 74, 83
Nicolau, Irina 74, 83
Niţu, Theodor 74, 83
Nogaj, Stanisław 147
Nolte, Ernst 33
Nowakowski, Tadeusz 147
Nowosielski, Jerzy 155

Obertyńska, Beata 90, 91, 96, 98, 101n10
Oja, Matt F. 3, 31
Oksanen, Sofi 67–68n25
Oleksy, Krystyna 159
Olszewski, Witold 90, 91, 92, 98, 101, 102
Olusoga, David 160n14
Opitz, Antonia 215
Orlea, Oana 74, 83
Orlowa, Raissa 247

Paju, Imbi 5, 51, 60–62, 63n18, 65n20, 66–67
Paleologu, Alexandru 81, 82
Pankowski, Marian 147, 153
Pantazi, Ion 75
Paperno, Irina 239n16
Park, Nick 156
Parks, Tim 42
Parnes, Ohad 243
Parrau, Alain 18, 139
Pastior, Oskar 212
Patel, Kiran Klaus 19
Pătrăşcanu, Lucreţiu 72, 84
Pavlovici, Florin Constantin 85
Pavlovici, Vlad 77
Pekić, Borislav 124n22
Perec, Georges 142
Perez, Marianna Eva 4n8
Peters, Uwe Henrik 253n2
Pető, Andrea 231n2
Petranović, Branko 106
Petrişor, Marcel 73
Pettai, Eva-Clarita 54n4, 61n14, 68
Pettai, Vello 64, 68
Piankevich, V. L. 197n18
Pica, Victor Ioan 73
Pinel, Vincent 139
Plath, Sylvia 156
Plato 81, 159, 173, 201
Plumelle-Uribe, Rosa Amelia 160
Podchlebnik, Mordechai 133n12
Podgórzec, Zbigniew 155
Poe, E. A. 158
Poetini, Christian 175
Pol Pot 19
Popović, Miroslav 7, 122n21, 123, 124
Popper, Karl R. 159
Posmysz, Zofia 153, 154
Prilepin, Zakhar 43
Prince, Gerald 18n11
Proust, Marcel 82, 95
Przyboś, Julian 155n9
Przybylski, Ryszard 159, 160
Putrament, Jerzy 150

Rawicz, Sławomir 101n9
Rechtman, Richard 53

Reif, Danielle 131n10
Resnais, Alain 7, 127, 128, 129, 132, 133, 134, 139
Ricœur, Paul 169
Rigney, Ann 43, 54, 67
Rigoulot, Pierre 209n1
Rizea, Elizabeta 74, 83
Robbins, Wendy 20
Robionek, Bernd 3n3
Rogovin, Or 25n27
Rogowicz, Jerzy 146, 147
Rohr, Angela [Pseudonym: Golnipa, Helene] 215
Rol'nikaite, Masha 35
Romanowiczowa, Zofia 147
Romański, Andrzej 100
Rooste, Jürgen 63
Rosenbaum, Alan S. 19n19
Rosenfeld, Alvin H. 153, 155, 156
Rosenfeld, Gavriel D. 19n14
Rothberg, Michael 2, 3, 32, 52, 64, 65, 216
Rothstein, Anne-Berenike 7
Roumette, Sylvain 129
Rousset, David 26, 40, 209
Rousso, Henry 18n12
Różewicz, Tadeusz 155
Russel, Bertrand 93
Rüütli, Hilja [Pseudonym: Helm, Aili] 55, 62
Rybakov, Anatolii 35

Saluri, Rein 56
Sandomirskaja, Irina 8, 192n7, 195n15, 202n24, 203n25, 205n26
Sariusz-Skąpska, Izabela 40, 97
Schlesak, Dieter 214
Schlögel, Karl 31
Schmid, Ulrich 170
Schmidt, Sibylle 169
Schmitt, Carl 110, 191n4
Schwarte, Ludger 210, 211
Scott, Walter 263
Segel, Harold B. 31
Segler-Messner, Silke 7
Segre, Cesare 187
Semprún, Jorge 26, 132n11, 153, 170, 214
Shalamov, Varlam 5, 7, 15n4, 16, 20, 21n18–19, 22–26, 30, 37, 38, 94–95, 104, 121–122n19, 124, 170n1, 171–172, 179–182, 209n1, 211, 215, 225, 233
Shaw, George Bernard 94
Shcherbakova, Irina 42
Shevchenko, Taras 257, 259n13, 260n15
Sidran, Abdulah 117n13
Siedlecki, Julian 89, 90
Sienerth, Stefan 213n9
Sienkiewicz, Witold 89
Siguan, Marisa 179, 186
Sikorski, Władysław 90
Simović, Dušan 107n5
Sîrbu, Ion D. 74
Skarga, Barbara [Pseudonym: Kraśniewska, Wiktoria] 92, 97, 100, 102
Skrzypek, Stanisław 98, 99, 100
Skultans, Vielda 59
Smith, Martin Cruz 43
Smith, Tom Rob 43
Snyder, Timothy 4, 16, 18, 20, 31, 33, 216
Solzhenitsyn, Aleksandr 5, 6, 16, 21–22n21, 26, 27, 31, 35, 37, 38, 42, 57, 62, 75, 76, 83, 84, 91, 93, 94, 97, 104, 159, 170, 233, 235n10, 236, 248
Spielberg, Steven 133n13
Spiridon, Olivia 213, 214, 215, 219
Spitzer, Leo 52
Staich, Tadeusz 148
Stalin, Joseph 6, 14, 18, 26, 31, 60, 93, 98, 101, 106–107, 118, 195, 205, 215, 232n4, 239–242, 247–98
Stannard, David E. 160n14
Stark, Meinhard 231, 237
Starobinski, Jean 173
Starzewski, Stanisław 89, 98
State, Aurel 74
Stefănescu, Alex 75
Steiner, George 19n14, 133
Steinhardt, Nicolae 6, 71, 74, 76, 77, 78, 84
Stevenson, Robert Louis 263
Strods, Heinrihs 61n14
Sturgess, Jim 101
Sturken, Marita 253, 254
Stürmer, Michael 33
Styron, William 156
Sucharski, Tadeusz 6, 31, 94, 97, 102n11, 233
Suderland, Maja 210n6

Sundhaussen, Holm 106
Susi, Arnold 57, 58
Swianiewicz, Stanislaw 95
Szajna, Józef 159
Szmaglewska, Seweryna 147, 150, 158
Sznaider, Natan 32, 33, 38, 52
Szymański, Tadeusz 146, 150
Szymborska, Wisława 155n9

Tamm, Marek 55n7
Tarand, Helmut 55n5
Taterka, Thomas 215
Taylor-Guthrie, Danielle 258
Taylor-Terlecka, Nina 88, 98
Thaidigsmann, Karoline 254n4
Thatcher, Nicole 135, 136
Thun-Hohenstein, Franziska 179, 191n3, 221, 233, 234, 242n19, 247
Tippner, Anja 5, 35
Tito, Josip Broz 6, 106, 107, 114, 116n12, 125
Titunik, Irwin R. 120n15
Todorov, Tzvetan 6, 18, 20, 33, 71
Toker, Leona 3, 5, 17, 20n17, 21n18, 31, 35, 36, 38, 39, 40, 41, 56, 58, 117, 118, 121, 122, 170, 215, 221, 225, 233, 234, 241, 244, 252, 254
Tołczyk, Dariusz 39, 247, 248n23
Tolstoi, Lev 37
Tomaziu, George 74
Torańska, Teresa 235, 238, 240, 242
Tougaw, Jason 34, 35, 43
Traverso, Enzo 3n6, 160n14
Trawiński, Zygmunt 237
Trepiński, Antoni 149
Troebst, Stefan 170
Tych, Feliks 233n6, 238n14

Uibo, Udo 56
Umiastowski, Jan Kasimierz 96, 98
Utitz, Emil 192n5

Valton, Arvo 56n10
Van Buskirk, Emily 197
van der Knaap, Ewout 129n7
Verne, Jules 263
Viola, Lynne 39

Vladimov, Georgy 104
Vogler, Henryk 147, 157
von Ribbentrop, Joachim 89

Wajdelota, Jan [Pseudonym: Sarnecki, Tadeusz] 148
Walter, Anton 239
Wańkowicz, Melchior 98
Warmund, Joram 17n8
Weigel, Sigrid 233
Weir, Peter 101n9
Werner, Andrzej 151, 160
Wesełucha, Piotr 161n15
White, Hayden 1
Wiechert, Ernst 153
Wielhorski, Władysław 89
Wiernik, Jankiel 149
Wiesel, Elie 19n19, 24, 36, 93n6
Wieviorka, Annette 52, 173
Williams, Philip F. 4n8
Wittlin, Tadeusz 90, 91, 100, 101, 102, 103
Wójcik, Władysław 147
Wojnar, Waldemar 152
Wolff, Lynn L. 190–191n2
Wordsworth, William 17n9
Wormser, Olga 129
Wu, Yenna 4n8
Wurmbrand, Richard 78n2, 79

Yezhov, Nikolai 15n5, 256, 265
Young, James Edward 2n4, 32, 134

Zabuzhko, Oksana 260n15
Zamorski, Kazimierz 89, 98
Zarembina, Natalia 149n5
Żaroń, Piotr 89
Zawada, Filip 156
Zborovs'ka, Nila 260n15
Zilber, Herbert (Belu) [Pseudonym: Şerbulescu, Andrei] 71, 72
Zimmerring, Karol 161
Zinoviev, Grigory 76
Zonik, Zygmunt 153
Zorin, Andrei 190n1, 197
Żywulska, Krystyna 148, 151

Index of Topics

Annihilation 2n2, 30, 33, 39, 111, 112, 176–177, 183, 193–194, 201, 203, 253
Anti-communism 244
Anti-Semitism 34, 176, 221, 222, 243

Baltic Republics 64
Blank space 7, 42, 127, 127–142

Camp 1–8, 18n12, 19, 23, 26, 30–43, 91, 94, 96, 100, 102, 103, 127–137, 147, 154, 158, 171, 174, 176, 178, 186, 209–212, 215, 225, 226, 231
Camp experience 1–8, 18n12, 23, 26, 30–43, 100, 103, 127–137, 147, 154, 158, 170, 171, 174, 176, 178, 186, 209–212, 215, 225, 226, 227, 231
Camp literature 2–7, 19, 30–43, 91, 94, 96, 102, 121, 122n20, 124, 146, 170, 227
Censorship 7, 56, 88, 91, 93, 116n12, 117, 154, 248
China 4
Cold 30, 36, 72, 81, 85, 119, 170, 183, 199
Collective memory 52, 134, 138, 157, 170, 195, 198, 225, 245
Communism 33, 42, 65, 71, 93, 95, 113, 170, 176, 232, 234, 239, 240, 241n18, 243n22, 244, 245–249
Comparison 2n2, 3n6, 4, 5, 16n6, 17–20, 26–27, 32–35, 39, 43, 123, 142, 190, 209–228
Concentration camp 1–9, 13–27, 30–43, 76, 107n3, 109, 110, 111, 114n9, 117, 124, 127, 129n6, 131, 132, 134, 146–161, 170, 176, 181, 182, 190, 192n5, 193, 196, 198, 201, 204, 209–210, 214, 220, 224, 255, 257
Confinement 2, 30, 36, 40, 41, 54–55n4, 72, 211, 214
Croatia 108, 117
Cultural memory 5, 39, 43, 54, 138, 228, 246, 266
Czech Republic/Czechoslovakia/ ČSSR 3

Deportation 6, 51, 53–59, 62, 63n17, 66n23, 67, 72, 88n2, 90, 96, 103, 129n4, 135, 154, 170, 193, 198, 200, 202, 212–220, 224, 241
Detention 4n7, 6, 71–85, 89, 182, 184, 235

Émigré community 55, 62
Enforced community 197–200, 201
Entangled histories 19, 26
Estonia 4, 5, 51–68
Exile 6, 56–57, 66, 83, 88n2, 89–92, 98, 112, 116n12, 148, 150, 224, 234, 238–241, 247, 257, 259
Extermination camp 110, 111

Fascism 218, 219, 243n22
Fictionalization 23, 130
Forced Labor 4, 8, 54–55n4, 60, 88n1, 146, 216, 221
Form, literary 128, 215
France 82, 94, 130n9

Gender 8, 51, 54, 59, 61, 68, 213, 219, 231–249
Generation 5, 42, 60–61, 63, 67, 96, 120, 138, 142, 157, 178, 215, 225, 232, 233, 234, 237–249, 261
Genocide 4, 19, 20, 33, 64, 152, 157, 159, 160, 221, 224
Ghetto 8, 16n7, 17, 155, 185, 190–206
Ghettoization 191, 198, 203, 205, 206
Great Patriotic War 8, 192
Grey zone 7–8, 169–187
Gulag 1–9, 13–14, 16–20, 23, 25–27, 30–43, 51–68, 71–85, 93, 94, 96, 97, 103, 106–125, 146, 169–171, 176, 179, 180–187, 209n2, 210, 215n16, 216, 220–223, 231–249, 252n1, 254, 257, 259, 267

Holocaust 2, 7, 16, 35, 36, 37, 41, 52–54, 60, 63–66, 127–142, 130–131, 153, 157, 267n21
Holocaust literature 2, 7, 35, 36, 37, 41, 127–142, 130–131, 153, 157, 267n21
Holocaust memory 2, 52–54, 60, 63–66
Holocaust survivor 16, 37

Hungary 42, 214n14
Hunger 36, 56, 58, 79, 80, 83, 148, 158, 192, 193, 196, 200, 203n25, 204, 205, 209, 237, 260

Ideology 8, 33, 109–111, 113, 115, 176, 216–220, 231–249
Italy 4, 37, 40, 118, 178, 183n4, 239

Jews 13, 14n3, 16n6, 19n14, 32, 89, 133, 135, 170, 177, 182, 185, 193n10, 194, 202, 204, 217, 221n21, 224, 237, 238

Labor 1, 4n7, 8, 22, 30, 38–39, 54–55n4, 60, 65, 73, 80, 82, 88n1, 89, 92, 97, 102, 111, 146, 148, 152, 160, 192, 206, 212n8, 216, 221–222, 255n6
Latvia 59

Memoir 16, 17, 21–22n21, 32, 34, 35, 37, 40, 41, 57, 58, 62, 72–75, 99, 100, 103, 122, 128n3, 147n1, 227, 231, 232, 234
Memory culture 52–55, 61, 63, 64, 65, 68, 169
Multidirectional memory 2, 32, 64, 65
Muselmann 25, 112–114, 177, 180

National martyrdom 6, 89, 98
Nazism 33, 64, 110, 112

Occupation 7, 51, 57, 89, 90, 101, 151, 155n9, 255, 256

Poland 7, 42, 89–92, 96, 102, 146, 147–151, 154, 169, 185, 233, 237, 238, 240, 243, 247, 256n9
Prison 2, 3, 6, 14, 15, 30, 36, 57, 61n14, 62n16, 71, 72, 74, 75, 77–85, 88–104, 107–109, 123–124, 159, 235, 236n11, 238–240, 256, 264
Prison narrative 30, 36
Propaganda 27, 39, 94, 146, 193–197, 217–218

Re-education 6, 38, 39, 106–125

Remembrance 1, 8, 32, 37, 41–43, 52, 58, 60, 65, 127, 129n4, 130, 132, 133n12, 136, 138, 142, 172–173, 215, 245–249
Repression 6, 33, 51–55, 57–58, 60–68, 72, 77, 80, 88, 89, 91, 147, 169, 185, 192, 199, 222, 237, 241, 244, 246, 247
Resistance 6, 14, 16, 26, 30, 34, 51, 53n3, 55n6, 58, 59, 61, 67, 71–85, 116, 118, 129n6, 148, 170, 171, 178, 182, 217, 222, 225, 243n22, 248n23, 256, 266
Romania 3, 4, 6, 8, 16, 71–85, 212, 213n9, 214n14, 215, 218

Second World War 1, 6, 51, 52, 64, 107, 117, 127, 142, 147, 149, 156, 160, 169, 212, 213n11, 256n9
Self-administration 195n16, 199, 203–205
Serbia 106n1, 109n6, 116n12, 117, 120, 124, 153
Soviet Union 16n6, 27, 32, 35, 41, 54–55n4, 57, 64, 89, 90–93, 98, 99, 102, 106, 148, 176, 186, 218, 221, 239, 240, 256–259, 262
Stalinism 1, 3n6, 4n7, 32–33, 55, 64, 110, 112, 192, 209, 221, 239, 240–241, 243, 246, 248, 261
Strojbaty (construction battalions) 6, 88n1

Testimony 5, 7, 13, 17–18, 21n18, 22, 30, 34, 40, 42–43, 52, 54, 56, 61–63, 65, 66, 71–75, 78, 92–93, 97–99, 104, 122n20, 124, 135, 141, 169, 171, 174, 176, 178, 179, 197, 205–206, 211, 212, 215, 233–249, 252, 267
Totalitarianism 30, 31, 33, 64, 71, 76, 159, 160, 209, 210, 215
Trauma 8, 35, 36, 42, 43, 51–54, 55, 59–61, 65–68, 124, 128, 131, 134, 152, 174, 177, 179, 252–267
Trauma narration 8, 252–267

Ukraine 212, 220, 253, 255, 256, 257, 259–262, 266
Uniqueness of the Holocaust 3, 18, 19n14, 32–33, 95, 113, 152, 235, 254

Yugoslavia 3, 106, 107n5, 109n6, 111, 117, 118, 124n22, 153

www.ingramcontent.com/pod-product-compliance
Lightning Source LLC
Chambersburg PA
CBHW031801220426
43662CB00007B/491